The Philosop|

'Vaihinger makes the ... very useful point that, as cognitively imperfect creatures, as not entirely reasonable, even at our best we can only build imperfect pictures of the world — which we recognize as imperfect. Though imperfect, these pictures remain the best we've got for the present purposes of guiding our actions and helping us decide what to do and how to bring about what we want to bring about.'

— *Kwame Anthony Appiah*

Hans Vaihinger (1852–1933) was an important and fascinating figure in German philosophy in the early twentieth century, founding the well-known journal *Kant-Studien*. Yet he was overshadowed by the burgeoning movements of phenomenology and analytical philosophy, as well as hostility towards his work because of his defense of Jewish scholars in a Germany controlled by Nazism.

However, it is widely acknowledged today that *The Philosophy of 'As If'* is a philosophical masterwork. Vaihinger argues that in the face of an overwhelmingly complex world, we produce a simpler set of ideas, or idealizations, that help us negotiate it. When cast as fictions, such ideas provide an easier and more useful way to think about certain subjects, from mathematics and physics to law and morality, than would the truth in all its complexity. Even in science, he wrote, we must proceed "as if" a material world exists independently of perceiving subjects; in behaviour, we must act "as if" ethical certainty were possible; in religion, we must believe "as if" there were a God. He also explores the role of fictions in the history of philosophy, going back to the ancient Greeks and the work of Leibniz, Adam Smith and Bentham.

The Philosophy of 'As If' was a powerful influence on the emerging philosophical movement of pragmatism and was groundbreaking in its anticipation of the central role that model-building and simulation would come to play in the human sciences.

This Routledge Classics edition includes a new foreword by Michael A. Rosenthal, which provides a fascinating and important background to Vaihinger's life and the legacy of *The Philosophy of 'As If'*.

Hans Vaihinger (1852–1933) was born near Tübingen in Germany. He made important contributions to epistemology, the philosophy of science and mathematics, and to the historiography of philosophy. Vaihinger produced groundbreaking work on Kant's philosophy, as well as one of the first serious philosophical commentaries on Nietzsche. He is best known as the father of the philosophical theory of fictionalism, which he sets out in his most famous book, *The Philosophy of 'As If'*, and his work also influenced the philosophical movement of pragmatism.

Routledge Classics contains the very best of Routledge publishing over the past century or so, books that have, by popular consent, become established as classics in their field. Drawing on a fantastic heritage of innovative writing published by Routledge and its associated imprints, this series makes available in attractive, affordable form some of the most important works of modern times.

For a complete list of titles visit:
https://www.routledge.com/Routledge-Classics/book-series/SE0585

Hans
Vaihinger

The Philosophy of 'As If'

With a new Foreword by Michael A. Rosenthal

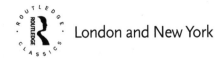

London and New York

First published in Routledge Classics 2021
by Routledge
2 Park Square, Milton Park, Abingdon, Oxon OX14 4RN

and by Routledge
52 Vanderbilt Avenue, New York, NY 10017

Routledge is an imprint of the Taylor & Francis Group, an informa business

Foreword © 2021 Michael A. Rosenthal

First published in 1924 by Routledge and Kegan Paul Ltd

British Library Cataloguing-in-Publication Data
A catalogue record for this book is available from the British Library

Library of Congress Cataloging-in-Publication Data
A catalog record has been requested for this book

ISBN: 978-0-367-55021-9 (hbk)
ISBN: 978-0-367-54994-7 (pbk)
ISBN: 978-1-003-09158-5 (ebk)

Typeset in Joanna
by codeMantra

CONTENTS

FOREWORD TO THE
ROUTLEDGE CLASSICS EDITION

There are philosophical works that when they are published are met with silence and disinterest, only to be acclaimed later for their greatness. And there are those that are heralded almost immediately as important and influence their generation, only to be lost to oblivion later. David Hume's *Treatise on Human Nature*, which the author famously lamented as "still-born" on its publication in 1739, is an example of the first category. Hans Vaihinger, *The Philosophy of "As If"*, is an example of the second.

The original German version, *Die Philosophie des Als Ob*, was published first in 1911 and there were more than ten editions of the work by the time Vaihinger died in 1933. Vaihinger had high ambitions for his work, on which he had worked since 1877. As the subtitle of C. K. Ogden's English translation of 1924 puts it, the book presents "A System of the Theoretical, Practical, and Religious Fictions of Mankind." Gerd Simon's detailed bibliographic chronology shows that there was an extensive and ongoing response, both critical and appreciative, of the book (Simon et al. 2013). Although Vaihinger was primarily known as a historian of philosophy—and the work provided interpretations of several key figures, most importantly, Kant—his work inspired a broad range of thinkers. It even provoked satire, frequently the mark of success. The German–Jewish humorist, Sammy Gronemann, published in

1927 his collection of anecdotes on Jewish life in the Weimar Republic, *Scha-let* (the German version of the Yiddish "Cholent" or sabbath stew), with the subtitle, "Contributions to the Philosophy of 'So What'" [*Beiträge zur Philosophie des "Wenn Schon"*] (Gronemann 1998).

The aim of the work, though, was always very serious. Vaihinger argues for a bold set of claims. Influenced by Darwin, he offers a kind of evolutionary account of human reasoning. In the face of an overwhelming complex world, we produce a simpler set of ideas that help us negotiate it. The ideas are not direct representations of the world but are always mediated by the other ideas and their function in our striving to persevere. Vaihinger focuses on a particular class of ideas, which he calls "fictions." True fictions are self-contradictory and cannot be true. Semi-fictions, which we also call "hypotheses," are internally consistent and might be true under certain circumstances. Fictions of both kinds exemplify the "as if" structure of thinking. We assume that the ideas refer to something in the world that exists independently of our minds, even though they either cannot (because no such things actually exist) or they do not yet (because we do not know if they exist). Although it seems that in the face of logical contradiction or empirical ignorance, we should abandon these ideas, nonetheless we maintain them because they are useful. Fictions are useful when they help us understand the world and act in it in some way. Unlike the pragmatists, with whom he has much in common, Vaihinger does not say that what is useful is true; rather, he asserts that they are useful precisely because they are not true. The burden of the book is to chart the theoretical contours of fictions in their many varieties and to show how they function in myriad domains of inquiry, such as mathematics, physics, and economics, and discursively structured action, such as morality and law. The philosophical investigation of the "as if" structure of thought is central to our very life as human beings.

This program was well on its way to success. Vaihinger founded a journal to propagate his ideas—the *Annalen der Philosophie, Mit besonderer Rücksicht auf die Probleme der Als-Ob Betrachtung* [Annals of Philosophy, With Special consideration of problems concerning the As If Perspective], which would later become *Erkenntnis*, a prominent journal of positivist philosophy of science, with Rudolf Carnap and Hans Reichenbach as editors (Carus et al. 2019: 291). A *Festschrift* published on the occasion of Vaihinger's eightieth birthday in 1932 contains essays on the philosophy of "as if" as applied to a range of areas, from law to statistics to religion (Seidel 1986). He had obviously struck a chord that resonated widely.

So why did Vaihinger's star fall so suddenly and dramatically? One reason was the rise of the Nazis to political power in 1933 and their efforts to transform the public sphere and the universities in terms of their politics. To understand why Vaihinger's work did not fit with the new vision of philosophy propagated by the National Socialists, we can look to a dispute that had occurred earlier with his co-editor of the journal, *Kant-Studien*, which he had founded in 1896 (Sieg 2013: 131–49).

Bruno Bauch was also a renowned scholar, coming out of the so-called "Southwestern" school of Neo-Kantianism, and a founder of the *Kant Gesellschaft* (Schlotter 2004). Like many he had been inspired by the outbreak of the First World War to dream of a new Germany. But as the war turned against the *Kaiserreich* in 1916, Bauch and others began to articulate a new nationalist agenda, both for society as a whole and for philosophy in particular (Schöning 2008). Bauch became openly critical of liberalism and what he claimed was the excessive influence of Jews (Sluga 1993: 83). The young Martin Heidegger weighed-in to complain about the editorial board of *Kant-Studien* that was "judaizing" [*verjuden*] the field (Sieg 2013: 136). Ernst Cassirer, the renowned student of Herman Cohen, the leading neo-Kantian of the Marburg school, strenuously objected to Bauch's views and efforts to turn Kant into a nationalist icon.

Vaihinger was forced to choose sides. Despite having his own agenda, which included, for instance, his attempts to form an alliance with Nietzsche's notoriously anti-Semitic sister, Elizabeth, whom he wished to nominate for a Nobel prize (Sieg 2013: 137), Vaihinger had generally liberal and pacifist views. In fact, a few years before, in 1913, Vaihinger, the son of a Protestant pastor, had already been accused by a right-wing journal, *Semi-Kürschner*, of being a Jew (Simon 2014: 31–32). He sued for defamation and won, but this incident foreshadows his work's later fate under the Nazis. In the dispute with Bauch, Vaihinger sided with Cassirer and the more cosmopolitan vision of Kant and German society. Bauch resigned from *Kant-Studien* and created a new philosophical journal, whose nationalist vision would eventually triumph. In 1929 Cassirer would take the stage in Davos with Heidegger in a debate that signified not only the profound split among philosophers and the future of their field but also the yawning abyss in society (Gordon

2012). In 1933 Vaihinger died, Bauch was soon to become the head of the German Philosophical Society, and Cassirer was forced into exile.

Vaihinger's work suffered not only because of his relation to and defense of the Jewish scholars in the Kant society, but also because his ideas were assumed to be "Jewish." What does it mean to have "Jewish" ideas in this period? For one thing, it meant that one was an exponent of political liberalism. The Nazis and their supporters attempted to undermine parliamentary democracy in the Weimar Republic through promoting a Manichean world view, in which they redescribed the middle-of-the-road practices of parliamentary democracy as the malign force of liberalism opposed to their nationalistic and pure authoritarianism. Several of those in the Kant circle associated with Vaihinger—most significantly, for instance, Ernst Cassirer—were supporters of parliamentary democracy and its institutions, in part because they realized the possibility of Jews as equal citizens in the German state. These political debates bear more than an incidental connection to this text. The Philosophy of "As If" asserts that the ideas at the heart of legal and political institutions are not "natural" in any sense—and certainly cannot be thought to follow from the nature of any particular Volk—but are in fact necessary artifices, whose effects can be judged in pragmatic terms.

In the case of Vaihinger and other intellectuals and artists, there was a more specific version of the problem: to be "Jewish" was to be a proponent of æsthetic modernism (Perloff 2016: 6). It was Robert Musil's novel, The Confusions of Young Törloss—and the interpretation of it by Achille Varzi—that provoked me to think about the literary quality of The Philosophy of "As If" (Varzi 2014). Early in the book, Törloss, while talking about religion with his schoolmate, says, "You always know that what you've said is a fabrication, but despite that there are times when it seems so credible that you stop short, caught by your own words, as it were" (Musil 2014: 22). This strikes me as what defines at least one aspect of literary modernism, which is a kind of philosophical irony, the ability to hold two, apparently contradictory, views in tension without denying one or the other, at least not immediately, and perhaps to be bound to always hold on to both without the ability to make an ultimate decision. Musil not only articulates the æsthetic principle behind Vaihinger's philosophy; his character, Törloss, also expresses precisely its ironic content: we know that what we think and say is a fiction yet we believe that it constitutes the fabric of our world. This committed detachment, cultivated in literature, art, and philosophy, was at the heart of a culture that the Nazis believed was degenerate and ripe for destruction.

Of course, the fate of a work may depend upon more than its reception by cultural and political authorities. We can identify at least two other, internal reasons why Vaihinger's work suffered neglect after its early splash on the philosophical scene. One might be, as its subsequent reception suggests, that it was too ambitious in scope. One aspect of the problem is that the ambition flows from the one big idea on which it is founded. If we reject that idea or find it distasteful in some way, then the rest of the edifice is going to come tumbling down as well. In a hostile review of the English translation, the American journalist, scholar, and satirist H. L. Mencken panned the work for its repetitive style and took aim at the central idea, which he thought was obvious and unoriginal. Even worse, because the philosophy of "as if" erased the distinction between fiction and fact, it made philosophers into liars (Mencken 1924). This is clearly a tendentious reading, which ignores the irony of the position and mistakes the necessity of fiction for deception. But it illustrates a liability in the grand conception itself.

Another problematic aspect of the project's ambition is the unlimited scope of application of that single idea. It is like using the idea of self-interest to explain all of political life. We can question whether self-interest is in fact the primal drive of a human being and we can also question, even if we accept that it is, whether it can explain all of political phenomena. The many counterexamples undermine our confidence in the idea. In our case, it seems that Vaihinger wants to turn all facts into fictions of some kind. At times, though, we want to maintain some kind of distinction between the two. Furthermore, there is the danger of a kind of fictional promiscuity. In order to account for all the various uses and applications of the idea, Vaihinger has to make so many distinctions among the various kinds of fiction that it is natural to question whether they all really refer to the same ultimate concept.

The revival of interest in Vaihinger's work in recent years reflects some of these conceptual ambiguities and a general philosophical ambivalence towards the kind of grand program that he envisaged and began to carry out in The Philosophy of "As If". The most important source of this renewal comes from the philosophy of science. As Arthur Fine emphasizes in his ground-breaking reappraisal, Vaihinger's book is "an effort to make us aware of the central role of model building, simulation, and related constructive techniques, in our various scientific practices and activities" (Fine 1993: 35). Although

Vaihinger was dismissed as an "idealist" and marginalized by the Vienna Circle—one of whom, Carnap, had studied under Bruno Bauch (Carus et al. 2019: xxxv)—he saw himself as an empirically minded positivist. Fine shows that the dispute is better understood as a debate over the nature of positivism itself. Fine argues that Vaihinger is relevant precisely because his version of positivism was not dominated by logical and syntactical analysis but has more in common with pragmatism and scientific practice.

More recently, Kwame Anthony Appiah has argued that Vaihinger is a crucial resource in debates over what he calls "idealization" (Appiah 2017). Like Fine, Appiah is aware of the flaws in Vahinger's approach—the proliferation of terms and examples, the logical problems in the discussion of contradiction, etc.—but instead of criticizing the philosophical ambition he applauds it and amends it when necessary (see also Stoll 2020). For Appiah, the fictional and the "as if" approach are essential to understanding recent developments not only in science, but also in decision theory and political thought. We find idealizations useful because these consciously false ideas help us to control the world and, more paradoxically, to understand it.

The other source of interest in Vaihinger comes from analytic metaphysics and is more ambivalent. A new field has been developed—fictionalism—which, like Vaihinger's project, cuts across several sub-areas, including the metaphysics of mathematics, language, æsthetics, and morality. Its defining idea is that "the aim of inquiry need not be the true representation of a putative domain of fact and that the acceptance of a theory need not involve belief in its content," which certainly seems close to the spirit if not the letter of Vaihinger's theory (Kalderon 2005: 2; Sainsbury 2010). However, as in most analytic philosophy the interest in the history of the field is quite limited. The editor of a recent anthology, Mark Eli Kalderon, dates the origin of fictionalism to 1980 and the publication of works in the philosophy of science by Hartry Field and Bas van Fraasen (Kalderon 2005: 1). In his survey of the history of the philosophical use of fictions, Gideon Rosen mentions Vaihinger but devotes most of his attention to others, such as Bentham (Rosen 2005). He notes that, although it is worthwhile to ponder the relation of contemporary fictionalism to past discussions of fiction, the philosophical relevance is often tenuous.

Contemporary fictionalism is less interested in adopting all of some grand theory from the past than in judging case by case whether some aspect of it can be relevant. We might expect some discussion of Vaihinger among those who are developing a fictionalist account of religion, but it is, somewhat surprisingly, absent (see Le Poidevin 2019). Other philosophers have argued that with the new distinctions developed by analytic fictionalism we can return to Vaihinger and find both anticipations of the contemporary views and perhaps even some new twists. For example, Döring and Eker have argued that, even if some of the leading exponents of moral fictionalism—such as Kalderon and Richard Joyce—do not refer to Vaihinger, the analytic distinction between "hermeneutic" and "revolutionary" fictionalism—that is, the claim, on the one hand, that we already do understand our concepts as fictions, and on the other, that we ought to understand them as fictions—can help us see the importance of Vaihinger to this topic (Döring and Eker 2014).

Although much of so-called continental philosophy has developed in the wake of Heidegger's perceived triumph in the Davos dispute, postmodernism, in its insistence that sign and signified are, if not entirely free from one another, in constant play or flux, might seem a fertile ground for an appreciation of The Philosophy of "As If". The common historical ground here may be more Nietzsche than Kant, but Vaihinger himself is scarcely mentioned, perhaps because of his rhetoric of scientific positivism (Friedman 2000). The most promising development in the use of fictions, partly inspired by Vaihinger, as a means of creative rapprochement among these various traditions, may be the recent work of Markus Gabriel, whose startling and apparently paradoxical claims—like the notion that the world as an objective fact does not exist and only the interpretations of it are real—result in part from reflection on the productive use of fictions (Gabriel 2020).

The resurgence of philosophical interest in fictions might yet lead to a more robust revival of interest in Vaihinger. It ought to. Even if we find some of the arguments faulty, the proliferation of categories undisciplined, and the ambition overweening at times, the book is a treasure trove of ideas that might be relevant to our understanding of many of the domains upon which he reflects. Moreover, if we think of the text as an example of philosophical modernism, then it would be worthwhile for us to maintain some elements of its eclectic style and, even more importantly, its ironic attitude.

Philosophy need not be mere puzzle-solving or the clever play of textual hermeneutics. It should not be relegated to the handmaid of science or elevated to a quasi-mystical intuition of the world. What we need more than anything is a sweeping form of philosophical irony in the sense defined by

Vaihinger; the possibility of taking our ideas seriously both as our creations and as descriptions of the world, believing in them because they help us navigate in a reality that always exceeds our grasp.

In his early work, Wittgenstein had realized the radical insufficiency of philosophy to grasp the world. His counsel was to limit ourselves to logical analysis and remain silent about the rest. It was part of the project of undoing philosophy. His use of irony—exhibited later most clearly in his mocking account in On Certainty of philosophers contemplating ordinary objects in vain—veered more toward satire and aimed at the destruction of contemporary academic practices (Wittgenstein 1972). In contrast, Vaihinger, though less rigorous to be sure, tended to use irony with a slightly optimistic twist. He presents a kind of permanent ironic seriousness toward the enterprise of philosophy as such. If we do not have any other choice than to use fictions, let us be aware of what we are doing with them, their limitations, and the joyous affirmation of a world we partly construct through them. In a world that is increasingly polarized, driven by both sincere and insincere certainties, the critical and æsthetic play at the heart of Vaihinger's ironic account of fictions may have its uses not only in philosophy but also in our everyday lives.

Michael A. Rosenthal, 2020

REFERENCES

Appiah, Kwame Anthony. 2017. *As If: Idealization and Ideals* (Harvard University Press: Cambridge, MA).

Carus, A. W., Michael Friedman, Wolfgang Kienzler, Alan Richardson, and Sven Schlotter (eds.). 2019. *Rudolf Carnap: Early Writings* (Oxford University Press: Oxford).

Döring, Sabine A., and Bahadir Eker. 2014. "Eine Morals des Als Ob? Moralischer Fiktionalismus heute und in Hans Vaihingers *Philosophie des Als Ob*," in Matthias Neuber (ed.), *Fiktion und Fiktionalismus: Beiträge zu Hans Vaihingers "Philosophie des Als Ob"* (Königshausen & Neumann: Würzburg).

Fine, Arthur. 1993. "Fictionalism," *Midwest Studies in Philosophy*, XVIII: 1–18.

Friedman, Michael. 2000. *A Parting of the Ways: Carnap, Cassirer, and Heidegger* (Open Court: Chicago and LaSalle, IL).

Gabriel, Markus. 2020. *Fiktionen* (Suhrkamp: Frankfurt am Main).

Gordon, Peter Eli. 2012. *Continental Divide: Heidegger, Cassirer, Davos* (Harvard University Press: Cambridge, MA).

Gronemann, Sammy. 1998. *Schalet: Beiträge zur Philosophie des "Wenn Schon"* (Reclam Verlag: Leipzig).

Kalderon, Mark Eli. 2005. "Introduction," in Mark Eli Kalderon (ed.), *Fictionalism in Metaphysics* (Oxford University Press: Oxford).

Le Poidevin, Robin. 2019. *Religious Fictionalism* (Cambridge University Press: Cambridge).

Mencken, H. L. 1924. "Philosophers as Liars," *The American Mercury*: 253–54.

Musil, Robert. 2014. *The Confusions of Young Törloss* (Oxford University Press: Oxford).

Perloff, Marjorie. 2016. *Edge of Irony: Modernism in the Shadow of the Habsburg Empire* (University of Chicago Press: Chicago, IL).

Rosen, Gideon. 2005. "Problems in the History of Fictionalism," in Mark Eli Kalderon (ed.), *Fictionalism in Metaphysics* (Oxford University Press: Oxford).

Sainsbury, R. M. 2010. *Fiction and Fictionalism* (Routledge: London and New York).

Schlotter, Sven. 2004. *Die Totalität der Kultur: Philosophisches Denken und politisches Handeln bei Bruno Bauch* (Königshausen & Neumann: Würzburg).

Schöning, Matthias. 2008. "Bruno Bauchs kulturphilosophische Radikalisierung des Kriegsnationalismus: Ein Bruchstück zum Verständnis der Ideenwende von 1916," *Kant-Studien*, 98: 200–19.

Seidel, August (ed.). 1986. *Die Philosophie des Als Ob und das Leben: Festschrift zu Hans Vaihingers 80. Geburtstag* (Scientia Verlag: Amsterdam, Netherlands).

Sieg, Ulrich. 2013. *Geist und Gewalt: Deutsche Philosophen zwischen Kaisrreich und Nationalsozialismus* (Carl Hanser Verlag: Munich).

Simon, Gerd. 2014. "Leben und Wirken Vaihingers," in Matthias Neuber (ed.), *Fiktion und Fiktionalismus: Beiträge zu Hans Vaihingers "Philosophie des Als Ob"* (Königshausen & Neumann: Würzburg).

Simon, Gerd, et al. 2013. "Chronologie Vaihinger, Hans". https://homepages.uni-tuebingen.de//gerd.simon/chrvai.pdf

Sluga, Hans. 1993. *Heidegger's Crisis: Philosophy and Politics in Nazi Germany* (Harvard University Press: Cambridge, MA).

Stoll, Timothy. 2020. "Hans Vaihinger," in *The Stanford Encyclopedia of Philosophy*, edited by Edward N. Zalta. Metaphysics Research Lab, Stanford University: Stanford, CA.

Varzi, Achille C. 2014. "Musil's Imaginary Bridge," *The Monist*, 97: 30–46.

Wittgenstein, Ludwig. 1972. *On Certainty* (Harper & Row: New York).

PREFACE TO THE ENGLISH EDITION

THE publication of this work in an English translation gives me very great pleasure. From early youth I have studied English literature, and later English philosophy. During the period when my philosophical views were taking shape, and especially in the years 1874–1876, it was David Hume and still more J. S. Mill whose influence on my thought was paramount. Thus I was early attracted by English philosophy, and I formed the project of writing a History of English Thought. But, like many similar hopes, this plan was destined to remain unrealized. I soon found that the importance of Fictions had already been partly recognized by English philosophers. English Nominalism of the Middle Ages showed traces of such a recognition. With John Duns Scotus, who died in 1308 in Cologne, when only in his thirty-fourth year, there began a sceptical movement which tended in the same direction. But it was in William of Occam, who took refuge with Ludwig of Bavaria, and died in Munich in 1347 at the age of 77, that we find for the first time a clear and definite treatment of the fictional nature of general ideas, developed in a manner which is still a model for to-day. He fully understood that ficta, as they were called in the writings of the Middle Ages, although their theoretical non-existence might be admitted, are practically necessary and must be recognized in this sense. On the other hand this was not realized by Bacon or even by Hume, though in Berkeley there are at least indications of an understanding of Fictions. But in Hobbes we find a considerable knowledge both of Fictions themselves and of the theory of their use. Empty space, the idea of a *bellum omnium contra omnes*, and of an "original contract" are for Hobbes conscious Fictions. A special study of Hobbes' theory of Fictions had been contemplated by my late colleague Professor Frischeisen-Köhler who was well versed in English philosophy and hoped to write a history of its development; but owing to his early death neither project was realized. Fictions, part of England's heritage from the Romans, have played a large part in English jurisprudence and political philosophy, both in practice and theory; more so than in other countries. There is room for a special monograph on this subject, covering the use of Fictions both in Adam Smith's political economy and in Jeremy Bentham's political philosophy. In the present work the methods of Adam Smith and Bentham have been treated in some detail, but they would appear in quite another light, if brought into relation with the whole history of English thought. Thus particularly in England conditions point to a favourable reception for the theory of Fictions as developed in *The Philosophy of 'As if.'* "Pragmatism," too, so widespread throughout the English-speaking world, has done something to prepare the ground for Fictionalism, in spite of their fundamental difference. Fictionalism does not admit the principle of Pragmatism which runs: "An idea which is found to be useful in practice proves thereby that it is also true in theory, and the fruitful is thus always true." The principle of Fictionalism, on the other hand, or rather the outcome of Fictionalism, is as follows: "An idea whose theoretical untruth or incorrectness, and therewith its falsity, is admitted, is not for that reason practically valueless and useless; for such an idea, in spite of its theoretical nullity may have great practical importance. But though Fictionalism and Pragmatism are diametrically opposed in principle, in practice they may find much in common. Thus both acknowledge the value of metaphysical ideas, though for very different reasons and with very different consequences.

It can be shown, and has been demonstrated at length in the present volume, that the theory of Fictions was more or less clearly stated by Kant, who was proud of his Scottish descent. Nearly 100 pages of the work are devoted to this question and it is there proved in detail that for Kant a large number of ideas, not only in metaphysics but also in mathematics, physics and jurisprudence, were Fictions. The metaphysical ideas were somewhat confused by Kant himself in his *Critique of Pure Reason* (Theory of Method), but were definitely called "heuristic Fictions." This was overlooked and not understood in Kant's own day and for a long time after; and Kant was quite right when he said of himself "I am a century too early with my works; it will be a hundred years before they are properly understood." That was in 1797. The hundred years of incubation which Kant prophesied for his theories have now gone by, and the times are ripe for this his profoundest contribution, which I may mention has now been given due value by Professor Norman Kemp Smith of Edinburgh in his admirable commentary on the Critique (recently published in a second Edition).

HANS VAIHINGER

AUTOBIOGRAPHICAL
THE ORIGIN OF THE PHILOSOPHY OF 'AS IF'

By Hans Vaihinger

I WAS born in a Swabian parsonage near Tübingen in 1852 and so I grew up in a very religious atmosphere. It was not exactly bigoted, but it had a limited horizon, for instance, the names of the Liberal Hegelian theologian Baur of Tübingen, the so-called "Heathen Baur" and his disciple, David F. Strauss, were spoken of with horror in our home. My father, who was the author of a good many theological works, had written a pamphlet against Strauss. When I was twelve years old I was given into the charge of an excellent master and teacher in Leonberg, Sauer, who was at that time a tutor and who became many years later one of the prominent figures at the Stuttgart Grammar School. Sauer awakened the ambition of his pupils by telling them how Kepler in the 17th century and Schelling in the 18th century had sat on the benches of that ancient school of Latin. I was his favourite pupil and he used to tell me too about his Sanskrit studies, which he carried on under the influence of Professor Roth of Tübingen University. He was especially interested in the great Mahabharata epic and occasionally at the end of the lesson in religion he would tell us how this Indian epic contained the same sort of legends as the New Testament. The stories of the Old and New

Testament had already awakened doubts in my mind, so I was gradually led to the conception of the ethical value of the myth. Generally speaking, Sauer's attitude was one of rationalistic theism with a solid moral basis. I had already reached this way of thinking at the time of my confirmation (1866). This ethical theism was a great help to me in those years, but from the time that I entered the Stuttgart Grammar School it gradually and imperceptibly evolved into pantheism, based on a deep love of Nature. During this period of transition, in 1868 I came across Herder's book on the History of Mankind, which appealed to my state of mind by its mixture of theism and pantheism, and to which I owe a great deal. It gives such a wide and lofty view of the whole development of the history of mankind, extending from the earliest origins onwards through all kinds and varieties of civilization. The idea of evolution became one of the fundamental elements of my mental outlook. Herder draws special attention to the evolution of spiritual life out of its first animal origins, and he regards man always as linked up with that Nature from which he has gradually evolved. Thus in 1869, when I first heard Darwin's name and when my school-friends told me about the new theory of man's animal ancestry, it was no surprise to me, because through my reading of Herder I was already familiar with the idea. In later years there has been much discussion as to whether Herder can be called a forerunner of Darwin. At any rate in my case Darwin's theory of descent added nothing new to what I had learnt from Herder.

Naturally I carried these studies further in later years, but from that time onwards one of the fundamentals in my philosophy has been this fact of man's animal ancestry. About this time I came under Plato's influence, which acted as a counter-balancing factor. I read the usual *Dialogues* and the *Apology*, but our Professor was old and though very thorough he was dull and kept us to the grammatical side. His routine teaching made nothing like the same impression on me as three lessons from a young teacher called Breitmaier, who came to replace him during an illness. He read to us in Greek the myth in the *Phaedrus* on the nature of the soul, and the description of the cave from the *Republic*. This opened up a new world to me, the world of "Ideas," and as be also spoke of Plato's myths, the seed was sown then of that conception which later I myself named the "World of 'As if'".

The Introduction to Philosophy which was customary at that time in South Germany, with its bare outlines of logic, psychology and ethics, played quite an insignificant part compared with the revolutionary ideas which I was discovering for myself. This was all the more marked because our professor was Gustav Pfitzer, the poet made notorious by Heinrich Heine. But I should like to pay him a tribute of admiration here, because he was a man of noble character and my feeling for him as a personality was one of absolute reverence. The opposition which I expressed in 1905 to the Introduction to Philosophy as a separate branch of instruction derives from my own earlier experience. In the same dissertation *Philosophy in State Examinations*[1] (1905) I urged on the other hand that philosophy should be the general principle of instruction in all subjects and I drew attention particularly to the "opportunist method" of philosophy, which emphasizes points of philosophical significance when the occasion arises in other branches of study. I found an example of this in 1870 in the excellent teaching of our Headmaster, K. A. Schmid, who has made a name for himself as the editor of a large Encyclopaedia of Education in many volumes. In an extra class of advanced pupils he used to hold grammatical discussions on complicated problems of Latin syntax and he taught us to overcome difficulties by a strict logical analysis of conjunctions and their various uses. The double conjunction 'As if' was not mentioned, but it was this accurate logical training which later enabled me to recognize in the grammatical formation 'As if' the Fiction which has such logical significance.

Last but not least I must mention Schiller's poems and treatises, for they too had an important influence on me at that period. Every earnest young student is inspired and fired by Schiller, but this Swabian poet had a special appeal for me, because he had played a great part in the history of my mother's family. My great-grandfather, Professor Balthasar Haug, was Schiller's teacher and his son, the epigrammatic poet Friedrich Haug, was Schiller's friend. Schiller's philosophic poems, in which he contrasts the ideal world of pure form with the empirical world, were easily linked up with the Platonic influences mentioned above. Many of Schiller's verses made an indelible impression on me, for instance the words "In error only is there life, and knowledge must be death",[2] words which in certain respects have become the foundation of my theory of Fiction. Schiller's philoshophical treatises were of course still too difficult for me to attempt, but I understood his theory of play as the primary element of artistic creation and enjoyment; and it had great influence on the development of my thought, for later on I recognized in play the 'As if', as the driving force of æsthetic activity and intuition.

Thus equipped, I entered the University of Tübingen in the autumn of 1870, as a student at the residential Theological College there. At Tübingen memories still linger of the many great figures who have passed through its University: Schelling, Hegel, Hölderlin, Waiblinger, Baur, Strauss, Vischer, Zeller and many others. In my time the University was run on very liberal lines and great freedom was, and still is, given to the students to allow them to develop in their own way. In the first four terms especially, they are given a very thorough grounding in philosophy. My first term was devoted to ancient philosophy, the second to later philosophy up to Kant, the third to the period from Kant to Hegel, and the fourth from Schleiermacher onwards to the philosophic foundations of dogmatism. First-rate coaches gave us careful instruction on an independent scientific basis and they also supervised the working out of philosophic treatises by the students, who were encouraged to think freely for themselves. No obstacles were placed in the path of my philosophical development. On the contrary, I was encouraged on all sides, especially when I started a prize essay for the faculty of philosophy on "Recent Theories of Consciousness."[3] For this work, which took me a year, I received first prize in the autumn of 1873, and this enabled me to travel in Switzerland and North Italy. This prize essay was also the decisive factor in making me abandon my theological studies which I had started with much hesitation. My transition to Pure philosophy was made easy for me in every way. Thus I have good reason to remember the Theological College of Tübingen with gratitude, particularly Professor Buder, the open-minded and kind-hearted Director at that time.

Sigwart was of course the most prominent of all the lecturers on philosophy. His lectures on the History of Philosophy, on Psychology, and above all naturally on Logic were splendid and I owe much to them. In exercises also, particularly on Schleiermacher, I learnt to admire his penetrating mind and his broad outlook. Yet I cannot say that I was a disciple of Sigwart, in the sense that I accepted the fundamentals of his philosophy. What did not appeal to me was his absolutely teleological conception of the universe, which was bound up with the theological, or rather theologising metaphysic that he had derived from Schleiermacher. Therefore, unlike me, who was spending more and more time in scientific study, he had little sympathy with the new scientific theory of evolution. Sigwart certainly revolutionized logic, but in the real problems of philosophy, particularly in the question of the mechanical conception of Nature, he was too timid for my taste.

With regard to this latter problem, Liebmann who was then a lecturer, helped me much, but unfortunately for me he was shortly called away. The other regular professor, Reeff, had built up a system of his own on the foundations of Schelling's teaching, but this had only a passing effect on my philosophical development. What I did retain, however, was the view which he frequently expressed, namely, that a philosophic system need not be regarded as true simply because it satisfies the emotions; whoever seeks this satisfaction must not go to the philosopher to find it; philosophy must give light, but it need not give warmth. Köstlin, an enthusiastic Hegelian, gave us brilliant and inspiring lectures on æsthetic questions, but when he tried to win me over to Planck, I refused to follow him.

So really I had only myself to fall back upon. In my first term the teaching of the Greek nature-philosophers made a great impression on me, because of their close similarity with the modern theory of evolution. Anaximander appealed to me especially also because of his profound words on the vengeance which all separate existences must suffer. An incomplete treatise *Anaximander and the Indeterminate*[4] resulted, and in it I anticipated much of what Teichmüller afterwards said about him. I also worked at Aristotle very thoroughly. In my second term Spinoza absorbed me by his consistency and his dispassionate conception of the universe.

But the impression made upon me by Kant was very different from the rest. In every respect he freed my mind, without fettering it. The bold theory of the ideality of space and time always liberates the mind from immediacy, from the pressure of the material world, even although one soon recognizes that in the long run it is not tenable in that form. But what impressed me most was Kant's discovery of the contradictions with which human thought is faced when it ventures into the realm of metaphysics. Kant's theory of antinomies had a profound influence on me. I derived permanent value not only from his theory of the limitation of knowledge to experience, but also from his doctrine that action, the practical, must take the first place, in other words the so-called supremacy of practical reason. This seemed to appeal to my innermost being.

Thus it was natural that the systems of Fichte, Schelling, and Hegel, in spite of their wonderful architecture and their wide range, could not hold me for long, although in accordance with the plan of studies of the College I had concentrated on these three systems. It was Fichte's preference for the practical and Hegel's theory of contradiction and its significance for human thought and reality that appealed to me most.

The official plan of studies passed from the "German Idealism" of Fichte, Schelling and Hegel direct to Schleiermacher. But I followed my own course and turned to Schopenhauer, who until then had been ignored, even despised by the Faculty. But I had got hold of E. von Hartmann's *Philosophy of the Unconscious*, which was making a great stir at the time, but which of course was officially non-existent for the College, and it led back to Schopenhauer, whose name was constantly being mentioned in all current literature. So I went straight to the source and studied Schopenhauer very thoroughly.

Schopenhauer's teaching gave me much that was new and great and lasting, pessimism[5], irrationalism and voluntarism. The impression which he made upon me was, although not extensively, yet certainly intensively greater than that of Kant. In order to explain this, I must go further afield. In all the systems of philosophy which I had hitherto met, the irrational aspect of the world and of life had not received attention, or at least adequate attention. The ideal of philosophy was to explain everything rationally, that is to say, by logical conclusions to prove it rational, in other words logical, significant, fitting. The Hegelian philosophy came nearest to this ideal, and it was considered the supreme achievement of philosophy. This ideal of knowledge, however, had failed to satisfy me, for my mind was far too keen and critical not to see the irrational element in Nature as well in history. From my earliest days I had come across countless manifestations of the irrational in my immediate surroundings. It may sound strange, but it is a fact that my physical constitution had much to do with this also. From the very beginning, extreme short-sightedness has hindered me in all my activities. Whereas my nature impelled me to action, to energetic movement, to activity in every form and aspect, this physical defect forced me into reserve, passivity, loneliness. This glaring contrast between my physical constitution and temperament has always struck me as absolutely irrational, and it has sharpened my senses to notice all the other irrational aspects of existence. I therefore considered it to be a lack of sincerity in most systems of philosophy, that they tried more or less to hide the irrational side. Now for the first time I came across a man who recognized irrationality openly and honourably, and who attempted to explain it in his system of philosophy. Schopenhauer's love of truth was a revelation to me. I did not follow his metaphysical constructions, because since I had studied Kant the impossibility of all metaphysics had seemed to me to be obvious. But that part of Schopenhauer's teaching which can be established empirically became my lasting possession and a source of fruitful inspiration, particularly in so far as it could be linked up with the theory of evolution, which was then much to the fore, and with the theory of the struggle for existence.

I have already mentioned that what appealed to me most in Kant and in Fichte was their emphasis on the practical aspect. In Schopenhauer I found this same tendency, but much clearer, much stronger, much more comprehensive. With him it was not the rather nebulous "practical reason", but the empirical psychological element of "the will" which was placed in the forefront. To me much that had hitherto been inexplicable seemed suddenly to be explained or at least explicable

What struck me most was his proof of the fact that originally thought is only used by the will as a means to its own ends, and that only in the course of evolution does thought free itself from the bonds of the will and become an end in itself. Schopenhauer has already shown how the brain of animals is quite small, yet is large enough to act as an organ for the execution of the will's purposes, whereas in the higher animals, and particularly in man, it has grown out of all proportion. Darwin's theory of evolution, which was being worked out at this time, corroborated Schopenhauer's contention, which gave me a fundamental insight into reality.

This theory of Schopenhauer's seemed to me to be so fruitful that it called for expansion and general application. In my notes of the years from 1872 onwards this universal "Law of the Preponderance of the Means over the End" is constantly recurring. Everywhere I found evidence that an original means working towards a definite end has the tendency to acquire independence and to become an end in itself. Thought, which originally serves the purposes of the will and only gradually becomes an end in itself was the most obvious special case of a universal law of Nature that manifests itself in new forms always and everywhere, in all organic life, in the processes of the mind, in economic life, and in history. Unfortunately at that period I never managed to publish this "Law" and said nothing more about it when many years later Wundt produced his theory of the "Heterogeny of Purpose," which expresses the same idea. I maintain, however, that the expression "Law of the Preponderance of the Means over the End" gives the idea of the theory much more clearly and distinctly.

This theory of Schopenhauer's, that fundamentally thought is dependent on the purposes of the Life-will and has developed into an end in itself only as it were against all laws, became linked up in my mind with Kant's theory that human thought is bound by certain limits and that metaphysical knowledge is impossible. This limitation of human knowledge to experience, which Kant emphasizes over and over again, no longer struck me as a deplorable deficiency in the human mind, compared with a potential higher form of mind, not bound by these limits. This limitation of human knowledge seemed to me now to be a necessary and natural result of the fact that thought and knowledge are originally only a means to attain the Life-purpose, so that their actual independence signifies a breaking-away from their original purpose; indeed, by the fact of this breaking-loose, thought is confronted by impossible problems, which are not merely insoluble to human thought while possibly soluble to a higher form of thought, but problems which are utterly impossible to all forms of thought as such. This conviction has become one of the most solid foundations of my conception of the universe, and since that time it has grown within me and has crystallized with the years into an ever clearer form.

Another powerful influence on these same lines made itself felt about this time (1872–73), when Adolf Horwicz' book *Psychologische Analysen auf physiologischer Grundlage* came into my hands. In this work Horwicz showed that all psychology is based on the so-called scheme of reflexes: sense-impressions following upon stimulation, ideas leading up to thought, expressive movement and volitional action. The simplest reflexes are motor phenomena following upon stimulation. These stimuli must result in elementary feelings, which release corresponding movements, representing the most elementary beginning of volitional actions. In the interval between these impressions on the one hand and the motor expression on the other hand ideas come to the surface, first in an elementary form, but growing more and more complicated, so that in their highest form they may be described as Thought-processes. Thus the idea and later on the thought appear as merely a bridge, an intermediary between impression on the one hand and expression on the other hand. This theory, which Horwicz worked out most carefully and comprehensively, fitted in very well with the idea that I had derived from Schopenhauer, namely that thought originally is only a means for the purposes of the will, and both ideas coincided with the conviction that I had gained from Kant as to the supremacy of the practical.

As I have already mentioned, I was at this time not only working at the study of philosophy and its history, but was chiefly occupied with the great ideas which were revolutionizing science at this time. Firstly, I was interesting myself in the application, in every sphere of Nature, of the mechanical theory, with special reference to the "Law of the Conservation of Energy," secondly I was studying the new aspect taken on by the organic sciences as a result of Darwin's theory of evolution[6] and the theory of selection involved in this, namely the mechanical, automatic selection of the fittest through the so-called "Struggle for Existence". In all branches of inorganic and organic science I endeavoured to get not only a general survey, but so far as conditions allowed, a special knowledge of the most important aspects. I seized every opportunity of keeping abreast of the movement, not only by reading the special books, but also by getting into personal touch with scientists. Thus I came into contact with Hüfner, the Professor of Physiology, and one day I had an interesting discussion with him, on the Life-force. With youthful prejudice I spoke very strongly against it, as an antiquated and useless theory. He granted that my objections were in part justified, but he pointed out that the application of this idea was expedient on practical grounds and might be not only permissible, but even necessary, although it might be regarded as false or at least not quite theoretically justified. He gave me his book on the Life-force which had just appeared.

A new seed was sown in my mind by all this and it has proved to be of the most lasting and decisive importance. It made me look carefully for arguments on the same lines and I collected examples from all the sciences. I had all the more opportunity for this, because I was not only studying many branches of science, but with real universality I was seizing every occasion of exploring new scientific fields, in which personal acquaintances had to help me as much as books.

In my last year at Tübingen, from the autumn of 1873 till the summer of 1874, I studied principally the classical languages, Greek archæology and Germanic philology. As I was able in the autumn of 1873 formally to give up the study of theology, which I had nominally carried on *ex professo* until then, according to the wishes of my parents, I had to become reconciled to the plan of lecturing in a university. So in this last year I attended classes in classical and Germanic philology. What attracted me most in classical philology was Greek art and in Germanic philology the evolution of language, which at that time, thanks to Schleicher's Indo-Germanic Grammar was

XXX THE ORIGIN OF THE PHILOSOPHY OF 'AS IF'

being treated in accordance with the theory of evolution. I also began the study of Sanskrit under Roth.

What interested me most in these classes and in the history class which I also attended, was the practical contact with the exact methods of science. Ever since I had come under Sigwart's influence, I had been interested in Logic, not only for its formal aspect but especially for methodology, and now I had a welcome opportunity of collaborating in the practice of scientific methods and the formulation of theoretical conclusions from them.

In the summer of 1874 I graduated from Tübingen with a prize dissertation on "Recent Theories of Consciousness",[7] in which classical and Germanic philology appeared as subordinate sections.

But now the ground was burning under my feet. I had spent four years in Tübingen. According to the regulations of the College I had to spend eight sessions there. All that I could get out of Tübingen I had richly gained with hard, honest work. Now it seemed advisable to complete my one year of voluntary military service, and for this, according to the custom of many of my South German countrymen, I chose Leipzig, in whose celebrated University I could learn so much that was new and important.

Before leaving my home, however, I was anxious to consult some men of learning about a question that was troubling my mind. At the grammar school in Stuttgart I had turned from theism to pantheism, and at the University of Tübingen I had evolved from pantheism by way of Kantian agnosticism to a position closely approaching Schopenhauer's atheism. Now the question arose, as to what attitude one should take on this basis of theoretical atheism towards the historical forms of the Church, and to religious dogma with its historical origins, and whether one was obliged to adopt an absolutely negative attitude towards the positive Church. To my mind this did not seem to be necessary. My studies in Greek mythology, particularly its expression in ancient works of art (at that time called "Art Mythology") had taught me that, according to the custom of the cultured Greeks and Romans, and as I had noticed earlier in Plato, one may regard and treat these myths as "myths" and yet (or rather just because of this) continue to esteem such fictions for their ethical and æsthetic value. On this matter I wanted to hear the opinion of the three wise men of Swabia, at that time her most famous sons:—David F. Strauss, who had analysed the stories of the Bible, particularly of the New Testament, and the formulæ of dogma as "myths"; Friedrich T. Vischer, who earlier had made a strong attack on the Church but who, as an historian of art, could not get on without the myths of the Church; and lastly Robert Mayer, who discovered the law of the Conservation of Energy and who combined a strictly mechanical conception of Nature with a strong religious sense. I already had relations with Strauss, whose *Old Faith and the New* was making a great stir at the time. It was easy for me to see him, but I found him on a bed of sickness which a few months later was his death-bed. So our talk could not go very deep, but he gave me an introduction to his old friend Vischer. This latter, however, would only talk on his one favourite subject of those days, "the decline of the German people since 1871", on which he had publicly spoken on various occasions. He wanted to hear my opinion as a representative of the younger generation. I would not at that time quite agree that it was a "decline", but I had to admit that even I had noticed signs in the younger generation of boasting and arrogance and also an underestimation of the neighbouring civilizations. The French, who had been so gloriously defeated, were underestimated both on the ethical and cultural side. But what seemed to me much more dangerous was the universal misunderstanding and even contempt felt for the English. From my earliest years I had known many English people, and I had learnt to recognize, together with their peculiarities, their ability and reliability. Moreover, I had the greatest admiration for their literature, and the names of Hume and Darwin had made the English doubly dear to me. But here in Vischer there seemed to me to be something lacking, because he only knew the English from a distance and had no admiration for Hume and Darwin. My visit to R. Mayer was accidentally prevented.

When I arrived in Leipzig, in September 1874, I presented myself at once for military service. But because of my eyes, which even then were abnormal, I was not accepted. From one point of view this was a great blow to me, because I was fond of all sports and particularly of the military gymnastics which the Swabian Professor Jäger had introduced, and I should have liked to develop this side of my active nature. On the other hand, I naturally welcomed with enthusiasm the free time which I saw ahead of me, and at once employed my leisure in carrying out a long-standing desire. In Tübingen I had become acquainted with nearly all the sciences, but of one I still knew no more than what I had learnt at school, namely mathematics; and this was a source of growing distress. Our teacher of mathematics in Stuttgart was Professor Reuschle (also a friend of David F. Strauss) who had made a name for himself by his theory of the prime numbers, but who had no gift for teaching. I had tried to get on by studying alone (I got the suitable text-books out of the public library), and I had achieved considerable success, but in Tübingen I had no time to follow up these studies. Now with real avidity I threw myself into analytic geometry and the infinitesimal calculus. Both these lines of study revealed wonderful new truths to me that had originated in the minds of Descartes and Leibniz. Besides this, they gave me striking examples of methodic fictions, which were of great importance for the continuation of the methodological investigations which I had started in Tübingen. So altogether these studies were very fruitful.

In another direction, these winter days of 1874–75 were of decisive importance. It was about this time that the second edition of Friedrich Albert Lange's *History of Materialism* appeared in its enlarged form and with the addition of much scientific material. I had come across the first edition of this work in Tübingen, and it had filled me with admiration, but it made no deeper impression on me because the scientific apparatus of the book in its original form was inadequate. Now, with that defect remedied, the material fell into my hands at the right moment. Now at last I had found the man for whom I had sought in vain during those four years in Tübingen. I found a master, a guide, an ideal teacher. The spirit which urged me onwards more or less vaguely, dominated him with complete clearness and perfection of form. On the one hand he had the highest respect for facts, and an exact knowledge of the natural sciences, together with mastery over the whole history of civilization; on the other hand he was an expert in Kantian criticism, with views modified and extended by Schopenhauer. Above all, he was a man of high ethical ideals, and with regard to religious dogma he combined the strongest radicalism in theory with the most broad-minded tolerance in practice. I had striven for this myself, but never before had I found all these qualities in one person. All that I had striven for and aimed at stood before my eyes as a finished masterpiece. From this time onwards I called myself a disciple of F. A. Lange.[8] Naturally I read his other publications, particularly his book on the "Labour question", and his activity in this sphere also showed me that he was a man of wide vision and warm heart.

What gave the *History of Materialism* its particular value for my special studies of this period was that from my point of view F. A. Lange was on right lines even in regard to the methodic problem of fictions. On the other hand he showed a certain hesitation and vagueness on this point, so that I hoped, on the basis of my further thorough research, to be able to go further than he in this special question.

About this time I found another source of help in the same direction. The two old disciples of Herbart, Drobisch and Struempell were then teaching in Leipzig. Herbart's name had hardly ever been mentioned in Tübingen, but now my studies led me to him and I found in him very valuable examples of a theory of fiction, which he tried to apply in a practical form to his own philosophy. At the same time I was naturally drawn to a much deeper study of Herbart's psychology, and psychology in general; and through the influence of that ardent disciple of Herbart, Dr Susanna Rubinstein, who was then living in Leipzig, I got to know Volkmann and Lazarus. All this strengthened me in the conviction that, without psychology, philosophy and also epistemology are and can only be a methodic abstraction, which can be brought to no systematic conclusion.

Avenarius, whom I got to know at "The Academic Philosophical Society" which he had founded, influenced me in the same direction. He advised me to read Steinthal, whose Introduction to Psychology became one of the bases of my philosophy. His theory of the transformation by apperception of the material given to the senses has remained with me ever since.

I derived great profit from Avenarius in so far as he was a pungent critic of Kant's theories. This prevented me from regarding Kant's philosophy as dogma, but anyway I was not inclined to do this. I could not follow Avenarius, however, in his radical empiricism, or rather positivism. He realized quite rightly that the ideas of substance, causality etc. are imposed subjectively by the psyche on the given, yet for this very reason, according to "the principle of the least energy", he wanted to eliminate them completely from human thought. But I held that they are suitable fictions, which must be retained because of their utility.

In the autumn of 1875 Wundt came to Leipzig. His first lecture was on logic and I listened to it with great interest and profit. He appealed to me in every way. For his sake I should have liked to remain on in Leipzig, and I had already planned a *Journal of Pure and Applied Logic*, in which I hoped to interest him. But family matters called me back to South Germany. I was only able to have one more term in the North, and that was to be in Berlin, where the Swabian, Eduard Zeller, was actively at work. The help which I got from him and from his friend Helmholtz, and also from Steinthal, Lazarus, Lasson and Paulsen was more or less valuable to me, but what was really important was that I came across the writings of Gruppe, who had died shortly before this, and they were most useful for my theory of fiction. My private studies were devoted mostly to David Hume and John Stuart Mill, whose exact knowledge was decisive for my philosophic attitude.

At the same time, during my Berlin days in the summer of 1876, my first book on philosophy was published, *Hartmann, Dühring and Lange*—a critical Essay on the History of Philosophy in the Nineteeth Century. It consisted of lectures which I had given in the Academic Philosophical Society at Leipzig. The author of the *History of Materialism*, with his Kantian tendencies, seemed to me to strike the happy medium between the spiritualistic metaphysics of E. von Hartmann on the one hand and the materialistic positivism of E. Dühring on the other hand. In Berlin I had got to know these two men personally. In my book I also announced the early publication of my investigation of Fictions.

For family reasons I had to choose a University near my South German home in which to take up my residence as a lecturer; so in the autumn of 1876 I moved to Strassburg, where I received a welcome from Laas. In his recent work on Kant's Analogies of Experience he had drawn a sharp line between himself and the Kantian, or rather Neo-Kantian, A-priorism or "Transcendentalism," and he was gradually approaching that radical attitude which he took up some years later in his three-volume treatise on Idealism and Positivism. He was the unprejudiced man of whom I stood in need. He was able to do justice to my own attitude. He was busy just then with the study of John Stuart Mill's *Examination of Sir William Hamilton's Philosophy*, in which I joined him, all the more readily because this was really a continuation of my Berlin studies of Hume and Mill. The resolution of so-called reality, from an epistemological or psychological point of view, into "Sensations and possibilities of sensation" seemed both to him and to me to be the correct analytical way. On the other hand Laas resembled Avenarius, who was related to him, in his positivist tendency to eliminate all further subjective additions as unjustified and useless, whereas I was always anxious to emphasize and keep hold of the practical value and use of these theoretically unjustifiable conceptions of the older idealism.

During the latter part of the year 1876, for my inaugural dissertation, I wrote down my thoughts in a large manuscript, to which I gave the title "Logical Studies. Part I: The Theory of Scientific Fictions." As I had been carefully collecting the material for several years and had gone into it most thoroughly many times, the writing of it did not take me long. I handed in my MS. in the New Year and at the end of February 1877 I received my *venia legendi*. The work which received this recognition from the Faculty is exactly the same as what was published in 1911 as the "Part I: Basic Principles" of *The Philosophy of 'As if'*. In it I developed the whole system of scientific fictions, that is to say the 'As if' treatment, applied practically to the most varied aspects of science, and I tried to give an exhaustive theory of this manifold 'As if' process.

But like Laas I regarded this dissertation only as a rough outline, in need of much supplementing and correction, so I made use of the next two years, so far as my lectures allowed me, to work at my MS. My father's death compelled me to look out for some more remunerative occupation,[9] and so I made a very advantageous agreement with the generous and far-sighted Stuttgart publisher, W. Spemann, to produce a Commentary on Kant for the centenary in 1881 of his *Critique of Pure Reason*. I had then just started a far more thorough study of Kant, particularly his 'As if' theory, and in the course of this I had found in his *Prolegomena* that "misplacement of pages" which had passed unnoticed by many thousands of Kant readers for nearly a hundred years, but which is generally recognized by science nowadays. So I hoped, by application of the philological method, and by penetrating logical analysis, to further the study of Kant. But, as I have said, this new work was only a means to an end, and I hoped in a few years to be able to return to my researches on Fiction.

The above-mentioned "Law of the Preponderance of the Means over the End", which unfortunately I neglected to formulate theoretically and publish at the right moment, has proved in a practical sense very momentous in my own life. When, in 1884, the first volume of my Commentary on Kant[10] brought me an appointment as special Professor at Halle, I hoped soon to be able to finish the other volumes there. But my lectures on the one hand and bad health on the other held up the publication of the second volume until 1892. In 1894 I was appointed regular Professor in Halle, and in 1896 I founded the *Kantstudien* as a means of helping on my work. But even this means preponderated over its own end. My work on the Commentary became secondary to the new periodical. When in 1904 the centenary of Kant's death was celebrated, circumstances seemed to make it my duty, in order to promote the *Kantstudien*, to start a Fund to defray the costs. This Fund was a success, but its organization necessitated the foundation of a Kant Society and this gradually became more and more an end in itself and took up too much of my time and strength, although I was fortunate in having most efficient help in all these undertakings. Thus the means always triumphed over the end for whose sake it had been called into being, and robbed the original end of its life-force.

In 1906, in the midst of all these curious complications and crossings of my original intentions, a misfortune unexpectedly brought a happy solution, and enabled me after twenty-seven years to return to my original plan, which I had given up in 1879. The misfortune was the weakening of my eyesight, so that it became impossible for me to continue my lectures, or the special classes which I particularly enjoyed. So I had to give up my official duties. The eyesight still remaining to me was just sufficient to allow me to publish my MS. I got my Dissertation of 1876 copied, and introduced a number of small editorial alterations. This comprehensive MS. now forms "Part I: Basic Principles" of The Philosophy of 'As if'. I also completed the revision which I had made between 1877 and the beginning of 1879 on the basis of the reviews of that time, and this forms the Part II (Special) of the complete work. This part took me two and a half years because of my bad eyesight, and Part III (Historical) took me another two and a half years. Between 1877 and 1879 I had made a note of the most important 'As if' passages in Kant's works, and I now completed this in an exhaustive manner, so that I was able to produce a monograph on Kant's 'As if' theory of nearly one hundred pages. The exposition of Forberg's religion of 'As if' also took me a long time, and so did the development of F. A. Lange's "Standpoint of the Ideal," with which I had much in common. But what took longer still was the final section on Nietzsche's theory of Fictions, which he had condensed into a few pages. It was the Spring of 1911 before the work appeared.

I called this work, The Philosophy of 'As if' because it seemed to me to express more convincingly than any other possible title what I wanted to say, namely that 'As if', i.e. appearance, the consciously-false, plays an enormous part in science, in world-philosophies and in life. I wanted to give a complete enumeration of all the methods in which we operate intentionally with consciously false ideas, or rather judgments. I wanted to reveal the secret life of these extraordinary methods. I wanted to give a complete theory, an anatomy and physiology so to speak, or rather a biology of 'As if'. For the method of fiction which is found in a greater or lesser degree in all the sciences can best be expressed by this complex conjunction 'As if'. Thus I had to give a survey of all the branches of science from this point of view.

But it was not only a methodological investigation that I was attempting. The study of fictional thought in all branches of science had led me gradually to extend these investigations to philosophy itself, particularly to epistemology, ethics and the philosophy of religion. Just as my investigations into the function of 'As if' had arisen out of a definite view of the world so again this developed independently into a universal system of philosophy—I gave it the name of "Positivist Idealism" or "Idealistic Positivism". As I have already mentioned, Ernst Laas had published between 1884 and 1886 a three-volume work on Idealism and Positivism, in which he attacked Idealism and championed Positivism. The positivist attitude was also represented in Germany by Mach, Avenarius and to a certain extent by Schuppe, and it found particular favour with the scientifically inclined (but the name Positivism was never placed in the forefront of any programme). The chief currents of German philosophy, however, were certainly idealistic, though in different ways. Between these one-sided views[11] it seemed to me that a compromise was necessary, all the more so because attempts of this kind had met with success in other countries. I considered that the time had come to announce the union of Idealism and Positivism. The result has proved that the right word was spoken at the right moment.

The term "Scepticism" has occasionally been applied to the Philosophy of 'As if' and its systematic doctrines; but this is not correct, for scepticism implies a theory which raises doubt or questioning to the dignity of a principle. The Philosophy of 'As if', however, has never had a trace of this attitude. In a simple and straightforward investigation it proves that consciously false conceptions and judgments are applied in all sciences; and it shows that these scientific Fictions are to be distinguished from Hypotheses. The latter are assumptions which are probable, assumptions the truth of which can be proved by further experience. They are therefore verifiable. Fictions are never verifiable, for they are hypotheses which are known to be false, but which are employed because of their utility. When a series of hypotheses in mathematics, mechanics, physics, chemistry, ethics or the philosophy of religion are shown in this way to be useful fictions and so justify themselves, surely this does not imply scepticism. The reality of these hypotheses is not doubted; it is denied on the basis of the positive facts of experience. The expression "Relativism" would be more applicable to the Philosophy of

"As if", in so far as it denies all absolute points (in mathematics just as in metaphysics) and shows a natural affinity with the theory of relativity both of the past and the present.

The use of the term "Scepticism" as applied to the Philosophy of 'As if', has no doubt been partly due to the doubt with which this philosophy regards metaphysical realities, particularly God and immortality. But the above consideration applies in this case also. In the Philosophy of 'As if' I have never attempted to hide the fact that I regard these conceptions as Fictions of ethical value. My conviction in this respect is clear, simple and decided.

Many people of course confuse the technical expression involved here and think that they can discover in the Philosophy of 'As if' not exactly "Scepticism", but "Agnosticism". This latter system teaches that human knowledge is confined within more or less narrow limits and speaks of the Unintelligible, the Unknowable, according to Spencer's definition. Naturally the Philosophy of 'As if' also holds that knowledge has certain limits, but not in the sense that these limits bound only human knowledge, while they are non-existent for a superhuman knowledge. This is the theory of Kant and Spencer. It is the old complaint that the human mind is confined by narrow boundaries, which do not limit the higher forms of mind. My opinion is that these boundaries of knowledge are not implicit in the specific nature of man as compared with other possible minds of a higher order, but that such limitations are part of the nature of thought itself; that is to say, if there are higher forms of mind, these limitations will affect them and even the highest Mind of all. For thought originally only serves the Will to Life as a means to an end, and in this direction also it fulfils its function. But when thought has broken loose from its original aim, according to the Law of the Preponderance of the Means over the End, and has become an end in itself, it sets itself problems to which it is not equal because it has not developed for this purpose; and finally the emancipated thought sets itself problems which in themselves are senseless, for instance, questions as to the origin of the world, the formation of what we call matter, the beginning of motion, the meaning of the world and the purpose of life. If thought is regarded as a biological function, it is obvious that these are impossible problems for thought to solve, and quite beyond the natural boundaries which limit thought as such. From this point of view, we have no inclination to fall back on the favourite old grievance about the limitations of human knowledge. At most we may complain that the Law of the Preponderance of the Means over the End has led us to ask questions which are as unanswerable as the problem of $\sqrt{-1}$. A moment of reflection will show that all knowledge is a reduction of the unknown to the known, that is to say a comparison. This proves therefore that this comparison or reduction will somewhere stop automatically. In no sense, therefore, can the Philosophy of 'As if' be called scepticism or agnosticism

In the same way we can dispose of another objection which is raised against the Philosophy of 'As if', namely that the concept of reality implied in it is not uniform: on the one hand all reality is reduced to sensations, or sensational contents (in the sense of Mill's theory of "Sensations and possibilities of sensation"); on the other hand the concept of reality in the natural sciences, which reduce everything to the movement of matter and the smallest constituents of matter, is constantly being employed, sometimes tacitly, sometimes expressly. And with this is bound up the question, how to unify these two concepts of reality represented by the Philosophy of 'As if'.

One might admire the perspicacity of this discovery of a twofold concept of reality in the Philosophy of 'As if', if one were not surprised at the short-sightedness of the subsequent question. I am going to ask a question in return. Has any philosophical system of ancient, modern or present times ever succeeded in bringing these two spheres into a logical, rational relation? These two hemispheres of reality, expressed briefly on the one hand as the world of motion and on the other hand the world of consciousness, have never been brought into a logically satisfactory relation by any philosopher. They will never be brought into a definitely unified association by any rational formula. We stand here at a point where an impossible problem confronts our reason. This question is just as impossible of solution by rational methods as the question of the purpose of existence. Although we, who ask this question, permanently unite in our nature these two halves of reality, or rather just because the divergence, or the obvious contradiction, between motion and consciousness runs all through our own being, our mind is not in a position to answer satisfactorily this fundamental question or this so-called world-riddle.

Therefore he who would criticize any system of philosophy, or the philosophy of "As if" in particular, for not answering this question, is in the same intellectual position as a man who would reproach a mathematician for not solving the problem of the squaring of the circle in his text-book of geometry, or a technical engineer for not dealing with the construction of the *perpetuum mobile* in his text-book of engineering.

In discussing ultimate world-problems, one is always coming up against this rationally insoluble antithesis between motions of matter and particles of matter on the one hand and on the other hand sensations, or rather contents of consciousness. For the philosopher who deals with the analysis of our contents of consciousness, this analysis ends everywhere with our sensations on the psychological plane and with our sensational contents on the epistemological plane. The world is to him an endless accumulation of sensational contents which, however, are not given to us and to him without plan, but in which certain regularities of co-existence and succession can be found. These sensational data—what Windelband calls "Gegebenheiten" and Ziehen "Gignomene"—these events crowd upon us more or less irresistibly; indeed they even cast a lasting fear over us, for we have to rule our lives according to them, in constant expectation of their appearance. This world of sensational contents is the material with which alone the philosopher as such can deal. But on the other hand, the philosopher must recognize for good or ill that the scientist constructs quite a different sphere of reality, the world of motion, the mobile world. To construct a rational relation between these two worlds is an impossible desire of our understanding, which fundamentally is not fitted for the theoretical solution of world problems, but only for the practical service of the will to live.

Naturally the human mind is tormented by this insoluble contradiction between the world of motion and the world of consciousness, and this torment can eventually become very oppressive. One would be well advised to remember how Kant had already pointed out that there are problems which mock us perpetually, but which we cannot get rid of. But there is one solution of this and similar torturing questions; for in intuition and in experience all this contradiction and distress fades into nothingness. Experience and intuition are higher than all human reason. When I see a deer feeding in the forest, when I see a child at play, when I see a man at work or sport, but above all when I myself am working or playing, where are the problems with which my mind has been torturing itself unnecessarily? We do not understand the world when we are pondering over its problems, but when we are doing the world's work. Here too the practical reigns supreme.

I will end by summarizing all the conclusions which are expressed in the Philosophy of 'As if', or which form its basis or arise out of it, as follows:—

(1) Philosophical analysis leads eventually, from an epistemological standpoint, to sensational contents, and from a psychological to sensations,

feelings and strivings or actions. Scientific analysis leads to another concept of reality, to matter and the smallest constituents and motions of matter. Naturally it is impossible for the mind as such to bring these two spheres of reality into a rational relation, although in intuition and experience they form a harmonious unity.

(2) The strivings which probably exist in the most elementary physical processes develop in organic beings into impulses. In man, who has sprung from the animal (and to a certain extent in all the higher animals) these impulses have evolved into will and action, which is expressed in movements and caused by stimuli or by the sensations arising from stimuli.

(3) Ideas, judgments and conclusions, that is to say thought, act as a means in the Service of the Will to Live and dominate. Thought is originally only a means in the struggle for existence and to this extent only a biological function.

(4) It is a universal phenomenon of nature that means which serve a purpose often undergo a more complete development than is necessary for the attainment of their purpose. In this case, the means, according to the completeness of its self-development, can emancipate itself partly or wholly and become established as an end in itself (Law of the Preponderance of the Means over the End).

(5) This Preponderance of the Means over the End has also taken place in thought, which in the course of time has gradually lost sight of its original practical purpose and is finally practised for its own sake as theoretical thought.

(6) As a result, this thought which appears to be independent and theoretical in its origins, sets itself problems which are impossible, not only to human thought, but to every form of thought; for instance, the problems of the origin and meaning of the universe. To this category belongs also the question of the relation between sensation and motion, popularly known as mind and matter.

(7) These endless, and, strictly speaking, senseless questions cannot be answered by looking forwards but only by looking backwards, by showing how they arose psychologically within us. Many of these questions are just as meaningless, as for instance the problem of $\sqrt{-1}$.

(8) If intellectualism or rationalism be identified with the assumption of an original theoretical reason as an inherent human faculty with certain problems to be determined by it, then my exposition must be termed

anti-rationalism or even irrationalism, in the same sense in which histories of modern philosophy, for instance that of Windelband, speak of "idealistic irrationalism".

(9) From this standpoint all thought-processes and thought-constructs appear a priori to be not essentially rationalistic, but biological phenomena.

(10) In this light many thought-processes and thought-constructs appear to be consciously false assumptions, which either contradict reality or are even contradictory in themselves, but which are intentionally thus formed in order to overcome difficulties of thought by this artificial deviation and reach the goal of thought by roundabout ways and by-paths. These artificial thought-constructs are called Scientific Fictions, and distinguished as conscious creations by their 'As if' character.

(11) The 'As if' world, which is formed in this manner, the world of the "unreal" is just as important as the world of the so-called real or actual (in the ordinary sense of the word); indeed it is far more important for ethics and æsthetics. This æsthetic and ethical world of 'As if', the world of the unreal, becomes finally for us a world of values which, particularly in the form of religion, must be sharply distinguished in our mind from the world of becoming.

(12) What we usually term reality consists of our sensational contents which press forcibly upon us with greater or lesser irresistibility and as "given" can generally not be avoided.

(13) In these given sensational contents (which include what we call our body) there is an abundance of regularity in co-existence and succession, investigation of which forms the content of science. By means of the sensational contents which we call our body, we can exercise greater or lesser influence on the rich world of the other sensational contents.

(14) In this world we find on the one hand a very great number of relations of fitness, on the other hand much that is not fitting. We have to take this as we find it, for there is little that we can alter. It is a satisfying Fiction for many to regard the world as if a more perfect Higher Spirit had created or at least regulated it. But this implies the supplementary Fiction of regarding a world of this sort as if the order created by the Higher Divine Spirit had been destroyed by some hostile force.

(15) It is senseless to question the meaning of the universe, and this is the idea expressed in Schiller's words: "Know this, a mind sublime puts

greatness into life, yet seeks it not therein" (*Huldigung der Künste* 1805). This is positivist idealism.

The journal which I founded in 1919 with Dr Raymund Schmidt, *Annalen der Philosophie* ("with particular reference to the problems of the 'As if' approach"), has been very useful in spreading and intensifying this positivist idealism or idealistic positivism. It represents quite a new type of journal, for its contributors include not only professional philosophers (Cornelius, Groos, Becher, Bergmann, Koffka, Kowalewski) but also eminent representatives of the most important branches of science, the theologian Heim, the lawyer Krückmann, the doctor Abderhalden, the mathematician Pasch, the physicist Volkmann, the biological botanist Hansen (†), the economist Pohle, and the art-historian Lange. It thus demonstrates in a practical way that philosophy can only advance in the closest co-operation with the individual sciences and that philosophy, although it has much to give to the individual sciences, yet has much more to learn from them. It is from this interactivity alone that a fruitful and lasting compromise and reconciliation between positivism and idealism can take place—at least in the manner in which this is the deliberate and fundamental aim of the Philosophy of 'As if'. The critical examination of the use of the different methods of the 'As if' system in the most varied branches of science must on the one hand promote the scientific theory of method; and on the other hand the right method must also be found of finally reconciling the positivism of facts with the "Standpoint of the Ideal" (F. A. Lange). This analysis and this synthesis must be mutually complementary.

NOTES

1 *Die Philosophie im Staatsexamen.*
2 Mauthner in his *Wörterbuch der Philosophie*, Vol. II (1911), p. 567, in the article "Truth" argues that these words of Schiller should not be claimed by biological Fictionalism. This may be so, but it remains historically true that it was these words which paved the way "in certain respects" for my Fictionalism.
3 "Die neueren Theorien des Bewusstseins."
4 *Anaximander und kein Ende.*
5 Schopenhauer's pessimism became in me a fundamental and lasting state of consciousness, and all the more so because of my own sad and difficult experiences. Even in earlier days I had been deeply affected by Schiller's lines

"Who can enjoy life, if he sees into its depths!" I have not found that this outlook tends to weaken biological and moral energy. On the contrary, I am one of those whom only pessimism enables to endure life, and to whom pessimism gives the ethical strength to work and fight for themselves as well as to help others. On the other hand, I believe that pessimism has given me a more objective view of reality. In particular, I regarded or rather judged the political situation of Germany even in those days, but especially in the last thirty years, in quite a different way from the great majority. I foresaw and prophesied for many years the World-war, its result and its consequences for us. I have also found that the people of other nations, who have been accustomed to a more realistic philosophy than the usual German idealism and optimism, had a far clearer view of reality. If Germany's leaders since 1871 had taken a lesson from Schopenhauer, Germany would not have fallen into this desperate condition. The development of the social question too might just as well have evolved towards the right as towards the left if Schopenhauer had been the guiding influence, instead of Rousseau and Hegel. Even in Kant, as I noticed in those early days, there is a strong under-current of pessimism. Therefore when E. von Hartmann described Kant as "the Father of Pessimism", I welcomed this description with enthusiasm. (Cf. *The Philosophy of 'As if'*, pp. 311 and 319). Kant's theory of "radical evil" in human nature is a direct contradiction of certain tendencies in extreme socialism.

6   In my excess of youthful zeal I produced a definition which at the time soon became a catchword, and also brought me much hostile criticism:— "Mankind is a species of monkey suffering from megalomania". The adverse comments which I had to listen to, even in scientific journals, were unjustified, in so far as the sentence was naturally a conscious and intentional exaggeration of a view justified on zoological and psychological, or psychiatrical, grounds.

7   According to the then prevailing custom in Tübingen, this dissertation has not been published.

8   There were two possible ways of working out the Neo-Kantianism of F. A. Lange. Either the Kantian standpoint could be developed, on the basis of a closer and more accurate study of Kant's teaching, and this is what Cohen has done, or one could bring Lange's Neo-Kantianism into relation with empiricism and positivism. This has been done by my philosophy of 'As if', which also leads to a more thorough study of Kant's 'As if' theory.

9   At that time I was also considering the plan of writing a History of English Philosophy, mentioned in my Preface to this translation. But there was then so little interest and understanding in Germany for the development of

English philosophy that on the advice of the experts of the time the publishers did not regard the suggestion with favour.

10 On my journey from Strassburg to Halle, I paid another visit to Friedrich T. Vischer, whom I had often seen in the interval. Our talk was concerned chiefly with his philosophical novel *Auch Eincr* (1897) in which he expresses his favourite idea of the decline of the German people since 1871. He had shown in this book how the Germans by their arrogance would become involved in a world-war, in which after hard struggles and a moral revival they would eventually be victorious. Even then I did not agree with this optimism, and my political pessimism grew stronger in the following years, particularly after 1888. After 1908, and particularly 1911, I contemplated following Leibniz' example and entering the arena of world-history with an anonymous pamphlet, *Finis Germaniac,* with the motto "Quos Deus vult perdere, prius dementat", and with the device of Schiller's Cassandra "The Thunderer's clouds loom heavy over Ilion". I thought of having this pamphlet printed in Switzerland, but my eyesight became rapidly worse and prevented me from doing this. I also said to myself that I would be a voice crying in the wilderness, for it seemed impossible to penetrate the blindness of my seventy million fellow-countrymen. I felt afraid too that the publication of my views might only increase the number of our enemies and the weight of their opposition and that my action might thus hasten the impending catastrophe. Even then I would have mentioned most of the factors that are recognized to-day—or at least ought to be recognized—as the causes of the disaster. An unjustified optimism (if I do not go so far as Schopenhauer in calling it a "criminal optimism") had for a long time been leading German policy astray in the direction of improvidence, rashness and arrogance. A rational pessimism might have saved us from the horrors of a world-war. World-philosophy and practical politics have a closer connection than is generally realized.

11 The growing tendency of the "idealistic" philosophers and the Neo-Kantians to return to Fichte and Hegel seemed to me to be becoming more and more dangerous. I was always convinced that this one-sided idealistic tendency, which was partly foreign and partly hostile to reality, was the more dangerous to the whole of German civilization in that it led our youth to underestimate foreign philosophy, and therewith the whole civilization of neighbouring peoples, their capacity and, in general, their mental and moral power.

GENERAL INTRODUCTION

THOUGHT, CONSIDERED FROM THE POINT OF VIEW OF A PURPOSIVE, ORGANIC FUNCTION

SCIENTIFIC thought is a function of the psyche. By the term "psyche" we do not understand a substance, but the organic whole of all so-called "mental" actions and reactions; these never come under external observation, but have to be partly inferred from physical signs, partly observed by the so-called inner sense. Psychical actions and reactions are, like every event known to us, necessary occurrences; that is to say, they result with compulsory regularity from their conditions and causes. If we would compare psychical processes with some group of external phenomena, the physical and in a narrower sense mechanical processes are less suitable than the functions of the organism. This statement is confirmed by the fact that so-called empirical utility is found in the psychical functions as well as in the organic functions of the bodily sphere. This utility is manifested here as there in a ready adaptation to circumstances and environment; in the maintenance of a striving and successful reaction of the physical or psychical organism to external impulses and influences; and in the adoption and acceptance or the repulsion of new elements. In the psyche there takes place not merely a mechanical play of ideas, but the movement of ideas fulfils to a great extent the demands of utility by its continual modification. All psychical processes are useful in the sense mentioned; above all the so-called theoretical processes of apperception. Scientific thought consists in such apperception-processes and is therefore to be considered from the point of view of an organic function.

Thus we would compare the logical or thought-processes with the organic creative processes. The appropriateness that we observe in growth, in propagation and regeneration, in adaptation to environment, in healing, and so on, in the sphere of the organic repeats itself in the psychical processes. The psychical organism also reacts fittingly to stimuli. It is not merely a receptacle into which foreign matter is simply poured, but may be compared to a machine with a chemical retort, which uses foreign matter most fittingly for its own maintenance and the maintenance of its motion, and appropriates it through assimilation, not through pure juxtaposition. And similarly consciousness is not to be compared to a mere passive mirror, which reflects rays according to purely physical laws, but "consciousness receives no external stimulus without moulding it according to its own nature." The psyche then is *an organic formative force*, which independently changes what has been appropriated, and can adapt foreign elements to its own requirements as easily as it adapts itself to what is new. The mind is not merely appropriative, it is also assimilative and constructive. In the course of its growth, it *creates its organs* of its own accord in virtue of its adaptable constitution, but only when stimulated from without, and *adapts them to external circumstances*. Such organs, created by the psyche for itself in response to external stimuli, are, for example, forms of perception and thought, and certain concepts and other logical constructs. Logical thought, with which we are especially concerned here, is an active appropriation of the outer world, a useful organic elaboration of the material of sensation. Logical thought is therefore an organic function of the psyche.

Just as the physical organism breaks up the matter which it receives, mixes it with its own juices and so thus makes it suitable for assimilation, so the psyche envelops the thing perceived with categories which it has developed out of itself. As soon as an external stimulus reaches the mind, which rapidly responds to it as though provided with delicate feelers, inner processes start, a psychical activity begins, the outcome of which is the appropriation of the thing perceived for some purpose.

To Steinthal is due the merit of having established and worked out this view of the organic function of the logical movements involved in knowing; we go a step further, in attempting to consider the organic thought-functions from the point of view of *purposive activity*. Sigwart and Lotze begin their Logic with this teleological point of view. Just as it is the purpose of the eye to transform the various ether-waves into an ordered system of fixed sensations, and, through refraction, reflection and so on of rays, to make reduced "images" of the objective world; and just as that organ is suitably arranged for the fulfilment of this purpose and is able to carry out independent movements of accommodation and modifications according to circumstances—so the logical function is an activity which suitably fulfils its purpose and *can adapt and accommodate itself to circumstances and objects for the fulfilment of this purpose*. It is the purpose of the organic function of thought to change and elaborate the perceptual material into those ideas, associations of ideas, and conceptual constructs which, while consistent and coherent among themselves are, as the phrase goes and as we can also say provisionally, "clothed in objectivity."

Since, however, we do not know objective reality absolutely but only infer it (and this is also an ordinary scientific view) we must revise our statement and say that thought has fulfilled its purpose when it has elaborated the given sensation-complexes into valid concepts, general judgments, and cogent conclusions, and has produced such a world that objective happenings can be calculated and our behaviour successfully carried out in relation to phenomena. We lay most stress on the *practical* corroboration, on the experimental test of the utility of the logical structures that are the product of the organic function of thought. It is not the correspondence with an assumed "objective reality" that can never be directly accessible to us, it is not the theoretical representation of an outer world in the mirror of consciousness nor the theoretical comparison of logical products with objective things which, in our view, guarantees that thought has fulfilled its purpose; it is rather the practical test as to whether it is possible with the help of those logical products to *calculate events that occur without our intervention* and to realize our impulses appropriately in accordance with the direction of the logical structures.

It is interesting to observe how Lotze in his Logic withdraws his first definition, p. 4 [E.T. p. 2], of the truth of thought, that is to say its final purpose: "Truth consists in the agreement of ideas and their associations with the objects presented and their own relations," and modifies it to: "Connexions of ideas are true, if they are in accordance with those relations in the matter of the ideas, which are the same for all consciousness, and not the mere occurrence and juxtaposition of impressions, which are different for each individual consciousness." But when Lotze claims as the final function of thought a general world-image that shall be the same for all (cf. Laas, *Anal. d. Erf,* pp. 95, 127: the objective world in "consciousness in general") he overlooks that such a general agreement would still offer no guarantee of the "truth" of combinations of ideas. Only the practical test is the final guarantee; but even here we can only conclude that combinations of ideas fulfil their purpose, and have been rightly formed. From the standpoint of modern epistemology we can therefore no longer talk about "truth" at all, in the usual sense of the term.

Helmholtz too, in several places in his works, as in the Optics, and particularly in his lecture entitled "Logical Principies of the Empirical Sciences" assigns the principal value to the practical proof demanded above.

We will not at this point settle the question, deeply rooted in metaphysics and in our whole practical outlook, whether the logical function, or, to put it otherwise, whether the theoretical activity is or should be an end in itself for man, or whether all theoretical functions have arisen solely from our impulses, and have therefore ultimately to serve only practical ends.

Schopenhauer in particular has taken this latter view in modern times. As the will, according to him, is the only metaphysical principle, and a will that is blind and illogical, so the brain with all its ideas is in his opinion essentially nothing but a tool, whose function it is to serve the will and preserve the life of the individual. The intellect occupies a subservient position in regard to the will. That Herbart adopted a very similar position is less well-known, but it is a natural conclusion from the relation of the psychical monads to the organism, which can well exist without them. He therefore calls the mind a "parasite of the body," exactly as Schopenhauer does; it serves chiefly to facilitate the preservation of the organism. They both regard the theoretical activity, consciousness, therefore, as a tool of the organism and a means to self-preservation. It is not, as such, essential to our subsequent enquiry how the relation of thought, of the theoretical and conscious thought-processes to the life of the instinct and will is understood; but, as we proceed, the treatment of thought as an instrument may prove useful in securing the right orientation. If thought only exists on account of the will, or as we may say with Fichte, on account of action, then knowledge is not the ultimate purpose of thought; it cannot, therefore, be an end in itself, but only a by-product, something emerging incidentally, as it were, from the workshop of thought. The practical value of thought would then rank first, and "knowledge" would only be a secondary and incidental motive, as

Schopenhauer also assumes. This point may be of interest in the course of our enquiry, when we come to treat of conceptual structures whose intellectual value is as questionable as their practical value is obvious. Steinthal pertinently develops the same view: "We need knowledge of the world of things, and of ourselves, and of the connection of things with each other and with ourselves, in order to be able to live." He mentions, quite in accordance with the modern attitude, three chief tasks for which knowledge is required: the search for food, cultivation, and protection from the elements. "Knowledge is therefore a necessary factor in Nature's economy. It combines with physical and chemical operations to render the existence of the human race and the animal kingdom possible; it facilitates the material conditions which are essential to life." Thought, then, must be regarded as a mechanism, as a machine, as an instrument in the service of life; and this way of treating it is more important for logic than appears at first sight.

For our more limited purposes we may be content with the definition given above, according to which the test of the correctness of a logical result lies in *practice*, and the purpose of thought must be sought not in the reflection of a so-called objective world, but in rendering possible the calculation of events and of operations upon them. For us the purpose of the logical function of thought is to keep us constantly in a position to deal with things so that, with given conditions, relations, stipulations, and circumstances, we may receive an exactly ascertainable sense-impression (for every determination of objective data ultimately rests on that, and can be scientifically established in no other way); and so that, by such and such an impulse under certain conditions, we may produce an exactly ascertainable effect, which in its turn cannot be observed except by means of certain sensations. Only through the reduction of the concepts "thought, action, observation," etc., to elements ultimately physiological, to sensations, do we obtain a correct standard for the valuation of logical work, which converts elements of sensation into logical structures. These latter again, in the last resort exist to be converted into sensations, or to serve to control impressions and adjust will-impulses, that is to say, nerve-impulses.

All purposeful activity manifests itself in seeking out, collecting, or producing the necessary and serviceable means for the attainment of its object. The organic activity of thought also manifests its purposeful nature in exerting itself to attain its aims by all the means at its command.

If sensations are the starting-point of all logical activity and at the same time the terminus to which they must run, if only to render control possible (and as we remarked above, it must remain undecided whether we must regard the logical functions between these two points as having some inherent purpose), then the purpose of thought may be defined as the elaboration and adjustment of the material of sensation for the attainment of a richer and fuller sensational life of experience.

In order to attain the purpose of its activity as completely and quickly as possible, namely, to deal with independent events and to render them possible for or dependent on our will, thought or the logical function employs the most diverse means.

> Thought is bent on continually perfecting itself and thus becomes a more and more serviceable tool. For this purpose it expands its province by inventing instruments, like other natural activities. The arm and the hand do the same, and most ordinary instruments are to be regarded as elongations and extensions of these organs. The natural function of thought, which we spoke of above as a tool, also expands its instrumentality by the invention of tools, means of thought, instruments of thought, one of which is to form the subject of our enquiry.

Thought undertakes ingenious operations, invents brilliant expedients, is able to introduce highly complicated processes. The material of sensation is re-modelled, re-coined, compressed, it is purged of dross and mixed with alloys from the fund of the psyche itself, in order to render possible a more and more certain, rapid, and refined solution of the problem of the logical function. All these very different and highly complicated processes and operations are governed by very few and simple laws, just as the complicated work of the physical organism and its apparently very different organs is reducible to remarkably simple, regular elementary forms and processes. It is the business of logical theory to reduce the complicated logical processes to such simple elementary processes, to a few, definite mechanical events. The rich life of the spirit, as it expands with its countless variations in the vast field of science, rests in its most complicated forms and processes on simple, primitive laws. It arises only as a result of the extraordinarily ingenious modification and specialization of these few elementary types and laws, which partly under the pressure of external causes and circumstances, and partly in obedience to immanent processes of development, expand into that rich and infinite system of knowledge of which man is so proud. Just as *Meleagrina margaritifera*, when a grain of sand gets beneath its shining surface, covers it over with a self-produced mass of mother-of-pearl, in order to change the insignificant grain into a brilliant pearl, so, only still more delicately, the psyche, when stimulated, transforms the material of sensation which it absorbs into shining pearls of thought, into structures. By means of these structures the logician follows the adaptable, organic, purposeful, logical function into its most secret processes, its most delicate forms of specialization. In both cases it is the ingenuity of the *purposive activity* which arouses our wonder and attention. We deliberately emphasize the utility of the organic function of thought, because we shall subsequently be dealing with logical structures in which this purposiveness is strikingly manifested.

So far in our exposition we have not yet touched on an aspect which is of great importance for the right understanding of the logical function: the fact, namely, that the organic function of thought is carried on for the most part *unconsciously*. Should the product finally enter consciousness also, or should consciousness momentarily accompany the processes of logical thought, this light only penetrates to the shallows, and the actual fundamental processes are carried on in the darkness of the unconscious. The specifically purposeful operations are chiefly, and in any case at the beginning, wholly instinctive and unconscious, even if they later press forward into the luminous circle of consciousness, which in course of time is able both as regards the individual and the general history of culture to bring under its control ever wider areas of psychical activity. Logic is specially concerned to throw light on the dark and unconsciously working activity of thought, and to study the ingenious methods and devices which that unconscious activity employs in order to attain its object.

However we may conceive the relation of thought and reality, it may be asserted from the empirical point of view, that the ways of thought are different from those of reality, the subjective processes of thought concerned with any given external event or process have very rarely a demonstrable similarity to it. We make this observation in order to emphasize that the logical functions are subjective but useful efforts which thought makes to attain the objects we have already described. Whatever objective reality may be, one thing can be stated with certainty—it does not consist of logical functions, as Hegel once thought.

The Hegelian system offers historically the most glaring and typical example of this general error of philosophy: the confusion of thought – processes with events, the conversion of subjective thought-events into objective world-events. (That the Hegelian dialectic is, however, based on a correct insight into the nature of logical development, we shall have occasion to remark later.)

Actually the greatest and most important human errors originate through thought-processes being taken for copies of reality itself;[1] but the ultimate practical agreement of our ideas and judgments with so-called "things" still does not justify the conclusion that the processes by which the logical result has been obtained are the same as objective events. On the contrary their utility is manifested in the very fact that the logical functions, working according to their own laws, do constantly coincide in the end with reality.

THOUGHT AS AN ART, LOGIC AS TECHNOLOGY (A COLLECTION OF TECHNICAL RULES OF ART)

WE have spoken of thought as an organic function. Every natural faculty, and this applies to all organic functions, can, through practice, development and hereditary transmission, be raised to an art. Only in this sense can thought be an art. Logic is sometimes called a technology.

Whoever calls logic technology must consider thought as an art.

It is inaccurate to consider logic itself as an art. Thought is an art, but logic is a science, and a technology in particular.

It need hardly be stated that in this use of the word and concept "art" we are taking the meaning in which the æsthetic side is not emphasized. We are not concerned with an artistic activity, but with an ingenious dexterity. So long as the organic activity of thought remains in the sphere of the unconscious (the "hypo-psychical" according to Laas) we call it preferably purposeful, just as we attribute a similar purpose without hesitation to all organic functions, without thereby raising the metaphysical problem of teleology; but when the organic activity leaves the sphere of the unconscious for more wakeful activities, when consciousness seizes the rudder, we choose to call this organic activity technical. The more the natural faculty of thought, the instinctive activity of the logical functions is improved and refined—the more the logical operations are specialized, and the finer logical functions fall to the lot of special individuals in consequence of the division of labour in the economy of nature—the more do these terms find justification in this fact. If thought is a wide spread activity, acquired by the individual in the course of his development, as so many other arts which are *necessary* to human existence, then the more difficult part of the logical problem is carried out by single individuals, specially gifted and developed for that purpose; but as soon as a common natural faculty becomes specialized in such a way that particular individuals practise it with particular dexterity, we call it an art. Certain technical rules are developed: the totality of these rules is called the technology; and such is logic, whose chief task is to present and establish the technical rules of thought.

THE DIFFERENCE BETWEEN THE ARTIFICES AND THE RULES OF THOUGHT

METHODOLOGY, as hitherto employed, has endeavoured to collect the technical rules of thought in their completeness and to employ them systematically. It has succeeded in registering, analysing and systematically establishing those technical operations and manipulations which are the most frequent, regular, and important. It is the operations whose skilful application, intelligent realization, and rational improvement are essential to the progress of modern science which have been raised from practice into theory and reduced to the simple and primitive forms of the logical function. The admirable methods of the empirical sciences, methods adapted to their object with an astonishing flexibility, and able to utilize and conform to all circumstances, as in the case of organic beings—these methods found a worthy and completely suitable expression in modern methodology, which has its most brilliant representatives in England, France, and Germany.

Meanwhile, as it seems to me, there are methods employed in scientific practice which have up till now not been duly considered and recognized in theory.

> I refer to the methods employed less in natural science than in mathematics and the ethico-political sciences, that is to say, in the most exact science and in fields where exactitude is definitely excluded. It is quite natural that since the methods of the natural sciences had been given a great deal of attention, the methods employed in other branches of science and

neglected in natural science should demand examination. In modern logic natural science is given undue prominence at the expense of the sciences mentioned, and to the disadvantage of logic. Mill pays scarcely any attention to the special methods of mathematics, and the methods of the moral sciences are too briefly treated. But the remarkable utility of the logical function is displayed in these two fields to far greater advantage than in the simpler methods of the empirical natural sciences, if only because in those fields the logical function encounters disproportionately greater difficulties and phenomena of a much more complex character than those of natural science. Just at the points where the empirical method of natural science converges on the methods of exact mechanics and abstract physics, and where on the other hand they approach the complicated phenomena of social life, the insufficiency of purely inductive methods is clearly manifest. It is here that methods begin which present a higher synthesis of deduction and induction, where, that is to say, both these methods are united in the endeavour to solve difficulties which can only be overcome indirectly.

The methods to which we refer may be described as irregular in contrast to the regular methods of ordinary induction. In other spheres also, however, the regular are systematically employed before the irregular, and the latter are left on one side. But where the methods in question have so far been met with, they have either been used too little and too superficially, or in the wrong place and the wrong systematic connection; or they have been confused with other similar forms, as is customary in every science; or, finally, they have been treated with timidity, as everything irregular is treated at first. In logic too a veil of secrecy was woven about such forms.

We make a distinction between *rules* and *artifices* of thought. In other functions also this distinction is of value; the *rules* are the totality of all those technical operations in virtue of which an activity is able to attain its object directly, even when more or less complicated. In logic too we call such operations, and in particular those of induction, "rules of thinking". The artifices, on the other hand, are those operations, of an almost mysterious character, which run counter to ordinary procedure in a more or less paradoxical way. They are methods which give an onlooker the impression of magic if he be not himself initiated or equally skilled in the mechanism, and are able indirectly to overcome the difficulties which the material in question opposes to the activity. Thought also has such artifices; they are strikingly purposive expressions of the organic function of thought. And as in certain arts and handicrafts such artifices are kept secret, so we notice that this is also the case in logic. We will give only one remarkable instance by way of illustration. When Leibnitz by an ingenious artifice of this sort (which we shall later take as our typical example and as one of the chief subjects of our analysis) discovered an amazingly simple and skilful solution of problems which up till then had passed for insoluble, he anxiously tried for a long time to keep this artifice secret; and those to whom he communicated it astonished mathematicians not yet acquainted with it by the solution of different problems. Newton acted similarly; and, so too, we are told, did the school of Pythagoras.

THE TRANSITION TO FICTIONS

WE are therefore dealing with a peculiar kind of logical product, a special manifestation of the logical function. We have already seen that this peculiar activity is expressed in what we call artifices, that its products are artificial concepts. We would here, anticipating the outcome, substitute other terms for these expressions: our subject is the fictive activity of the logical function; the products of this activity—*fictions.*

The fictive activity of the mind is an expression of the fundamental psychical forces; fictions are *mental structures.* The psyche weaves this aid to thought out of itself; for the mind is inventive; under the compulsion of necessity, stimulated by the outer world, it discovers the store of contrivances that lie hidden within itself. The organism finds itself in a world full of contradictory sensations, it is exposed to the assaults of a hostile external world, and in order to preserve itself, it is forced to seek every possible means of assistance, external as well as internal. In necessity and pain mental evolution is begun, in contradiction and opposition consciousness awakes, and man owes his mental development more to his enemies than to his friends.

Meanwhile, in the interests of greater clearness and intelligibility we may premise the following remark:

By fictive activity in logical thought is to be understood the production and use of logical methods, which, with the help of accessory concepts — where the improbability of any corresponding objective is fairly obvious— seek to attain the objects of thought. Instead of remaining content with the material given, the logical function introduces these hybrid and ambiguous thought-structures, in order with their help to attain its purpose indirectly, if the material which it encounters resists a direct procedure. With an instinctive, almost cunning ingenuity, the logical function succeeds in overcoming these difficulties with the aid of its accessory structures. The special methods, the by-paths, of which thought makes use when it can no longer advance directly along the main road, are of many different kinds, and their explanation is our problem. They often lead through thorny undergrowth, but logical thought is not deterred thereby, even though it may lose something of its clearness and purity. It is relevant also to remark here that the logical function, in its purposeful instinctive ingenuity, can carry this fictive activity from the most innocent and unpretentious beginnings on through ever finer and subtler developments right up to the most difficult and complicated methods.

NOTE

1   Cf. Kant, *Prol.*, §40: "All illusion consists in holding the subjective ground of judgment to be objective." Reason falls into error "when it mistakes its destination, and refers transcendentally to the object what only concerns its own subject and its guidance in all immanent use." Cf. *Prol.*, § 55.

PART 1
BASIC PRINCIPLES

GENERAL INTRODUCTORY REMARKS ON FICTIONAL CONSTRUCTS

The normal and most natural methods of thought always have as their primary object the formation of those particular apperceptions that are of a final and definitive character; and only such ideational constructs are formed as can be shown to correspond to some kind of reality. It is in fact the essential object of science to develop only such ideas as have an objective correlate and to eliminate all admixture of the subjective.

Such a task is, however, not easily accomplished, for many difficulties are encountered. The ideal, in which the world of ideas consists exclusively of congruous, well-ordered and non-contradictory constructs is only to be attained slowly and with difficulty. The way to this ideal is through methodology.

The first and the natural task of methodology is to suggest in what direction representations possessed of real validity are to be sought.

Our natural tendency is to adjust all our representations, to test them by comparison with reality, and to render them free from contradiction. This is the most natural and obvious method, and it appears to be the only way of advancing a scientific theory of knowledge. This would hold true even if our mental constructs were direct reflections of reality. But the customary modes and results of thought already contain so many subjective and fictional elements that it is not surprising if thought also strikes out along other lines. It must be remembered that the object of the world of ideas as a whole is not the portrayal of reality—this would be an utterly impossible task—but rather to provide us with an *instrument for finding our way about more easily in this world.* Subjective processes of thought inhere in the entire structure of cosmic phenomena. They represent the highest and ultimate results of organic development, and the world of ideas is the fine flower of the whole cosmic process; but for that very reason it is not a copy of it in the ordinary sense. Logical processes are a part of the cosmic process and have as their more immediate object the preservation and enrichment of the life of organisms; they should serve as instruments for enabling them to attain to a more complete life; they serve as intermediaries between living beings. The world of ideas is an edifice well calculated to fulfil this purpose; but to regard it for that reason as a copy is to indulge in a hasty and unjustifiable comparison. Not even elementary sensations are copies of reality; they are rather mere gauges for measuring the changes in reality.

Before entering on our task it is necessary to make a distinction that will subsequently assume considerable importance. Ideational constructs are in the strict sense of the term real fictions when they are not only in contradiction with reality but self-contradictory in themselves; the concept of the atom, for example, or the "Ding an sich." To be distinguished from these are constructs which only contradict reality as given, or deviate from it, but are not in themselves self-contradictory (e.g. artificial classes). The latter might be called half-fictions or semi-fictions. These types are not sharply divided from one another but are connected by transitions. Thought begins with slight initial deviations from reality (half-fictions), and, becoming bolder and bolder, ends by operating with constructs that are not only opposed to the facts but are self-contradictory.

A

THE ENUMERATION AND DIVISION OF SCIENTIFIC FICTIONS

CHAPTER I ARTIFICIAL CLASSIFICATION

THE most widely used of those "provisional methods" which we have called "semi-fictions" is *artificial classification*. The ultimately valid construct corresponding to it, and eventually to take its place, is the *natural system*. All cosmic objects present special forms which are theoretically expressed in some classification, and when this specification corresponds with reality in every respect then it is a natural system. The natural system is in itself one of the most complicated problems of philosophy and of natural science, and from it arises the vital question of the nature of species.

A natural system is one in which entities are arranged according to the principles apparently followed by nature in their development. To put it briefly, the natural system of classification must be a copy corresponding to the actual origins and the mutual relationship of all things. This is the goal of science and any direct method must work straight towards it.

It is at this point that all the considerations so far advanced are justified. The material at our disposal puts so many formidable obstacles in the direct path that the logical function strikes out along by-ways. It makes use of an artifice; it creates artificial classes. Now what does this mean? In our psychological terminology it means that it *provisionally substitutes for the correct constructs others which do not directly correspond to reality*. It then operates with these fictional classes as if they were real ones. We can here only draw attention to the well-known fact that the artificial and fictive classification always selects from a whole group of characters some one that is particularly prominent, and bases its division upon this without paying any attention to the way in which these characters are naturally determined by one another. These provisional classificatory aids not only serve the practical purpose of permitting objects to be arranged and brought under definite rubrics, and provide at the same time a sort of mnemonic device, but they also possess a theoretical value, in so far as they perform a *heuristic* service by preparing for and facilitating the discovery of a natural system. Artificial systems are generally based on these concepts of species, which themselves only bring a superficial order provisionally into the confused mass of phenomena.

Heuristic methods based upon dichotomy, etc. are but special subdivisions of this artificial method of grouping. The artificial classifications, however, themselves follow in certain essential respects another theory than the natural one; i.e. the methodological rules which appertain to them and which determine their applicability are clearly of a different nature from those that hold for natural classification. These rules relate particularly to the prevention of the mistakes that necessarily spring from artificial divisions: mistakes which are due not only to the fact that the natural arrangement of phenomena cannot be forced into this artificial edifice and does not coincide with it, but also to the fact that through this artificial system impossible sub-divisions arise which cannot exist in actual reality.

As examples we have among others the Linnæan system and many later classifications of animals, plants and men, all of which have been framed with a more or less conscious feeling of their artificiality. Lamarck, in particular, is to be praised in this respect. In the technical rules given in his *Philosophie Zoologique* concerning "Artificial devices" [E.T. Part I, Chap. I, p. 19] he discusses this subject in detail. And with him may be mentioned Cuvier, Blumenbach, Kant and a large number of scientists who either applied these artificial classifications themselves or dealt with their theoretical basis.

This artificial classification is almost the only one of the accessories to thought which has had the good fortune to be thoroughly studied by logicians. It was, of course, quite obvious in this case that we were not directly and immediately dealing with reality but with *indirect and provisional ideational constructs and modes of thought*. The various features characteristic of all fictions are here already clearly manifested: the fact, in particular, that all such fictions in the last analysis lead to contradictions, is worthy of special consideration, and later on we shall emphasize it more specifically.

As long as such fictions are treated as hypotheses without a realization of their nature, they are *false hypotheses*. They derive real value only if it is realized that they have been deliberately constructed as provisional representations which at some future time are to make room for better and more natural systems.

CHAPTER II ABSTRACTIVE (NEGLECTIVE) FICTIONS

I INCLUDE under this term various methods in which the deviation from reality manifests itself specifically in the neglect of certain elements.

The factor common to all fictions in this class consists in a neglect of important elements of reality. As a rule the reason for the formation of these fictions is to be sought in the highly intricate character of the facts which make theoretical treatment exceedingly difficult owing to their unusual complexity. The logical functions are thus unable to perform their work undisturbed, because it is not possible here to keep the various threads out of which reality is woven, apart from one another.

Since, then, the material is too complicated and confused for thought to be able to break it up into its component elements, and since the causal factors sought are probably of too complicated a nature for them to be determined directly, thought makes use of an artifice by means of which it provisionally and temporarily neglects a number of characters and selects from them the more important phenomena.

A standard example is the well-known assumption of Adam Smith, according to which all human actions are dictated by egoism. We shall try to give an especially typical example of every variety of artifice, and to use it in order to study by the most thorough analysis both the scheme of the construct and the methodology of the artifice employed. As regards artificial classification, by far the most typical historical example is the botanical system of Linnæus; while of abstractive fictions based on the neglect of certain elements the best is Adam Smith's assumption, which was long regarded as an hypothesis.[1]

Neither Adam Smith nor Linnæus regarded himself as dealing with more than a fiction. The proof of the statement that Adam Smith intended his assumption to be merely a provisional fiction was given by Buckle in the introduction to his *History of Civilization in England*, and this view has been expressly emphasized in Germany by F. A. Lange.

The empirical manifestations of human actions are so excessively complicated that they present almost insuperable obstacles when we try to understand them theoretically and to reduce them to causal factors. For the construction of his system of political economy it was essential for Adam Smith to interpret human activity causally. With unerring instinct he realized that the main cause lay in egoism and he formulated his assumption in such a way that all human actions, and particularly those of a business or politico-economical nature, could be looked upon *as if* their driving force lay in but one single factor—egoism. Thus all the subsidiary causes and partially conditional factors, such as good-will, habit and so forth, are here neglected. With the aid of this abstract cause Adam Smith then succeeded in bringing the whole of political economy into an ordered system. He presented it as an axiom and deduced from it the relations involved in trade and commerce, which followed with systematic necessity. The assumption of a "harmony" of all individual interests is intimately bound up with this; and it is an assumption which, though of great value as fiction, is positively ruinous as hypothesis or dogma.

But these are only provisional assumptions, which, however rigorously applied, are to be sharply differentiated from hypotheses. They are, or at least should be, accompanied by the consciousness that they do not correspond to reality and that they *deliberately substitute a fraction of reality for the complete range of causes and facts.*

These artificial methods are applied wherever there are complex situations of this kind, particularly in the treatment of political economy and social and moral relations.

There is one more domain where the application of this method has yielded exceedingly fruitful results, and that is theoretical mechanics.

The phenomena are here so intricate that frequently these abstract causes alone are assumed to be causal factors while others are for the time being neglected. It is precisely in the determination of the mechanical relations of bodies that subsidiary causes are neglected in order to simplify matters, and all mechanical motion, etc. is interpreted, *as if* it were only dependent upon the abstract factors.

> In physics we find such a fiction in the fact that masses of undeniable extension, e.g. the sun and the earth, in connection with the derivation of certain basic concepts of mechanics and the calculation of their reciprocal attraction are reduced to points or concentrated into points (gravitational points) in order, by means of this fiction, to facilitate the presentation of the more composite phenomena. Such a neglect of elements is especially resorted to where a very small factor is assumed to be zero (cf. Bacon in his *Nov. Org.*, II, 146. Particularly remarkable is the passage in Book II, § 36, where he raises the question whether "certain movements of the heavens have been conceived merely with the object of simplifying our calculations").

There are many other fields of inquiry where this method has been applied with some success. There are, for example, all the ideational constructs deriving from Condillac's fiction[2] of a statue, resuscitated for instance by Steinthal in order to simplify psychological inquiry.[3]

Psychological conditions in particular are so intricate that, a priori, just those fictions are on the whole possible and conceivable here which in the main emphasize only one point and neglect others in order thus to make the treatment more practicable. Ever since the analogy of psychical phenomena with mechanical processes was admitted this method has found a place in abstract psychology. The laws of Herbart as well as a number of other assumptions can also be shown to be fictions of practical value, and not hypotheses as hitherto supposed.

> The first attempt to treat the Herbartian formulæ as provisional, abstract fictions was made by Lange, particularly in his monograph on the *Grundlegung der mathematischen Psychologie*. More recently Steinthal has experimented with this method and formulated theoretical propositions at which he arrived only by neglecting numerous empirical factors. Glogau in his work *Steinthals psychologische Formeln* agrees that these formulæ were reduced to an extremely simple expression chiefly by the neglect of empirical factors.

A priori, no objection can be made to this procedure; indeed, it is very likely that something of real importance might be gained by it. Abstract mechanics is full of just such formulæ, obtained only by discarding a large number of empirical data, and events are always interpreted *as if* dependent upon these formulated laws. But at the same time it is clear that these fictions approximate closely to simple experiments, i.e. experiments where purely arbitrary values are provisionally assumed in the treatment of mathematical problems and then gradually "tested" one after another.

It is still often an open question whether such an assumption is an hypothesis or a fiction; but a regrettable lack of scientific understanding is apt to appear in the conclusion frequently drawn that because such constructs are devoid of reality they are to be regarded as devoid of utility. This is just as incorrect as the reverse inference—from their utility to their validity. Any true insight into the psychological setting and origin of knowledge proves that many things may be theoretically wrong and yet from a practical standpoint be fruitful in results, taking the term "practical", of course, in a wide sense.

A disputed point of this kind was the question whether *linguistic roots* ever really existed, whether there ever had been a period in the history of speech in which only roots were found, or whether these uninflected roots are to be regarded merely as grammatical points of reference. The controversy between Curtius and Pott would form an instructive subject from which to develop a discussion of methodological rules for this type of method. The same holds for the assumption of a period in man's history in which language did not exist. According to some authorities this is a legitimate hypothesis; according to others, e.g. Steinthal and J. B. Meyer, it is merely a fiction for simplifying the psychological study of man, because the conditions involved here are of an extremely intricate nature.

In recent times the number of such fictions has been multiplied to excess, though some useful constructs are to be found among them. Such, for instance, is the fiction of a *world containing only a single individual*, in order thus to get a better idea of linguistic and psychological evolution. A necessary element is, of course, neglected in such a procedure, namely, relationship to other individuals. Synchronous causes are here treated as if operating in temporal succession, in order by thus isolating the individual, to enable their operation to be more easily studied. Such a treatment of scientific material, as we remarked, serves sometimes more or less practical ends.

> The ideal isolation and division of what is given, and its separation in reflective analysis into different aspects, is one of the devices of thought most frequently employed.
>
> A fiction based upon an abstract isolation is that of "the ideal case presupposed by the Galilean axiom of inertia, for this is not to be found in any material entity whatever, nor in any system of such units in absolute isolation, nor is its characteristic peculiarity noticeable in such a system." This example provides an excellent illustration of the manner in which general laws may be formulated by means of such fictions. Incidentally, the fiction based upon this law has of late been frequently called in question. The Galilean postulate that a moving body can retain the initial motion imparted to it without change for ever, has the mark of a fiction from the very fact of its appeal to the concept of infinity.

Fundamentally related to the foregoing are fictions of the *mean*, i.e. fictions where the mean deviation of a group of gradually differing phenomena is selected and serves for purposes of calculation. This average is an imaginary figure only used for calculation, and such methods are very commonly employed in applied mathematics (also in statistics, meteorology, etc.). Here, too, minute differences of fact are ignored. Rigidly applied, such fictions lead to contradictions with reality. The confusion of such assumptions, and of the results flowing from these methods, with hypotheses is not infrequent, though not so common as in the case of the abstractive fictions mentioned above.

> A celebrated statistical fiction is the *homme moyen* of Quetelet, i.e. the fiction of a normal, average man. This fiction is not of value for statistics alone, for in medicine we meet with the concept of an absolutely healthy individual, of an average man in whom all abnormal deviations have disappeared. We may compare Jevons, *Principles of Science*, I, 422, on fictitious means. Here we may also include all the arbitrary determinations found in science, such as, for example, the meridian of Ferro, the determination of the zero point, the selection of water as the measure of specific gravity, of the movements of the stars as an index of time. In all these cases certain points of reference are taken and lines similar to co-ordinates drawn in different directions for the determination and classification of phenomena.
>
> We might also remark here that the whole conceptual classificatory system, and in general the differentiation of concepts, is based upon abstractions of the most one-sided nature, as Lotze has clearly demonstrated in his Logic, cf. Pfleiderer, *Der Moderne Pessimismus*, p. 81: "Light and darkness, black and white, life and death are merely the artificial products of rationalistic abstraction; they may be necessary, with all their inaccuracy, for purposes of reference, but when applied to reality they must always be used with caution."

A number of other methods may be included as sub-divisions of the group we have been describing, e.g. the method of *approximation*, where an abstract solution of a problem is first posited, and this solution (a concept, number, etc.) then gradually brought into harmony with reality by tests and experiments. This method is particularly common in the mathematical sciences, where the complicated nature of the problem does not permit of any other treatment. In principle, these trial methods or tentative fictions are not different from the neglective ones. The Socratico-Platonic method of seeking to obtain definitions by first selecting any definition at random and then bringing it gradually nearer to reality, is also, in principle, the same.

CHAPTER III SCHEMATIC, PARADIGMATIC, UTOPIAN AND TYPE FICTIONS

Schematic Fictions.—This sub-group was already in evidence in the two types already described. Both in classification and in the abstractive fictions we have the postulation of schematic, general types conceived as absolutely bare and deprived of all those characters of reality that might interfere with the procedure. Nevertheless they quite legitimately form a subgroup by themselves. Whereas in the case of the abstractive fictions a certain portion of reality is cut off and set aside, and only the remainder taken into consideration, in the case of schematic fictions a scaffolding, that is to say, the skeleton of a definite complex is erected and thought proceeds in relation to this bare picture which is devoid of many of the features of reality. The distortion of reality has, however, progressed further here than in the preceding sub-groups. Here too a subjective and abstract representation is formed in order to base theoretical procedure upon it and not upon the far more complicated reality. To a certain extent the laws of nature are here studied by means of simpler models, containing, it is true, the essentials of reality but in a much simpler and purer form. The *schematic drawings* employed in many sciences give us an idea of this method which here finds extensive application.

> Schematic drawings are very frequently employed in geology, as well as in mechanics and in physiology. (They are incorrectly called "ideal" presentations, especially in geology.) A great dispute as to the nature, justification and application of schematic drawings arose between Haeckel, His, Semper and others. Cf. Semper, *Offener Brief an E. Haeckel,* Hamburg, 1877, and Haeckel, *Ziele und Wege der heutigen Entwickelungsgeschichte,* Jena, 1875. Cf. also V. Baer's schematic drawings. "They are fabricated, deviate from reality and distort the facts," Haeckel himself admitted.

These forms might also be called the fiction of *the simple case.*[4] A typical example is what is known as "Thünen's idea," a fiction which was introduced into economics at the beginning of the nineteenth century by Thünen and led to a reform of the subject. It is also the most famous historical example of this type of methodological expedient. It consists in postulating an imaginary city, in order the better to determine conditions of agriculture, transportation, etc. Around it in concentric zones are arranged the different spheres of activity from which the necessary means for supplying the requirements of the city are drawn. With the aid of this ingenious artifice all agricultural and economic laws are then systematically deduced. Fictions of this type are specially common in political economy. The schematic fiction of an isolated man, an isolated city (or island), an isolated state, etc., belongs to the same category. Similar schemata are employed in all the social sciences for the operation and deduction of theoretical laws. Dühring,[5] in particular, was very successful in his use of this method in his economic works, where from the fiction of schemata of the simplest cases conceivable he deduced the fundamental social laws by very simple processes.

Closely related to these forms are *paradigmatic* fictions or imaginary cases. It is particularly in demonstrative arguments that cases are assumed where what is to be proved is referred to as though it existed.

This method of imaginary cases is a favourite one in all sciences. Locke, for example (III, 6, 44), employed this method in order to make the origin of names of substances intelligible. An extremely frequent sub-division which belongs here is that of *rhetorical* fictions where cases are created merely for purposes of demonstration.

Another group, though one which may be treated as a variety of the schematic fiction, is formed by *Utopian* fictions. The name given to this group derives from the Utopias and fictions so prevalent in earlier times, such as those depicted by More and Campanella. Plato's ideal state may be mentioned here as historically the first example of this method. To the same category belongs the fiction of a primeval state, which was particularly popular in the eighteenth century and still played an important part in the writings of Fichte.

The idea of a primordial or world spirit also belongs here; such as that so happily employed, for instance, by Dubois-Reymond in his well-known address,[6] for the elucidation and theoretical development of a strictly scientific train of thought. And here too we must place the Platonic idea of a (hermaphrodite) original man, and all those fictions of primordial laws, religions, pacts, traditions, and the like that once were or still are of importance. Indeed it is just in this field that scientific phantasy often manifests itself most freely. As long as such fictions are taken for what they are and not called hypotheses, they can frequently be of great service to science.

Another species of fiction closely bound up with the above is the *type-fiction* or the imaginary *original form*. Here a picture of a species or type is built up from a series of organisms, and then not merely are the laws governing particular organisms deduced from it, but all these organisms themselves are regarded as modifications of the type. In this group the interplay of fiction and hypothesis is often remarkable. The classical example is Goethe's idea of an original plant and an original animal, a question in which interest was revived in modern times through Darwinism. The first question is what Goethe understood by a "plant archetype", whether it was a fiction or an hypothesis; and we may also ask whether in the present state of our knowledge the historical existence of such an "archetype" can be assumed, or if the mere imaginary postulation of such an original form still serves any scientific purpose. Characteristic, and not without significance for the theory of this kind of fiction, is the well-known phrase of Schiller, "this original plant is merely an idea", whereby he stated in Kantian terminology that it was an ideal or typical fiction.

CHAPTER IV SYMBOLIC (ANALOGICAL) FICTIONS

THERE is another variety of fiction important for science which I call *tropic* fictions; they may also be called *symbolic* or *analogical*. They are closely related to poetic similes as well as to the myth.[7] In these fictions the mechanism of thinking is as follows: A new intuition is apperceived by an ideational construct in which there is a similar relationship, an analogous proportion to that existing in the observed series of perceptions In such cases relationships constitute the apperceiving power. This is also the formal origin of poetry.

Fictions of this variety are particularly popular in scientific theology, Schleiermacher's application of the method being the most important.[8]

> Similar tendencies are already noticeable in Fichte and Hegel. Fichte's re-marks are interesting *(Wesen des Gelehrten*, first lecture [E.T. 1847]):—"If we speak of the life of the absolute, that is merely a method of speech (cf. Leibniz' *modus dicendi*) for in actual fact the absolute *is* life." And again in

the second lecture he says: "On the analogy of our mind we picture God as thinking, and the ethical life of man as the sole purpose for which he is in existence; not at all as if it really were so, and as if God thought after the manner of the finite, but simply because we cannot grasp the relationship in any other way." (The "As-if" does not in this case belong to the fiction but together with the negation merely serves to exclude error.) In the fifth lecture he says: "What, regarded as a *philosophical question,* constitutes the nature of a scholar, means how would God have to conceive the nature of a scholar, if he thought? For a philosophical attitude grasps things as they are in themselves, i.e. in the world of pure thought, of which world God is the original principle; accordingly, therefore, such as God would have to conceive it if thought were attributed to him."

Socrates too had already taken an attitude towards popular myths resembling that of Schleiermacher towards the dogmas of Christianity. Cf. especially in this connection Mendelssohn's Introduction to the Phaedo, where he inquires whether Socrates' daimon was not a conscious fiction.

The remarkable thing is that Schleiermacher and his school regard most dogmas as analogical fictions, provisional auxiliary constructions, because the actual metaphysical relationship remains incomprehensible to us. Thus, for instance, the relationship of God to the world, which for the philosopher Schleiermacher is completely unknowable, is conceived of by the theologian Schleiermacher on the analogy of the father-son relationship; and so on. This is not a rationalistic reinterpretation of dogmas but a subtle epistemological manœuvre by means of which Schleiermacher held thousands of people to Christianity. "God" is not the "father" of men but he is to be treated and regarded *as if* he were. Such an interpretation is of tremendous importance for the practice of religion and worship, and by means of it Schleiermacher similarly transformed all dogmas from hypotheses into fictions. How close these analogical fictions are to myths I have already pointed out. With this attitude in mind Schleiermacher's philosophy of religion can be understood from the standpoint of method. He himself was well aware of the artificial and artistic aspect of his method, although he did not describe it quite as we do. How intimately related this interpretation is to the Kantian philosophy so assiduously studied by Schleiermacher is evident, although it has never been definitely emphasized; and the Kantian philosophy in general will assume a fundamental importance in the subsequent development of our thesis.

The analogical method is natural to metaphysics no less than to theology and metaphysics. In the theory of knowledge categories are examples of such analogies. They are simply analogical fictions, and, as such, are grouped with methodological classifications where they find their proper place. Reality is, and must be thought of, on the analogy of human and subjective relations. All knowledge, if it goes beyond simple actual succession and co-existence, can only be *analogical*.

> Grün is therefore quite right when he says that metaphysics is metabolic, *metaphoric*. What Grün calls metaphors are in the main indispensable fictions.

Substance, above all, is such a fiction and Fichte indicates its nature somewhat naively when he says (*Wesen d. Gelehrten*, Lecture 6): "The ceaseless change in the tream of time must be given something of a permanent and unchangeable nature to support it."

We have here the main elements of what might be called a *theory of understanding* and comprehending. All cognition is the apperception of one thing through-another. In understanding, we are always dealing with an analogy and we cannot imagine how otherwise existence can be understood. Anyone acquainted with the mechanism of thought knows that all conception and cognition are based upon analogical apperceptions. The only ideational constructs by means of which existing things can be apperceived are either the corresponding general conceptions or other concrete objects. But since these are in their turn inconceivable, all these analogies only give rise to an apparent understanding. From the mechanism of thought, as Steinthal in particular described it, there follows with absolute certainty exactly what Kant so laboriously demonstrated in his theory of cognition, namely that it is utterly impossible to attain knowledge of the world, not because our thought is too narrowly circumscribed—this is a dogmatic and erroneous interpretation—but because knowledge is always in the form of categories and these, in the last analysis, are only analogical apperceptions. This powerful demonstration of the unknowable and incomprehensible nature of the world showed clearly the lines on which knowledge should proceed and put a stop to all dogmatic speculation. By taking an entirely different path we thus reach the conclusion of the Kantian philosophy, that categories are of no assistance in grasping reality and that as analogical fictions they cannot provide us with any true knowledge.

The realization that categories are merely analogical fictions was facilitated by Locke, Leibniz, Kant, and others.

In particular, it must be pointed out that the special investigations on the subject of symbolic knowledge (a term introduced by Leibniz) which were a by-product of eighteenth-century logic are intimately related to the above contention.

Maimon's treatment of this question deserves praise in this connection. All the eighteenth-century discussions, which were often very subtle, have been forgotten in the confusion caused by dogmatic philosophy of absolutism. Maimon, in particular, quite correctly sums up all the results of the Kantian philosophy when he says that only *symbolic knowledge* is possible.

> Among those who have made *symbolic knowledge* the subject of investigation, Lambert is worthy of mention. Of the immediate predecessors of Kant, as of the successors of Maimon, he is the most acute. Lambert's *Organon*, Part II, contains a detailed section on symbolic knowledge in which many of the results of Kant are already anticipated. All discursive thinking is symbolic in two respects: first, in so far as it operates with symbols in the mathematical sense; and secondly, in so far as all knowledge gained thereby forms but a kind of simile, image, or counterpart of reality, but does not enable us to obtain knowledge of reality itself, or at least not in any adequate form. A recognition of reality in an adequate form leads us to the concept of intuitive knowledge or intellectual perception, brings us again, in other words, to a fictional concept of methodological but not objective value.

Had this path been pursued further, the conclusions of Kant would have been preserved in their purity. But the great philosopher stained his glorious discoveries by clinging to effete rationalistic dogmas and thus himself contributed to the fate of his true achievement which was consigned to oblivion.

Thus we see how all logical results gain a significance for the theory of knowledge at the same time. When the categories are regarded as *analogical fictions*, the whole theory of knowledge takes on a different complexion.

They are then recognized as simple representational constructions for the purpose of apperceiving what is given. Objects possessing attributes, causes that work, are all mythical.

We can only say that objective phenomena can be regarded *as if* they behaved in such and such a way, and there is absolutely no justification for assuming any dogmatic attitude and changing the "as if "into a "that."

As soon as these analogies are interpreted as hypotheses we get all those systems of theology and philosophy whose object is the explanation of the resultant contradictions. We have only to recall the time and trouble spent in elucidating the father-relationship of God to Christ; and the simplicity of Schleiermacher's solution! Of still greater interest are the endless attempts to determine the nature of substance and its relation to its attributes, of cause and its relation to effect, etc.

> All such ideas as "possible", "necessary", etc., belong here. Thus G. H. Lewes in his *History of Philosophy,* Vol. I, p. 319 (1880), says of the Aristotelian idea of potential existence: It is a fiction; useful, it may be, in the department of Logic, but dangerously illusive in Metaphysics. And he deals in the same way with "the actual" as well as with the idea of στέρησις. These are the formal or relational ideas which Aristotle had already posited as categories, which the Sceptics had treated as πρός τι, as added mentally and which, in an increasing degree, have been recognized as fictions by modern philosophy.
>
> These and similar ideas form the basis of discursive thinking. "The error which makes us so guilty in the sight of God is that, by our concepts, we are always assigning limits of which nature knows nothing." Engel, *Philos. für die Welt,* p. 26.

Such analogical fictions are very widespread and popular in other sciences. Quite frequently however the vital question arises as to what extent such an analogy is "real", to what extent *hypothetical,* to what extent *fictional.* This question is important, for instance, in the popular modern analogy whereby the state or a society is compared with an organism.[9]

It is in just such questions that the lack of a logical theory of the method involved is so regrettably obvious. Even where such analogies are purely fictional, as, for example, in the comparison of society with the human organism, they are often of service in arriving at true theoretical laws.

From the same source arise many errors, in which these fictions are thought-lessly treated as true analogies and the laws deduced from them uncritically substituted for reality. Error is due to exactly the same causes as truth, and just as in nature the same blind laws may bring what is either helpful or harm-ful, according to circumstances—for they cut in both directions—so in the mental field both good and evil spring from the same laws. It is all the more the duty of logic to explain error because the dividing line between error and truth is not sharply drawn, as was clearly shown above; for the application of a fiction can be based partly upon truth, partly upon (conscious) error. The logicians of the eighteenth century always regarded it as their duty to include error in a general way within their logical systems. We must therefore, as we have already stated, distinguish between *real analogies*, where discovery is the work of induction and hypothesis, and purely *fictional analogies* due merely to subjective method. That I expect one phenomenon to be immediately and necessarily followed and preceded by another, according to the law of causal-ity, is a real analogy; for I have so often observed that all phenomena precede and follow others, that I am justified in inferring analogically that in the present instance also this can be assumed. But the fact that I call this whole relation of unalterable sequence "Cause and effect", and apperceive it under the category of causality, constitutes an analogical fiction; for although the relation of will to its activity is a real analogy with an unchangeable sequence, we are not entitled to designate the constituent members of this sequence by names taken from the realm of the subjective. The form of the relation is in this case really analogical, but the material equating of the unchangeable se-quence with action following volition is an analogical fiction.

CHAPTER V JURISTIC FICTIONS

A SPECIAL form of the foregoing is presented by the legal fiction. The term fiction has hitherto been nowhere better known than in jurisprudence where it forms a favourite subject of discussion. In principle these fictions are identical with those which we have just considered. The psychological mechanism of their application consists in subsuming a single case under a conceptual construct not properly intended for it, so that the apperception is, in consequence, merely an analogy. The basis for this method is as follows: since laws cannot include within their formulæ all particular instances, cer-tain special examples of an unusual nature are treated as if they belonged to them. Or else, because of some practical interest, an individual instance is brought under a general concept to which it does not really belong. Anyone conversant with the method of jurisprudence will easily understand how important this artifice is for legal practice. It is just as essential for law as for mathematics. It is true that the logicians, with negligible exceptions, have allowed this example to escape them because they quite failed to realize that logic must take its material from living science. Apart from mathematics there is hardly any domain more suitable than law for the deduction of logical laws and their illustration, or the discovery of logical methods. This fact is due to the similarity in principle existing between the two subjects. What makes such methodological considerations attractive and profitable is that they enable us to observe how the mind employs the same principle even in fundamentally different fields. It is therefore not at all strange, but even natural, that up to the present these fictions have been subjected to extensive theoretical examination only in mathematics and law, and then only by authorities in these sciences themselves. What is remarkable is the casual way in which the logicians have allowed this domain to escape them. The a priori method of establishing laws must necessarily be supplemented by purely inductive observations of the logical procedure within the sciences themselves. Only a very close familiarity with the method of the special sciences can qualify a person for framing fruitful logical laws and such laws have consequently been the work of those who were exceptionally well acquainted with special sciences, men like Aristotle and Bacon. The English no less than the German logicians of the eighteenth century achieved very important results in this respect. Only an all-embracing knowledge of scientific procedure in all fields renders it possible to make logical discoveries.

It is exceedingly interesting to see how phenomena apparently so remote as juristic fictions are, in principle, identical with those pertaining to the theory of knowledge treated in the preceding paragraphs.

The firm bond determining the order that exists here is simply and solely the *method and its principle*. Our classification, no matter how it may seem to jumble together the most varied types of things, will at once appear as fundamental, necessary and correct, as our criterion of the methodological principle, the only point of real consequence here. We shall thus be able to see how the logical function in very different fields always continues to apply the same devices.

Fictiones juris cover a wide field. But for that very reason they offer, methodologically, extremely fruitful material and reveal the wonderful mechanism and contrivances of thought. It is just as impossible to avoid a consideration of juristic detail as in the case of mathematics, political economy, theology, epistemology, etc. Logic has hitherto occupied itself far too little with the detailed analysis of complete systems of scientific thought and method. Only a sympathetic appreciation of the ways of thought can enlighten us about the method of the logical function and the astonishing by-paths it often takes.

In the fictio juris, too, something that has not happened is regarded as having happened, or vice versa, or an individual case is brought under an analogous relationship violently in contradiction with reality. Roman law is permeated throughout by such fictions, and in modern countries it is in England especially that juristic fictions have undergone additional development.

A further point of particular interest in this connection is the relationship of the fictio juris to the praesumptio juris. The latter is the juristic hypothesis, the former the juristic fiction. They have both often been confused in juristic theory and practice, and the distinction between them has become a favourite juristic problem. The praesumptio is a conjecture, the fictio an intentional and conscious invention.

The enormous practical advantages of this method are indeed so great that it is repeatedly applied. For instance, in the new German Commercial Code, Art. 347, we find a provision that goods not returned to the sender within the proper time are to be regarded as if the recipient had definitely authorized and accepted them. Such an example enables us to study to advantage the identity in principle of analogical fictions, such as the categories, with juristic fictions.

Where the acceptance of the goods by the consignee is admitted, the question of the time within which no return or complaint is made becomes of importance. This time-relationship is treated as in the similar case of a recipient who is unwilling to accept the goods but yet neglects to send in a complaint within the specified time. Here, therefore, a purely analogous time-relationship between two cases becomes the basis of an actual material identification of content. This method is just as necessary in the interests of practice in jurisprudence as in the theory of knowledge. In the one field comprehensibility, in the other a practical treatment of individual cases, would be impossible without an analogous appercep- tion. The formal behaviour of the psyche in both instances is absolutely identical, and an understanding of this formal identity is important be- cause it is so difficult to get accustomed to attaching equal value to both types of behaviour. From a practical standpoint, the importance is great and almost incalculable. Theoretically, however, not only has nothing been gained thereby, but there has been a *deviation from reality.* Without such deviations thought cannot attain its purposes, and this is quite natural, for how otherwise could thought manipulate and elaborate what is given? It is just the deviation that, in the end, appears to be the natural procedure, and it is absolutely necessary constantly to stress this fact and draw attention to it. Generally, as has already been stated above, the opposite view is taken and reality is attributed to all logical acts until their unreality is demonstrated. Our methodological principle is the reverse. The eye of the philosopher is thereby able to recognize more readily the tremendous difference between the formal processes of thought and the objective reality of external events.

CHAPTER VI PERSONIFICATORY FICTIONS

ANOTHER type of analogical fiction deserving of special treatment is the *personificatory fiction.* The analogy under which phenomena are apprehended is, in this case, the group of ideas connected with a person. The preceding type of fiction was an application of an analogical fiction to a special field; that which we are about to examine represents a special form of apperception.

The principle common to both is the hypostatization of phenomena in some way or another, whatever the extent to which the picture of the personality is involved. This is also the true determining factor in the category "thing." Here, too, belong a whole series of well-known concepts, such as *soul, energy, psychic capacity.* While formerly these ideational constructs were taken to be the expression of real things, to-day they are regarded as mere abbreviations, as the comprehensive expression for a series of interrelated phenomena and processes. Moreover, all the more specific forces are to be included here, such as *gravitation,* which Newton himself only looked upon as a fiction. The phenomena are, of course, real, but the attribution to them of gravitational *force* is simply a summary expression for the regularity of the phenomena.

We may compare particularly Heinr. Boehmer for the treatment of force as a fiction, in his excellent but neglected work, *Entwicklung der naturwissenschaftlichen Weltanschauung,* Gotha, 1872, pp. 163 ff. and 166. Boehmer quotes the following from Du Bois-Reymond: "Force is

simply a disguised outlet for the irresistible tendency to personification; a rhetorical device, as it were, of our brain which seizes upon a
figurative expression because the idea is not clear enough to be directly
formulated."

It is the same with the *vital force* and a large number of other forces. The
former, in particular, was once universally regarded as a relatively secure
hypothesis: to-day it is almost as universally regarded as a fiction (certain
theologians and theological scientists excepted). Liebig, in his *Reden und
Abhandlungen*, declared that unknown causes are merely products of the
imagination: for example, the *spiritus rector*, phlogiston, sound stuff, and
the catalytic energy of isomeres. The vital force is for him an invention
of the mind, a spectre, etc. On the other hand, used as an auxiliary word
it is still extensively employed as a concise summary, and as a nominal
fiction (auxiliary word) it can hardly be dispensed with. Apart from this,
however, the vital force has no use; and for any further purpose it is a
bad fiction.

It is true that this fiction has here deteriorated into a purely nominal one,
i.e. the idea serves no practical purpose but that of bringing a number of
entities under one head and simplifying our methods of expression. Nothing
is stated by such words except what the individual phenomena themselves
could state.

To suppose that by means of such words or ideas anything has really been
understood—a naïve attitude that has not so very long been discarded — is
to forget that they are all tautologies.

> The same is true if it is believed that the inevitable sequence has been
> understood when it has been apprehended as causality. This is simply a
> tautology, for causality is an analogical fiction and ultimately nothing but a
> word. To-day, at least, this idea has sunk to the rank of a mere word for the
> philosopher, whereas previously everything was regarded as understood if
> it could be brought under the category of causality. Thus all so-called proof
> and understanding is no more than tautology.

Various other concepts are to be regarded as nominal fictions of this kind.
For example, chemistry includes many processes under the term "catalytic
energy," which is sometimes also ascribed to them.

The eighteenth century, in particular, was responsible for many such ideas in all the sciences, and at that time it was believed that something was actually being understood by this means. But a word of this sort is a mere shell preserving and holding together the essential content, and just as the shell always adjusts itself to the content and simply reflects it as an external counterpart, so these words or concepts represent tautologies that repeat the essential facts under another guise. The best-known example is the *vis dormitiva*. In general it must be remembered that most of what is called knowledge, not merely in ordinary life but also in science, consists of such shells, of ideas in which the facts as they actually exist are grouped together without producing any new knowledge. The so-called riddles of the universe can never be solved, because most of what appears puzzling to us consists in contradictions created by ourselves, and arises from trifling with the mere forms and shells of knowledge.

CHAPTER VII SUMMATIONAL FICTIONS *(GENERAL IDEAS)*

THE fictions just discussed bring us to *general ideas*, which perform in a general way the same service as that of the fictions already discussed for special cases.

> The service rendered by these fictions to the psyche and to its logical operations is constantly approximating more closely to that rendered by language and words to thought. That general ideas are, of all fictions, the first to suffer the common fate of being hypostatized, is well-known. Compare the correct and very good account given of the relationship of Plato and Aristotle in this respect by Lewes *(History of Philosophy,* Vol. I, p. 298). Taine still further elaborated this treatment of general ideas.

We spoke of general pictures and concepts above—from a strictly nominalist standpoint—as fictions, because these artificial ideational constructs render a great service to thought. But since they nevertheless correspond indirectly to reality and embrace a series of similar phenomena, they are here included under provisional constructs which as comprehensive expressions are substituted for a series of particular phenomena. Concepts and schematic ideas are likewise artificial constructions, conceptual knots formed by thought for mnemonic purposes. They are pure *summational* fictions, i.e.

expressions in which a number of phenomena are grouped together according to their chief characters. In so far as these expressions are regarded as copies of things which are supposed to be real, they may also be regarded as personificatory fictions; or, in so far as only the essential characters are retained and the unessential neglected, they may be termed abstractive fictions. The different classes merge into one another.

According to Spencer "abstract ideas" do not represent actual experiences, but are symbols signifying groups of such experiences, aggregates of representations and re-representations.

Meynert very correctly observes (*Mechanik des Gehirnbaus*) that "a concept is always the designation of something impossible to imagine; it is rooted not in the world of ideas, but in language as a word."

For the metaphysical side of the problem (the question of species) cf. Spitzer, *Nominalismus und Realismus*, 1786, especially pp. 102–103. Only nominalism is right: "The assertions of theological metaphysics are recognised as *fictions*." Fiction is here used in a derogatory way instead of its only correct meaning of an expedient invention. Species, for instance, are certainly partially expedient fictions even if, like all fictions when strictly adhered to, they lead to logical nonsense and to contradictions with reality.

General ideas are practical fictions, i.e. assumptions by means of which the practice of thinking is made easier but which correspond to no actual metaphysical reality. They are for logic ideals, postulates, i.e. *fictions*, fictional ideals. In logic, in particular, many bad fictions are to be found; such, for example, as *quidditas* and other medieval entities.

CHAPTER VIII HEURISTIC FICTIONS

ANOTHER type of fiction to be examined is the heuristic. It is true that a number of those already considered also have heuristic value, but the fictions which we specifically group together under this term serve heuristic purposes to a particularly marked degree. In the fictions hitherto discussed the deviation from reality consisted in a more or less arbitrary alteration of it; in those now to be treated we have something absolutely unreal definitely substituted for something real. Here the most important condition is that this conceptual construct should not be self-contradictory, as is the case with fictions to be mentioned later on. It may, however, be a type of construct not to be found in the real world, and one which, if consistently adhered to, leads to contradictions with reality. For the explanation of a complex of real events the assumption of unreal causes is first made, and when this has been systematically worked out, not only is order brought into the phenomena but the ground is also prepared for the correct solution of the problem; and for this very reason the method has heuristic value. But such assumptions, in so far as they do not belong to the methods hitherto mentioned or to purely experimental ones, and in so far as they are of a tentative nature, are not directly created for the purpose but arise wherever the hypotheses hitherto employed prove insufficient and erroneous; and such discarded hypotheses frequently still continue to perform good practical and heuristic service. The history of science provides a number of such cases of a very instructive nature. It can be proved that the Ptolemaic cosmic system was already regarded by the Arabs of the Middle Ages as a fiction and not an hypothesis. The same is true of the Cartesian vortex-hypothesis, which, in the eighteenth century, particularly in France, was still adopted as a fiction, a fact that led to interesting theoretical discussions of the method of hypotheses and fictions. The same thing holds true to-day for the ether hypothesis, which is supposed to explain the phenomena of light and is still for many scientists only a fiction. All these discarded hypotheses are useful as fictions, including the teleological hypothesis, which from a theoretical standpoint is without value, at least in its earlier form.

> Teleology if taken metaphysically and hypothetically is certainly a "sorry shift", as Goethe says in commenting upon this tendency to explain things by their final causes. On the other hand, it forms a very good auxiliary if used only heuristically for the purpose of discovery. Compare Kant's *Kritik der Urteilskraft;* and also, for the "As-if" in this connection, Grün, *Philosophie,* 184 ff. According to Kant, teleology is only a *modus reflexionis* (*modus dicendi*), a makeshift, a crutch, a mere regulative and subjective auxiliary principle.
>
> The ideal of an "ascending scale of sentient beings" is likewise a heuristic principle.
>
> The earlier *geological Periods* are to-day frequently only regarded as *artificial divisions* or "schematic" fictions. Here too a natural system of stratification is being sought.

Surprise was caused by Neumann's declaration that the Newtonian laws of gravitation were fictions of this kind.

In all modern science there is a tendency to depose hypotheses hitherto regarded as firmly established and to degrade them to the position of useful fictions. Neumann's attitude has found support in the claim that the Newtonian laws were formulated without taking into consideration the resistance of the ether and are only empirical. As soon as empirical laws are declared to be actual laws, and treated as if they were really objective, then they become fictions. Compare Wundt, *Aufgabe der Philosophie*, p. 6: "It was thus quite natural that all hypotheses concerning the ultimate basis of physical phenomena should come to be regarded as mere *aids* for their concrete understanding or treatment, and that no one should therefore have been disturbed when changes took place in the hypotheses prevalent in the various divisions of natural science concerning the constitution of matter."

Neumann also called the law of the conservation of energy, as well as a number of mathematical axioms and postulates, mere fictive assumptions. Criticism of fresh hypotheses often terminates in a willingness to permit these assumptions to stand as heuristic fictions but not as hypotheses. This is especially the case in the denial of Darwinism.

This theoretical and methodological question is intimately connected with a problem that has received particular attention in England. We know that Newton distinguished in his methodological rules between a *causa vera* and a *causa ficta*. The discussion of this somewhat obscure distinction dealt with precisely the point on which we have been insisting. Another of Newton's remarks, *hypotheses non jingo*, which still continues to form a subject of discussion, is here relevant. As is well known, it has always been objected that Newton himself advanced hypotheses. It is strange, however, that everyone has overlooked the fact that Newton laid stress upon the "*jingo*" and not upon the "*hypotheses*." Even Mill and Whewell, who comment on the phrase, did not see that Newton was not denying that he framed hypotheses of any kind, but explaining that he declined to invent them.

In this utterance Newton is attacking the dilettantism very widespread in his day, of formulating entirely arbitrary and phantastic hypotheses, impossible of verification. This led to the well-known dislike felt by many natural scientists and logicians for hypotheses in general. But hypotheses are admittedly indispensable; and that there are also fictions which are as justifiable as they are useful, is precisely what we wish to demonstrate. We shall indeed have at every step to oppose *bad fictions*, just as formerly *bad hypotheses* were opposed.

Newton's theoretical and methodological postulates, then, are not unassailable. From our point of view fictive assumptions are permissible if consciously advanced as such and nothing more; and they can be of great service. To this class belong a number of historically famous examples: e.g. Locke still used the Cartesian theory of "animal" spirits as a propaedeutic and heuristic fiction. Spinoza's assumption of a complete parallelism of psychical and physical events, which to-day has many adherents, is on our view not only untenable but valueless as an hypothesis—whereas as a fiction it is of incalculable value.

More recent examples of this type of heuristic fiction are not hard to find: e.g. Zöllner advanced such a fiction in his well-known assumption that the atoms or the mass-particles of a given system move "*as if* they wished to produce the smallest degree of discomfort." But for the most part these fictions represent former hypotheses which render services to science even in their present emaciated condition. It is still an open question whether some of the assumptions advanced in the form of axioms or postulates will not sink to the level of hypotheses, and so to that of fictions. Such gradual degradation has, in fact, frequently occurred. Even in mathematics or mathematical physics these pillars are now being shaken, and it is not at all unlikely that elements may here be shown to be fictional that have hitherto been regarded as axiomatic.

CHAPTER IX PRACTICAL (ETHICAL) FICTIONS

WITH the class of fictions just described may be associated another group which we call *practical fictions*. With this class we depart, it is true, from our classification, but we shall not be able to adhere to this any longer. We are here in the presence of assumptions which not only contradict reality but are in themselves contradictory. They cannot be referred to any of the classes so far discussed, or reduced simply to abstractions or analogies—the two main factors in the formation of fictions—for different fictional forms have co-operated in their construction. The ideas to be treated here are of so intricate a nature that they cannot be brought under homogeneous formulæ. Their psychological structure is exceedingly complicated.

Very diverse psychical processes have contributed to the formation of these complicated concepts, which serve to present the most important problems in science.

We encounter at the very threshold of these fictions one of the most important concepts ever formed by man, the idea of *freedom;* human actions are regarded as free, and therefore as "responsible" and contrasted with the "necessary" course of natural events. We need not here recapitulate the familiar antinomies found in this contradictory concept; it not only contradicts observation which shows that everything obeys unalterable laws, but is also self-contradictory, for an absolutely free, chance act, resulting from nothing, is ethically just as valueless as an absolutely necessary one. In spite of all these contradictions, however, we not only make use of this concept in ordinary life in judging moral actions, but it is also the foundation of criminal law. Without this assumption punishment inflicted for any act would, from an ethical standpoint, be unthinkable, for it would simply be a precautionary measure for protecting others against crime. Our judgment of our fellow-men is likewise so completely bound up with this ideational construct that we can no longer do without it. In the course of their development, men have formed this important construct from immanent necessity, because only on this basis is a high degree of culture and morality possible. But this does not prevent our realizing that it is itself a logical monstrosity, a contradiction; in a word, only a fiction and not an hypothesis. For centuries liberty has been regarded not merely as an hypothesis but as an unassailable dogma. It then fell to the rank of a disputed hypothesis, and to-day it is already often regarded as an indispensable fiction. A bitter struggle was necessary before we attained our present attitude, which for a long while was far from general. On this modern view there is nothing in the real world corresponding to the idea of liberty, though in practice it is an exceedingly necessary fiction.

Hoppe takes a similar view in *Die Zurechnungsfähigkeit,* (Wurzburg, 1877). Only the absence of the word "fiction" distinguishes his view from ours. On page 32, he says, with reference to the question of responsibility, that absolute freewill and responsibility are impossible. Nevertheless we must allow everyone the ideal wish which they embody, for every "false concept" has the value of an ideal. "An individual is to be condemned for offences in proportion to the ideal feeling of responsibility he may possess." And again "the ideally imagined responsibility does not stand the test; nevertheless men desire responsibility in its ideal form, and they should and must desire it." Let me add here that the perfect and ideal constructions of mathematics are comparable with the above; e.g. there is no ideal roundness in nature, but the mathematician requires it and proceeds as though it could exist. For this reason Hoppe holds that ideal responsibility is a justifiable assumption in spite of its impossibility.

From this we may conclude that just as science, and especially mathematics, leads to the imaginary, so life leads us to the impossible, which is quite justifiable—to absolute responsibility, absolute freedom and good actions for their own sake (absolute). Thou art a man and shouldst possess these noble sentiments—such is the command of the idealist and of society.

The imaginary (the absolute, ideal) is therefore justifiable in spite of its unreality. Without the imaginary factor neither science nor life in their highest form are possible. The real tragedy of life is that the most valuable ideas are, from the point of view of reality, worthless. The value of reality is thus reversed. F. A. Lange has also pointed out that the ideal and the real interchange their rôles; that the ideal, the unreal, is the most valuable: that men must "demand the impossible", even if it leads to contradictions.

That the idea of absolute responsibility, in particular, leads to a contradiction has also been shown by Hoppe (Ibid., pp. 52 ff.): "Absolute responsibility, like the demand for absolute perfection (together with the categorical imperative) is only a desire, an ideal striving for the non-existent." It is "an ideal creation of mankind" (Ibid., pp. 86 ff.). "Freedom is only an entity of thought", but mankind must retain this imaginary ideal, just as the mathematicians, for example, retain imaginary ideal points in spite of their inner contradiction.

Adolf Steudel takes a similar attitude in his Philosophie im Umriss (II, Praktische Fragen, A, Kritik der Sittenlehre; published in Stuttgart in 1877). Steudel completely refutes the doctrine of freedom but believes that his theoretical refutation does not affect the theory of morality. He states this expressly, p. 589: "Even though we live, think and act as if we possessed absolutely free control over our volitions and actions, natural law fulfils itself with certainty just the same."

It is both important and instructive to exhibit the different forms which this dispute has frequently assumed. The wellknown statistician, Rümelin, delivered an address in Tübingen in the autumn of 1876, November 6, "On some psychological presuppositions of Criminal Law".[10] He starts with the view that freedom and responsibility form necessary presuppositions of criminal law and continues in the following strain: freedom, it is true, is an idea that has been challenged, but it must be remembered that if freedom is to be denied theoretically and on the other hand made, in practice, the basis of criminal law, an intolerable divergence of theory from practice must arise. Such a divergence appears to him unlikely from both points of view: for if a theory is right and the practice based upon it wrong, then such things as *barren truths* should exist, but if the theory is false and the practice based upon it right, then we must allow that there are *fruitful errors*. But, the speaker asks, can we really admit this? He thinks that this question can be easily answered in the natural sciences, for experiment and empirical demonstration are there possible. It is more difficult to answer in other fields of inquiry; in law, for instance. Criminal law is concerned with the idea of responsibility and of free-will as necessary ethical and psychological presuppositions. For if there is to be punishment there must also be guilt. But this cannot exist where responsibility and freedom are denied. Determinism in its various forms gets rid of this concept and attempts to justify punishment in other ways. But the theory of punishment as a deterrent is contrary to our moral feeling, which looks upon wrong as guilt and regards punishment as atonement and expiation. A judge must necessarily act according to the following presuppositions: he must assume (i) the existence of the soul as a real inner governing principle, determining the instincts and actions of man and thus constituting his freedom of choice; (ii) that character is not an objective power determining the will, but a product of the will; and (iii) that there exists in everyone a conscience, a feeling of right and wrong, the consciousness of an ethical compulsion whose disregard demands expiation and atonement. These, says Rümelin, are absolutely essential presuppositions in a judge, for he certainly could not allow a criminal to plead the necessity of his act. But, he asks, can we draw any inference as to the truth of these theoretical postulates from this procedure of the judge in the practice of criminal law? And he answers in the affirmative. It is essential to demonstrate and establish the unity of practice and theory. There are, he concludes, no fruitful errors.

Our answer to this question would naturally have been the reverse. A thinker who is dealing with a particular concept may well find it difficult to declare so important a concept a fiction; yet in the whole context of our investigation it forms only a fractional element, and where more important concepts have to be given up this one, too, can readily change from an hypothesis to a fiction.

The above method of argument is typical of current procedure and provides an example of *logical optimism*. We may certainly grant that the judge need not first indulge in meditations upon the nature of freedom. Yet, though for our part we not only admit, but even strongly contend, that freedom is a necessary presupposition of punishment, we must also insist that the term "presupposition" has two meanings. It may be an *hypothesis*, but it may also be a *postulate* or a *fiction*. Undoubtedly there is a conflict between theory and practice; and undoubtedly there are *fruitful errors*. The logical optimist, of course, does not like to admit this, but in the end the facts cannot be shut out. The history of mankind is full of examples proving the existence not only of fruitful errors (take the religions alone, for example) but also of *harmful truths*. Rümelin, himself, spoke of "barren truths." But the choice of this expression to contrast with "fruitful errors" obscured his thought, for harmful truths correspond far more closely to fruitful errors. The logical optimist, it is true, does not accept this, for from his youth up he has been impregnated with the belief that the *good* is also the *true* and that *truth* is always *good*. The identification of the Good and the True—as Lange[11] has already clearly shown—is an ideal. Instead of ideal we say "fiction," for all ideals, logically considered, are fictions.

Logical optimism cannot accustom itself to the fact that in the domain of science there are certain counters that the ordinary man takes to be real facts. It is just the most fundamental principles of many sciences that are insecurely grounded.

Let me in passing also take exception to Rümelin's statement that such a question is more easily answered in the natural sciences. Apart from the examples already adduced, we shall find many cases of conceptual constructs in natural science where theory does ultimately prove to be as unfertile as practice is fruitful. It is precisely the most important and most fruitful ideational constructs that are full of contradictions.

Among moderns, R. Seydel in his Ethics has shown a tendency to regard liberty as a fiction, and a fiction in our sense of the term, i.e. admittedly contradictory but nevertheless an exceedingly fruitful and necessary basis for ethics; and not in the sense, in which it is often used, of a mere error.

Kant's treatment of this problem presents points of particular interest.

Kant was well on the way towards regarding liberty as an "idea," i.e. as a fiction. Indeed his conception of intelligible freedom was at first probably thought of as a fiction, but his reactionary tendency, also found elsewhere in Kant, induced him in the end to make an hypothesis out of a fiction; and this was naturally transformed by his followers into a dogma, and as such enthusiastically disseminated. This conception is actually only of value if treated as an expedient fiction, since all these fictions are, after all, manifestations of the organic purposive activity of the logical function. On the other hand, the logical paradox, the contradiction contained in this idea, prevents it from functioning as an hypothesis with something objective corresponding to it. Here also belong, in part, the ideational constructs which were grouped above under the term "symbolic fictions," in so far as they influence practical behaviour. Thus, according to Kant, man is not merely to be judged in his conduct *as* if he were a free agent, but should conduct himself *as* if, at some time or other, he were to be held accountable for his acts. Although Kant himself would not have agreed, Schleiermacher allows that prayer is a practical act, so long as there is still a consciousness of its being interpreted *as* if God would hearken to it. It is well-known, however, that this very concept of prayer contains antinomies which destroy its objectivity. In prayer, at least in Islam and Christendom, there is an insoluble contradiction between the omnipotence of God, who can hearken to the prayer, and his omniscient government of the universe, quite apart from the contradictions insolved by the ordinary idea of prayer in relation to natural laws.

In the category of practical fictions a number of other moral concepts and postulates are also to be enumerated, such as the concept of duty, of immortality, etc.

Cf. in particular, for the idea of immortality, Biederman, *Christliche Dogmatik,* §§ 949–973; Biederman admits this idea as a fiction but attacks it as an hypothesis, i.e. as dogma. A person of really noble character does not require it.

The most sublime *fiction* of this kind is the "moral world-order"; and there is also the idea of infinite perfection, le progrès indèfini, both for individuals (Leibniz) and in the history of the world.

Mill says quite correctly in his essay on Theism that the ideas of God and immortality are for Kant 'incentives,' methods of inciting, of stimulating and of educating. The "imaginary good being" he regards as a norm to be venerated.

All this is intimately connected with what Darwinism calls useful illusions formed by natural selection, a fact specially emphasized in Hellwald's *Kulturgeschichte.*

Here belong all the so-called "ideals" of ordinary life. From a logical stand-point they are really fictions, but in practice they possess tremendous value in history. The ideal is an ideational construct contradictory in itself and in contradiction with reality, but it has an irresistible power. *The Ideal is a practical fiction.*

This gives us a clear expression of the principle that Lange called the *stand-point of the ideal.* He still lacked the logical terminology with the aid of which we are enabled to formulate the principle simply, as follows: Ideals are not hypotheses. They would be hypotheses if they were attainable or had been realized in any part of the world; but they are fictions.

We include as fictions not merely indifferent theoretical operations but ideational constructs emanating from the noblest minds, to which the no-blest part of mankind cling and of which they will not allow themselves to be deprived. Nor is it our object so to deprive them—for as *practical fictions* we leave them all intact; they perish only as *theoretical truths.*

Lange's idea of imaginative creation, which has been frequently misun-derstood, appears from this point of view as a vague expression of what we call fiction. We can thus probe to the real psychological source of these con-structions of human imagination. We have discovered the common logical procedure that lies at the basis both of these vast conceptions of mankind and of utterly indifferent logical and scientific methods. From this insignif-icant logical device—the formation of conceptual constructs which serve practical purposes though they are of no further theoretical value—all logi-cal methods as well as the most important practical ideas of mankind arise. The common element in them all is, however, the immense practical value which all these constructs possess although there is no corresponding ob-jective reality.

The logical optimist will be depressed by this formula compressed into a few sentences, but this can in no way alter the facts of the case. The pro-gress of science is relentless. Anyone who finds such knowledge terrible, who regards it as a harmful truth and therefore feels constrained to cast aside his ideals as valueless—such a man has never really believed in his ideals with all his heart. We are here stating, in our own terminology, what constitutes the real principle of Kantian ethics, namely, that true morality must always rest upon a *fictional* basis. All the *hypothetical* bases, God, immor-tality, reward, punishment, etc., destroy its ethical character, i.e. we must act with the same seriousness and the same scruples *as* if the duty were imposed by God, *as if* we would be judged therefor, *as if* we would be punished for immorality. But as soon as this *as if* is transformed into a *because*, its purely ethical character vanishes and it becomes simply a matter of our lower interests, mere egoism.

Thus, before our very eyes, does a small psychical artifice not only develop into a mighty source of the whole theoretical explanation of the world — for all categories arise from it—but it also becomes the origin of all the idealistic belief and behaviour of mankind. This is generally ascribed to the imagination, but that is just as useless as to ascribe the organic processes to a "vital force." What is wanted is an account of the fundamental processes. In virtue of purely mechanical psychical laws these constructs have an immense practical importance and play an indispensable intermediary role. Without them the satisfaction of understanding, the ordering of our chaotic material, would be impossible; without them all advanced science would be impossible, for they serve as its instruments both in the process of thought and in the preparatory stages; without them, finally, all higher morality would be impossible. In spite of the enormous importance of this function, its products—these very ideational constructs—must only be regarded as fictions, without any corresponding reality, as free representations, arising by immanent necessity from the mechanistic play of ideas, as aids and tools created by the purposive logical activity with the object of lightening and perfecting its labour, whether in relation to science or to life. Thus fantasy becomes "the principle of the world-process," but in a different sense from that of Frohschammer, the author of a book with this title.

CHAPTER X THE FUNDAMENTAL FICTIONAL CONCEPTS OF MATHEMATICS

MATHEMATICAL fictions must be treated as another special field. We have already pointed out that, in addition to jurisprudence, it is in mathematics that the importance of fictions has already been recognized. In both fields the particular is often subsumed under the general, and the characters of the general case are later re-applied to the particular. But the latter resists this subsumption, for the generalized statement is not so comprehensive that it can embrace the particular case. In mathematics, for instance, curves are subsumed under straight lines, which has the immense advantage of allowing us to operate with them. Jurisprudence deals with the problem of bringing a single case under some law in order to apply its theory of rewards and punishments. In both instances a relation which cannot be realized is represented as actually realized. Thus the curved line is regarded as straight, the adopted son as the real son. Actually both are absolutely impossible. A curved line is never straight, an adopted son never a real son. To give other examples: a circle is thought of as an ellipse; in jurisprudence the defendant who does not put in an appearance is regarded *as if* he admitted the charge, and an heir who is deemed unfit to inherit is regarded *as if* he had died before the testator.

Jurisprudence, however, has an easier task in dealing with its fictions than has mathematics, for its cases are covered by arbitrary ordinances, and a transference is easily made. We have only to think of the case *as if it were so*. In mathematics, however, the more stubborn material of spatial relationships resists such mistreatment by artificial devices; and the logical function then makes use of an ingenious expedient which particularly appeals to the logical observer. This artifice is one of the most remarkable ever devised. Anyone acquainted with mathematics and its astonishing methods knows how the psyche proceeds in these cases: the circle is regarded as an ellipse, the distance of whose foci is zero (this is a method to which mathematicians are very partial). When the curve is subsumed under the straight line, it is thought of as made up of an infinite number of straight lines.

The fundamental concepts of mathematics are space, or more precisely empty space, empty time, point, line, surface, or more precisely points without extension, lines without breadth, surfaces without depth, spaces without content. All these concepts are contradictory fictions, mathematics being based upon an entirely imaginary foundation, indeed upon contradictions.

Upon these foundations the psyche has constructed the entire edifice of this amazing science. Mathematicians have occasionally realized that they were dealing with contradictions, but seldom or never was this made the subject of any profound study. The frank acknowledgment of these fundamental contradictions has become absolutely essential for mathematical progress. The efforts frequently made to conceal this fact have all worn threadbare.

The concept on which the whole of mechanics is based of *empty time* as a firm and lasting construction, a form, as Kant also assumed it to be, is a fiction based on an abstractive and one-sided isolation. But it is instructive that empty space and empty time should be indispensable fictions both for mechanics and for the theory of knowledge.

Moreover, it is generally accepted that the "mathematical ideal conceptions" which are "aroused by reality," "but to which reality never exactly corresponds," are also fictional. A perfect circle, an absolutely straight line, etc., are ideals, i.e. fictions. Laas includes the absolute line, constant velocity, the unconditioned, totality, the infinite, consciousness in general, and the "Ding an sich" as ideals, i.e. as *fictions*. Cf. the Geometrical Imagination, *Ibid.,* p. 208.

Special mention may be made of Michelet's work on Natural Philosophy, § 174; nor should we forget that Plato had already called the point a δόγμα γεωμετρικόν, in the sense of a fiction, and points, like atoms, are only "limiting concepts." A "limit" itself is a fictitious assumption if hypostasized.

That the line is made up of points is likewise a mathematical fiction. Cf. again, Michelet, who also treats asymptotes as imaginary constructions. In his *Logic,* § 75, Michelet further showed how and why much that is accepted as possible was logically impossible.

The philosophy of mathematics, especially in Michelet, provides many other examples. If the circle is regarded as a polygon, this is a formal identification at the expense of a qualitative difference, the circle being regarded *as if* it were a polygon consisting of an infinite number of sides, infinitely small.

That such fictions lead to contradictions is clear from the inferences drawn by Zeno, which were based upon the fact that the fiction of spatial and temporal atoms (infinitely small divisions of space and time) was taken seriously and transformed into reality. The fiction became an hypothesis and the crudest contradictions followed.

Mathematicians are fond of making such fictions in order to deal more effectively with reality; e.g. the fiction "of an infinitely thin shell, ellipsoidal, and bounded by two similar surfaces" or the "fiction of an infinitely thin layer."

Empty space is a pure mathematical fiction, and yet all science is concerned with an attempt to reduce the world-processes to movements of atoms in empty space. That the atom in all its various forms is also a fiction we may here affirm in anticipation of our later conclusion, and so give expression to an important idea, namely, that the reduction of all happenings to atomic movements in space, which is the goal of all science, is in fact an attempt to reduce all existence to ideational constructs of a purely fictional nature.

To understand is to reduce to known ideational constructs. Empty space, and atoms interpreted in a material sense, seem to be such constructs, but in actual fact they are only fictions. If, however, we succeed in reducing everything to these fictions then the world seems to be understood. It *seems* to be!

These apperceptive constructs are fictions, the product of the imaginative faculty. All events are reduced to this known measure; and just as reductions made from one system of measurement to another, e.g. into the metric system, cannot be undertaken without residual fractions, so it is with this immense reduction to apparently known constructs.

Thus the immense work of modern science reduces all existence, which in the last analysis is absolutely incomprehensible, to an entirely subjective and purely fictional standard.

We are now for the first time in a position to understand the full significance of Kant. According to him space is subjective and all reality is unknown. The Kantian proof of this statement is inadequate, the only true proof being the following: space is a subjective construct because it is full of *contradictions*. It is a character of all true fictions that they contain contradictions and the concept of space is simply riddled with them. The conceptual construct of space has been invented and given form by the psyche with a view to bringing order into the events which it encounters—the chaotic and contradictory mass of sensations. Space is a construct with which we have become gradually familiar, and which on account of its familiarity appears to be real and entirely harmless. The cosmic process has stimulated the development, within the psyche, of this concept of tri-dimensional space in order to create an illusion that something is being understood. Real events are incomprehensible to us but are projected into this space.

It is true that attempts have recently been made to do away with these contradictions by the invention of artificial spaces, but this always leads to the same contradictions. Moreover, the idea of such n-dimensional spaces is based upon a new device of thought whereby far more generalized structures are conceived than are actually given.

CHAPTER XI THE METHOD OF ABSTRACT GENERALIZATION

THE method of abstract generalization is another of the brilliant devices of thought, but also one which is not free from contradictions. Its value consists in the invention of highly generalized relations which simplify the systematic study of special relations actually existing. In mathematics three-dimensional space is thought of as a special case, since, in the abstract, more than three dimensions are conceivable. By the formation of such spaces, of such conceptual constructs, which are, however, contradictory, it is then possible to grasp the particular in its relationships more definitely.

> This fiction has found many opponents, among them Dühring (*Cursus*, 68) who calls it mystical. (The reproach of mysticism, as we know, is encountered again in connection with the atom, the differential, the *Ding an sich*, and energy — in short in connection with all fictions.) These concepts are mystical only if they are regarded as hypotheses. As conscious fictions they are valuable. We must therefore not only distinguish between fiction and hypothesis, but also protect the fiction against its detractors. The fiction, like the hypothesis, has many opponents, and we admit that many fictions have been bad ones. But the opposition is due mainly or in part to the fact that these fictions are interpreted as hypotheses, just as the objection to hypotheses is due to the fact that they at once take on a dogmatic form.
>
> Laas criticizes these fictions on the ground that they do violence to the facts and are dangerous. But this is characteristic of all fictions, and so is the fact that they cannot be given concrete form, which here reaches the point of contradiction. Laas very justly adds that they are fruitful in practice, when used for purposes of calculation. This well describes the essence of the fiction, but whether the fiction of a space with more than three dimensions is really valuable raises a different problem. The criterion of a good fiction is simply its fertility in practical use. The *fictional possibility* of spaces with more than three dimensions must never be confused with its *hypothetical possibility*.

Abstract generalization is a product of the far more liberal attitude taken towards things by man to-day. But it is based solely upon the fact that the special examples in question are merely products of the imaginative faculty, and it is only applicable where this is the case. All these special instances were instinctively developed in the pre-scientific period; and to-day scientific thought makes use of the same imaginative faculty that created the primary elements, and conceives other more generalized cases which can be thought of in abstract terms, such as a space with n-dimensions. It is while trying to discover why any given case, e.g. space of three dimensions, has been retained and selected, that we find the causes and motives that have guided thought in making such constructions. It is best adapted to objects, and, in short, it is the only survivor of various other possible spaces and, by selection, has proved to be the most suitable.

We are now at last in a position to appreciate fully the uses of generalization. This generalization breaks up the very constituents of existence and puts them together again in a far more general manner, in the process discovering the many possibilities which might still—have been possible. Then the laws of *compossibilitas* (in the sense of Leibniz) are studied and the particular is thus more profoundly understood.

We have already had an example of this abstract generalization in the idea of a world-spirit to whom all cosmic movements would be known.

This method of abstract generalization is one of the most brilliant devices of thought; it is applied in all fields, the existent and particular being taken generally and thought of as a special instance of many other possibilities. This device is not only the basis of scientific progress but of the whole practical progress of mankind. The great reformers of social life always think what exists as a special case among many possibilities.

In this manner chimerical constructs easily arise. On the other hand, the realization that imagination also plays a great part in science is one of the main advances of modern epistemology. In this respect Kant was quite correct and circumspect when he spoke of a "transcendental imaginative faculty." The realization of this fact has recently passed from philosophy to other sciences, although admittedly never on the same scale as here, where so many fundamental concepts have been shown to be fictional, i.e. products of the imaginative faculty, of the free creation of the psyche, though the psyche is, of course, always tied down by the actual sequence and co-existences of sense-data. If the creation of fictions is to be of value we must always be able to find our way back to actuality again.

CHAPTER XII THE METHOD OF UNJUSTIFIED TRANSFERENCE

MATHEMATICAL fictions, and the methods connected with them, are not exhausted by those so far described. One method in particular, that of *unjustified transference* as I would like to call it, of which some examples were given above (subsumption of the curve under the straight line, of the circle under the formula of the ellipse), is very common in mathematics and is applied with great success in the generalization of formulæ.

> Formally, we have a special case of this sub-division in every ideational construct in which a relationship extending to two members is ascribed to one of them (generally the first), as referring to itself, i.e. where one member is fictively doubled. Thus there is "duty to oneself", and *causa sui,* and similarly sin against oneself (to be one's own enemy, etc.). Duty is a relationship of A to B and so is *causa.* If then A is doubled (A = A) then the same relationship can be attributed to A itself alone.
>
> These fictions are not only necessary from a practical standpoint in a theory of duty, but also theoretically in metaphysics, and they contain within themselves an irrational element. It is, for example, irrational to be one's own cause, and it is irrational to have duties (or rights) towards (or on) oneself.
>
> The expression "duty to one's self" is formally exactly the same as, e.g., $\sqrt{1}$, since 1 is not a composite number. Similarly the statement that $1 = 1.1$, is a fiction, i.e. an unjustifiable extension. A product can only be a plural number; the proposition $1 = 1.1$ is therefore an unjustified retrospective extension. "Rights on oneself" are legal fictions just as "duties to oneself" are moral fictions.

The so-called *zero cases* are of importance here, as we saw in the case of the circle (in order to be able to bring it under the formula of an ellipse, the circle, as we know, is thought of as an ellipse whose two foci have the distance 0). In a similar manner this zero-method is utilized to bring the straight line under the category curve, the former being treated as a curved line with a curvature whose radius = 0. This method is related to that of abstract generalization and has its basis in the ascription of existence to zero, which is an entirely fictional construct.

The same method plays a part in the formation of *negative* numbers, *fractions,* and *irrational* and *imaginary* numbers. The very names of these constructs indicate their logical significance:—they are fictional constructs possessing great value for the advancement of science and the generalization of its results in spite of the crass contradictions which they contain. This will be shown in the more detailed discussion where particular attention will be paid to their history. At the same time they support the assertion made above that such irregular constructions and concepts are generally surrounded by a certain mystic halo. The history of mathematics is full of examples of the superstitious awe with which these number-constructs were regarded even as late as the eighteenth century. To-day they are universally recognized as fictional, though exceedingly valuable and fruitful. The basic principle here also is an illegitimate application and transference of a logical method to cases that cannot properly be subsumed under it, or the treatment of such constructs as numbers when they are not true numbers at all. Negative numbers are self-contradictory as all mathematicians admit; they are the extension of subtraction beyond the logical possibility of its application. Fractions are a product of the same method in division and so are the irrational numbers in taking roots. The most preposterous of these number-constructs are the imaginary numbers, and the constructions given to them by Gauss, Drobisch, and others have in no way altered their fictional and contradictory nature.

Indeed all mathematics, even arithmetic, rests on a purely imaginative basis, just as do measurement and similar mathematical methods. Mathematics, as a whole, constitutes the classical instance of an ingenious *instrument*, of a *mental expedient* for facilitating the operation of thought.

That all number-formation is imaginative is shown not only by the possibility of an infinitely large number of conceivable numerical systems but also by the fact of the infinity of the numbers themselves. The concept of infinity will occupy us at a later stage.

Another ingenious mathematical method is that of considering lines and surfaces as composed of line and surface elements of infinitely small extension. This method is applied in two ways; first, as we shall see, in order theoretically to justify the use of numbers in measurement at all—a necessity first recognized by the modern mathematicians—and then in order to benefit by a single type of measurement for all lines, more particularly so that curved lines can be measured and dealt with. Even the attempted subsumption of curves under straight lines, i.e. the concept of the length of a curve is, as Lotze rightly noted, a fiction.

Perhaps none of the questions falling within our domain has so general an interest or so great a scientific attraction as that with which we are here concerned. The historical treatment of the attempts made by the logical function to clear away the difficulties which it encountered is among the most instructive in the whole history of the sciences, and especially that of mathematics. The object was to bring the curve under the concept and the laws of straight lines, and it was brilliantly achieved in two consecutive stages; the Cartesian reform of analysis, and the infinitesimal calculus of Leibniz and Newton's fluxions. With regard to the first, the fundamental point was the reduction of curved lines in general to straight ones. This Descartes accomplished by means of an extremely ingenious method which, by its simplicity and originality, generally makes the same astounding impression upon the beginner in mathematics as is made upon the young philosopher when introduced for the first time to the fundamental ideas of Kant. In both cases we seem to be suddenly in the presence of a wonderfully bright and clear light.

This parallel is likely to be more appropriate and fruitful than the comparison made by Kant himself of his fundamental thought with that of Copernicus. The Cartesian idea rests upon the fiction of co-ordinates. By means of this fiction it is possible to bring curved lines under the laws of straight ones. The character of the fiction is shown by the fact that it requires the idea of infinity, always the surest indication that the logical function is treading dangerous and forbidden paths. The justification for equating the Cartesian idea with that of Kant is based upon the following reasons (which can only be briefly indicated here): just as Descartes measures curved lines by means of reduction and the use of coordinates in terms of abscissae and ordinates, so Kant reduces the "world" to a relationship between the two epistemological co-ordinates, subject and object. But curves cannot be completely reduced—the forbidden concept of infinity always being involved—and it is likewise impossible to reduce the world to a relation of subject and object without residuum. The "Ding an sich" remains a mystical incomprehensible entity. Thus there is to be found in Kant, too, an unjustified transference of a subject-object relationship from a sphere where it is valid to one where it no longer holds. Sense-impressions can, it is true, be reduced to a subject-object relationship, but the attempt to reduce the whole world to such a relationship leads to nonsense. And yet this idea has had a remarkably illuminating influence.

Our view, then, is as follows:—The reduction of a series of phenomena, e.g. colours, tones, tastes, etc. to a subject-object relationship is justifiable and illuminating and removes all the contradictions that arise for sensation. But the attempt to reduce matter and everything else to this relation leads finally to the assumption that everything we can conceive exists only within us, including causality. But what we conceive is caused by some "Ding an sich"; hence the contradiction in the "Ding an sich", (i.e. it is postulated as an absolute cause whereas the concept of causality is supposed to be purely subjective).

Reality can be more easily understood if reduced entirely to subjective relationships which are contrasted with an unknown *x*. To this *x* there corresponds as the other co-ordinate an unknown *y*. But just as in the final results of the mathematician the co-ordinates disappear—for they are merely artificial lines—so in the theory of knowledge do *x* and *y*, i.e. the subject-object relation, disappear. In other words:—

Ultimate reality is to be thought of as a single stream of sequence and co-existence. By drawing the artificial lines *x* and *y*, subject and object, we try to understand and deal with this stream. This fiction of an *x* (object) and *y* (subject), which are opposed to one another by Kant, disappears when they have fulfilled their function. This brings us simply to the standpoint of Hume, adopted in more recent times by Avenarius, that nothing exists except sensations which we analyse into two poles, subject and object. By means of this polar analysis we obtain in the domain of epistemology what in the theory of curves is obtained by means of co-ordinates, particularly polar coordinates. In other words the ego and the "Ding an sich" are fictions; what actually exists being what lies between them, the sensational mass, at one end of which we place the subject and at the other, the object. By this interpolation we are enabled to deal with reality. The separation into an inner and an outer is an expedient of the psyche.

But though reality is thus rendered more amenable to treatment contradictions arise. The Kantian reduction of the world to the subject-object relation is thus to be compared to the idea of Descartes. The fictional "as-if" plays a great part here (as it does in Kant). Descartes regards the curved line *as if* it had originated from the reciprocal movement of two straight lines; Kant regards the world *as if* it had originated from the relative movement of two things (subject and object).

The second stage in the method designed to bring the curve under the concept of the straight line was due to Leibniz and Newton. Especially interesting is the investigation of the remarkable preliminary attempts to solve the problem in the work of their predecessors, particularly that of the Englishman Wallis and the Italian Cavaleri. The real completion of the method occurred through the development of an ideational construct which appears as an aid and an intermediary, and which provides the standard example of a fiction, namely *differentials* or *fluxions*. These are purely fictional, contradictory constructs by means of which, however, it is possible to subsume the curve under the general concept and the laws of the straight line. This amazing method is the finest example of the partially unconscious purposive activity of the logical function which we have described in detail above. Neither Newton nor Leibniz was entirely clear in his own mind as to what he was doing logically when he invented these ideational constructs. Exactly how they really wished their concepts to be understood is a problem on which much has been written. Nowhere does the purposive function of the logical impulse reveal itself in a more brilliant and inventive manner than in this branch of mathematics. The whole of the controversy which followed and which has been in progress for two hundred years is concerned with the question whether the differentials or fluxions are hypotheses or fictions. All the acute criticisms of the method have concerned the impossibility of such constructs possessing an objective existence and the contradictions involved by this method. That this is no objection must surely now be obvious in view of the examples already adduced of constructs which, in spite of their unreality, are still of great service to thought. That contradictions are thereby engendered is also no objection as soon as we accustom ourselves to our new principle and reject the old prejudice that thought progresses and achieves its results only by non-contradictory operations. We have tried in the above to put our new view, which was foreshadowed by both Hegel and Lotze, on a firm basis.

We are very far, even to-day, from having resolved the contradictions involved in the infinitesimal method. For two hundred years mathematicians, together with the philosophers, endeavoured to show that there were no such contradictions. We reverse the position, and insist from the opposite point of view that these contradictions are not only undeniable but *are the very means by which advances have been made.*

Among the opponents of infinitesimals, a fact forgotten by mathematicians and philosophers alike, Berkeley stands pre-eminent. He revealed the contradictions involved in the method with a wonderful clarity and elegance, and it is remarkable that he also showed that thought attains its ends in spite of these contradictions. But he never made any use of his discovery, and on the contrary even rejected the method as contradictory. It was only in the nineteenth century that this discovery was made once more, in France by Carnot, in Germany by Drobisch, though it did not attract the attention which it deserved. Both, however, failed to extend it to the general method of thought on the lines of the present work. The discovery in question is that thought proceeds to correct the error which it makes. This simple statement contains the whole principle of fictions, and we shall subsequently return to it again.

CHAPTER XIII THE CONCEPT OF INFINITY (WITH SOME GENERAL REMARKS ON CRITICAL POSITIVISM)

CLOSELY related to the phenomena discussed in the previous section is a type of ideational construct which has not only been the crux of all mathematics up to the present day, but has also caused philosophers not a little trouble. By bringing it under our general principle, this concept, the concept of infinity, can perhaps be both clarified and explained.

> That the infinite itself is a fiction, whether as infinitesimal or as the infinitely great, is demonstrated especially by the startling contradictions that follow from it, as well as from the illusory problems which it engenders (cf. the Eleatic sophisms, which arise from the fact that the infinitely small is treated as an hypothesis instead of as a fiction).

The idea of infinity proves to be an auxiliary introduced by thought to facilitate its operations; and just because of its immanent contradiction, it makes successful thinking possible. This is the case, for instance, in mathematics, where the symbol ∞, used for "infinity," is simply a fiction by whose means mathematical thinking more readily attains its purpose. The gradual elaboration of this concept constitutes one of the most fascinating and instructive themes in the history of science. (The Greeks with a strange but easily explicable fear, avoided all fictions, including this one, and tried to get along without having recourse to these fictional constructs.) Indeed the gradual historical development of all these fictional concepts provides one of the most remarkable spectacles in the history of the human mind. We get here a good notion of the way in which the logical function at first gropes clumsily in the dark, how it gradually moves forward tentatively, and forms the structures which subsequently render such incalculable service.

Hence, too, instructive light is shed upon the philosophical idea of the infinite. It, too, is an auxiliary idea of which an injurious misuse has frequently been made but which has, nevertheless, rendered certain services to thought.

This important construct owes its origin entirely to the imaginative faculty and possesses no objective value whatever. The very contradictions which it contains show that it is purely fictional, and that its application to the real world is a misuse The strongest proof of the subjectivity of space and time lies in their being infinite, and the ordinary concepts of space and time are thus unmasked as fictional, as mere auxiliary ideas, helpful pictures, developed by the logical function to bring order into reality and to understand it. It is precisely the subjective operations which admit of the abuses to which these concepts have been subjected; only a subjective operation can be constantly thought of as if it were without end and were yet complete. All these products are therefore pure forms of thought, purely subjective operations. It would indeed be strange if these concepts or ideas were actually pictures of objective reality. We have only to make clear to ourselves what this term, *picture* or *copy*, is supposed to mean; and to ask how the logical functions could be copies of events or processes. No! All these concepts are not pictures of events, but are themselves events, a part of the cosmic process. They occur of necessity at a certain stage of organic development; the cosmic process is continued in these ideas. They are indeed psychical products, psychical processes, and psychical events are certainly a part of the cosmic process. The world as we conceive it is only a secondary or tertiary construction, arising in our heads through the play of the cosmic process and solely for the furtherance of this process. This conceptual world is not a *picture* of the actual world but an *instrument* for grasping and subjectively understanding that world.

It is only an auxiliary construct gradually formed by the logical function in order to take its bearings. This construction can be substituted for the actual world, and in practice we all do that; but it is not a picture of true reality, it is only a sign used in order to deal with reality, a logical expedient devised to enable us to move about and act in the real world. In practice we can substitute the conceptual world for the real one, but theoretically the two must be distinguished. The conceptual world is only a secondary product of the real world itself, a construction, which the organic beings of this world develop from within themselves.

The treatment of ideational forms and of the whole conceptual world as mere products of the imaginative faculty was originally accomplished by Hume and Kant, and continued by Schopenhauer and Herbart. But to treat them as fictions in our sense is to include the idea that these constructs are, from a logical point of view, identical with scientific fictions, i.e. with constructs that, from a practical point of view, are useful and necessary, though theoretically they are false. This point is not stressed by Kant and Hume. For them the conceptual world is only a creation of the imagination. But what is characteristic of our account is our insistence on the fact that it is an exceedingly useful construct and must logically be regarded as a fiction. This shows how necessary a theory of fictions is, for in order to look at the conceptual world as a fiction, we must first methodologically establish what a fiction is, what it can accomplish, and how it is constituted.

The view here briefly outlined we call Critical Positivism.

CHAPTER XIV MATTER AND THE SENSORY WORLD OF IDEAS

MATTER is a fiction of this type. It contains contradictory elements, but it is as serviceable as the fiction of force. That matter is really such a fiction is to-day generally agreed. The contradictions inherent in it were conclusively shown by Berkeley in particular, and therein he revealed a remarkably profound insight into the nature of the logical function. The numerous controversies which have developed round this concept always bear upon a point which we have already encountered on several occasions—whether matter is an hypothesis or a fiction. The concept of matter can be elaborated as much as we like; but we can never get rid of the contradictions which have so often been discovered in it. The unknown element at the basis of matter is not thereby denied. What is denied is its identity with the conceptual structure that we call matter.

How closely matter is connected with the concept of substance is obvious, for it is supposed to be substantial, the bearer of forces. That such an idea can only be fictional has gradually become an almost universal assumption since the eighteenth century, and is due especially to Hume. In Germany, Platner in the second edition of his *Aphorisms* (which were influenced by Kant and Hume) expresses himself as follows (Vol. I, p. 415): "Substance is force itself, and a substantial subject containing attributes and force is but an illusory idea of the imagination; for that would lead to the infinite." Modern physics approximates to this view in reducing all phenomena to functions of energy.

This conceptual construct, matter, is made up of quite contradictory elements, but it is very useful for scientific thought, as a fiction. It is therefore quite wrong to follow Berkeley and reject these concepts as useless as soon as their objective impossibility has been recognized. This shows the very prejudice which still dominates philosophy to-day, namely, that because a concept is logically contradictory, it is for that reason of no value. For precisely the contrary is true, and these contradictory concepts are the most valuable. Many of the fundamental ideas with which science operates are fictions, and the problem is not how to do away with these contradictions— that would be a futile undertaking—but to show that they are of utility and advantage to thought. It is wrong to imagine that only what is logically non-contradictory is logically fruitful. Such an attitude—since so many of the fundamental concepts of science are contradictory—if consistently adhered to would bring us to the conclusion of Agrippa of Nettesheim, that all science is valueless. Our position must be sharply distinguished from this. It is, of course, true that many fundamental scientific concepts are fictional and contradictory and are not a reflection of the world of reality—a world quite inaccessible to us—but this in no way renders them valueless. They are psychical constructs which not only give rise to the illusion that the world is being comprehended, but which make it possible, at the same time, for us to orientate ourselves in the realm of actuality.

It is because our conceptual world is itself a product of the real world that it cannot be a reflection of reality. On the other hand, it can serve as an instrument within reality, by means of which the higher organisms move about. It is a symbol by means of which we orientate ourselves; and it is in the interests of science to make this symbol more and more adequate and utilizable, but a symbol it always will remain. There is no reply to the argument that because the conceptual world is a product of the real world, it cannot be identical with it. There is no identity of thought and reality, for the "world" is merely an instrument of thought and, for that reason, the world of ideas is not the ultimate goal of thought. The actual purpose of thought is not thought itself and its products, but behaviour, and ultimately *ethical behaviour*. The means thereto is the objective world in the form of a world of ideas. With Fichte, we can therefore say that the world is the material of ethical behaviour. Fichte erred only in allowing this material to be produced by the ego itself; its form alone is a product of the psyche. The world of ideas is essentially an expedient of thought, an instrument, for rendering action possible in the world of reality.

> We *deny*, then, that the world as conceived by us has value as knowledge; and we deny, too, that differentials, etc. have any such value. On the other hand, we *insist* that they have practical value, and we regard them as serviceable products of the logical function, as a useful device. Whenever such artificial constructs are consistently used, contradictions arise—the surest sign of a fiction.[12]

The true and final purpose of thought is action and the facilitation of action. Looked at from this point of view the world of ideas is, taken as a whole, simply a means and its constituent elements are also merely a means. What we have here is a system of expedients of thought which mutually help and support one another and whose final product is a scientifically purified conceptual world. It is just an extremely sensitive machine constructed by the logical instinct, and related to a pre-scientifically developed world of ideas as a modern iron hammer to the prehistoric stone hammer of tertiary times, or steam-engine and railway to the crude wagon of the countryside. Both are only instruments, and though very different as regards delicacy and elegance are yet identical in kind. They are instruments, products of the logical instinct, of the logical activity. The entire conceptual world lies between these two poles of sensation and motion. The psyche continually adds new members between these two points, and the delicacy and elaboration of its interpolations, pictures and auxiliary concepts, develop with the growth of the nerve-mass and the increasing isolation of the brain from the spine. Our conceptual world lies between the sensory and motor nerves, an infinite intermediate world, and serves merely to make the interconnection between them richer and easier, more delicate and more serviceable. Science is concerned with the elaboration of this conceptual world, and with the adjustment of this instrument to the objective relations of sequence and coexistence which make themselves perceptible. But when science goes further and makes of this instrument an end in itself, when it is no longer concerned merely with the perfecting of the instrument, it is to be regarded strictly as a luxury and a passion. But all that is noble in man has had a similar origin.

When we say that our conceptual world lies between the sensory and motor nerves we are making use of fictional language for, in actual fact, we only have sensations. Our ideas both of movement and nerves, that is to say, of matter, are constructs of our productive phantasy, of fiction. The whole conceptual world is, in other words, inserted between *sensations*; these alone are ultimately given. Only certain sequences of sensation are given to us. The conceptual world is thus a structure made up of elementary sensations and their residue, and serves the purpose of creating easier lines of communication between the various sensory centres. The conceptual world has its origin in all those processes by means of which the elementary sensations are changed, and in accordance with elementary laws. By reason of the condensation, interconnection, etc. of sensations, which takes place within the brain, *i.e.* within that part of reality which we regard as the brain, a more advanced and more developed structure is created for the enrichment and perfection of human activity. In principle, it is irrelevant whether we regard the fictive activity as contemporaneous in origin with the construction of the concept of space, or later: what is fundamental is the recognition that all the more advanced conceptual constructs are merely means for facilitating the intercourse of sentient "beings." The theory of fictions teaches us, however, that the utility of such fictions constitutes no proof of their objective truth; the duty of a logical theory of fictions being to discover the mechanism by means of which these constructions perform their service.

We must therefore regard it as a pardonable weakness on the part of science if it believes that its ideas are concerned with reality itself. It is dealing with reality only to the extent of establishing the inevitable sequences and co-existences. But the concepts which encompass and embrace reality are of a fictional nature, the additions of man, and form merely the frame in which man encloses the treasure of reality in order that he may thus manipulate it better. Science has thus two tasks: (1) to determine the actual sequences and co-existences; (2) to give the ideas with which we invest reality a more concise, more adequate, more useful and more harmless form. This weaving of ideas, on the lines favoured by Aristotle and the Scholastics, is extremely harmful, because it hides the real and turns attention away from reality to the glittering but hollow framework of ideas. Without their aid we could admittedly not deal with the world, nor would we be able to act; they are, in fact, a necessary evil. There have been great thinkers who have regarded concepts and all discursive thought as a necessary evil without whose help reality could not be grasped. The freeing of reality from all concepts, all discursive modes of approach, leads to the attitude of the Greek sophists and sceptics, who believed in suspending all judgment. These philosophers undoubtedly went too far in questioning the material validity of general judgments; for the establishment of an unchangeable sequence and co-existence (or at any rate one that has never changed within our field of observation) is certain knowledge. It is only the formal expression in the judgment that is erroneous and fictional, for in the judgment we always have the separation into subject and predicate, substantive and verb, i.e. into thing and attribute, cause and effect. It is therefore impossible for us to express the sequences which we observe without the intervention of discursive thought. But to regard this as an expression of reality is an antiquated attitude.

> We must, therefore, accept as actually real only certain sequences of sensation, from which there arise, in accordance with definite laws, structures that are treated as fictions. These develop from sensations in certain sensation-centres and help towards a richer interconnection.

It is, however, not possible without the aid of discursive thought to make ourselves intelligible to others or even to think or calculate. Without this discursive aid we should be disarmed, and there would be nothing left for us to do but to remain silent and stare vacantly into space, after the manner of certain sceptics. We make use of the means which present themselves for dealing with reality, but these additions and supplements are afterwards laid aside, just as in mathematics we drop an imaginary quantity that has been introduced.

A clear-cut distinction is, however, only possible if we definitely decide to regard the discursive aids as subjective instruments.

We are thus gradually led on, and have gradually removed, from above, the scaffolding that man has erected around reality. In order to do this, we have always had to rest on the successive rungs and steps of the scaffolding; but again and again we have broken these off, until we have come at last to the basic pillars of the framework itself—to space and matter. This successive breaking-off of the scaffolding of thought is typical of the structure itself and of the gradual manner in which it has been erected in the course of time during the historical evolution of mankind.

The logical function, when it has reached its goal, abdicates of its own free will; the scaffolding is cast away when its purpose has been achieved.

The importance of the logical function does not prevent it from recognizing its own nothingness. Man's most fallacious conclusion has always been that because a thing is *important* it is also *right*.

> This is the same fallacious conclusion to which we have repeatedly called attention. We may not argue from the utility of a psychical and logical construct that it is right; differentials are useful constructs, and yet no one would claim that they exist. As soon as the mechanism by means of which these concepts perform such efficacious service is disclosed, the illusion of their truth disappears, for this only persists as long as the mechanism is concealed.

The logical function is already at work in the production of the elementary basic principles. Psychology shows how the constructs of space, matter, etc. arise out of elementary sensations. The work of discursive thought begins at this point, and it is for this reason that these products of the psyche must also be regarded as fictions created by the logical impulse in order to attain its goal. Thus the logical impulse builds up its products only to destroy them in the end of its own accord. This need not, however, lead to pessimism, for the metal-caster also destroys his mould as soon as the object has been cast. The logical function similarly destroys its fragile framework as soon as it has attained its goal—the establishment of unchangeable relations and connections.

This attitude alone can free us from the pressure of the logical contradiction so constantly concealed in the basic principles and processes of science. It is not these which really matter, for they are but a means. Discursive thought creates more and more delicate means of encompassing and dealing with reality, and it is a logical error to confuse the means, the instrument, with what the instrument was created to deal with.

> When the logical mechanism is revealed, its claim to so-called objectivity disappears; for the question, why it happens that we are able to deal with reality by means of fictional constructs, has then been answered. In the last analysis, this must rest upon a few fundamental mechanical processes of psychical life. If when once this mechanism has been disclosed it is still claimed that these constructs are real, we can only recall the well-known story of the peasant, who after having had a steam-engine explained to him asked if he might see the horse which drew the locomotive.

The mechanism of a locomotive can certainly not be understood without a knowledge of the purpose it fulfils. In the same way the mechanism of thought is not intelligible without a knowledge of the purpose it serves. This purpose can only be that of facilitating conceptual activity, of effecting a safe and rapid connection of sensations. What we have to show, therefore, is how fictional methods and constructs render this possible; for that is exactly the nature of the mechanism of thought, and in the end its goal can only be that of facilitating the interrelation of sensations, i.e. of rendering action easy. We must show, then, how action is made easy thereby, and remember in this connection that the whole mechanism of thought is an articulated system of expedients which mutually support one another, so that fictions serving primarily to perfect the instrument itself become in due course an accessory of this very instrument.

CHAPTER XV THE ATOM AS A FICTION

Our task of revealing the ultimate bases of the framework of thought has not yet been fully accomplished, for there are still some fictional ideas and expedients to be examined, and in particular the atom. This is a modification of the general concept of matter to which it bears the same relation as does the fiction of the differential to the fiction of the length of a curve; matter being conceived as made up of infinitely small constituents. A lively controversy has arisen in connection with the atom, the point at issue being whether it is an hypothesis or fiction. This is our own description of the problem, for the disputants themselves are, for the most part, not clear what it is all about. The opponents of the atom are generally content to point to its contradictions and reject it as unfruitful for science. A rash form of caution, for without the atom science falls. And yet, with it, true knowledge and understanding are impossible. It is a group of contradictory concepts which are necessary in order to deal with reality. Of late it has been recognized that the atom is a fiction, a fictional counter, as has been clearly shown, among others, by Liebmann.

O. Liebmann, *Zur Analysis der Wirklichkeit*, pp. 290 ff. particularly p. 295. "The atom is a transitional idea whose provisional character is obvious. Its imaginary conceptual existence is due to a conceptual equilibrium of a peculiarly unstable character." Cf. also what he says, page 296: "It is true that the atom is a mere theoretical counter, a provisional fiction, an interim-concept, but for the present it is an exceedingly useful interim-concept." Whether the concept can be dispensed with entirely is an open question. To judge from the present state of the problem, apparently it cannot; and to-day, at any rate, the atom is used by both the chemist and the physicist for the co-ordination of their laws, which they cannot yet formulate in a purely abstract manner.

The fiction of a simple element, of the atom, is still retained, in spite of the fact that the "material" has long since "evaporated into energy" (as von Hartmann puts it). Cf. Cooke, *Die Chemie der Gegenwart,* 1875. This book is based entirely on the atomic theory, and yet the author is not a believer in the atom. Cf. for the chemical concept of the atom, Lothar Meyer, *Die Moderne Chemie,* p. 15.

For the opinion of scientists themselves about the atom, cf. Lange, *History of Materialism,* and the same author's *Beiträge,* 51, where he says that atoms are a means to an empirical treatment of nature and to orientation.

All this only becomes valuable in relation to our general principle, which has deprived many another concept of its dignity as an hypothesis and shown it to be fictional and subjective. The dispute about the atom will also provide an instructive and exceedingly interesting theme for subsequent treatment, for it involves the whole of the modern philosophy of nature.[13] For the most part, the participants adopted a wrong method of attack. The defence was always anxious to show that the alleged contradictions were only apparent and that the concept therefore possessed objective validity and could be applied. Their opponents, on the other hand, demonstrated the contradictions and so refused to allow the concept any legitimate place in science; in other words, they poured out the baby with the bath, while the defence accepted it—unwashed. The final result was always that the idea persisted in spite of all criticism, but its contradictions invariably called forth fresh contradictions.

The recognition that there is right and wrong on both sides generally comes at the end of a discussion—the concept in question is contradictory, but necessary: for most of the fundamental concepts are of this character. It is remarkable that in the course of time the realization that these contradictions exist becomes blunted through the use of the concepts. We need only note the extent to which mathematicians and physicists have accustomed themselves to differentials and atoms and no longer notice the contradictions inherent in them. Yet though the contradictions in ideas to which we have grown accustomed are no longer noticed, they are at once recognized in new constructs. The introduction of the infinite, of differentials, gave rise at one time to the same opposition as that which the introduction of an n-dimensional space encounters to-day at the hands of competent thinkers. The irrational and imaginary numbers had the same fate in mathematics.

CHAPTER XVI FICTIONS IN MECHANICS AND MATHEMATICAL PHYSICS

JUST as mathematics owes its remarkable advance in modern times exclusively to the introduction of appropriate fictions and the ingenious methods based upon them, so, apart from observation, mechanics and mathematical physics owe their progress in the last few centuries mainly to the introduction of fictions. Such fictional concepts as the rigid line, the Alpha body (as the immovable central point of absolute space), the centre of gravity, *actio in distans*, forces, etc., are at the very basis of modern mechanics.

> Cf. the famous address of C. Neumann, *Über die Prinzipien der Galilei-Newtonschen Theorie* (Leipzig, 1870), p. 20, on the Alpha body, defined by him as an unknown rigid body to which all changes of position are related.

Duhamel has done more than anyone else for the theoretical presentation of these fundamental physical principles in his methodological works, though he treats this aspect of theoretical mechanics rather inadequately. If logicians would only take the trouble to study the methods of physics and learn how logical operations are actually carried out, they would see in what an arbitrary manner fictive ideational constructs are formed in this field. Theoretical mechanics is for the most part a tissue of such purely arbitrary ideas, and these are used by physicists for practical purposes, as auxiliary ideas, points of departure, theoretical preliminaries — in short, as fictions. Modern logic is not sufficiently familiar with mathematics and its surprising methods. It must learn more of the methods of mathematics and mechanics, so that it can observe exactly how the logical function proceeds in order to deal with reality, for artifices abound in these sciences. All mathematics, indeed, is only a device, which tells us nothing about what actually exists.

It is not an end in itself, but its main purpose is to be a method and an aid. Mathematics itself is really the most ingenious method for determining reality and assists in the development of that scale of measurement to which we refer the whole world—space, and motion in space. That the idea of motion is itself a fiction was already evident from the contradictions discovered by the Eleatics; and these contradictions are still so far from a solution that they confront us with the same abruptness as in ancient times. Motion is only an ideational construct, an idea, by means of which we attempt to bring objective changes (which in the last analysis are only given as sensory modifications) into an ordered system. That this system of motion in space together with all its subsidiary concepts is only a fictional conceptual construct follows both from the contradictions in the concept of motion itself and from those in the concept of space, upon which it is based. We are dealing here with a closely woven net, a fine tissue of subjective and fictional concepts in which we envelop reality. We achieve a passable success; but that does not mean that the content must necessarily take the form of the net woven round it.

The ideas of an absolute and an infinite space are also based upon fictions, like that of absolute motion—indeed this whole procedure of creating absolutes is a form of fiction which is connected with that of ascribing infinity to an element.

CHAPTER XVII THINGS-IN-THEMSELVES

BEFORE turning to the idea of the absolute we must discuss one other idea, the Ding an sich. From all that has preceded it is fairly clear what our attitude must be—that the "Thing-in-itself" is not an hypothesis but a fiction. By the use of this formula we have solved many of the difficulties hitherto encountered. Kant is the originator of this concept, which is a product of the logical function as an imaginative activity. The first point which arises from this is the historical understanding of Kant himself. All the ambiguity that Kant developed in connection with this concept was due essentially to his hesitation, his wavering between the Ding an sich as an hypothesis or a fiction. Thus in the first edition of his Critique of Pure Reason, Kant in one place calls it "a mere idea," i.e. a fiction. In constructing this concept Kant was throughout hardly clearer than Leibniz with his differentials. The term limiting concept also receives an important elucidation from the above; for as a fiction the notion of a Thing-in-itself represents a limiting concept in the same sense in which we speak of the method of limits in mathematics, the limit being elevated by a fiction into something real and treated as such. Thus the whole controversy about the *Ding an sich* in the early days of Kantian philosophy, as conducted by Reinhold, Schulze, Maimon, Jacobi, Fichte, and others, and renewed recently during its second efflorescence, at once becomes clearer. It is simply a question whether the concept is a fiction or an hypothesis. It was Maimon who realized this most clearly. Schulze saw the contradictions in the idea and rejected it; Maimon saw the contradictions and retained it as a fiction. We must certainly follow his example. To Maimon also is due the brilliant comparison of the Things- in-themselves with imaginary numbers, i.e. with $\sqrt{-a}$. $\sqrt{-a}$ is the symbol of a mathematical fiction, the unjustified extension and transference of a mathematical operation to a case where the nature of the material forbids its application and renders it meaningless. Nevertheless, mathematics often requires this idea, and proceeds with it *as if* it symbolized a reality, a number that could be expressed; but, be it remembered, this fiction always drops out as valueless at the end of the procedure.

This is what also occurs in the case of the *Ding an sich*.

It arises from the unjustified application of a logical operation. The illegitimate extension of the mathematical operation in the formula $\sqrt{-a}$ is the extracting of a root, and here the parallel logical operation consists in the application of the categories, *thing* and *attribute* (and causality) to what makes their application meaningless, namely to actual and ultimate *reality*. If it be admitted that all categories are merely subjective, then this category, too, cannot be applied to actual reality. But, as we know, there is another category involved here, the category of *causality*. This, too, is unjustifiably applied to a something where its application is not legitimate, namely, to actual reality. If, with Kant, we agree that this category is subjective, then it is a contradiction to ascribe it to actual reality. Such an application belongs to the group of illegitimate transferences or extensions where a quite different case is brought under some unsuitable construct. The analogy of this illegitimate extension of mathematical operations is particularly illuminating here, for in this case also the extension is to an unsuitable field, to actual reality. Only within the limits of discursive thought do these categories possess a meaning and a justification, for here they serve to introduce logical operations. Only within the world of our ideas are there things, things that are causes; in the real world these ideas are but empty echoes.

The idea of causality is entirely inapplicable to reality itself. Actual reality will not tolerate this category. If sensations are, in fact, essential reality, then their reduction, together with space, matter, etc., to the impact of some unknown object, is an unjustified extension of the concept of cause and effect.

But everything that is reduced to this category seems to be grasped, and the Thing-in-itself allows the category of causality to be applied to actual reality. This, on our view, is the world of sensation. When, therefore, Kant reduces sensations, together with space, time, etc., to the system of co-ordinates of cause and effect, object and subject, the whole world appears to be understood as an effect.

The fiction of the *Ding an sich* would thus be the most brilliant of all conceptual instruments. Just as we introduce into mathematics and me-chanics ideas which facilitate our task, so Kant introduces a device in the form of the concept *Ding an sich,* as an *x* to which a *y,* the ego, as our organ-ization, corresponds. By this means the whole world of reality can be dealt with. Subsequently the "ego" and the *Ding an sich* are dropped, and only sensations remain as real.

From our point of view the sequence of sensations constitutes ultimate reality, and two poles are mentally added, subject and object.

In spite, then, of its numerous contradictions the idea of the Thing-in-itself cannot be dispensed with in philosophy, any more than can imaginary numbers in mathematics. If we wish to speak of the real world at all, we must use some category, for otherwise it is not only unthinkable but even inexpressible.

The result of our whole inquiry is that the subjective and fictive method culminates in the *Ding an sich.* In order to explain the world of ideas which exists within us, Kant assumed that the actual world consisted of Things-in-themselves, mutually interacting, and on the basis of this interaction he explained the genesis of sensations. We must, however, remember that Kant only had the right to say, and in the first instance only wanted to say, that we must (compelled thereto by reason of our discursive thought) regard real existence as if Things-in-themselves really existed, as if they influenced us and thus gave rise to our idea of the world. In actual fact this is all he had the right to say according to his own system; and in that case the *Ding an sich* was a necessary fiction, for only thus can we imagine actual reality or think and speak of it at all. Kant, however, did not adhere to this definite stand-point, but his *Ding an sich* became a *reality*, in short an *hypothesis*, and hence his hesitating discussion of the concept.

CHAPTER XVIII THE ABSOLUTE

We now reach the last and greatest fiction, a modification of the *Ding an sich* when it is expanded into *the Absolute, or absolute substance, absolute cosmic-energy,* etc. In so far as thing, substance, cause, energy, are themselves only conceptual constructs full of contradictions, they have already been discussed and dealt with; but the addition of *absolute* makes the fiction more pronounced. The contradictions in the idea of the Absolute are so conspicuous that they have already been often described. The English metaphysician, Mansel, in par-ticular, did much to reveal these contradictions.

The Absolute is a metaphysical aspect of the mathematical concept of in-finity. Both these constructs have the same value. In so far as the Absolute is supposed to be a thing beside or above the world, it partakes of all the contradictions involved in the "thing". To conceive it as energy leads to further contradiction. Whether this fiction is a valuable construct is still an open question, but of its tremendous practical utility there can be no doubt. We only know what is relative, changeless relations and laws of phenom-ena; all else is subjective addition. The division of the world into Things-in-themselves = *Objects* and Things-in-themselves = *Subjects* is the primary fiction upon which all others depend. From the standpoint of Critical Posi-tivism, then, there is no Absolute, no Thing-in-itself, no Subject, no Object. All that remains is sensations, which exist, and are given, and out of which the whole subjective world is constructed with its division into physical and psychical complexes. Critical Positivism asserts that any other, any further claim is fictional, subjective and unsubstantiated. For it, only the observed sequence and co-existence of phenomena exist, and upon these alone it takes its stand. Any explanation going beyond this can only do so by using the accessories of discursive thought, i.e. through fictions. The only fiction-less doctrine in the world is that of Critical Positivism. Any more detailed or elaborate claim about existence, as such, is fictional. Moreover, any system built upon it is valueless, for it can move only within the circle of aids, aux-iliary concepts and instruments of discursive thought.[14]

B

THE LOGICAL THEORY OF SCIENTIFIC FICTIONS

CHAPTER XIX INTRODUCTORY REMARKS ON THE POSITION OF FICTIONS AND SEMI-FICTIONS IN THE LOGICAL SYSTEM AS A WHOLE

WE have now completed our description of semi-fictions and real fictions and have found confirmation for our view that there is a continuous and gradual transition from the one to the other, though, logically, they must be kept rigidly distinct. The semi-fiction first encountered was that of artificial classification and the method of abstraction and we then concluded with a discussion of real fictions — the Atom, the Infinite, and the Thing-in-itself. The transition between the two is represented by the practical fictions (IX), and at this point the pure fictions begin. The semi-fictions confirmed the general principle stated above, namely that they are methods and concepts based upon a simple deviation from reality. Here, however, the deviation is of a *material* nature, whereas that of fictions in the narrower sense is of a *formal* character as well; for in their case not only are concepts constructed which are at variance with the content of reality, but the newly-constructed concepts contradict the formal principle of reality, the law of identity and contradiction, i.e. they are self-contradictory.

When we examine the enormous scope of these methods we may very well ask why they have hitherto not been treated in logic. We generally find in logic that these phenomena are either subsumed under similar but not identical cases, or they are simply ignored. Fictional assumptions have usually been discussed as *hypotheses* and yet, as has been clearly shown above, these are fundamentally distinct despite their apparent similarity. In so far as the above fictions appear in the form of interpolated *concepts*, and as assumptions externally resembling hypotheses, they have been treated as hypotheses. But in so far as they are *methods*, they have been grouped—if considered at all—with some inductive or deductive method. In actual fact they were generally passed over. This silence was as much due to a fear of the difficulties which appeared to be involved as to ignorance of the methodological details of science.

It should, therefore, cause no surprise, after what we have said above if, taking fiction in its broadest sense of *fictive activity*, we place it on an equal footing with deduction and induction as a third member in the system of logical science. To us it does not seem correct simply to include the methods we have been discussing under *induction*; for in the first place they do not belong merely to the inductive sciences, and secondly, their whole nature and procedure are quite at variance[15] with the rules of induction.

We regard it as essential, therefore, to treat fiction, at the very least, as an independent appendix to the older logic of induction, although we believe that it may claim to occupy an independent division of its own.

Induction shows the direct route by which our goal is to be approached and obstacles overcome, whereas fiction points out the indirect ways, the by-paths. Induction is thus a methodology of the descriptive sciences; fiction, a method of the exact mathematical and the ethico-political sciences, and with hardly any application at all in the domain of the descriptive or historical sciences. In the case of the latter we are not concerned with the theoretical understanding as in the mathematical, but with a determination of causal connections, which is only possible through careful observation and objective description. Indeed one of the main tasks of logic and methodology is to reveal the differences in the methods of the various sciences and to explain them.[16]

Deduction is certainly intimately connected with fiction, though not more closely than is induction; and, especially in certain cases, it is as closely related to the axiom as to the hypothesis, although fundamentally distinct from both. The axiom and the hypothesis, for instance, endeavour to be expressions of reality. The fiction, on the other hand, is not such an expression nor does it claim to be one.

This is connected with a point already mentioned and on which we must here lay particular stress; namely, that the true fiction, formulated in a strictly scientific manner, is always accompanied by the *consciousness* that the fictional idea, the fictional assumption, has no real validity. The fictions most important historically, e.g. the Linnæan system, Adam

Smith's theory and, in part, the atomic theory and the differential calculus, demonstrate this fact.

It may be added that the consciousness with which scientific fictions are framed also extends to the realization that they are either merely provisional concepts destined to be replaced later or corrected, or are simply there to facilitate logical communication. The first alternative is more usual in semi-fictions, the second in real fictions: the former are historically provisional, the latter, logically provisional fictions. The former *disappear* in the course of time, the latter are *omitted* in the course of the operation.

If we mean by a *mistake* a deviation from reality, and by an *error* a contradictory concept, then we can call the semi-fictions "conscious mistakes" and the real fictions, "conscious errors" or "conscious contradictions," the one group tending to serve purely practical purposes, the other theoretical. The former are used more for logical "operations," the latter for "understanding"; and while the semi-fiction leads us back to methodological motives, the real fiction leads to those connected with the theory of knowledge. The first is more in the nature of an indirect method, the other more in the nature of an incorrect concept: the one is essentially ingenious, and substitutes something conceived for what is actually given; the other is essentially artificial and blends the given with the unthinkable. Semi-fictions assume the unreal, real fictions the impossible. The former avoid difficulties by deviating from reality, the latter, on the other hand, create new difficulties and are much more free with the given; for while the semi-fiction only falsifies reality with the object of discovering truth, the fiction proper makes reality incomprehensible—in order that it may be comprehended. Semi-fictions are only by-ways and cover the same ground, while fictions proper leave the earth and reality altogether and move about in the air. The former behave contrary to, the latter in contradiction with, the facts; the former substitute something different for reality, the latter interpolate impossible elements. Semi-fictions are generally simpler than reality appears to be, real fictions more complicated. Mistakes due to the former must be corrected if there is to be a real advance, while, in the other case, errors can only be avoided if the concepts are afterwards dropped. Mistakes due to semi-fictions are in conflict with the objective state of affairs, while with real fictions we get essentially formal mistakes in thought, logical mistakes. The former proceed along byways and short-cuts, the latter along forbidden paths. And finally, whereas semi-fictions modify what is given, real fictions infect it, to a certain extent, with elements which do not belong to it but yet serve to render it comprehensible.

CHAPTER XX THE SEPARATION OF SCIENTIFIC FROM OTHER FICTIONS, PARTICULARLY FROM THE ÆSTHETIC

HAVING introduced a certain order into the differences between the various fictions themselves, we must now indicate the boundaries which separate scientific fiction from what is also often designated by the same term.

Fictio means, in the first place, an *activity of fingere*, that is to say, of constructing, forming, giving shape, elaborating, presenting, artistically fashioning: conceiving, thinking, imagining, assuming, planning, devising, inventing. Secondly, it refers to the *product* of these activities, the fictional assumption, fabrication, creation, the imagined case. Its most conspicuous character is that of unhampered and free expression.[17]

Mythology, in so far as it may be regarded as the common mother of religion, poetry, art and science, shows us the first expression in free constructive activity of the inventive faculty, of imagination and of fantasy. It is here that we first find products of fantasy which do not correspond to reality. On the other hand, the psychological genesis of fictions is the same in all fields of inquiry. Steinthal has sufficiently emphasized this fact. As a rule, we speak not only of all gods as fictions, but more particularly of all constructs which are freely fashioned out of empirical elements. The favourite examples are, Pegasus, the sphinx, the centaur, the griffin. Here we have the free creative play of psychical activity, expressing itself in arbitrary combinations and alternations of elements existing in the world of fact. However interesting these and other fictions, such as angels, devils, pixies, spirits, etc. may be for the logical theory of existential propositions, they are of minor importance for our present theme. At most they concern us only in so far as such a judgment as, "matter consists of atoms" or, "the curved line consists of infinitesimals" is to be understood only as a fictive judgment in which no existence is predicated. Otherwise (i.e. if the judgment be not taken to mean that matter is to be regarded *as if* it consisted of atoms), then a correct fiction is changed into an incorrect judgment, in other words, into an error. The primary meaning of fiction = mythological entity, is thus distinguished from the scientific fiction, and this covers all the specifically religious fictions. On the other hand, we saw above that definite theological fictions could be of value for the scientific study of fiction. Here, too, we have a gradual transition from poetry to science.

Closely related to the mythological and religious fictions are the *æsthetic*, which, in part, simply represent poetic adaptations of the former, but in part are newly created. The æsthetic fictions not only include all similes, metaphors and comparisons, but also those ideational forms that deal even more freely with reality. Here we must group not only all personifications, but also allegories and all idealizing forms of thought. The æsthetic fiction and its theoretical explanation are, in part, closely related to the scientific fiction; and this is quite natural when we remember that the same elementary psychical processes contributed to the construction of both. Æsthetic fictions serve the purpose of awakening within us certain uplifting or otherwise important feelings. Like the scientific, they are not an end in themselves but a means for the attainment of higher ends. This parallel might be pressed further and is exceedingly instructive. Just as the introduction of scientific fictions gave rise to a violent controversy, both in general and as regards particular concepts, so in the case of the æsthetic fiction—as everyone acquainted with the history of æsthetic theory well knows—there has been a bitter conflict. It is the old dispute, still carried on intermittently, as to the degree in which the imaginative faculty may deviate from nature, how far it must be imitative and how far freely creative. As in science so in poetry, of which we are here speaking in particular, fictions have been greatly abused, and this has frequently led to reactions, based on exactly the same grounds as those resulting from the misuse of scientific fictions. The real criterion as to how far such fictions are to be admitted into either field, and one which has always been adopted by good taste and logical tact alike, is simply the practical value of such fictions.

As the æsthetic fictions have been attacked, so also have the scientific. Dühring, for instance, combats the extension of the concept of space (meta-mathematics). It is interesting to find the same writer opposing poetic fictions (use of myths and tropes) and, like Plato, refusing to tolerate poetry in his ideal state.

But Plato and Dühring (if the reader will pardon the juxtaposition) entirely misunderstand the psychical influence of the poetic fiction, and Dühring, in particular, that of the scientific fiction. Its excessive employment may certainly cause great injury and demoralization; for anything may prove to be double-edged. The æsthetic fiction may also be very harmful, but it is a mistake to reject it entirely. The poet shows us imaginary figures, pictures and individuals, especially in the drama (against which Dühring like Plato protests). Yet the poetic fiction (in the case of the drama it is a double one, since the actors represent imaginary individuals and deliver imaginary speeches) is of the highest æsthetic importance.

How easily the fiction can transform itself into an hypothesis can be seen by the fact that the audience and the reader are not able to maintain the psychical tension of the *as if* indefinitely.

Another type of fiction is furnished by those used in conventional social intercourse. Most of the phrases of social intercourse are fictions. Von Hart-mann in his essay, "On the Insincerity of Modern Life," certainly showed that most conventional phrases as well as those employed in politics, etc., are "lies," but he forgot to note that these are not merely legitimate but *necessary* fictions, without which the more refined types of social intercourse would become impossible, and which, for that reason, have always existed. We might call this type the *poetic* fiction.

Thus here, too, we have the same principle, namely, that certain forms of speech and thought, which in themselves are purely formal and unreal, make social intercourse easier. Polite fictions might also be called "conventional fictions." If I conclude a letter with the words "Your obedient serv-ant," that does not mean "I am your servant," but "regard me *as if* I were your servant." Thus the *as if* is indispensable in practical life also. Without such fictions no refined form of life would be possible.

This brings us to "official fictions" as they might be called. It may, for in-stance, be in the interest of a government to create an official fiction. Von Hartmann quite unjustly criticizes such forms also, for only when they de-generate are they really deserving of opprobrium. This is a matter for moral tact, just as æsthetic taste and logical tact decide the application of fictions in their respective fields.

Fiction thus enters profoundly into our practical life. Here, too, what were originally hypotheses frequently become fictions. Such cases can have enor-mous practical importance. Take, for instance, the question of oaths. With the current formula, everyone who swears without believing in a God is indulging in a permissible fiction. The phrase, "I swear by Almighty God," then means, "I swear *as* if a God heard me." Such fictions are not merely permissible, but under certain circumstances are necessary, and resistance is ridiculous.

Our theory of practical fictions—and it is only the outcome of a critical attitude toward the world—certainly has many dangers, as von Hartmann, for example, rightly pointed out. But it must not be forgotten that such fictions are necessary; they are a consequence of human imperfection, and, like the various aids to reflective thought, are by no means an unmixed blessing (as Nicolai, for instance, well insisted). Whether they are merely consequences of imperfection must remain an open question. But the importance of our theory for practical philosophy is obvious. All the nobler aspects of our life are based upon fictions. We have already contended that a *pure ethic* can only be established by the recognition of its fictional basis. How closely truth and illusion thus approach one another is apparent. We shall have occasion in the sequel to point out how "truth" is really merely the most expedient type of error. It is an error to suppose that an absolute truth, an absolute criterion of knowledge and behaviour, can be discovered. The higher aspects of life are based upon noble delusions. Thus our theory clearly leads to a practical view of the world very different from the ordinary one.

CHAPTER XXI THE DIFFERENCE BETWEEN FICTION AND HYPOTHESIS

WE have already shown that the fiction is generally treated as an hypothesis (although, methodologically, it is entirely different). The explanation for this lies in the fact that fiction and hypothesis are externally very similar; that they cannot always be strictly separated in actuality; and, finally, that a logical theory in general can really only take form some time after the development of a scientific procedure.

An hypothesis is directed towards reality,[18] i.e. the ideational construct contained in it claims, or hopes, to coincide with some perception in the future. It submits its reality to the test and demands *verification*, i.e. it wants to be proved true, real, and an expression of a reality. Every hypothesis without exception endeavours to establish a reality, and even though we are still uncertain as to the actual occurrence of something hypothetically assumed, we yet entertain the hope that the assumption will eventually prove to be true. If, therefore, we put forward the hypothesis that Man is descended from the lower Mammals, we are definitely insisting upon the actual existence of direct and indirect ancestors of Man, we are expressing the *belief* that had we lived at that time—a fiction impossible from the practical standpoint but logically necessary—they would have presented themselves to perception, and the hope that the remains of these vanished links may still be discovered. We are compelled to frame this hypothesis by the law of causality. For according to this law, to which there has hitherto been no known exception, every phenomenon is to be explained by some other, unless it be an elementary one. And since the human organism shows every indication of *not* being an elementary phenomenon, it must be regarded as the result of other phenomena. We therefore infer the existence of a still unknown link—the missing link—a necessary causal relation on the analogy of interconnections otherwise known to us. What we infer and hypothetically assume is the existence of an intermediate form from which the men of to-day are directly descended according to unalterable laws of sequence. This is an *hypothesis*.

We are now in a position to deal with the *fiction*. When Goethe introduced the idea of an animal archetype on the analogy of which all animals were to be treated and explained, and as modifications of which all known animal species were to be regarded, this invention of an animal archetype was a schematic fiction. For Goethe did not desire thereby to assert the actual existence of an animal archetype or to imply either that it would ever be perceived, or could ever have existed; he was merely stating that all animals should be regarded *as if* they were modifications of an archetype. The fictional element in a fiction of this kind is that we are invited to proceed *as if such an animal could have existed*; the hypothetical element—for it is a semi-fiction—being the statement that all animal forms are reducible to a single type. This is an assertion based upon observation, and its correctness would have to be demonstrated inductively by showing that all animal forms, as a whole and in particular, should be treated as modifications of such an ideal type.[19]

The value of Goethe's fiction is quite clear. It suggests an entirely new classification of animal forms and also prepares the way heuristically for the truth. It was recognized, after a time, as a heuristic fiction, but it has now been given up because the correct view has taken its place in the Darwinian theory, which assumes that all animal forms develop from one another and that an animal archetype can at most be thought of as a unicellular organism. Thus Goethe's fiction prepared the way heuristically for the Darwinian hypothesis. Whereas Darwinism asserts the actual existence of such animal archetypes, Goethe definitely denied it.

Goethe wanted his idea to be regarded as a fiction. And this was not an error on his part, as might perhaps be supposed, for Goethe's animal archetype was a useful fiction, in that it included the protozoa and assumed an original form, an original type, for all forms, and regarded them as modifications of it. Whether this fiction is useful now is another question. The primitive animal of to-day (Monera, Bathybia) is very different from the animal archetype of Goethe, who did not understand thereby beings so formless as these, nor did he claim that it had actually existed. He had in mind a single form, a type (not an animal archetype, but *the* animal archetype, said Goethe). His fiction was not concerned to assert a real fact but something by means of which reality could be dealt with and grasped, and this is actually the case in the example given. This example also serves to show how readily fiction and hypothesis can be confused and how essential is a sharp, logical distinction here.

The function of an hypothesis is, of course, only provisional—but the goal which it has ultimately in view is to be theoretically tested and established by the facts of experience. The hypothesis has also to be discarded, but this is because the hypothetical idea has become fully qualified for admission into the circle of what is accepted as real. The provisional object of the fiction is quite different; for the fiction, in so far as we have termed it a provisional auxiliary construct, ought to drop out in the course of time and make way for its real function; but in so far as it is a pure fiction, it ought, at any rate logically, to disappear as soon as it has done its duty.

Closely related to this is the question how far, on occasion, it may be doubtful whether a given assumption is a fiction or an hypothesis—where, for instance, an hypothesis is of so general a character that, in the end, it cannot possibly coincide with actual reality, and where some modification, as well as a verification of its general part, is expected. Thus we may still call Adam Smith's assumption an hypothesis, in so far as it actually expresses, in part, a real fact and a modification of the general assumption by further conditions is expected. But it is always better in such cases to avoid all possibility of error by calling such an assumption a fiction. On the other hand, it may sometimes be advisable not to include a given assumption immediately under the category of fiction, especially where there is still some doubt as to the possibility of its corresponding to something real. We must be careful not to bar the road to verification by the use of the term fiction, and still less must we commit the more obvious mistake of labelling an assumption a fiction through sheer laziness, in order thereby to avoid the laborious task of verification. In particular instances it may be very questionable whether a given assumption is a fiction or an hypothesis, and in any given case we can adopt the *hypothesis that it is only a fiction*. The possibility of this interlacing is the best proof that fiction and hypothesis should be distinguished. If, then, there is some doubt as to whether a given assumption is a fiction or an hypothesis, a detailed and specific examination should be undertaken to decide the point.

Thus the real difference between the two is that the fiction is a mere auxiliary construct, a circuitous approach, a scaffolding afterwards to be demolished, while the hypothesis looks forward to being definitely established. The former is artificial, the latter natural. What is untenable as an hypothesis can often render excellent service as a fiction, and of this we have given many examples above. On the other hand, a fiction may become superfluous in the course of time, and we know that thought is always glad to throw aside its crutches. But the main types of true fictions are never repudiated by thought, for without them reflection and analysis would be quite impossible.

The hypothesis has ultimately only a theoretical object, that of connecting facts and filling up the gaps in the connection, which experience shows to be numerous; and of establishing what is ultimately and primarily unalterable. On the other hand every fiction has, strictly speaking, only a practical object in science, for it does not create real knowledge. The hypothesis endeavours to do away with actually observed contradictions, while the fiction calls logical contradictions into existence. For that reason both their tendency and their method of application are quite distinct. The hypothesis tries to discover, the fiction, to invent. The former is therefore often also called a *découverte*; whereas the differential calculus is generally (by d'Alembert for instance) called an *invention*. Thus natural laws are *discovered* but machines *invented*. Fictions, as scientific mental instruments without which a higher development of thought is impossible, are invented. It is, however, well known that discovery and invention cannot always be sharply differentiated, any more than can hypothesis and fiction. The atom is not a discovery of natural science but an invention.

We spoke above of the necessity that every hypothesis should be confirmed by verification. But must not something similar take place in the case of the fiction?

To the *verification* of the hypothesis corresponds the *justification* of the fiction. If the former must be confirmed by experience, the latter must be justified by the services it renders to the science of experience. If a fictional construct is formed, its excuse and justification must be that it is of service to discursive thought. This justification is always a matter of special proof, like verification. Fictions that do not justify themselves, i.e. cannot be proved to be useful and necessary, must be eliminated, no less than hypotheses that cannot be verified.

The construction of fictions is as justifiable and indispensable a means of scientific investigation as that of hypotheses. What A. Lange says of hypotheses holds, *mutatis mutandis*, also of fictions: "The wise man is not he who avoids hypotheses, but he who asserts the most probable, and who knows best how to estimate the degree of their probability. If we substitute here fictions for hypotheses, and expediency for probability, this holds absolutely for fictions. Indeed the very objection that is rightly urged against those who despise hypotheses, namely that even the most common assumptions of man are based upon hypotheses that have simply attained a high degree of probability and often not even that—this same objection can and must be urged against those who, like Dühring, disapprove of fictions. For it is unquestionable that not even the most ordinary assertion can be made without the creation of fictions, such, for example, as the very categories and general ideas without which no proposition can be asserted; though in the course of time they have become so matter-of-fact that their fictional nature is no longer recognized. In reality they are fictions that daily justify themselves anew by the services which they render.

It is quite natural that the fiction should have an entirely different methodology from that of the hypothesis. The methodology of the latter consists essentially in this, that the assumption is not merely possible for thought but also actually possible, and that the facts of experience agree with it. One single fact at variance with it can destroy an hypothesis. This does not hold at all in the case of the fiction: neither its contradiction of experience nor even logical objections can disturb it, or at any rate they disturb it quite differently from an hypothesis. The principle of the rules of hypothetical method is the *probability of the conceptual constructs*, that of fictional method is their *expediency*. The rules can be deduced from this general principle, but they can be better reached inductively from the observation of particular fiction and of the procedure by which they are successfully applied. Expediency not only determines the acceptance or rejection of a particular fiction but also its selection from among others. If a fiction has finally been accepted, the principal requirement is that of being careful not to transform it either into an hypothesis or into a dogma, and not to substitute for reality what has been deduced from the fiction, without having first made the necessary corrections. A far more important requirement, however, is that we should not permit ourselves to be misled or disturbed by the contradictions of the fiction with the world of experience or its inconsistency with itself, and that we should not infer so-called world-riddles from these contradictions. In other words, we must not become attached to these fictions as though they were the essential thing, but we must recognize them as fictions and be content with this knowledge, and refuse to allow ourselves to be enticed and confused by the illusory questions and illusory problems arising out of them.

To indulge in subtleties over these contradictions involves us in the most serious aberrations of thought and we must guard against losing ourselves in sidetracks and mazes of this kind. All this is very different from the rules which hold of the hypothesis. As Lotze well puts it (*Logik*, p. 399), "every hypothesis claims to be not only a figure of thought, or a means of making thought concrete, but a statement of fact." "Everyone who sets up an hypothesis believes that he has extended the series of real facts by a happy divination of facts not less real though falling outside the range of his observation." "The fact under consideration must be thought of as an existing actuality." "*Fictions*, on the other hand," he says [E.T. p. 351], "are assumptions made with a full realization of impossibility of the thing assumed, whether because it is internally contradictory, or because on external grounds it cannot be a constituent of reality." Lotze here not only states quite correctly the distinction between fiction and hypothesis but also indicates the difference between the two kinds of fiction.

CHAPTER XXII THE LINGUISTIC FORM OF THE FICTION. ANALYSIS OF "AS-IF"

WE must now also examine in its proper context a question which has already been brought to our notice from time to time—namely, the way in which fictions are expressed in language. This, too, will show the profound and fundamental distinction between fiction and hypothesis. Indeed, the marked difference in their respective forms of linguistic expression should alone have prevented any confusion. Grammar as a whole is certainly a field in which logic may collect material; for though thought and speech are not identical, speech is nevertheless a means of which thought makes use, and the study of the subtler developments of this instrument is therefore an exceedingly important task and at the same time offers a fruitful field for logical theory, but though speech and thought are not identical there is yet a connection between them. Aristotle was thus quite right in linking his Logic with his Grammar. Among modern writers Lambert alone, who made a thorough examination of the logical meaning and value of individual particles, has shown any originality. Yet the connections of sentences through particles are the real logical joints by means of which the individual members are held together. A whole chain of thought is often compressed into a particle, and a logical analysis of a given chain must therefore direct particular attention to the connecting particles.

We have already encountered the fictional forms of expression on different occasions. For instance, every curved line is to be thought of (may be thought of, must be thought of) *as if* it consisted of an infinite number of infinitely small straight lines. Here we have a strange combination. We will not, for the time being, stress the fact that the first clause can be stated either problematically, assertively or apodictically; let us rather concentrate our attention upon the strange combination of particles, *as if*, and compare the form it takes in different languages: Latin, *quasi*, also *sicut*; French, *comme si*, *que si*; German, *als ob*, *wie wenn*; Greek ὡς εἰ [ὡσεί], ὡς εἰ τε.

Our assertion that in the last analysis all fictions derive from comparative apperception, is supported by their linguistic form. For what is implied by the combinations of particles, *as if*, *als ob*, *wie wenn*, etc.? First, clearly a comparison; that is quite manifest, for *als*, *wie* are particles of comparison. Thus the curved line, to take the special case, is treated *as* a series of infinitesimals; here we have the first *comparative apperception*, the curved line being apperceived by means of the conceptual construct of the infinitesimal. But this comparison is then modified by the *wenn* and the *ob*. It is, of course, not a simple comparison, not a mere trope, and yet it is not a real analogy. The comparison lies midway between a trope and a real analogy; in other words, between a rhetorical comparison and actual equivalence. It is thus quite a different kind of comparison from that of comparative anatomy, for instance, where the organism of a man is compared with that of the gorilla, or of comparative philology, where the structure of the Germanic is compared, say, with that of the Romance languages. These are real analogies, comparisons on the basis of a common descent, and common laws of structure. And it is also a comparison of a different order from that of a mere trope, as when, for example, the curved line is compared with the crooked ways of a burglar. This is a trope. A real analogy would be the comparison of four conic sections with one another. But what if I regard the curved line as a straight one? Is that a trope? It is certainly something more. Is it a true analogy? Assuredly it is less than that. It is a fiction. The comparison is only possible indirectly through the intermediate idea of the infinitesimal. If it were an analogy or a trope, the simple *as* (*wie*) would suffice. As it is neither one nor the other, to the *as* (*wie*) is added the *if* (*wenn*), to the *als* the *ob*. And what is implied by this addition? In the *if* lies the assumption of a condition, and indeed, in this instance, of an impossible case. In this complex of particles there lies, in fact, the whole process of thought proper to a fiction. Let us carry the analysis further. Taking the *if* as the starting-point, the sentence would read, "If *there were* infinitesimals then the curved line could be treated as made up of them"; or, "If *there were* atoms, then matter could be treated as made up of them"; or to take another example, "If egotism *were* the only incentive to human behaviour, then we ought to be able to deduce social relations from it exclusively."

In the conditional clause something unreal or impossible is stated, and yet from this *unreality* or *impossibility* inferences are drawn. In spite of its unreality or impossibility the assumption is still formally maintained. It is regarded as an apperceptive construct under which something can be subsumed and from which deductions can be made.

What, then, is contained in the *as if*? There must apparently be something else hidden in it apart from the unreality and impossibility of the assumption in the conditional sentence. These particles clearly also imply a decision to maintain the assumption *formally, in spite of* these difficulties. Between the *as* and *if*, *wie* and *wenn*, *als* and *ob*, *comme* and *si*, *qua-si*, a whole sentence lies implied. What, then, does it mean if we say that matter must be treated *as if* it consisted of atoms? It can only mean that empirically given matter must be treated *as* it would be treated if it consisted of atoms or that the curve must be treated *as* it would be if it consisted of infinitesimals. Or finally, that social relations are to be treated *as* (*wie*) they would be if (*wenn*) egotisms were the only incentive to human conduct. There is, then, a clear statement of the *necessity* (*possibility* or *actuality*) of an *inclusion* under *an impossible* or *unreal assumption*.

The same result naturally follows from the German form, *als ob. Ob*, in Middle High German, is *wenn*. Consequently we have—matter is to be treated *as* (*als*) it would be treated "if" ("ob") it, etc. So in French—*comme si*; and in Greek, *ὡς εἰ*, etc.

This formula, then, states that reality as given, the particular, is *compared* with something whose impossibility and unreality is at the same time admitted. It depends upon the type of conditional sentence what fiction, in each case, is actually used. For example, in the juristic fiction the formula runs as follows: This heir[20] is to be treated as he would be if he had died before his father, the testator, i.e. he is to be disinherited. Or starting with if:—If the person in question had died before his father he would be treated as all such persons are treated, i.e. he would not inherit anything. The person in question is to be treated like such, just as they are treated, *as* such. We have here primarily a *comparison*, i.e. a proposal to make a comparative or subsuming apperception. Such a sentence really asserts nothing more than is asserted by such a sentence as "man is to be treated like a gorilla." Why? Because he is similar to one. The same holds true for all these cases; there is a proposal for a comparative apperception. Together with this proposal the comparison is also declared to be based upon an impossible condition. Instead, however, of abandoning it, it is *nevertheless*, for other reasons actually made.

We can now also understand the linguistic similarity of the fiction to *error* and to *hypothesis*.

As is well-known, the grammatical formula for error is exactly the same. That is why the fiction is so frequently confused with error. We say, for instance, that Descartes regarded the idea of God and the Absolute *as if* they were innate; but that is an error, etc. Here the error is marked by the same formula, and psychologically it has the same formation as the fiction. Fiction is, after all, merely a *more conscious, more practical and more fruitful error*. Something else must, of course, be understood here. It is not asserted that the comparison is *nevertheless* to be maintained, but it is rejected as useless.

We thus see how many subtle trains of thought are expressed in this pair of particles, and how they can serve different purposes.

From the above analysis the relationship to the hypothesis also becomes apparent. The form of the atomic fiction is that matter must be treated *as* it would be, if there were atoms of which it was imagined to be composed. The form of the hypothesis connected with this assumption runs thus: only on the presupposition that atoms exist and only if they do exist, can the empirical appearance of material phenomena be explained. In this more expanded method of expression we see how different the two ideas really are from a linguistic point of view.

In spite of this occasional ambiguity of language, the grammatical difference between fiction and hypothesis is very remarkable. Linnæus did not say that the world of plants *was* objectively divided according to his species, nor did Leibniz say that the curve *consisted* of infinitesimals, and modern scientists, in so far, at least, as they have had some philosophical training, do not say that matter *is* composed of atoms. Kant never directly stated that the world consisted of a majority of free, intelligent beings. They all interpolate the *"as if"* in some form or other. Leibniz, for instance, says that his infinitesimals are a *modus dicendi*; while Kant speaks of an Idea;[21] and natural scientists speak of ideational aids, conceptual aids, etc. In all these expressions, which could be greatly increased in number, an *"as if"* is somewhere hidden, and they are all merely other forms of fiction, other forms of expression. Linguistically, therefore, it is not at all easy to confuse fiction and hypothesis; and were we instead of "this must or can be regarded as if"—to say "is," it would either be a mere abbreviation or definitely an error. But the sciences usually employ the more accurate expression. No mathematician says: "Every plane *is* made up of triangles," but in his fundamentals of trigonometry he says: "by drawing auxiliary lines, every plane can be *conceived* as if it were made up of many triangles, and can be treated as such." A careful psychologist and jurist does not say that man *is* a free agent, but that man must, at any rate legally, and from the moral standpoint, be regarded and treated *as if* he were free.

In a *fictive judgment*, as we might call this composite judgment, the possibility or necessity of a comparison or judgment, is stated, together with the assertion that this judgment has only subjective validity and not objective significance. It is easy to see that in the above verbal formulations there is actually expressed: first, the denial of objective validity, i.e. the insistence upon the lack of reality or the impossibility of what is stated in the conditional clause; secondly, the subjective validity, the assertion that this judgment, although subjective, is permissible or even necessary, for the human observer.

From this it follows that scientific fictive judgments (as distinct from the æsthetic fiction) can appear only at a high stage of human intellectual development. The fictive judgment has in its essentials only developed in modern times, partly in connection with the progress of mathematics, mechanics and jurisprudence, and partly side by side with the recognition that objective events or entities and subjective attitudes may coincide in the final result, and yet not be identical. The ancient philosophers, on the other hand, in spite of their scepticism, were still bound by a naive theory of knowledge (cf. Chapter XXXIII). An elaborate judgment of this type is, therefore, only possible in a period of advanced mental development.

CHAPTER XXIII COLLECTION OF EXPRESSIONS FOR 'FICTION'

Now that we have studied the various linguistic means of expressing fictions, it will be useful to collect the various terms under which the fiction has hitherto been treated and which have been applied, more or less correctly and appropriately, to it. There is quite a large number of these designations, some of which have already been encountered. Fictions are frequently referred to by terms simply translated from the Latin: *inventions, conceits, figments of the brain, phantasies, phantastic ideas, imagination, imaginary ideas.* We also speak of *quasi-things* and *quasi-ideas.* Thus Kant's "Ding an sich" has always been termed a quasi-thing, i.e. an imaginary, fictional thing. This sometimes means an erroneous idea or an erroneous designation, and sometimes a scientifically valuable fiction. In the latter sense jurisprudence, in particular, uses it occasionally in connection with *quasi.* Thus we speak of a quasi-contract. Such contracts refer to legal relations which, because of a certain similarity, are treated on the analogy of a contract, though they do not in fact rest on any real contract; for example, guardianship or financial transactions entered into without any actual contract. In jurisprudence we find also quasi-affinity, quasi-delictum, quasi-possession. (Cf. Chapter V on Juristic Fictions.) Other terms are derived from the fact that fictions are an *aid* to thought:—*conceptual aids, auxiliary words, auxiliary operations, makeshifts;* and, for special purposes, *auxiliary lines, auxiliary divisions, auxiliary methods, auxiliary concepts, auxiliary formulas.* Others again arise from the ingenious character of the process: *expedients, devices, artifices* (particularly in mathematics), *artificial ideas, artificial concepts, artificial methods, counterfeit ideas, stratagems, dodges, contrivances, by-ways, approaches, short-cuts,* etc. Some names derive from the function of the device, such as *instrumental or intermediate ideas, bridges, props, ladders, crutches, surrogates, substitutes, suppositions, scaffoldings,* etc. There are also various other terms:—*chimæra, distorted concept* (Dühring), *accessory or auxiliary concept or method transit-point for thought,*[22] *instrument* (for theoretical and practical purposes), *arbitrary concept, play-idea* (v. Kirchmann) *deceptive idea, doubtful idea, unjustified method, schema, provisional idea, heuristic idea, vicarious or substitutive idea, "provisional"* (Dühring), *technical idea or method, regulative idea, accessory hypothesis,* etc.

We also find: *Illusory idea* (Lambert), *Figure of thought* (Lotze), *Modus dicendi* (Leibniz), *"Mere idea"* (Kant), *Interim-idea, Counter* (Liebmann), *Limiting concept, Boundary-idea, Theoretical concept, By-path, Starting-point for investigation, Provisional assumption, Means of orientation* (Lange).

This approximately complete collection of names used for fiction shows how important they have always been, and how a really central term has hitherto been lacking. This we shall now try to supply by the introduction of the term, *fiction*.

CHAPTER XXIV THE MAIN CHARACTERISTICS OF FICTIONS

Before presenting our provisional attempt at a logical theory of fictions, we have still to indicate the *general characteristics* of a fiction; and the logical theory will, in part, be deducible from these. Most of them have already been mentioned in other connections.

The striking feature of semi-fictions is their arbitrary deviation from reality, that is, their contradiction of it, a contradiction which in the case of fictions reaches the point of self-contradiction. This contradiction with reality shows itself both in the form of the ideas and judgments involved, that is to say in the premises, which do not harmonize with facts, laws and phenomena otherwise known, and also in the conclusions drawn from these ideas and judgments. These are always in contradiction with immediate reality, and though the opposition is often hidden it reveals itself to deeper analysis. In the case of true fictions this self-contradiction discloses itself particularly in the antinomies to which they give rise (cf. Kant's antinomies of the infinite, by means of which he proved that the idea of infinite space was subjective, or, in our terminology, fictional). When, therefore, in the history of science, objections have been brought against important achievements on the ground of self-contradiction, we may suspect that as often as not we are dealing with valuable fictions; this was the case with Leibniz and Newton, with the atomic theory, etc. Where stress is laid rather upon the opposition to experience, we are often really concerned with semi-fictions, e.g. in the case of Linnæus, Adam Smith, etc.

> This first characteristic is identical with the violence which marks such an assumption. The special character of a fiction is not only its arbitrariness but also its violence. Violence must be done not only to reality but (in real fictions) also to thought itself. The arbitrary way in which thought operates

corresponds to the violence to which it subjects reality and the logical Law of Contradiction.

I find this confirmed with regard to the fiction of the general idea in Flügel, *Probleme der Philosophie*, p. 136. "Logical concepts are in reality never finished and completed concepts but rather demands upon thought, logical ideals where the greater the degree of the abstraction the greater the *violence* done to thought!"

This does *not* in itself constitute any reason for rejecting such fictions, as is often supposed, when some idea is referred to as forced or arbitrary. It is not in this but in expediency that we shall find the criterion of a useful concept.

A second main character is that these ideas either disappear in the course of history or through the operation of logic. The former holds for semi-fictions, the latter for true fictions. Of course, if there is a contradiction with reality, then the fiction can only have a value if used provisionally until experience has become richer, or until the methods of thought have been so refined that these provisional methods can be replaced by definitive ones. In the same manner the discarding of true fictions in the course of a given mental operation follows necessarily from their contradictory character—for, after all, our aim is to obtain non-contradictory results. Contradictory ideas are thus only there to be finally eliminated; moreover, in spite of these contradictory ideas, correct results are obtained in thought and calculation, and these fictions must somehow be eliminated and their contradictions cancelled.

The third of the main features of a normal fiction is the express awareness that the fiction is just a fiction, in other words, the consciousness of its fictional nature and the absence of any claim to actuality. I say "of a normal fiction" advisedly, for this character holds only for such fictions as these are supposed to be. But as we have already seen, in the historical development of the sciences such cases are relatively rare, and for this reason the first authors of a fiction are always hesitating between fiction and hypothesis. This is to be explained by the fact that the ordinary man takes everything that is asserted as undoubtedly natural and true and, at first, not only supposes that the concepts of thought are representative of reality, but regards mental methods and processes as identical with the processes and laws of reality itself—an error subsequently canonized by eminent philosophers. Only in the course of time is it observed that subjective methods are quite distinct from objective happenings. It is because of this that the first inventors of such fictions so frequently hesitate. With Linnæus and many mathematicians, there is a lively awareness of the fictional nature of such ideas and methods. Newton and Leibniz, on the other hand, both wavered. In a large number of fictions we have the situation described above, namely, that they are first adopted as hypotheses and the realization of their fictional nature only develops later.

A further essential character of fictions, i.e. of scientific fictions, is that they are *means* to a definite end, in other words that they are expedient. Where there is no expediency the fiction is unscientific. Thus when Hume called the categories fictions, he was right *in fact*, though his idea of a fiction was very different from ours. His idea of the "fiction of thought" was that of a merely subjective fancy, while ours (borrowed from the usage of mathematics and jurisprudence) includes the idea of its utility. This is really the kernel of our position, which distinguishes it fundamentally from previous views. For us the essential element in a fiction is not the fact of its being a conscious deviation from reality, a mere piece of imagination—but we stress the useful nature of this deviation. This utility constitutes the transition from the pure subjectivity of Kant to a modern Positivism. If we simply say, "The whole world is our idea and all forms are subjective", we get an untenable subjectivism. But if we say: "Conceptual forms and fictions are expedient psychical constructs", then these are closely related to "cosmic agencies and constituents" (Laas), for it is they that call these expedient forms into existence in the organic being.

The four main characteristics thus enumerated fully suffice to distinguish fictions from hypotheses. With this "warrant" every fiction can be at once recognized and examined; and if a survey of the whole field of science were made to-day many fictions that we have not mentioned here would certainly be discovered.

CHAPTER XXV OUTLINE OF A GENERAL THEORY OF FICTIONAL CONSTRUCTS

THOUGHT is circuitous: herein lies the real secret of all fictions. The primary object of a logical theory is to separate these devious ways from the essential starting-points and goals of thought. Fictions are mere temporary halting-places for thought and have no bearing on reality. We have repeatedly pointed out that the whole world of ideas, the whole subjective conceptual edifice of man, lies between sensation and movement (which in the end can also be reduced to sensation).

The ultimate attitude of logic with regard to fictions is and must remain to regard them as points of transition for the mind. But we have treated thought as a whole, with all its auxiliary apparatus, its instruments and devices, in other words, the entire theoretical activity of man as a mere transit-point with practical utility as its ultimate goal, whether this be taken to mean ordinary action or ideally interpreted as ethical action. Thus we are here modifying the fundamental concept of Fichtean philosophy to suit our present purpose. Ideas as transit-points are also the joints by means of which the connection between sensations is established. The whole conceptual world is a system of such articulations, of such mechanical arrangements for suitably connecting sensations. The comparison of psychical with mechanical events must, however, be taken seriously. We must not think merely of mechanical processes in the sense of purely physical phenomena, but look upon them as mechanics regard its appliances for practical purposes and for the increase of power, that is to say, lever, pulley, screw, inclined plane, etc. In the mechanics of the mind similar events also take place.

Psychical phenomena are not mechanical only in the sense that they take place of necessity and according to law, that the combinations, fusions and apperceptions occur mechanically, but because they also follow the laws of their own special mechanics; in the sense that, through appliances such as those of physical mechanics, the elementary natural forces are worked over and made use of. The psyche must therefore be regarded as a machine, not only because it works according to psycho-mechanical and psycho-chemical laws, but in the sense that its natural forces are intensified by these mechanical processes. A machine is an appliance of practical mechanics by means of which a given movement is accomplished with the least expenditure of energy. This is a requirement which the human psyche, regarded as a psychical machine, fulfils to a high degree and that is why its activity is to be looked upon as purposive. The work demanded of the human psyche is movement in the widest sense of the term, primarily purely external movement and also reflex movement, and in the second place voluntary movement for the purpose of preserving the organism. The whole psychical machine, then, must be looked upon as an energy-saving device, as an arrangement enabling the organism to perform its movements as effectively as possible, i.e. quickly, neatly and with the least expenditure of energy.

But the machine taken as a whole is composed of single parts which, within the machine, have the same task as had the whole machine in relation to a complex of phenomena. And so it is with the psyche. Individual psychical acts are to be regarded from the same standpoint, as mechanisms for saving energy, which perform the desired work as quickly and efficiently as possible. And, finally, we must also remember that man is continually perfecting his machines so that they do their work ever more quickly, better, more effectively and with greater economy of energy (we have only to recall the evolution of the steam-engine); and in the same way the psyche is always perfecting its mechanisms.

Thus the psyche is a machine which is continually improving itself, and whose purpose it is to perform as safely, expeditiously and with the minimum expenditure of energy, the movements necessary for the preservation of the organism; movements in the broadest sense of the word, as the ultimate objectives of all our acts. All our mental life is rooted in *sensation* and culminates in movement; what lies between are mere points of transit. This gradual improvement of the mental machine is clearly expressed, for instance, in the law of the condensation of ideas, a psycho-mechanical process which materially increases the rapidity, safety and efficiency of ideas. It is to be compared with the efficiency of compressed steam, for example, whose power varies directly with its so-called "tension." Condensation is of no less importance in the psychical machine than in the more material machines of mechanics. The whole formation of concepts may be reduced to a condensation-process by means of which its working-capacity is considerably heightened. We must, however, remember in this connection, that it is not the machine that is of primary importance but its work. The same is true of the psyche and its special machines. Its purpose is the performance of expedient movements or, ideally expressed, of ethical actions. To regard ideas as ends in themselves is an error; and in the last analysis the theoretical is only a means to the practical. As soon as we treat the problem seriously from this standpoint, which was first adopted by Kant and Fichte, light is thrown on quite a number of problems and obscurities.

Thus far our treatment, strange and forced though it may appear, in reality merely transfers to the psychical sphere a method of approach which has long been current among physiologists in regard to the organic function of the brain, especially since the law of the conservation of energy has given us a deeper and more correct insight into organic processes. Moreover, our treatment is only a special application and a more serious development of what can already be found in Kant, Herbart, Fichte and Schopenhauer.

We cannot accept the ordinary view that thought is an end in itself. Thought serves as a means of communication with others and its individual mechanisms must all be regarded as mechanical expedients. The reduction of the whole conceptual world to such mental expedients is the proper task of epistemology, their methodology forms the subject-matter of logic. All logical methods, including the fictive, are only aids and accessory arrangements of this machine whose mechanical structure and output we have attempted to exhibit above.

The proper task of methodology is to teach us to manipulate this instrument, this thought-machine. We have already pointed out that a methodology of this kind might be content, at first, with external rules of routine, put together empirically, while a scientific methodology must, in the end, be based upon a theoretical analysis of the mechanical operations of the mind. Such an analysis would eventually bring the whole complicated procedure of thought back to such simple basic principles as, for instance, the principle of the lever. We have found fictions in general to be elementary aids to thought, simplifying the movement of thought and of the larger ideational masses with mechanical mental work as their object. These fictions play the same role in the mechanism of thought as the elementary mechanical expedients play in the physical theory of machines. The various kinds of fiction correspond to the various kinds of aids to physical motion. The most complicated of these aids to the movement of thought, e.g. the idea of the infinite, must be reduced to simple, mechanical principles of the same sort.

The two elementary psycho-mechanical principles which stand out most prominently in a psychological analysis, are the formation of fixed nuclei by means of *categories* and of fixed centres by means of *general ideas*. By the reduction of all phenomena and their relations to a few primitive analogies, continually decreasing in number, namely the categories, the movement of thought is given a definite and fixed direction. In this way psychical levers are formed, and through their instrumentality a free movement of ideational masses is first rendered possible. Pulleys also are created in the form of conceptual constructs and thus allow particular sensation-complexes to be connected with one another and to interact. The chief interest in all these processes lies in the question why a simplification of mental movements should be created by these arrangements, and how it happens that in spite of these fictional intermediary elements thought does attain the goal of its logical activity. When whole complexes of similar elements, centres of similarity, are formed, as happens in the case of the categories, which must be regarded as analogies, and of the concepts, the psychical movement of ideas is thereby naturally increased, facilitated and intensified. A centre of this kind has a far greater capacity for attraction than a single element. By means of these centres the comparison of single phenomena is simplified and accelerated. For example, directly a single phenomenon appears, it need not be attracted by every similar sensation, but it will be drawn to the powerful centre of similarity with greater force, and its approach to this centre will be correspondingly more rapid. By this movement, however, an extremely quick comparison with sensation-complexes containing and constituting the similarity-centre becomes possible. It is thus obvious that the only object of these centres is to facilitate and accelerate the comparison of particular sensations. It thus serves merely to enable and accelerate psychical movement, and fulfils its purpose when this is achieved. From this it necessarily follows that the centre of equality can in the end serve only as a point of transition for movement, so that the essential interest is only in the reciprocal movement of the particular sensations themselves. This movement is facilitated by the centres to which we refer.

The elementary mechanical processes taking place in the psyche during thinking and understanding also furnish the answer to the question why in spite of these fictional, subjective ideas, we nevertheless succeed in arriving at reality. These ideas, and the often very extensive fictive methods connected with them, are after all only transit-points to assist psychical movement, which is accomplished by their means but in such a manner that they are subsequently cast aside. As soon as the centre has performed its service, i.e. made the movement of particular sensation-complexes and ideas possible, it has achieved all it can and is no longer taken into account. Its work ends as soon as it has performed its function as intermediary.

In this elementary mechanism, the formation of a similarity-centre, lies the secret of all fictions, whether they be simple like the artificial classifications, or complicated like the idea of infinity.

For us, all the higher concepts are delicate mental accessories of this kind, parts of a machine in the marvellous mechanism of thought, and our task here consists in going back to the elementary mechanical laws of psychical life.

The points of transition represent deviations from reality, which, when we proceed in a purely theoretical manner without regard for the reality of phenomena, must of necessity lead to those contradictions with actuality which we described above as characteristic of fiction. The first feature, namely, that historically they disappear and logically are cancelled, follows necessarily from the character of fictions as transit-points of thought.

We must here firmly adhere to the principle of the mechanism of thought, the principle that all ideas and complexes of ideas of an advanced type, in so far as they do not directly coincide with reality, merely support, accelerate and facilitate the ideational mechanism. On the other hand, we must always be on our guard against attributing reality to these mental complexes and accessories; for only what is felt, what confronts us in the world of perception, whether it be internal or external, is real. If we assume these fictions to be real, all those antinomies and contradictions follow which run through the history of philosophy from its origins to the present day.

All the other common methodological principles for the fiction flow with necessity from these relations: for example, the necessity of destroying the subjective logical scaffolding of thought when its actual purpose has been accomplished, of destroying it historically or logically so that false and imaginary ideas do not disturb our vision of reality.

The above theory of centres of similarity can now be extended from the elementary fictive processes of the formation of general ideas and general ideational forms, to the more special fictions. In every case groups of ideas are formed which act as intermediaries for the connection, comparison and adjustment of concepts. Fundamentally we are dealing with a variation of one and the same basic process, the formation of ideational constructs that are interpolated in the stream of thought in order to assist and facilitate it. And in so far as all thinking ultimately aims at an equation, fictions enable this equation and comparison to be effected where otherwise they would be impossible.

The tremendous importance of fictions is obvious from all this. They are, as Lotze correctly insists, of extraordinary "importance for the processes of discovery." They are, in fact, a part of that *ars inveniendi* which, in former times, was usually appended to Logic.

Apart from the general warning not to confuse fictions with reality, we may also call attention to the fact that every fiction must be able to justify itself, i.e. must justify itself by what it accomplishes for the progress of science. It must be shown in each case that the particular form, the particular structure is not superfluous, that it performs a service, and the extent of its influence must also be determined. The gulf between reality and fiction must always be stressed, and care must be taken to confuse neither the fiction itself nor its immediate consequences with reality. With all these precautions before us, the fiction can be regarded as a "legitimatized error," i.e. as a fictional conceptual construct that has justified its existence by its success. On the other hand, it would be wrong to argue from the success of such a logical procedure to its logical purity or real validity. Fictions are and must remain circuitous and indirect mental paths, which cannot, because they conduct us to our goal, be regarded as really valid or free from logical contradiction. This is indeed the fundamental mistake which we have already so repeatedly censured, of arguing from logical success to logical purity. It was once contended that since the differential calculus leads to correct results, there must be real differentials and that the idea of differentials could not be contradictory. This conclusion is, as we have said, false. Even those fictions, such as the categories, which are absolutely necessary from a subjective point of view, if we are to think discursively at all, are not thereby rendered objective. The subjective necessity, for instance, of regarding everything that we observe in terms of things, is not a criterion of objective validity.

> Aenesidem quite correctly reduced Kant's philosophy to the following formula:—Kant demonstrated that the necessity of being thought is by no means the same as existence. The reason is to be sought in the fact that thought requires mental aids in order to attain its purpose, aids that up to Kant's time had been confused with reality. It is true that Locke, Berkeley and Hume had partially recognized this better and more clearly than Kant. In Kant we look in vain for that definitely modern point of view which regards thought as a means to an end.
>
> For him the main question was not how it comes to pass that the purpose of thought is accomplished by these means, but the falsely-framed question, what justification have we for formulating a priori laws about nature that shall be valid for all experience? These questions are clearly related but are by no means identical. We do not regard it as a fact that we enunciate a priori laws—for this proved to be illusory; but it is a fact that ends are attained by logical means, and what we want to know is how this happens, what is the mechanical process by which these means set about the attainment of their

purpose. What is to us a fact is the actual empirical correctness of the results of our mental operations, and we want to know how these mental operations attain such correct results. We know, on the other hand, that the ways, the methods and the procedure of thought are subjective, i.e. fictional.

For us moderns the question is, what are the mechanical laws according to which purposive-organic processes develop and run their course; through what psycho-mechanical processes do categories and fictions arise out of sensations; and finally, by what psycho-mechanical means do these structures actually make themselves useful? It is the particular merit of Kant to have shown that most ideational constructs are purely subjective. That they are fictions in our sense, i.e. fictions as a means for attaining certain purposes, he no more realized than Hume.

The importance of fictions for the theory of knowledge we have already sufficiently stressed. Here again the main emphasis is to be laid upon the fact that these epistemological fictions, i.e. the categories, in particular, are absolutely indispensable for thought, for otherwise thinking could not be discursive at all. The epistemological fiction of the categories is, however, of particular value, because their unjustified transference to the world as a whole leads to all those philosophically important ideas, such as world-substance, cosmic energy, cosmic causes, which are a necessary logical illusion. The existence of an unavoidable logical illusion was asserted before Kant, but it was he who first discovered it completely.

As regards the relations of phenomena we can speak of things and attributes, causes and effects; but behind and beyond these phenomena this conceptual approach has no justification. Its application in this field gives rise to the illusion of real things "as-such", real causes "as-such". Even Kant did not entirely escape this illusion. In actual fact, we have only sensations and the unchangeable coexistence and sequence of phenomena. We may call these "things" and "causes" as long as we are conscious of the fact that such forms of expression and conception are chosen merely for purposes of convenience. But as soon as we assume real transcendental "things-in-themselves" we are victims of the logical illusion which not even Kant entirely avoided. These *Dinge an sich* are admittedly necessary from a subjective and conceptual standpoint, in order to enable us to think of the world discursively at all, but they are nothing more, as Maimon first recognized.

The main result of our investigation is, then, that *contradiction* is the driving force of thought and that without it thought could not attain its goal at all; that it is immanent in discursive thought and is one of its constituent elements.

We have repeatedly insisted above that the boundary between truth and error is not a rigid one, and we were able ultimately to demonstrate that what we generally call truth, namely a conceptual world coinciding with the external world, *is merely the most expedient error.*

> Of course what we understand here by the content of truth is not the estab-lishment of unalterable sequences, but the forms of thought.

The conceptual world is, as we both assumed and found to be the case, subjective in its forms: only the observed and the unchangeable are real. The whole framework in which we place what is perceived is only subjective; *subjective is fictional; fictional is false; falsehood is error.* It is the ambition of science, we saw, to make of the world of ideas an ever more useful instrument for dealing with things and for action. The world of ideas which results from this ambition, and which we generally call "truth" is consequently only the most expedient error, i.e. that system of ideas which enables us to act and to deal with things most rapidly, neatly and safely, and with the minimum of irrational elements. The limits between truth and error are therefore just as movable as all such limits, e.g. those between cold and warm. Cold is a degree of temperature that is unsuitable for us, warm that which is most suitable. The difference between them objectively is merely one of degree. Subjectively the differences can be shifted according to circumstances and the nature of the object concerned. In the same manner, truth is merely the most expedient degree of error, and error the least expedient degree of ideation, of fiction. We call our conceptual world true when it permits us best to gauge objectivity and to act therein. So-called agreement with reality must finally be abandoned as a criterion.

CHAPTER XXVI THE METHOD OF CORRECTING ARBITRARY DIFFERENCES OR THE METHOD OF ANTITHETIC ERROR

HAVING now proved that the logical theory of fictions is based upon a psychological analysis, and attempted to sketch the importance of fictions and their methodology for various questions, our next task must be to examine, from a specifically logical point of view, the logical mechanism of thought connected with fictions. Our treatment hitherto was primarily psychological; what follows will have to be primarily logical.

We have repeatedly asserted that in fictions thought makes deliberate errors, in order thereby to understand the nature of Becoming. All departures from reality are mistakes and all self-contradictions are logical errors of the first degree. We added on several occasions that these errors must be cancelled, because otherwise the fictions would be valueless and harmful. Thus when Adam Smith dealt with the human activities by means of his fiction of egoism, he began with an error because actually egoism is not the only source of human action. When, therefore, he came to apply the laws derived from this fiction to concrete reality, compensation had to be made for the difference.

Expressed in general terms we have the following:—If, in fictions, thought contradicts reality, or if it even contradicts itself, and if in spite of this questionable procedure it *nevertheless* succeeds in corresponding to reality, then—and this is a necessary inference—*this deviation must have been corrected and the contradiction must have been made good.*

In so far, therefore, as a *correction* must be made (in the case of semi-fictions), the procedure of the logical function in this respect can be called the method of correcting deviations made arbitrarily; in so far, however, as self-contradiction is a logical error and this error must be corrected, which can only be accomplished by an equivalent error of an opposite nature, then this procedure can be called the *method of antithetic error.*

Under this seemingly strange designation those familiar with mathematics will immediately be reminded of certain mathematical methods where the procedure is the same, for all methods of thought find their purest expression in mathematics.

The correction required may vary from the simple remark that the results obtained by fictional methods are not to be confused with reality to the actual necessity of making a logical mistake of an opposite nature.

The simple correction generally takes place in semi-fictions. As found in artificial classifications, it is limited to the simple remark that this artificial system is not to be taken for reality but represents a preliminary system designed for heuristic and practical purposes. But of course the procedure is not always so harmless. There are cases where the first error made by thought in artificial classification has to be balanced by one made in the other direction;

and with artificial classifications this involves a necessary deviation from the artificial system itself. Thus not only do errors spring from these artificial systems but they must be partially cancelled by errors of an opposite nature. And in this case the procedure is very simple. To the arbitrary deviation from reality made in the artificial classifications and in their formation—where a character selected at random is made the *fundamentum divisionis*—there must correspond on the other side a correction, if the classification is to be utilizable at all, and if impossible elements are to be got rid of and all real ones included.

That the same correction is required for abstractive and neglective fictions is clear; the neglected elements must come into their own again if errors are to be avoided. The same is true of schematic fiction as well as of paradigmatic, Utopian and type-fictions—all these conceptual constructs only possess a value for an understanding of reality when real values are substituted for ideal representations. The conditions here are quite simple: the correction, and its necessity, possibility and reality are all obvious. In the case of juristic fictions, on the other hand, such a correction does not seem at all necessary, nor is it in fact. For here it is not a question of dealing accurately with a real object, but of subsumption under an arbitrary law—the creation of man—and not a law of nature or a natural relation. In the case of heuristic fictions we have the same situation, the essential point being not to regard the fictional cause, the *causa ficta*, as a real one.

It is quite different with other kinds of fiction: for whereas in those hitherto mentioned, which are based on deviations from reality, the correction of this deviation alone suffices, a different type of procedure is required when the fictive subsumption occurs not directly but through the mediation of a fictional conceptual construct. In the case of the above constructs only fictional ideational forms and methods are involved; here we have fictional ideational constructs.

In the ordinary course of events only one method of correction is possible; the constructs must simply drop out in the final result. The error must be cancelled by having the fictively introduced construct simply rejected again. If, however, its appearance was due to a logical error, then its rejection can only be accomplished by means of another logical error. That is why we call this the *method of antithetic error*. Strictly, the name only fits those mathematical examples which we have already enumerated. But it will fit all logical sequences of thought, when these are examined from the point of view of the law of contradiction.

In practical fictions the discarding of these intermediate links is quite simple. If the object is attained they simply drop out. Of course they do not drop out of the psyche itself but only out of the thought-process. Thus, for instance, in the fiction of liberty the judge uses this fiction only in order to arrive at a sentence. The purpose is the legal sentence which is obtained by means of the fiction that man, here in the form of a criminal, is free. Whether man is actually free is a matter of indifference. The intermediate idea of liberty drops out, as does the middle term in every syllogism. The judge concludes that every man is free, and therefore if he has sinned against the law, he must be punished. A is a man, a free man, and has transgressed; he is therefore liable to punishment. First A is subsumed under the idea of a free man, then under that of liability to punishment. The idea of freedom, however, drops out here; it has only served to make the sentence possible. But the premise, whether man really is free, is not examined by the judge. In actual fact this premise is only a fiction which serves for the deduction of the final conclusion; for without the possibility of punishing men, of punishing the criminal, no government would be possible. The theoretical fiction of freedom has been invented for this practical purpose.

The same holds true for the fiction of a social contract. This also serves only as the basis of a criminal code (and not, as in the case of freedom, of the moral right to punish). It is assumed that every inhabitant of a country has tacitly entered into a pact with society to obey the laws. According to these laws any infringement of the pact itself is punishable. If then A has transgressed these laws, he has broken the contract and is thus liable to punishment according to the law. This whole fiction has as its object merely the theoretical establishment of public criminal law, for it is an open secret of political science that the criminal code cannot be established in any other way. Whence the community (or an individual representing it) can derive the right to punish others, is far from obvious.

> That it has the *power* to do so is another matter. But the state does not desire to base its currently enforced criminal law upon might, nor simply on utilitarian motives, but wishes to prove its actual juridical right. That is only possible by means of the fiction of a contract, for the jurist knows of no rights except those arising out of contracts.

Since then we are unwilling to reduce punishment to a mere question of power, and to say that the stronger party, the community, may inflict a punishment on the individual for which there is no legal or moral justification, an attempt is made to justify criminal law theoretically by the fiction of a contract. Similarly, in earlier times, and to some extent even to-day, the attempt has been made to establish theoretically both the right of the monarch, of the crown, and also that of the people to revolt; for it cannot be asserted absolutely that the state has any right whatever to punish, the ruler to govern or the people to revolt. Thus the contract forms the intermediate idea from which the rights in question can be theoretically deduced.

In the conclusion itself, however, the intermediate idea drops out, and so it drops out from the completed thought-process.

Before pursuing this idea further, we would draw attention to the fact that the nature of the necessary correction depends upon the nature of the various fictions; and there is a great variety of forms. Where unjustified transferences, etc. take place, e.g. where the circle is defined as an ellipse, the fictional conceptual structure itself represents not the first but the second error; when, for instance, I say the circle is an ellipse this is a self-evident error. If, however, I say that the distance between the foci $= 0$, then the assertion becomes intelligible. How? Through another error! That a distance $= 0$ is logically nonsense. A distance equal to 0 is no distance at all. The non-occurrence is simply regarded as an occurrence in the negative sense. Here, therefore, two mistakes have been committed; first, the assertion that the circle is an ellipse—which is compensated for by the second, that a distance $= 0$, though this, if taken literally, is logically the same kind of a contradiction as the assertion that the circle is an ellipse. The concept distance $= 0$ represents the intermediate idea that subsequently drops out. The conclusion is then as follows: Every figure which, among other things, possesses two foci separated from one another by a certain distance is an ellipse. Thus we see how the fictional intermediate idea drops out in the conclusion. The result itself was the purpose to be accomplished; to attain a generalization of the idea ellipse or to subsume the circle under an entirely different construction. This also reveals the subjectivity of all our classificatory terms. In this way I can subsume all contrary ideas under one another, which is in direct contradiction with ordinary logic.

A number of corrections are connected with the fact that a variation, made at the beginning on the basis of the actual situation, is cancelled when the process is finished. This is particularly true in mathematics. For example, let us take the following problem:—the line a is to be divided into two parts x and $a - x$ so that $x^2(a - x)$ shall be a maximum. This historical problem appeared for a long time insoluble until Fermat solved it by the following device. He substituted for x the part $x + e$, in other words an absolutely arbitrary part larger than that required. The expression

$$x^2(a - x)$$

was thus transformed into

$$(x + e)^2 \cdot (a - x - e)$$

This expression he then compared with the former *as if both were equal though in reality they are not*. Their respective values are clearly different; for example, $6^2(9-6) = 108$, whereas $(6-1)^2(9-6-1) = 50$. This comparison he calls an *adaequalitas* (Diophanti παρισότης). Fermat, in other words, gives the following equations:

(I) $x^2(a-x) = x^2a - x^3$

(II) $(x+e)^2(a-x-e) = \left(x^2 + 2ex + e^2\right)(a-x-e) =$
  $ax^2 + 2aex + ae^2 - x^3 - 2ex^2 - e^2x \ -ex^2 \ 2e^2x - e^3$ **L**

As stated above, he then equated (I) and (II). From this follows,

(III) $x^2a - x^3 = ax^2 + 2aex + ae^2 - x^3 - 2ex^2 - e^2x - ex^2 - 2e^2x - e^3$
  $2aex + ae^2 = 3ex^2 + 3e^2x + e^3$
  $2ax + ae = 3x^2 + 3xe + e^2$

But what came next?

Fermat now simply cancels the previous error by saying that the $x + e$ was merely a fiction to facilitate the calculation. In actual fact I must be equal to II. That however is only possible if $e = 0$.[23] All the expressions containing e therefore drop out, and we have

$$2ax = 3x^2$$
$$2a = 3x$$
$$\frac{2a}{3} = x$$

For example: let the line a have a length 12. Then $x = 8$, $a - x = 4$. Only in this case would $x^2(a - x)$ be a maximum, i.e. $8^2(4) = 256$. Every other division gives a smaller result, e.g. $7^2(5) = 245$; $6^2(6) = 216$; $5^2(7) = 175$. etc.

In this remarkable example we have a picture that is typical of all fictive and discursive thought. Fermat considered the matter as follows:—The imaginary quantity $x + e$ is not equal to that of the quantity x, if e is *real*, but it is equal if $e = 0$. The whole method is thus based on a *quaternio terminorum*, where e is first assumed to be real and then equated with 0. The equating of the two quantities $x^2(a - x)$ and $(x + e)^2(a - x - e)$ is quite impossible. That is why Fermat calls it an *adaequalitas*, an approximate and not a complete equation. Nevertheless he proceeds *as if* the equation were complete, although according to the strict code of mathematics and logic x can never be equal to $x + e$.

Yet the correct result is obtained by this procedure, by interpolating the fiction $x + e$ and equating it with x.

What then did Fermat actually do? He simply cancelled his first error in the course of his procedure, by allowing the auxiliary quantity e to drop out. The equality in the final equation is then no longer an imaginary one, like the first, but an actual one. By this fiction, by this method of antithetic operation an exceedingly important result was here obtained.

Exactly the same method, although somewhat simpler, is followed by mathematical thought in solving equations of the second order. Take the equation

$$x^2 + px = q$$

Thought can do nothing with this. Progress can only be made by means of the method of antithetic operations. But how does thought begin? It introduces the *auxiliary quantity* $\left(\dfrac{p}{2}\right)_2$, and then puts

$$x^2 + px + \left(\frac{p}{2}\right)^2 = q$$

But that would be an error and the antithetic operation is therefore immediately performed by adding the same term to the other side. Thus

$$x^2 + px + \left(\frac{p}{2}\right)^2 = q + \left(\frac{p}{2}\right)^2$$

Now the equation can be solved, for

$$\left(x+\frac{p}{2}\right)^2 = q+\left(\frac{p}{2}\right)^2$$

$$x+\frac{p}{2} = \pm\sqrt{q+\left(\frac{p}{2}\right)^2}$$

$$x = +\sqrt{q+\left(\frac{p}{2}\right)^2} - \frac{p}{2}$$

How did mathematical thought arrive at such a result? By the introduction of the auxiliary quantity $\left(\frac{p}{2}\right)^2$ which is added to both sides of the equation. By adding $\left(\frac{p}{2}\right)^2$ to the right side I cancel the error committed on the left. It is a general mathematical rule that I cannot quantitatively alter one side of an equation, without error, without destroying the equation. I make this error but immediately nullify it by another in the opposite direction.

Formally this procedure is almost identical with that of Fermat. In mathematical terminology we call this a *device* or *artifice*. The second of these devices gives a clear picture of a *semi-fiction*. Here reality is altered, but here the peculiarity of the subject requires an immediate corrective, a remedy, whereas in the other semi-fictions this only takes place later.

In the first mathematical example, too, the correction only takes place later. Yet it provides an example of a true fiction, for here a contradiction occurs. Either $x^2(a - x) = (x + e)^2 (a - x - e)$, i.e. $x + e = x$ and $e = 0$ (the device consists in the use of 0, which is not a number); or x is not equal to $x + e$, and in that case the equation is false. But it is false in the first case too, for $x + 0$ has no meaning. It is then simply equal to x, and what is an 0^2 doing? We should never be able to disentangle ourselves from contradictions in this way. The subtlety of mathematics consists in nevertheless operating with meaningless symbols, like 0, *as if* they were actual numbers.

I maintain that every fictive operation is formally identical with the above mathematical procedure. The identity of the first form, the mere alteration of reality (without any self-contradiction), is quite manifest. As in our second example the term in the equation $x^2 + px$ is arbitrarily altered by the addition $\left(\frac{p}{2}\right)^2$ (it cannot, of course, be quite arbitrary for it must stand in some relation to it), so the psyche, in artificial classification, abstractive or "neglective" fictions, etc., neglects reality, neglects the given perception. But in order that the result may agree, an antithetic operation is undertaken. In the case of our mathematical example this occurs immediately, in other cases subsequently. I am not claiming to have reduced the logical functions to mathematical ones, but to have shown the formal identity of scientific methods in the various fields of scientific inquiry, and in particular of methods which attempt to attain their goal by an alteration of the given facts, by an arbitrary deviation from reality. The mathematical example given merely happens to be the most transparent and shows how it is conceivable that thought should be able to progress precisely *because* of such deviations from reality. The logical function finds itself faced by the stubborn data, the material of thought; but without allowing itself to be frightened thereby it arbitrarily alters the facts, sets the ideas in motion and then quietly changes the mistakes it first made. The formal identity of these logical devices is thus quite obvious.

Berkeley, whose work has been forgotten, reduced the differential calculus to the schema of Fermat and demonstrated (without referring to Fermat's example) that the calculus might be explained in the same way. He came to the conclusion that a double error had been made. The objections of Berkeley are contained in a neglected work, *The Analyst*, and developed at length in fifty sections. Berkeley rendered a great service in pointing out these contradictions in the method of fluxions. Yet he himself fell into an exceedingly amusing error. He exhibits in detail the device by which the mathematicians attained their results, namely by committing a *double* error. Instead, however, of recognizing in this brilliant discovery, which is much more profound than the discussions of the problem by Newton and Leibniz, the reason for the correct result and the *justification for its application*, he rejects the whole method as illogical, as contrary to the traditional code of logic. History has given him the lie, for we still make the same errors to-day, contradictions with the same devices, and rightly. Berkeley made the same mistake elsewhere and in an even more amusing fashion. He proved, quite correctly and with wonderful insight, that practically all the fundamental principles of mathematics were contradictory. From this he drew the conclusion that the mathematician had no right whatever to scoff at the incomprehensible elements and mysteries of Christianity, since their own subject had the same defects. The method of fluxions appeared to him to be such a contradiction and he rejected it for this reason. Like a good Englishman, however, the Bishop of Cloyne did not realize that he would then also have to reject the basic principles of Christian theology.

He actually had the key in his hands! Here then we have a strange spectacle, and one not likely to occur again in the history of science, of a thinker with a key to a problem in his hands—but without the problem itself!

The explanation is this. Berkeley was irritated because some of the "free-thinkers," who were mathematicians, expressed themselves sceptically about the incomprehensible elements in Christian dogma. His whole endeavour was to prove that the mathematicians should sweep their own doorstep first, and that "people who live in glass houses should not throw stones." His object was merely to demonstrate that fluxions were full of contradictions; and it was quite by chance that he discovered and demonstrated that the method cancels one error by another and thus arrives at a correct result!

Berkeley had an unscientific tendency. The real problem was and still remains this:—How comes it that in mathematics a correct result can be obtained by means of contradictions such as those involved in fluxions? Instead, Berkeley sought merely to show the contradictions themselves. But he accomplished more than he intended. For he also discovered the answer to a question that he had never asked. And yet this answer should have led him to the correct question. We certainly have here an unusual occurrence in the history of science.

The answer to the problem is that the correct result is obtained by the method of antithetic error.

The details of this extremely interesting discovery of Berkeley's concerning fluxions (which Drobisch and Carnot subsequently rediscovered) will have to be relegated to a special section. For us this method follows quite naturally from our principle and forms only part of the general fictive methods of thought. The auxiliary quantities introduced drop out later. In mathematics this is only possible by means of antithetic operations of the kind discussed. The real solution of the secret lies in the fact that dx and dy in one case $= 0$, in another $=$ something real, even though this is thought of as very small. That is the mathematical solution. Why correct results are obtained by the fiction of dx, dy and ds can be answered in a number of entirely different ways according as we wish to attack the problem from a purely mathematical standpoint or to explain it by means of discursive ideas. Mathematically this fiction is a simple artifice and the members dx, etc., drop out in the end because an error of the opposite kind has been made, the *quaternio*; they are first equated with something real and at the end with 0. Expressed in logical and discursive terms, we call to our aid the concept of the "infinitely small" which is merely a discursive conceptual construct, but which in the mathematical calculus itself is treated as a mere symbol; in the differential calculus when treated purely mathematically, it is not even necessary. Many attempts have already been made to rid the differential calculus of this concept; there is no need to remove it from the mathematical calculus, since, correctly understood, as Berkeley rightly showed, it is not present there. The whole matter rests on a mathematical device. But critical interpretation endeavours to justify mathematical procedure by this illusory concept. And rightly. Fermat's method can be justified thus:—we say that $x + e$ differs merely *in an infinitely small degree* from x, and they can then be equated. But this is no justification for mathematicians, for no matter how small e is $x + e$ is nevertheless different from x. A purely mathematical treatment, with no discursive elements, can deal with the Fermat method and with that of infinitesimals quite apart from the concept of infinity. Just as e is simply a symbol $= 0$, taken at first as equal to something real, and then to 0, so are ds, dx, dy, first equated with something real and very small (*not* infinitely small), and afterwards with 0. By means of this simple and ingenious mechanism the result is attained. In contrast with this mathematical justification we find a critical justification arising out of a distorted concept of the infinitely small. It is quite correct to say that this can be dispensed with in these methods, but this will not get rid of the contradiction, for we either work with 0 as a number or we first postulate e and ds as very small and then equate them with 0. These are devices whose correct results rest entirely upon the method of antithetic error. First e is introduced, then discarded; and the same with the differentials. The explanation by means of the concept of the infinitely small belongs entirely to the domain of discursive thought and there is some possibility of entirely dispensing with this concept now that we know it to be superfluous. But even if this does not happen, it is and must remain a recognized fiction. What is important is to show how in these fictions the actual result is obtained by errors of an opposite nature. Even if we take e and ds, dx, dy as infinitely small, the method is the same as the above; a fictional construct is thus introduced, for an infinitely small thing is logical nonsense, the bastard offspring of nothing and something. The whole secret is thus finally reduced to the ridiculously simple method of considering a concept in one case as something, in another as nothing.

The infinitely small is a fiction. It is true that by means of this fiction (which is justified by the method of antithetic error), the world of reality can be broken up into its elements; and this makes progress in calculation possible. Thought progresses by means of antithetic operations. The inclusion of these antithetic operations under one concept creates the fictions which are only the symbol of such antithetic operations and antithetic errors. The contradictions found in such ideas are thus both explained and justified at the same time. What matters is not these concepts themselves but the antithetic operations which find expression in them and by means of which thought progresses. How that is possible we have seen from these mathematical examples, and shall see again subsequently. The whole progress of thought rests entirely upon such antithetic operations or errors. Logical progress consists entirely in this to-and-fro movement, not in a straight line but by continually tacking against an unfavourable wind.

We have endeavoured to show in the above mathematical examples how ingeniously the psyche proceeds in order to solve certain difficult problems, by simply turning aside to evade difficulties and attempting to attain its goal indirectly. The examples given were certainly striking, yet they alone were able to reveal to us the actual mechanism of thought, the psychical mechanism of thinking. If all categories and general ideas are, as we have contended, merely fictions, something similar must, of course, take place here. And that it does take place has already been pointed out but must be stressed again. By the interpolation of a category, as we saw, not only is the illusion of understanding developed but a certain order is introduced into the phenomena and the treatment of the data of experience is made possible. Incidentally, I do not see what advantage the grouping of the phenomena into boxes such as categories has over artificial division. From a practical stand-point this grouping is quite valuable, but who to-day would insist that it has led to any actual knowledge, or deny that this division leads to incongruities and contradictions, to "impossible terms", as Lotze calls them.

Our categories are therefore a purely artificial classification of things and the principle of this grouping is exclusively that of the analogy of the succession and simultaneity of unchangeable phenomena with subjective relations. Conspicuous instances are selected from among these to form centres of similarity round which the other similar cases congregate. But in the course of the operation they actually drop out.

The position as regards the second of the main fictions of the logical function, the general ideas, is not very different. They too drop out at the end of the thought-process, just as "*e*" and δs, δx, δy dropped out, because they are fictional, interpolated conceptual constructs without true objective significance. Let us follow such a process throughout its whole course and analyse the psychological mechanism involved therein. Take the case—an old text-book example—that we are to prove Socrates to be mortal because every individual man, and mankind in general, is mortal. The problem here is to predicate of the special phenomenon something that can be observed in many thousands of similar cases. We have, then:

> M—P—Man is mortal.
> S—M—Socrates is a man.
> —————————————
> S—P—Socrates is mortal.

What have we done here? With the help of the intermediate concept "man" we have performed a mental operation whose result is—Socrates is mortal. The intermediate concept itself has dropped out. We are after all only concerned with the individual case of Socrates, of comparing this special phenomenon with innumerable others so that a common coexistence or sequence could be inferred, i.e. could be perceived if the special case ever came within our sphere of perception. In reality this conclusion is an hypothesis formed on the basis of analogy. Because many men, i.e. all men are mortal, Socrates is also mortal. But this mere analogy—and in fact all our knowledge is such—is assisted and facilitated by the intermediate concept "man."

As soon as the result is attained the intermediate concept drops out.

The antithetic operations therefore consists first, in the fact that the general concept "man" is constructed at all, and secondly that Socrates is subsumed under it. In this way the dropping out of the intermediate concept is made possible.

These antithetic operations, however, we also called antithetic errors. We shall now examine this more closely, and perhaps we shall find a further and quite unexpected result. The first error consists in the formation of the concept "man in general." What is this "in general"? It is a pure piece of imagination, a fiction, a fictional conceptual construct. From the innumerable men whom we observe there gradually emerges a general picture, a type, a scheme, in which the most general "characteristics" of these similar phenomena are fused. This picture is a mere ideational construct, for in reality only particular men exist. This construct is known as the general concept "man." Since such a construct does not exist the proposition, "man is mortal"—logically considered—is false, for only individual men are mortal, the individuals A, B, C, D, . . . An assertion concerning "man" is, from a strictly logical standpoint, false, a deviation from actual reality because reality gives us no "man" as such.

The second premise S —M is, however, also false, for in it an individual being is equated with a general concept. The M as a general concept is after all different from the Mabc (abc being the series of individual determinations in accordance with Lotze's terminology), which forms Socrates. Let us call this M^1. In the second premise we have S predicated as M. But that is not true, for S is M^1.

Just as in the above we have a *quaternio terminorum* in the case of e (which in Fermat's work was first equated with something real and then with 0), so here also. In fact, the method of antithetic operations consists in the *quaternio*. First all M^1, M^2, M^3 are grouped together into M by means of an arbitrary abstraction, to which the characteristics observed in the former are ascribed. And *vice versa*, a given M^1 is identified with this M, i.e. the opposite error is made. By this error the arbitrary deviation is again righted and the intermediate concept drops out.

Every conclusion, therefore, where the intermediate concept is a general concept, rests on a *quaternio terminorum*.

Thus in the case of general ideas, too, the method and mechanism of thought is brought back to the general method of antithetic operations which we have been considering.

We must add a corollary to the above. Expressions where the antithetic operation has not yet been completed are strictly speaking just as false as x^2 $(a - x) = (a - x - e)$, where the antithetic operation has *not yet* taken place.

That applies indeed to all general propositions, for the only function of proposition is to serve as an intermediary in a mental operation. The proposition "man is mortal" is then, as many sceptics have already asserted, false, because "man" has no real existence. It is an unreal statement requiring completion like one part of a page torn in half.

Lotze (and similarly Steinthal before him), made the same observation in relation to all the concepts contained in the categories, and certainly with full justice. Steinthal repeatedly calls attention to the fact that the judgment primarily affords a relief from the tension introduced into thought through the formation of individual concepts. And we should naturally agree, for all concepts, all relations put into categories, are fictions. The tension and contradiction result from putting down in isolation a single term of the relationship, a fiction. "Tree" and "green," are examples; separated and isolated they are fictions. But if I say "This tree is green," then the tension is released in the judgment.

> The real principle which leads to the completion of isolated concepts and general judgments is the fact that they are only means to an end, without which they would be valueless. To treat the means without reference to their purpose leads only to tension and contradiction.

This whole matter is, however, only a special instance of a more general phenomenon involved in all fictions. We have repeatedly called attention to the fact that if the fictions, the intermediate links, are taken out and treated separately, we get the husk and the kernel is lost. As soon as a fiction is regarded apart from the ground on which it has developed and apart from the purpose it fulfils, then it is a husk without content such as $\sqrt{-1}$, δy, δx, e,[24] etc., and not merely have we loaded ourselves with husks but with contradictions and illusory concepts. They possess validity only in relation to reality; without it they are dead; regarded apart from their purpose they are valueless. Whole epochs were content with the husks of things; the Middle Ages, for instance, when men were occupied exclusively with concepts unrelated to the living reality where alone they fulfil their purpose. All preoccupation with fictions as such is valueless and harmful because fictions only possess value in their relation to a purpose. The observations made above are only a special application of this general law—which follows with absolute necessity from the nature of the fiction itself, and at once explains so much in the history of science. Concepts and general judgments based upon them have naturally no value except in relation to particular phenomena and their context. That is why the concept demands to become a judgment, because in itself it is incomplete i.e. a fictional conceptual construct. In the proposition, however, the error committed is corrected by the fact that the phenomenon which is torn from its connection in the categories, is reunited again in the individual judgment. In our previous example, "The tree is green" or "Sugar is white", "sugar", "white" are in themselves fictions. On the other hand the judgment, "Sugar is white" expresses a fact. Of course, as we saw above, such a general judgment, regarded from a higher standpoint, is also strictly speaking false, for only particular pieces of sugar exists, not sugar in general.

Our view gains real importance and value primarily through its application to the favourite ideas of philosophers, God, liberty, immortality, *Ding an sich*, the Absolute, etc. and a whole series of other concepts and methods. These are here considered for the first time from this comprehensive standpoint, and they only gain their true significance when they are denied significance for truth. The real value of our inquiry lies, therefore, in the rigorous application of this theory to certain popular concepts and famous ideas, as well as to the whole world of thought, this being the only way in which Critical Positivism can arrive at a complete and consistent result. Not only are these individual concepts, a great number of methods, and all discursive thought fictional, but so is the whole world of ideas. The only thing that is real and will remain real is the observable unchangeability of phenomena, their relations, etc. Everything else is a mere illusion with which the psyche plays about.

CHAPTER XXVII THE LAW OF IDEATIONAL SHIFTS

WE have now obtained enough data to enable us to formulate and psychologically justify an additional law concerning fictions. I shall call this the *law of ideational shifts*. Formulated in general, it is to the effect that a number of ideas pass through various stages of development, namely those of fiction, hypothesis and dogma; and conversely dogma, hypothesis and fiction. The law expressed in this general formula follows as a direct corollary from the psychological nature of the stages in question, just as the law of sound-shifts follows from the nature and the laws of the physiological nature of the sounds themselves. Our purpose demands that we again summarize briefly the nature of the forms in question and describe the condition of the psyche when it takes on one of these forms.

The psychical elements, as we saw, can be divided into fixed and well-established ideas and groups of ideas on the one hand, and on the other hand the ideas whose inclusion in this group still remains a problem.

On one side we have groups of ideas which are without hesitation regarded as the expression of reality; on the other, ideas as to whose objective validity there is doubt. The former are dogmas, the latter hypotheses.

If then we first compare the dogma with the hypothesis, we notice that the latter involves a condition of tension which must be exceedingly disagreeable to the mind. The mind has a tendency to bring all ideational contents into equilibrium and to establish an unbroken connection between them. An hypothesis is inimical to this tendency in so far as it involves the idea that it is not to be placed on an equality with the other objective ideas. It has been only provisionally accepted by the psyche and thus interferes with the general tendency to adjustment. An idea that has once been accepted as objective has a stable equilibrium, the hypothesis an unstable one. The psyche tends to make every psychical content more stable and to extend this stability. The condition of unstable equilibrium is as uncomfortable psychically as it is physically.

This condition of tension, involving as it does a feeling of discomfort, quite naturally explains the tendency of the psyche to transform every hypothesis into a dogma. The only way to transform an unstable into a stable equilibrium is to support the body in question. In the psyche this takes the form of making the hypothesis more stable through repeated confirmation. This, the only legitimate way, may, in the case of certain ideas, not merely involve centuries of labour, but in many cases be quite impossible. So the psyche circumvents it by simply transforming the hypothesis into a dogma by illegitimate methods. The transition from hypothesis to dogma is a psychical process so commonplace that we need not dwell upon it here. It occurs daily not only in each individual but also in communication with others: what one man imparts as an hypothesis, the other accepts as a dogma. Examples of this kind can be found in all fields of human activity and not merely in science. We do not, of course, mean here the gradual verification of the hypothesis but its illegitimate transformation into a dogma. In the latter case the idea is shifted one place in value either gradually or suddenly, and this may therefore be called the law of ideational shifts.

One such, that of *hypothesis* to *dogma*, has thus been demonstrated; and we may now turn to that from *fiction* to *hypothesis*. This is to be explained as due simply to the external similarity of both constructs as we have described them above. Nothing is more natural than that constructs so similar should be interchanged. Two things must be taken into consideration here, however; first that the transformation of a fiction into an hypothesis (not the reverse process) is a natural one; and secondly, that a fiction readily becomes a dogma without the intervention of the hypothesis. Both are easily explained.

If fiction and hypothesis are compared, the condition of tension developing in the psyche due to the fiction is far more important than that resulting from the hypothesis. Consider how complicated a construct a real scientific fiction is. We are asked to assume something that we are convinced is not the case at all; we are to regard it *as if* it were such and such. This means that a conceptual form has been completely included among the others, for it serves in the determination of reality. And yet the psycho is expected during the very process of application to burden itself with the fact that this ideational form is only subjective. Indeed a form of this kind is a positive hindrance and definitely interferes with the tendency toward an equilibration of ideational constructs. The hypothesis only hampers this adjustment negatively and indirectly, but the fiction hampers it directly and positively. The simplest way of preventing this unpleasant condition of tension is to give to the whole idea that has thus been dragged along subjective validity only—to let it drop out entirely; and since the ideational form is, otherwise, on a basis of equality with the others, to recognize it as a dogma. Thus fiction becomes simply a dogma, and the *as if* a *because* and a *so that*. The other method, which is just as frequent, passes through the stage of the hypothesis; the ideational form receives the smaller tension-coefficient of the hypothesis; and the *as if* becomes *if*.

We have thus considered one series of phenomena produced by the law of shifts; the fiction becomes an hypothesis, the hypothesis a dogma. Sometimes, in cases which will be mentioned later, the fiction becomes a dogma immediately. The driving-force in this transformation and shifting is the equilibratory tendency of the psyche which is impatient to rid itself of the uncomfortable condition of tension. We should remember that this tendency towards the stabilization of ideas is quite natural. Yet however necessary this tendency is and must be for science, to precipitate the transformation is bound to give rise to error.

Before adducing examples we may append to the above discussion an account and justification of the second process. If the first process, in virtue of its precipitate nature, is an unscientific process of transformation, the second is a scientific process of regression.

When science begins its work, it finds in the psyche innumerable dogmas not all of which are religious in character. These are in a stable condition, to which, after minor disturbances, they always return. It is different when experience and reflection have gradually made these dogmas doubtful. The psyche still tries to adhere to them in obedience to the law of inertia, and does actually adhere to them; and when this is no longer possible with a stable equilibrium, when the position has been too much shaken, then it contents itself with the unstable equilibrium of the hypothesis. The dogma becomes an hypothesis and the idea is reduced in value by one degree.

New doubts, new shocks follow; and here again the psyche has but two paths available. Either the idea is simply eliminated and falls to the ground— science having completed its destructive work, the false ideational constructs are discarded; or the other way may be taken. The idea may possess such a theoretical and practical value that the psyche will not readily reject it; it cannot do without it for ever, or even indefinitely. The conceptual construct is then transformed from an hypothesis into a fiction, either into a permanent, persistent fiction, or into a provisional one, so that in the end if not permanently necessary it fades away. According to the law of persistence of concepts, the psyche will, if it is at all possible, prefer the second alternative. Ideational constructs that once become firmly rooted are retained as fictions rather than discarded.

This then is the law of ideational shifts, a law which receives its best confirmation from the history of civilization and the history of science, while on the other hand it explains and groups together a series of phenomena. Finally we must add that a single idea can run through both processes, i.e. through the process of transformation as well as through that of regression.[25]

The law of the "transformation of ideas," as this phenomenon may be called, covers three epochs, three stages in the life-history of an idea (naturally not of all but merely of a number of ideas). These three stages are the *fictional,* the *hypothetical* and the *dogmatic.*

> It is not only figuratively that these stages can be called "epochs in the life-history" of an idea, but to say that they constitute stages in the organic development of ideas is quite justified. They are products of an organic activity, for as such we have recognized the logical function, and are therefore organic products with a quite definite evolutionary history.

As in the laws of sound-shifts only certain changes and inversions have, for specific reasons, made themselves felt in many words, so with ideas.

The first process, the transformation of a fiction into an hypothesis and of an hypothesis into a dogma, is particularly frequent in history. Every historian can give numerous examples where what were at first conscious myths (and such myths are built up psychologically in the same way as fictions) become transformed into historical hypotheses and then into historical dogmas, or the reverse.

> This historical law was enunciated by Zeller in his address on "Literary and Historical Criticism." Conscious fables and myths first became historical hypotheses, then dogmas, and *vice versa*. Zeller quotes the legend of the "Four hundred and sixty Pforzheim burghers" as an instructive instance. This was first a fable, then an hypothesis and then a dogma.

Additional examples can be found in the mythology and legendary history of every people. Frequently these myths omit the stage of the hypothesis and become dogmas immediately, but the intermediate links have often been lost. All myths are fictional creations, similes, etc., which were not infrequently built up by individuals quite consciously and later gave rise to hypotheses and dogmas. We find the regressive process also very clearly developed in this field. These dogmas are at first retained until critics cast doubt on them and they become hypotheses; and if the doubt becomes so strong as to disturb the idea of their objectivity, then the idea is thrown aside. If on the other hand such ideas are of value as tribal legends, like the Tell legend, they are retained as fictions, as symbols.[26] These examples taken from history are, however, not the most instructive, because the ideas concerned generally arose as myths of unconscious origin. But they serve as parallels illustrating the law and making it more concrete. For, actually, the same psychical laws are operative in this transformation.

The philosophy of religion yields better examples. Myths, similes, even the conscious fictions of the founders of religions either become dogmas to the founders themselves, or to their adherents among the people, and rarely pass through the stage of hypothesis. On the other hand, during the decline and break-up of a religion all three stages stand out very clearly. At first all religion consists of general dogmas (the dogma has itself perhaps developed from an hypothesis or even from a fiction). Then doubt appears and the idea becomes an hypothesis. As doubt grows stronger, there are some who reject the idea entirely, while others maintain it either as a public or a private fiction. This last condition is typical of every religion so far known when it has reached a certain age. It can be seen to great advantage in Greek religion, where the Greek folk-deities were at first general dogmas, though for Aristotle and many other philosophers they were only hypotheses. Subsequently they became fictions for the educated classes, who adhered tenaciously to the worship of God, or rather of the gods, although convinced that the ideas represented nothing real. This was also the case with certain philosophers whose contradictory utterances about the gods can be explained only in this way. We find the same development in Christianity. Its original dogmas became hypotheses for the philosophers of the seventeenth and eighteenth centuries. But what were they to men like Kant or Schleiermacher? Merely fictions!

Even in philosophy and science themselves we find these gradual transitions both with single individuals and throughout whole epochs. The Platonic myths (of the transmigration of souls, etc.) were originally fictions, which in the mind of their originator had already been transformed from μῦθος to, λόγος i.e. had become hypotheses under the influence of the equilibration of psychic tensions.[27] With his followers, for example the Neoplatonists, they became true dogmas. Later on they resumed the status of hypotheses, and to-day, to students of Plato, they are pure fictions, mythical ideational forms.

At first the Platonic ideas were probably only regarded as fictions by Plato himself, yet it was he who converted them into hypotheses and after that they were dogmas for many centuries, later becoming hypotheses again. Dühring well called attention to the fact that they were probably merely fictions originally.

A valuable confirmation of this view is found in Herbart who (according to Flügel, *Probleme* 140) asserted that logical general ideas (which for Herbart, as is well-known, were only logical ideals, i.e. fictions) are first hypostasized and then converted into mythological entities.

The same thing happened to Kant's *Ding an sich* as we have already indicated. It passed through various stages for Kant himself. In his strictly critical period it was probably a mere idea, i.e. a fiction in our terminology. But the process of transformation into an hypothesis had already taken place in his own mind. To his disciples and to Herbart and Schopenhauer, the *Ding an sich* had already become a firm dogma. Then it became an hypothesis again, and now many Kantians like Stadler and Lange are prepared to recognize it as a mere fiction, as a construct useful in practice but without any real theoretical value for knowledge. Others reject it altogether.

As we know, various ideas are necessary at an earlier period (for certain purposes), "from which a more enlightened age frees itself entirely" (Dühring, *Kr. Gesch, d. Philos.*, p. 317). Thus an idea like immortality may be necessary for a time in order to give birth to moral ideas. But once these have been developed, the scaffolding, i.e. the concept in question, can be demolished.

We saw in the special case of heuristic fictions, how what were formerly dogmas become hypotheses, and what were formerly hypotheses became fictions. That was the fate of teleology, and the fate, too, of the Ptolemaic system. On the other hand it cannot always be determined historically whether such dogmas were originally meant to be taken merely as fictional.

Linnæus and Adam Smith built up their respective systems as purely artificial ones. Their followers either turned them into hypotheses or interpreted them as hypotheses (for it requires a high degree of mental training to recognize an idea as fictive), and then these hypotheses themselves at once became dogmas. Adam Smith's system was later regarded as an hypothesis, and since Buckle's convincing demonstration it has been treated almost universally as an artificial system built up on a fiction. But the idea was regarded earlier so definitely as an hypothesis or dogma that it was believed not only that all actions were egoistic but that it was actually necessary so to act, as has been well shown by Lange.[28]

This is, of course, even more the case with fictions which have been formed by the psyche unconsciously and then present themselves to consciousness as fully developed dogmas; the whole division of things into categories, for instance. Originally a dogma, this became an hypothesis; and since Hume and Kant its fictional nature has been firmly established, for categories were of course originally mere fictions. Similarly, a number of constructs, which at first were fictional, have in the course of time become hypothetical, particularly ideals and fictional archetypal forms. Thus, for example, an original ideal state was conceived as a fiction; yet in a moment it became historical.

This is clearest in tropic and analogical fictions. The fictional analogy of the state with a contract is transformed into the assumption of an historical social pact, primeval historical rights; in short the theoretical foundations immediately develop into the assumption of historical instances. Then out of these hypotheses fictions are later developed.

Thus with Newton and Leibniz themselves, fluxions and differentials became hypothetical entities, and later, dogmas. After that there was a regression.

In the same way Kant's assumption of intelligible freedom had become an hypothesis even in his *Kritik*, while for Schopenhauer the hypothesis was already a dogma.

The same or something similar has been the fate of the atom, of the infinitely-small and the infinitely-large (an unjustifiable generalization), and of the Absolute.

Gradually, however, the fictions that have become dogmas are recognized as fictions again, and the process of ideational shifting comes to an end.

> This law thus cuts across Comte's law of the three stages of development in the sense that Comte's law stresses the material content of the ideas, which gradually alters (mythical material becomes metaphysical and this becomes positive); whereas our law stresses the *formal* change of the ideas themselves, whose content remains always the same, whereas according to Comte it changes.

Some of these fictions are immortal, those that make discursive thinking itself possible—the categories and general ideas. But this is only in their capacity as fictions, with the consciousness that they are fictions.

Progress can be discerned not only in the logical conscience of mankind in that the contradictions in fictions are noticed, but also in the logical capacity. For to maintain a fiction as a fiction implies a highly developed logical mind, one that does not surrender too precipitately to the equilibratory impulse but carefully distinguishes between means and end. To maintain the purely critical standpoint as represented by Hume and Kant, considerable mental energy is required. All attempts subsequent to Kant are nothing but attempts, and very premature attempts, to resolve that condition of tension which though uncomfortable at least disturbs mental slumber.

> To what an extent the tendency to get rid of this unwelcome condition (both doubt as well as fiction belong here) is connected with the "principle of least energy" is a matter for special treatment. This law, formulated by Avenarius for the psyche, is considered by him only in connection with its beneficial effects. But it can also be injurious, as for example in the attempt at a

premature resolution of tension. Thus the neo-Kantians often over-hastily convert Kant's fictions straight into hypotheses and even dogmas; as for example, in the case of the Kantian fiction of intelligible intuition. Thiele, in his work *Kants intellectuelle Anschauung* (Halle 1876), fails entirely to recognize that this was for Kant only a fiction which his followers naturally transformed into an hypothesis, and which for Thiele himself becomes a false dogma. The same holds true for the so-called concept of an "identity of thought and existence," for "absolute knowledge" and many other fictional concepts. Thiele altogether failed to realize that such concepts, "the infinite" included, are but auxiliary concepts formed by Kant. It is undoubtedly true that Kant, by his inexact method of expression, was responsible for these and similar misunderstandings, and that, in part, he himself made the same mistake.

Compare on this point Riehl, *Kritizismus,* Vol. I, 437. "In one place in the *Critique of Judgment* Kant described the whole conception of another kind of intuition, such as the intelectual . . . as a mere auxiliary concept for making clear the independence of the idea of Thing from the forms of intuition arising in the subject. Thus interpreted, the idea is a good one; in fact, it serves as a passage through the realm of imagination, to render more concrete the theory of intuition as an appearance of things. The possibility of a super-sensuous world is exclusively dependent upon this concept, which is useful only for methodological purposes. And yet Kant made a positive use in practical philosophy of the idea of this imaginary world!" Here we have a good description of the transition that took place in Kant himself without his knowledge. The idea of intellectual intuition which was at first only a methodological fiction, developed into an hypothesis and then into a dogma.

This law of the resolution of psychical tension not only dominates the special law of ideational shifts but also a large part of all intellectual development, and, like all natural laws, operates for good or evil, according to the circumstances.

One beneficial effect is that by this tendency to adjustment dogmas and hypotheses are, where possible or expedient, transformed into fictions. For so long as these ideational constructs are supposed to have objective value, contradictions and difficulties arise which disappear if we regard them as mere fictions. This is the critical method for which Kant prepared the way.

Thought conducts us automatically to certain illusory concepts just as in vision there are certain unavoidable optical errors. If we recognize this logical illusion as necessary, if we accept the fictions established thereby with a full realization of their significance and, at the same time, see through them (e.g. God, liberty, etc.) then we can cope with the logical resultant contradictions as necessary products of our thinking, by recognizing that they are the inevitable consequences of the inner mechanism of thought itself. No capital, then, can be made out of this for ordinary scepticism on the ground, for instance, that human thought is too weak for a knowledge of truth. But since thought cannot get along without these fictive auxiliary concepts, it must necessarily accept the contradictions that go with them. Even though we recognize these fictions as such theoretically, they yet remain from a practical standpoint necessary elements in our thought. Thought of its very nature necessarily develops these fictions, and thanks to its special combination of instinct and ingenuity, it also creates the contradictions which accompany them. Thought of its own accord twists the threads furnished by experience into knots. These sometimes aid it but may also entrap it, especially if they are supposed to be something in objective experience itself, instead of what they really are—subjective auxiliary constructs.

C

CONTRIBUTIONS TO THE HISTORY AND THEORY OF FICTIONS

PRELIMINARY REMARKS

THE THEORY AND PRACTICE OF FICTIONS

OUR historical task falls into two parts which must be kept strictly apart. The first consists of a presentation of the scientific and practical utilization of the fiction in the course of the historical development of science, the second of a description of the gradual discovery and theory of these fictions. In the introduction to this book we laid down the principle that logical theory must take its empirical data from scientific practice. Our enumeration of the fictions found in present-day science showed quite clearly that they do actually occur. It is, however, also one of the tasks of logic to follow, in connection with the general history of science, the gradual evolution of scientific practice in general and that of each scientific method in particular. Hitherto this task has always been confused with another, that of describing the gradual development of logical theory. The slow development of a cognitive instrument presents features of the greatest interest, and a history of method is consequently an indispensable complement and preliminary to any methodology.

CHAPTER XXVIII THE FICTION IN GREEK SCIENTIFIC PROCEDURE

THE scientifically valuable fiction is only a recent growth. If the hypothesis, which is, after all, a very simple method, a form of thought lying near the surface, has but recently been correctly applied and developed in science, and if we have had to wait for modern science to show us how hypotheses are to be built up and how valuable they are for serious research, we may assume that the fiction, which presupposes an artificial and sophisticated form of thought, came into use much later. We know that in other fields also man first tried all the natural means before making up his mind to use artificial ones. Indeed it took a long time for the scientific fiction to appear in a pure form and it is exceedingly interesting and instructive to observe how the human mind gradually embarked on these artificial and dangerous methods.

To employ such an instrument, a freedom and independence of logical thought is necessary, an emancipation from ordinary prejudices, such that we can only expect to find a productive utilization of this method where the logical function has really freed itself from the idea of its identity with reality, and where it is more or less aware of the chasm between its own operations and the actual state of affairs. The Greeks lacked the independence of thought necessary for the application of such an instrument, an independence that shows itself above all in an ability courageously to tear oneself away from reality and yet, in spite of this deviation, not lose hope of returning to it again. The Greek recoiled before the bold flight of thought which seeks to attain its goal by arbitrary and contradictory ideas. Where, however, in classical times the realization of this deep chasm between thought and reality was awakened—and it has probably never been so fully awake as among the Greek sceptics—it resulted in a marked theoretical depression. The logical function had not yet achieved those tremendous scientific feats which are distinctive of modern times. As soon, therefore, as the split between thought and being, between the logical operations and the actual operations in the world of fact was realized, the natural consequence was a scepticism which in spite of its childishness has something magnificent about it. The problem already stated, as to how it happens that in spite of the application of mere subjective thinking full of contradictions, we nevertheless arrive at a correct determination and treatment of actual phenomena—a problem of which Kant was already aware—this problem could not be formulated in ancient times simply because thought had not proved that it could perform any great feat. The Greeks were still so closely and slavishly bound to the world of immediate perception that when this world was shaken they often despaired of all thought. Where the ancient sceptic found thought beginning to pursue its own path and departing from reality, he immediately supposed that he could declare all thinking void, without reflecting that thought yet leads to correct practical results. He did not dare to strike out boldly along this path and discover whether, in the end, it did not lead him back to reality.

This is particularly clear in mathematics where the ancients probably attained their best scientific results. Even their most complicated methods are cumbrous in comparison with modern ones. The best example is to be found in the method of exhaustion, and here I base myself on the judgment of authoritative mathematicians. In this connection a remark made by Drobisch is particularly interesting.[29] He expressly states that the Greeks were particularly careful to avoid these very methods which are used to-day for the solution of the same problems, the fiction, for instance, that the circle consists of an infinite number of triangles, or that it is a polygon with an infinite number of sides, a fiction by means of which we attain the result that the diameter is to the circumference as 1 : 3. 1416, far more neatly than did the Greeks. The Greek mathematicians purposely avoided every concept which involved a contradiction, particularly that of the infinite, and they were afraid of these fictions because of their contradictions, whereas modern mathematicians make use of this fictive method without worrying about the contradictions.

The ancients, however, did employ fictions, not merely in the form of hypotheses, which were in reality only fictions, but conceptual forms accompanied by a consciousness of their subjective and fictional nature, though, of course, in a crude and incomplete form.

In the later period of Greek mathematics and mechanics we find various beginnings of scientific fictions, all of which may be regarded as crude attempts to utilize this form of idea scientifically. In politics we meet with Plato's Utopian fiction of an Ideal State. The legal fiction was hardly employed among the Greeks. The Socratic method is only an approximation-method, and belongs to the semi-fictions, the only kind that really come in question. We have already dealt with the Platonic Idea as a fiction which developed into an hypothesis and even into a dogma in the mind of its own author. Plato's mythical fictions are a very good type of fiction. The *as if* is here very clearly in evidence. Yet, on the whole, they are far more in the nature of poetic similes than scientific fictions. At best they are of equal value logically and ethically with the tropic fictions of modern theologians.

Here too belongs the fact that Plato constructed allegories, that of Heracles at the cross-roads, for example, and that the old dogmas of folklore were retained as useful fictions, or actually regarded as such—assuming, that is, that they were originally only fictions which later developed into articles of faith.

We must not forget the religious allegorical symbolism which so attracted the Greeks, i.e. the procedure common to philosophers like Pythagoras, Parmenides, Empedocles, Anaxagoras, Metrodorus and others, who continued to employ the traditional religious dogmas as fictions. Later on, the Stoics, in particular, very often allowed the creations of popular religion to continue in the form of fictions; and so did the Neoplatonists. The same is true of the Platonic myths, which contain certain hitherto neglected elements of the critical theology and the religious philosophy of the Greeks, with a conscious appreciation of the fictional or symbolic nature of the religious ideas.

The only really useful fiction from a purely methodological standpoint, though it has no material value whatever, is a thought of Parmenides which has caused his interpreters a good deal of trouble, but which fits very well into our theory and can only thus be properly understood. Parmenides, as is well known, held that multiplicity and change were meaningless illusions; there was no beginning; all change and all separation were not true Being but Not-Being, something unreal and unthinkable. Only Being eternally at rest, unchanging, and unmoved, only what persisted in eternal, divine Sameness, was real. Existence is an indivisible whole, a uniform continuum, limitless and absolute. The world of sensory appearance, on the other hand, is mere illusion, and unreal. Becoming and passing away are but a delusion of the senses. Phenomenal nature is the sphere of the nonexistent.

Parmenides appended to this account of his cosmology a further exposition which the historians of philosophy have sought in vain to reconcile with his main thesis and which they finally agreed to call a "hypothetical" view. The world of illusion is, in this supplementary view, treated as having Being, and as consisting of two principles, light and darkness, or fire and earth, and all things are only a mixture of these. To call Parmenides' physics "hypothetical" seems to me inexact and inadequate. It would be hypothetical were it not for the first part of his metaphysics, where all change and the whole empirical, divisible world is declared to be mere illusion. Parmenides cannot, without being self-contradictory, assume the real existence of these elements, i.e. they are not hypotheses but mere fictions. Parmenides does not say, "the world of appearance consists of fire and earth"; he can only say, "the world of appearance may be regarded *as* if it consisted of fire and earth." These two elements are for him only fictional constructs to which everything can be reduced.

Only in this way can sense be made of his philosophy. Fire and earth are thus not hypotheses for Parmenides, but fictions. And whether his comparison of Being to a self-contained sphere is anything more than a symbolic-analogical fiction, is doubtful. I would treat this comparison simply as evidence that Parmenides proposed to regard absolute Being from the point of view of its perfection and self-sufficiency as a sphere, and they are only related for purposes of comparison. The spherical form of Being is for Parmenides not an hypothesis but a fiction.

This is the most notable example of a really scientific use of a fiction by the Greeks, but owing to the inadequate expression of the original text the real meaning of Parmenides is essentially conjectural.

CHAPTER XIX BEGINNINGS OF A THEORY OF FICTIONS AMONG THE GREEKS

AN investigation of the scientific theory of fiction among the Greeks is not much more fruitful. Before there could be a logical theory of fictions, they had first to be created and employed in scientific practice—for if there is any field where theory does not precede practice, it is here. The scanty beginnings of a practical employment of the fiction in ancient times hardly sufficed for the creation of a theory, and had anyone in those days really been struck by the peculiar characters of the fiction, he would certainly have at once confused it with an ordinary assumption or hypothesis. The view that we can and must think, without thereby necessarily implying anything as to the nature of existence, and yet be able to attain correct practical results, was one to which the ancients never attained. That we are compelled to think of something was always regarded as a proof of the reality of what was thought of. That what we are (apparently) compelled to think of, is not objective but can only be a means—such an idea is an entirely modern product. The form of the conscious fiction only developed after people had learnt by experience, long enough and often enough, that thought does not mirror reality and yet does arrive at reality; that mental processes are ultimately adequate. It was then that the idea arose that the phenomenal world was not a mere illusion, but a symbolic and expedient conceptual construct enabling us to move and to orientate ourselves in the world of the unknowable and the unrealizable, without knowing it as it is. We do this by forming in its place a conceptual construct which has become more appropriate and suitable through a progressively richer experience, and which we can substitute for the unexplained world, at any rate *practically*; though theoretically this conceptual world with its contradictions cannot be a mere reflection of reality but only a subjective instrument.

Since, however, the fiction has generally been confused with the hypothesis until to-day, or has been frequently symbolized by the same word, a few remarks as to the meaning of the Greek ὑπόθεσις will not be superfluous. We will not embark here on a philosophico-lexicological excursus, but the little we have to say may perhaps throw some light on the subject.

The use of this term by the ancient philosophers is of such a nature that even in a particular instance we often cannot decide whether an hypothetical or a fictional method is meant. As a rule it refers to a purely rhetorical, stylistic fiction that has not as yet attained a true scientific value. Plato, in particular, likes to play with a number of possibilities, leaving it open whether we are dealing with hypotheses or fictions.

Plato is also fond of employing the ὑπόθεσις as a method of first granting an opponent the truth of a proposition, in other words, of assuming its truth, i.e. thinking of it *as if* it were true, and then of developing from it certain consequences to prove its falsity. Here this hypothetically assumed proposition, this proposition fictively set forth as true, forms the foundation for a *reductio ad absurdum* in an indirect proof. This is of course particularly suitable for a dialogue, though it later also finds a place in actual scientific discussions. Two processes must be distinguished here: first the statement of the proposition itself as an assertion made by an opponent or as the opponent's objection; and, secondly, the provisional statement of this proposition *as if* it were true, for the purpose of subsequently proving its falsity from its consequences.

The forms mentioned so far have clearly very little interest for our purpose, and we must turn to Aristotle for more light.

> Where Aristotle speaks of ὑπόθεσις in the logical sense, he understands thereby in its wider meaning generally a proposition on which some inference is based. Such are the premises of a conclusion, and the axioms. An ὑπόθεσις of this type is made with the full consciousness of its falsity and might perhaps better be called a logical fiction. In apogogic proof, a proposition which is notoriously false is provisionally accepted as true. This in itself, however, is of little importance for our question.

Apart from the word ὑπόθεσις Aristotle (Met., XIII, 7) speaks of absurd and fictitious assumptions, πλασμαῶδες = τὸ πρός ὑπόθεσιν βεβιασμένον (he proposed to call "fictitious" what is brought in forcibly to suit an hypothesis). By this term he admirably expresses the essence of error and also that of fiction.

> It is a "violent" assumption, for instance, in this sense, if Aristotle accepts in one place "pure form" (without matter) which in another he declares to be really impossible. The assumption of "pure matter" (without form) is, however, for Aristotle a fiction and not an hypothesis. It was his followers who transformed it into an hypothesis. Perhaps this throws light on Plato's doctrine of matter, which in one place he calls ἀληθινὸν ψεῦδος, a kind of conscious error, i.e. a fiction. This is the sense in which Plato is probably speaking when he says of matter that it can only be attained by means of a spurious conclusion νόθῳ συλλογσμῷ. Here we have a part of the early history of fiction which has never been investigated.

With regard to fundamental notions of geometry Aristotle approximates to the view that they are to be regarded not as hypothetical but as fictional. Whether this can safely be assumed from the passage (Met., XIII, 8) where he speaks of Plato's "indivisible line", is doubtful. On the other hand, Met., XIII, 3 is worth attention, where he speaks of the fact that if we suppose things separated and treat them as separated, this does not lead us into error; any more than when we draw a line on the floor or call it a foot long, when it is not really so. There is nothing false in such presuppositions. Indeed everything can best be studied by supposing separate what is not separate as the arithmetician and the geometer do. The idea of the abstractive fiction is fairly accurately developed here. Aristotle is trying to justify the procedure of mathematics against the reproach that its subject-matter is a non-existent entity and not something independent.

The term ὑπόθεσις takes on a special meaning later where it is employed, particularly in mathematics, as the equivalent of αἰτήματα = postulala, petitiones and by mathematicians, uti: punctum carere magnitudine et esse individuum. Formally, these assertions are mathematical postulates; in content, however, as this example shows, they are fictions. The new meaning of ὑπόθεσις is here quite clear and distinct. The word does not signify an assumption with regard to reality but a presupposition that is only admitted "on sufferance".

The original indefiniteness of ὑπόθεσις = "assumption" tends to be differentiated into the two possibilities; in the one case it agrees with reality and in the other it expresses propositions which, though they serve as premises and as the basis of further conclusions, can yet only be postulated, for they are really, in our terminology, fictions. This ambiguity is inherent in the concept of "assumption" and is quite manifest in Aristotle. It is only by degrees that we get a clearer differentiation between hypothetical and fictional assumptions.

It is obvious from the above that the Greeks made no clear-cut distinction between hypothetical and fictional assumptions and that, as they expressed it at any rate, the confusion is undeniable, and the ambiguity cannot in every case be avoided. In so far as the expression ὑπόθεσις applies to fictional assumptions, these always refer only to rhetorical or stylistic fictions or to assumptions which provisionally provide the ground for a chain of argument and which may therefore be called *syllogistic fictions*. True methodological fictions in our modern sense are thereby excluded.

But it is worth remarking that among the post-Aristotelian sceptics we find an intimation that assumptions may from a scientific standpoint be intended only as fictional. Unfortunately this particular period in the history of Greek philosophy has not yet been adequately studied. Our sources are far too meagre to allow us to form an accurate opinion. We may, however, recall the argument of Sextus Empiricus (*adv. Math.*, IX, 207) against causality, and his claim that it belongs to the relative. The relative (πρός τι) however, has no existence (ουχ ὑπάρχει) but is merely added (ἐπινοεῖται μονον) mentally. Here we have the first glimmerings of the view that the categories are not a hypothetical expression of reality but merely fictive means to enable us to understand it. But if a theory of fictions can be found anywhere in Greek philosophical literature it will only be among the Sceptics, who were well aware of the chasm between thought and existence although they were unable to advance from sceptical negativism to a critical positivism. The Sceptics repeat and amplify certain assertions of the Sophists who clearly had an understanding, however distorted, of what to-day we call a fiction. Thus we everywhere encounter the deficiency mentioned above, namely, that the Greeks were so dependent on immediate reality that when they seemed to be losing touch with it they at once fell into a theoretical apathy, and failed to take the further step to the positive concept of thought as an instrument, and of the world of ideas as an expedient symbol.

CHAPTER XXX THE USE OF THE FICTION AMONG THE ROMANS

ONE type of scientific fiction was fully developed among the Romans, namely the juristic. Their complicated legal relationships made this necessary. In the formulation of legal decisions certain cases occurred which could not be treated according to the existing statutes. These were treated as analogous cases and forced quite arbitrarily under certain laws. To quote Forcellini (*Lex. Tot. Latinit.*, II. 287 ff.) on the *fictio legis*. "Fictio legis dicitur, cum per legem aliquam cuipiam conceditur, ut alia conditione censeatur atque in praesenti est: v. gr. lex Cornelia sanxit, ut, qui apud hostes morerentur, eorum testamenta perinde valerent, ac si in civitate decessissent. Itaque lex quodammodo *fingit*, eos in civitate testamentum condidisse, *quamvis* inter hostes fecerint." Here then we have an obvious *as if*, which we have called the external sign of the fiction. *Fictio*, we read in Pauly's *Realencyclopädie* (Vol. III. p. 473) was the term used by the Romans for a facilitation and cir- cumvention of the law, created by praetorian enactment, and consisting in the fact that something, strictly necessary in law, might, under certain circumstances, be regarded as having happened or as existing, even if it had never happened or did not exist. In this way certain legal conclusions follow even if the relations presupposed do not occur as the law prescribes. Thus, to follow the *Reallexicon* further, there were certain charges which could be made by a *peregrinus* acting as though he were a *civis*, which as a *peregrinus* he had no right to prefer. A person who had lost something before complete *usucapio*, was treated *as if* he had secured *usucapio* and could therefore prefer charges. A *capitis deminutus* was regarded under certain circumstances *as if* he had not suffered *capitis deminutio* (Gaius, III. 84). The *honorarius emptor* may appear as a plaintiff *qua* fictive heir. Such *actiones*, which were extended by fictions to other cases not covered by the law (and therefore an illegitimate extension), were called *actiones utiles* (Gaius, IV. 32–38).

CHAPTER XXXI BEGINNINGS OF A THEORY OF FICTIONS AMONG THE ROMANS

FOR our purposes the gradual development of the expression *fictio*, which we employ to-day in contrast with the Greek term ὑπόθεσις, is very important. We must therefore pay some attention to it.

The most noteworthy feature here is the fact that the Romans very clearly realized the ambiguity inherent in the Greek expression ὑπόθεσις, and for that reason translated the Greek word in two different ways. Since the Latin terminology remained in force from that time on and lasted throughout the whole of the Middle Ages, so that its influence continues even to-day, the clear-cut division made by the Romans between hypothetical and fictional assumptions has had very important consequences. So it cannot be denied that the Romans performed a useful service for science in this respect. Not only did they independently develop the legal fiction in practice, for it was only known in embryo to the Greeks, but they quite clearly distinguished these assumptions and thus made a theory possible. They recognized that the fictional assumption must be strictly separated from the hypothesis. The practical and sober sense of the Romans was quite correct here; much more so than the imaginative faculty of the Greeks. For the latter entirely confused the two forms of assumption and their otherwise rich language had no expression for fiction, just as it presented other awkward features which in Latin are happily overcome. The Romans translated ὑπόθεσις sometimes by suppositio, sometimes by fictio—so that here we find a strictly logical distinction instead of the confusion of the Greek.

The most natural translation of ὑπόθεσις is suppositio.

CHAPTER XXXII MEDIEVAL TERMINOLOGY

A FEW words must also be devoted to the Middle Ages. There can, of course, be no question here of a scientific method, so we must not look for any scientific fiction in the strict sense. That the Arabs regarded the Ptolemaic system as a fiction (cf. p. 36 above) is probable though not absolutely certain, but it suggests that there may have been certain tentative beginnings.

Nominalism naturally declared all general ideas to be ficta, fictiones, without, however, attaching to fiction the positive meaning which it has for us and which was already contained in the legal fiction. The "negative sense" of the fiction we call the assumption, for instance, that general ideas are expressions for something unreal, i.e. definitely invented and fabricated, whereas by its positive sense we mean the realization that these fictions have nevertheless great practical value, that they serve as the means for acquiring knowledge. This is assuredly the meaning of scientific fiction: an assumption, namely, whose complete falsity or impossibility is admitted, but which is adopted, nevertheless, for certain practical or theoretical purposes. The explanation of general ideas by the Nominalists suffers, like that of the ancient Sceptics, from the fact that they stop short at negativism and do not proceed to a critical, positive standpoint, to a realization that these instruments of thought are absolutely necessary and useful acts of the intellect, which though more or less worthless theoretically, still fulfil certain practical purposes, facilitate thought and accelerate its movement. Yet there was a profound significance in the *fictio rationis*, as these general ideas are called, for it marked a great advance on Platonism, a great advance in epistemology as a whole, that Nominalism should have opposed the exaggerations of medieval Realism. According to this latter view every general concept was supposed in Platonic fashion to have some existing transcendental thing corresponding to it. It was the path of Nominalism which was later taken by Locke.

The obvious comparison of the *fictiones rationis* with the *fictiones juris et legis*, a comparison that would unquestionably have led to interesting results, did not strike the Nominalists, for otherwise they might have discovered that the *fictiones rationis* perform the same service for knowledge that the *fictiones legis* do for jurisprudence, and that both are *actiones utiles*. (Leibniz seems to have been the first to make such a comparison in his *Nouveaux Essais*.)

All the further uses of *fictio* come from this medieval expression, and particularly that prevalent in English philosophy from Locke to Hume, whose "fiction of thought" leads to exactly the same mistakes as the nominalistic *fictio rationis*, namely a one-sided negative rejection of the concepts designated as fictions, instead of a realization of their positive utility and necessity.

CHAPTER XXXIII THE USE OF FICTIONS IN MODERN TIMES

WE now proceed to an account of the use of the scientific fiction in modern times. Here its employment is incomparably more extensive.

So far we have found in the *legal* fiction the only really scientific fiction. We should, however, remember in this connection that jurisprudence is not really a science of objective reality but a science of arbitrary human regulations. Moreover the fiction was applied rather in the practice of law. On the other hand it was not yet as extensively employed as in modern law, where it has been used specifically in the foundation of Public law and where, moreover, the fiction of juristic persons is very widely adopted, even to the extent of including the *State* itself in so far as the State can be regarded as a juristic person. Both in the special *practice* and in the *theory* of law, the fiction has been far more extensively employed in recent times than in the classical period. In England especially it has been much used and abused. The fiction serves to subsume a given case under some general rule, when the case in question can thereby be treated juristically. For instance, it is assumed that a husband is the father of a child if he was in the country at the time of the child's conception, i.e. since every single case cannot be investigated, the general assumption is made that every husband is to be regarded as the father of a child if he was in the country when the child was conceived. This example is given by Leibniz in his *Nouveaux Essais* [E.T. p. 260], but it is rather a *praesumptio* than a true fiction. A fiction in the juristic sense can only be spoken of if a husband, whose wife has committed adultery, is nevertheless regarded, if he was in the country at the time, as the father of the child. He would then be regarded *as if* he were the father of the child, although he is not and although we know he is not. This last addition is what differentiates the *fictio* from the *praesumptio,* for in the *praesumptio,* a presupposition is made until the contrary is proven, whereas the *fictio* is the acceptance of a statement or a fact although we are certain of the contrary. An example of a real fiction is the fact, for instance, that in England (in the eighteenth century) every crime could be treated *as if* personally directed against the king, and every plaintiff had the right to bring his action under this fiction. The practical value of this fiction lay in the fact that trials under this fiction were far more stringent than those under the ordinary laws, for charges thus made were brought before a special court. Here we have the "*as if*" in all its force. The Code Napoleon also allows a number of legal fictions; for example, the household goods of a woman are regarded as *immobilia*. Similarly we find fictitious property, etc. and under certain conditions an "enfant conçu" can be regarded as "né" if important legal consequences are involved.

In legal practice the employment of fiction may lead both to benefits and also to the grossest forms of injustice, as when all women were treated *as if* they were minors.

In legal theory the fiction was particularly used in the theory of contract, in so far as the State was regarded as the result of a contract and was treated as a juristic person.

This fiction, which was already known to the ancients, has been very extensively used in recent times.

Another favourite method was the *ideal* or *Utopian* fiction. In the nineteenth century the French Socialists, Fourier, for example, were still employing this method of spreading their ideas by the description of towns and states *as* if the ideas they promulgated had been there realized. Such a method passes very easily over into the realm of phantasy and forms the transition from a scientific treatment to pure poetry. But this whole group of scientific methods must not be overlooked, though they are neither very important nor do they present any theoretical difficulties.

With the growth of science the fiction began to be more extensively employed.

The first of the main fields where really great results were achieved was *mathematics*. Modern mathematics is characterized specifically by the freedom with which it forms these fictional constructs. A careful study of the development of mathematics brings to light a number of such fictions. We do not so much mean thereby such *substitutions* as the employment of letters instead of figures as a notation, though even this simple method is strictly speaking a fiction. By the fiction that a, b, c, x, y are *numbers*, and by treating them *as if* they actually were, enormous progress is made; results can be generalized and calculations simplified. This is usually called an application of symbols, but taken logically, we are dealing here with a substitutive fiction. Thought itself, in general, when operating with words instead of perceptions, makes use of such symbols.

But quite apart from this, fictions have been more and more used in recent mathematics. Their most famous and most fertile application was in the measurement of curves by Descartes, Leibniz and Newton. This is really the classical example. By means of the fiction of coordinates, of artificial lines (all artificial lines are fictional methods), and by means of differentials or fluxions, a treatment of curves became possible.[30]

The methods of unjustified transference, of zero-cases, of abstract generalization, etc. are modern mathematical devices. They were generally known by these names; great mathematicians have always been distinguished by the invention of devices, and these devices are always essentially based upon fictions. Even the drawing of artificial lines is such a device. Schopenhauer called attention to the fact that no real knowledge can be obtained by their means. But such devices are not meant for this but for *practical* purposes.

It is upon such devices and fictions that the concepts of the infinitely large, and of negative, fractional, imaginary and irrational numbers, are based, all of them serving the purpose of simplifying calculation and all in a strict sense logically contradictory.

The utilization of these devices, to which the progress of modern mathematics is due, has continued right into our own time, and every really new discovery in mathematics rests upon such a device. The device of abstract generalization has now been applied to space, and spaces of more than three dimensions have been imagined.

The method of determinants depends on such an artifice.

Of special interest are the fictions of line, surface and volume elements as a foundation for the use of measure-numbers. Mertschinsky, in particular, has utilized the fiction of minima of constant size for this purpose. This fiction had already been employed by Giordano Bruno in his *De triplici minimo et mensura*, and *De monade, numero et figura*. But Bruno still hesitates whether to treat his minima as fictions or hypotheses. The same uncertainty is found in Leibniz who, on the one hand, declared that *minima infinite parva* were only a *modus dicendi*, but in the interests of his monodology was inclined to assume that they were hypotheses. Whether Leibniz hit upon his idea through the influence of Bruno has not yet been determined. It is not improbable. But Bruno's principle of application was different, for he used his minima in order to lay the foundations of mensuration, while Leibniz was concerned with the measurement of curves.

Other mathematical fictions refer particularly to the infinite; as, for instance, infinitely distant points, infinite stretches, limits of infinite surfaces, convergence at infinity, etc.

In modern mathematics the employment of such fictional concepts is quite general, but mathematicians and philosophers have so far not developed any methodology for these devices, though such a methodology would certainly be very illuminating as regards the use both of the infinite and the absolute from a philosophical standpoint. Generally speaking, these fictions are methodological accessories for arriving at results which could otherwise not be obtained at all or only with great difficulty.

Extensive application of the fiction is also made in mechanics, in mathematical physics, and even in chemistry, all of them sciences which have been fully developed only in modern times.

Numerous other examples of the modern use of fictions have already been given in our classificatory chapters. We there saw how a number of sciences have successfully utilized the scientific fiction in all its different forms. The true nature of these devices was frequently realized, but they were often employed quite instinctively without any methodological understanding. Hence a number of famous controversies, turning on the question whether certain concepts were legitimate or not. This question has already been partly discussed in detail above.

The fiction may find some employment in philosophy too, but here if anywhere caution is necessary. It can never serve as an explanation of anything but only as a means of simplifying thought and for the purposes of practical ethics.[31]

Maimon put forward the view that Leibniz' monodology and pre-established harmony were only fictions; but with this we cannot agree, for Leibniz interpreted his doctrines otherwise. But had they been fictions they certainly would have been very useless constructs. It is one question whether Leibniz desired his doctrines to be understood in this way and quite another what value we are to attach to such constructs. Leibniz undoubtedly regarded his doctrines as hypotheses and not as fictions. Whether after they have ceased to function as hypotheses they can still be used as fictions—as we saw was possible in other cases—is doubtful. This is more likely to hold for Spinoza's theory of parallelism. For us this is only a fiction but one of tremendous scientific and heuristic value. On the other hand, metaphysically the relation between the physical and psychical can scarcely be such as Spinoza and the modern Spinozists, such as Bain (following Hartley), Lange, Wundt and others, assume.

Whether Kant's fiction of a Ding an sich is still really of value to us requires a special investigation. But a sharp distinction must be drawn between Kant's realization that the Ding an sich is a fiction and his actual employment and utilization of this fiction. He himself employs it for scientific purposes and in his own hands it was transformed into an hypothesis.

We have then to distinguish two facts, first that Kant recognized the employment of the Ding an sich up to his own time as based upon a fiction, and secondly, that he himself created the same fiction. What he recognized in others he did not recognize in himself, namely, that his Ding an sich was also a fiction.

This error prevented him from recognizing actual sensations as the sole reality and from discovering that all real knowledge comes only from observation of the sequence of sensations.

Kant allowed the tacit provisional assumption that there are egos and Things-in-themselves, to remain as a scaffolding. Had he destroyed that scaffolding and rejected them both he would have found that sensation was the sole reality left.

When, therefore, Jacobi says that "without the presupposition of objects as Things-in-themselves, and of ideational faculties upon which they work, it is not possible to enter the Kantian system, though with them it is quite impossible to remain in it"—in other words that the beginning and the

continuation of the Kritik are mutually "destructive"—he was quite correct. Kant, after having discovered and asserted in the Kritik that Things-
in-themselves are merely fictions, had only to recognize frankly that these
presuppositions of his were nothing more than provisional devices for the
purpose of arriving at his conclusions; he had only to recognize, in other
words, that there is only empirical knowledge, and he would have been
left, as was Maimon, with sensations as the sole reality. But he allowed his
schematic frame to stand; and whenever fictions do not drop out they lead
to contradictions.

We see from this that Kant had an importance for our subject in two
respects:

1. He discovered that the categories are fictions. We must, however, add
    that he obscured this point in so far as he allowed the methodological
    device of the ego to remain and attributed them to it as innate forms of
    the ego instead of removing the ego. This point is of unusual impor-
    tance. With the aid of his methodological device, the *ego* and the *Ding
    an sich*, Kant discovered the fact that the categories were subjective, but
    by retaining the *ego*, he made the categories into innate forms, and by
    retaining the *Ding an sich*, he failed to recognize the reality of the world
    of sensation.
2. He himself employed the method of fictions, many of his concepts
    being artificial. He employed an artificial classification, the method of
    abstract generalization, and the methodological device (introduction
    of fictional concepts)[32]— and yet he was not clear as to what he was
    doing.

Kant thus used a number of devices which were transformed into hypotheses both for himself and many of his followers. That a thinker should be
far from clear about his own methods and discoveries, is a phenomenon of
frequent occurrence in science.

Kant's method was extraordinarily acute and bears to the methods of
others who have arrived at the same result the same relation as does the
procedure of a modern mathematician to the ancient methods, in the measurement of the circumference of the circle, for instance.

But this is obscured by Kant's reactionary tendencies, as shown in his justification of rationalism as well as in his defence of certain dogmas. Kant's
real scientific objects were, however, the determination of the limits of

thought and experience, the proof that the conceptual and ideational forms had merely subjective value, and the proof that only immediate experience is real. His opponents have frequently recognized his weak points. He allowed his methodological device to stand. That was his main error, and in mathematics, too, it leads to contradictions.

On the other hand a device which is subsequently dropped is an absolutely legitimate artifice. Without it we cannot philosophize at all. Thus in all thinking we necessarily proceed from the illusion of the contrast of things and the ego, and later on this device is itself eliminated. The comparison of thought with calculation is far more correct and legitimate than was formerly supposed. It is a detailed knowledge of the remarkable methods of mathematics which first enables us to realize that thought employs the same methods.

The same is true of Kant's practical philosophy. He proves first that the ideas of practical philosophy are merely fictions. He himself consciously employs them in this sense until eventually they are again transformed into hypotheses.

We cannot, of course, expect more from his disciples than from the master himself. The post-Kantians made the same mistakes as Kant; only in a more marked degree, both in theoretical and practical philosophy. In theoretical philosophy only Maimon, and in practical philosophy only Schleiermacher, have even approximately recognized the truth.

The law of ideational shifts can be very clearly demonstrated from the fate that befell the Kantian concepts among his disciples. The fictive device tends more and more to become a (false) hypothesis. The maintenance of the pure result is, after all, quite difficult; for man has an inclination towards dogmatism. The study of Hume and Comte has proved a corrective to the errors of Kant and his successors.

Fictions were first extensively employed from the seventeenth to the nineteenth century, particularly in the fields of mathematics, physics, sociology and philosophy, where their different forms and methods have developed in great variety. Gradually, fictions of ever greater importance make their appearance, though it must be admitted that every now and then misapplications occur of methods which it is certainly easy enough to misunderstand.

We would dwell particularly on the gradual evolution of the fiction and the continuous extension both of its area of application and of its varieties. This process had already begun in the sixteenth century and reached its climax in the seventeenth. In the eighteenth the logical theory began to assert itself, though not markedly. In the nineteenth, their application increased, particularly in mathematics and physics, as well as in political economy. Hypotheses recognized as false were still retained in large numbers as heuristic fictions. Present-day text-books and monographs on higher mathematics, mathematical physics and sociology, contain many good examples of fictions.

CHAPTER XXXIV THE THEORY OF FICTIONS IN MODERN TIMES

LEIBNIZ in his *Nouveaux Essais* tried to explain the legal fiction methodologically. The Port Royal *Logique* on the other hand attempts neither a methodology nor a theory of fiction, though its theory of abstraction is of value for one group of fictions. It was Hobbes who introduced the comparison of "reason" with "reckoning"; he did not, however, discuss the fiction.

Condillac's *Logique* is valuable because it emphasizes the method of antithetic operations (analysis and synthesis).

Wolff, the first logician to discuss the fiction, did so with considerable insight, and his work as a whole has been undeservedly neglected. Zeller has recently endeavoured to do him justice. Wolff was qualified to undertake such a methodology, not only as a pupil of Leibniz, but as a mathematician of independent views.

He both appreciated the importance of mathematical fictions and discussed them, though in a rather cursory manner, according to present-day standards; and in his metaphysics he dealt with certain fictional concepts and operations. Thus, in his Ontology, § 404, he inquires whether the fiction $\frac{1}{1}$ is a fraction; cf. § 77 on the fiction of the "land of Cockayne," and § 797 on the fiction of the infinitesimal (*non sunt verae quantitates sed saltent imaginariae*), and again § 804.

In his *Elementa Matheseos universae* (Halle, 1741) he gives a very acute analysis of a number of mathematical fictions, and treats them as parallel to legal fictions. He is particularly interested in the *arteficia analytica*. Wolff was thus the first logician to deal with these fictions.

But it was Maimon who paid most attention to the fiction in all his writings, from the point of view of its interest both to methodology and to epistemology.

He stressed this point in almost every one of his now almost forgotten works; and even where his writings are cited, this point is entirely overlooked. In the account of Maimon's doctrines given by Erdmann and Fischer and later by Witte, the point is passed over in silence.[33] And yet this is Maimon's only real achievement, and is closely connected with his attitude to the *Ding an sich*.

Among the later logicians, Herbart in particular developed this point in his *Lehrbuch zur Einleitung in die Philosophie*, § 152, where the "chance aspects" as well as the auxiliary concept of space and various mathematical methods are dealt with. The theory of fictions was also clearly stated by Herbart in the same passage and he well remarks that thought must have certain transit-points, "that it pursues its own way in order subsequently, at the main points, to get once more into touch with the nature of things."

In the division of Herbart's book devoted to natural philosophy, the mathematical and physical fictions are frequently mentioned; in particular, § 160, the fiction of the divisibility of the mathematical point and the fiction of regarding it as a magnitude; similarly § 161.

But the most important fact is that mentioned in § 162 (Hartenstein, I, 319), where for the first time in philosophy the difference between the fiction and the hypothesis is clearly, definitely and fully developed. "Fictions like that of the centre of gravity are extremely useful and deceive no one."

Lotze, who is often in agreement with Herbart, is the only modern logician who has included the fiction in the sphere of logical discussion.

Bain in his two-volume work on logic also made an investigation of fictions. but in an inadequate and incomplete manner.

Yet Bain, who had clearly grasped the idea of a methodology of all science, should have felt the necessity of assembling material from all the sciences for this purpose.

We must devote a few words in conclusion to the gradual application of the concept of fiction to the theory of knowledge.

Locke here comes first. He declared a number of concepts to be subjective; but no more than Hume, in whose writings the expression "fiction of thought" occurs repeatedly, did he succeed in attaining a positive realization of their value as useful fictions. Hume merely succeeded in proving negatively that the categories were subjective.

Kant started to prove the value of these subjective concepts and to elevate them to the position of real logical fictions in our sense, but his system failed because he was hemmed in by false tendencies and prejudices. The real progress Kant made beyond Hume was his proof not only that the categories arose merely as conveniences, but that they were actually produced by the psyche itself—thereby subscribing to a false a priori philosophy; and also his attempt to show the real advantage of these subjective concepts.

Kant wanted to allow the subjective concepts some part and value in the acquisition of knowledge—in contrast to Hume who regarded them in a one-sided and negative way as imaginary—by showing how through these subjective concepts the objective world first comes into existence.

But he became entangled in a false position because he regarded the subjective conceptual forms sometimes as fictions, sometimes as hypotheses, and sometimes as an unfortunate cross between the two.

Modern positivism is on the way to asserting—indeed it has in part already asserted—that all categories are for it only symbols and fictions, that "discursive thought," as Maimon says, "is a fiction."

But in order to know what is meant by the statement that anything is a fiction, logic must first show at length and methodologically the characters of a fiction, the service it performs and where it can be applied. The application of the logical distinction between fiction and hypothesis to the theory of knowledge will then become profitable.

D

CONSEQUENCES FOR THE THEORY OF KNOWLEDGE

CHAPTER XXXV THE BASIC PROBLEM OF THE THEORY OF KNOWLEDGE

FROM the chaos of sensations emerges differentiated perception. No concept of a particular thing is as yet discernible in this chaos, for the vast, vague, nebulous mass of sensations only gradually takes on a rotatory movement and only gradually do the individual elements that belong together combine to form perceptual objects and intuitions of the particular. In intuition we already have a union of sensory data, due to the psychical attraction of the elements. The forms in which this union occurs are the relations of the whole and its parts, of the thing and its attributes. Here the logical function has already begun.

Before proceeding further, however, we must add something that is bound to be decisive for our inquiry. The psyche works over the material presented to it by the sensations, i.e. elaborates the only available foundation with the help of the logical forms; it sifts the sensations, on the one hand cutting away definite portions of the given sensory material, in conformity with the logical functions, and on the other making subjective additions to what is immediately given—and it is in these very operations that the process of acquiring knowledge consists—and it is all the while departing from reality as given to it. Indeed it is inherent in the very idea of working over, of elaborating, the data, that those data should change, that immediate reality should be altered. The sensations produce within the psyche itself purely subjective processes to which on the modern view nothing in reality—picture it as we will—can correspond.

Here, therefore, we see the tendency of the logical function to alter reality and deviate from it. What we must insist upon, consequently, is that even in the elementary logical processes a deviation from reality takes place. The very fact that Thought tries to describe Being, that it serves to maintain and facilitate the relations of living beings, goes to show that Thought and Being cannot be one, that ways of thought cannot be those of reality. It is improbable and unnatural that two processes on such different bases, those of subjective thought and objective events, should take the same form. But at the same time it is hard to imagine to what precisely in reality these subjective forms should correspond, once we have recognized that reality is essentially an ordered system of movements. Ever since nature presented this side to us, all the subjective additions which we have made in the form of logical trappings, i.e. the categories in the widest sense of the term, have been more and more clearly recognized as such. And only when these ornaments were laid aside and nature stood before us naked and undistorted, did we ascribe to the psyche itself the additions with which—whether out of unselfish generosity or childish self-deception—it had bedecked the external world. This deviation from reality increases in the higher stages of psychical development, and eventually reaches so high a point that it is recognized as such. But it is not for that reason discarded as worthless. Indeed, in dealing with its data the psyche always deviates more and more from reality. Yet quite apart from the fact that at a certain stage of intellectual development these deviations (which are at first handed over to the objective world as its property) are recognized as such, they do not usually make themselves felt either in practical action or in the results of thought. Although the course of thought deviates from that of reality, thought tends constantly to reunite with reality. We have already mentioned this on several occasions and set forth the problem arising from it. It does not merely mean that we wish to know what there is in the nature of objective existence that enables thought, when proceeding in accordance with the laws of logic, to reunite with fact when it has run its proper course. Such a formulation seems to us inadequate. The proper formulation of a problem is, as is well known, half the solution. On the other hand, to put a question falsely is to go half way towards error; and this in our opinion is the case with the above method of putting the problem, for it presupposes that the field of inquiry in which the solution is to be sought belongs exclusively to the "nature of things," whereas in fact the reverse is true, and the solution is to be sought in the nature of thought itself. The nature of real events is sufficiently well known for us to be compelled to think of them as dominated by an unalterable regularity. Objective processes take place with an absolute unchangeable necessity, no matter how we interpret them, and the subjective world is linked up with these objective events in a manner not yet explained.

If, therefore, subjective events depart from reality and alter it either by subtracting from or adding to it, and if, in spite of this, correct practical results are obtained and the final outcome of thought tallies with reality—from these two contradictory statements there arises the important problem: How does it happen that although in thinking we make use of a falsified reality, *the practical result still proves to be right?*

The solution must lie in the thought-process, which must therefore be subjected to a special examination. The course of nature is unchangeable and proceeds according to hard and unalterable laws. Nature has an iron will; but thought is an adaptable, pliant, and adjustable organic function.

CHAPTER XXXVI THE FALSIFICATION OF REALITY BY THE LOGICAL FUNCTIONS (*LOGICAL OPTIMISM, PESSIMISM AND CRITICISM*)

Where the logical function actively intervenes, it alters what is given and causes it to depart from reality. We cannot even describe the elementary processes of the psyche without at every step meeting this disturbing—or shall we say helpful?—factor. As soon as sensation has entered the sphere of the psyche, it is drawn into the whirlpool of the logical processes. The psyche quite of its own accord alters both what is given and presented. Two things are to be distinguished in this process: first, the actual *forms* in which this change takes place; and secondly, the *products* obtained from the original material by this change.

The organized activity of the logical function draws into itself all the sensations and constructs an inner world of its own, which progressively departs from reality but yet at certain points still retains so intimate a connection with it that transitions from one to the other continually take place and we hardly notice that we are acting on a double stage—our own inner world (which, of course, we objectify as the world of sense-perception) and also an entirely different and external world. There are then exchange centres, where the values of one world are changed into those of the other and the active intercourse between both worlds is made possible, where the light paper currency of thought is exchanged for the heavy coin of reality, and where on the other hand the heavy metal of reality is exchanged for a lighter currency which nevertheless facilitates intercourse.

For the ponderous processes of matter the swift-winged operations of ideas are substituted. An ever greater condensation takes place, with the sole object of animating, facilitating, and enriching the interchange. Only after paper-money had been invented did trade expand on a vast scale, and only with the progress from the ponderous processes of the lower world to the ever more delicate processes of thought and the introduction of the thought-instrument did the organic world develop into the history of human beings. The difficulty in either case lies entirely in the reduction of one system to another, in effecting the exchange. Large quantities of false paper-money, many false ideas, that cannot be changed into material values, find their way into circulation; the nominal value of paper-money is not always paid, but the price which rules on the market. But all higher speculation and the whole of our intricate system of exchange are only possible by this expedient and by these fictional values.

> "Fictional value" is the name given in political economy to paper-money and such ideas as, for instance, the pound sterling, etc. The paper is regarded *as if* it had the value of metal; the computation is made *as if* we were really dealing with "pounds sterling." Our analogy has thus a real basis. In the same way Littré in his Dictionary, Vol. II, p. 1664, says, "Le papier-monnaie est une valeur de fiction; monnaies fictives d'une valeur imaginaire, de fiction, par convention." In particular the term serves to provide a real basis for analogies of which we have made frequent use. Concepts too are merely conventional signs. The main question here is to recognize specifically the identity of the formal logical activity which is operative in all these instances, whether it is as simple and uncomplicated as paper-money, or as complicated and important as categories and general concepts. In every instance it is the fictive function that is here at work.

Highly differentiated transactions are only possible by this means, even if we are forced to admit that there has been many a "swindle" in the realm of thought, where people have given up valuable material goods for value-less paper, for valueless thoughts. It is from this point of view that thought is comparable to paper-money. The deviation from reality or the fiction can according to circumstances work either for good or for ill, as is also the case with the paper-currency selected for purposes of comparison. The laws which govern the organic function of thought, like those governing nature, are all indifferent to us, all work blindly. Whether they work for our advantage or disadvantage depends upon circumstances. In themselves they are double-edged. The alteration of reality in the logical processes, the change of the given ponderous material into the light and evanescent thought which so little resembles it, involves dangers as numerous as the possibilities which it opens up for rapid mental operations. The degree of confidence we have in thought, in its work and its products is exceedingly important for our investigation. At any rate we must leave behind us the naive belief *that what is thought of really exists*, that the forms and methods of thought can be rediscovered in the world of fact. This naive and happy faith, this unquestioning confidence of the trustful, simple, natural man in the products of the logical function, i.e. in *his own* world is rudely disappointed by bitter experience. Thinking and the logical function do not constitute the central point where the radii of the world meet; are not the axis on which the world turns. Rather does the logical function play a modest role in nature's economy and the changes in the real world which result from its products—powerful and extensive though they may be from the human standpoint—are, in comparison with cosmic changes, of ridiculous insignificance. But though they may be small when contrasted with the grandiose and powerful agencies of the real world which operate and work under the dictates of a hard and clumsy necessity, like blind giant energies, this conceptual world is -nevertheless *our world*, in which we live and feel. Only we must not put any philosophical system in the place of reality, led away by the fact that it seems to us enchanting, ideal, glorious and noble. The thinker who indulges in this high flight, is committing, formally at any rate, exactly the same mistake as the most primitive savage when he objectifies the creations of his thought. These remarks are designed to encourage an attitude of mind essential for the proper understanding of the logical functions and their products; we must be neither dogmatic nor sceptical, but critical.

Dogmatism is a form of logical optimism which approaches the logical functions and their products with unbounded confidence, regards thought with an admiration and satisfaction so exaggerated that doubts are not raised at any point. The logical infallibility of thought is adhered to by the logical optimist as though it were a Gospel in which he blindly believed; and with the same intolerance that accompanies religious superstitions he regards the logical form in which he happens to think as better than any other.

This logical optimism is harmless and innocent enough when found among primitive people, but it is a questionable attitude and becomes definitely dangerous and disastrous when encountered in men of a more advanced type. The logical edifice, even if it be but a house of cards, is so carefully protected against contact with the fresh breezes of doubt, that no one thinks of mistrusting the logical function. Optimism here becomes conservative, reactionary and injurious like everything that outlives its usefulness. It becomes superfluous and dangerous—though for primitive man it was a necessity, unless he was to die of starvation while pondering on the problem whether the space through which he shot his arrow was real, or infinitely divisible, or whether "the arrow was ever stationary." Like Achilles he overtakes his "tortoise" without allowing the infinite divisibility of the space between them to mislead him. Had primitive man already begun to doubt the objectivity of his logical forms he would never have become civilized. But if a thinker at a higher stage of civilization does not question this objectivity, he becomes a primitive man again and, in the worst sense of the word, an uncritical man.

An instructive contrast to the behaviour of the logical optimist is presented by the logical pessimist or sceptic. He may rise to the mistrust of a Gorgias, or sink to the mysticism of a Huet or to the emptiness of an Agrippa of Nettesheim. He can find no words severe enough to characterize the uncertainty, invalidity and unreliability of thought. With the Solipsists he doubts the existence of the external world and in the end is not even certain of his own existence. Thought is regarded as an extremely defective instrument which falsifies reality, and leads us astray and deceives us. But if dogmatism, in spite of its naive products. is not fruitful, scepticism is definitely barren. Yet this mistrust, in addition to being strongly motivated, is of considerable service in preparing the way for the critical attitude which we ought to adopt towards our world, i.e. to the logical functions and products. The service rendered by this logical pessimism cannot be overestimated; it destroys naïve and unquestioning faith and, as against the assertion or naïve acceptance of the identity of thought and reality, insists strongly on their absolute distinction. It discredits the frequently used and abused simile of "the reflection of the external world within the psyche" which is supposed to portray the objective world truthfully and without alteration. The logical pessimist would prefer to regard thought as though it distorted reality like a pair of coloured spectacles or a concave mirror.

True criticism or logical positivism proceeds to examine the thought instrument dispassionately and objectively. With logical pessimism it frees itself from childish beliefs in the power and unlimited validity of thought, and with optimism it holds firmly to the fact of the ultimate practical coincidence of thought and existence. The valuable outcome of pessimism is the habit of seeing in these conceptual constructs primarily nothing more than subjective products. Instead, therefore, of demanding with the dogmatist that we accept their reality until their unreality is proved—a thesis that from a practical point of view is the only useful one—it reverses the process and *mutatis mutandis* applies the juristic formula "Quisque praesumatur malus, donec probetur bonus", demanding that every logical product and every logical function be taken for what it actually is, a mere logical construct; and insisting on a special proof before the reality of any given mental construct or logical form is assumed. Theoretically this is the only valid and useful principle.

CHAPTER XXXVII CATEGORIES AS FICTIONS (*WITH A GENERAL DISCUSSION OF THE PRACTICAL PURPOSE OF THOUGHT*)

BETWEEN the reception of sensations into the psyche and its processes, and the resolution of concepts and the final thought-constructs into sensations as the result of practical activity and of a theoretical comparison of mental operations with real happenings—between these two gates, the entrance and the exit of the mind—lies the psychical world. Everything that takes place between these two points belongs exclusively to the wide domain of the psyche.

As soon as the sensations have found their way into the psychical processes they are, as has already been noted, worked over into concrete pictures.

The differentiation of the chaos of sensations into "thing-and-attributes," into "whole-and-parts," etc., is a purely subjective achievement. These are all merely forms of apperception into which sensations group themselves and combine.

By observation we can discover whether the combination of these concepts in the psyche is based upon an inner relationship, for we find certain sensations always recurring in the same connections. One single instance of simultaneity or immediate sequence of concepts is no guarantee for the psyche that these sensations belong together and will always recur in the same way, nor is there any reason for assuming this. On the other hand, when there is a frequent recurrence of the same combination of concepts, the psyche feels itself called upon to distinguish this amidst the chaos of sensations. We believe that this would not occur without some practical stimulus, and that it was necessity, in the widest sense of the term, which awakened the tendency to form a special category for this persistent conjunction of concepts. In addition to the material of sensations as such, the time-relations in which they occur, and the rhythm in which the interplay of perceptions and sensations takes place, are also given. In this temporal sequence of sensations, those sensation-units become conspicuous in the stream of perceptions which always recur in the same combinations. This recurrence can take a double form—it can be either simultaneous or successive. Here we are concerned in the first instance with simultaneous combinations. Perceptions of landscapes, animals, plants, all pass before the psyche in chaotic confusion. Yet, however much the stream of perceptions may change, the combination of a certain configuration with a definite colour always recurs; the figure of a branching plant with green leaves. These particular combinations are constantly repeated.

The branching plant always appears connected with the same sensation of green, and this definite combinations of sensations is for the mind at first accidental. But it does not remain so. From the mechanism of sensation comes the form of Thing and attribute. There arises the object "tree" and its attribute "green." The first group of sensations—that of the shape— represents the object, the other—green—the attribute. The particular units of this relationship are then apportioned to the different sensations. But the matter by no means ends here. The leaves drop off—the tree becomes leafless. How, after that, can the relation of the object to its attribute be applied to the residual perception of the branching plant? Apparently only because the visible is regarded as a property of an invisible thing. Not only, then, is the general relation (thing and attribute) mentally added to the world directly given, but one member in the relationship is projected into the realm of the imaginary and changed into pure fiction.

Let me here call attention to the shifting and interchangeable nature of the categories. What is at one time thought of as an object is afterwards thought of as an attribute. From this capacity of shifting from one thing to another (for instance, cause and effect, whole and part, reality and appearance) we may infer that the categories are subjective; and it also enables us to explain how one member can be projected outside the realm of experience so that what is experienced comes to be its correlate. It is thus that we get the fiction of a substance, supposed to exist outside the realm of experienced objects, which then become mere *attributa* or *modi* of the substance. In the same way there arises the fiction of an absolute cause of which the world of experience is supposed to be the effect; and also the fiction of the macrocosm whose parts are supposed to constitute the objects of experience; and finally we get the fiction of an absolute "Thing-in-itself" which is supposed to be the essence of phenomena. All these are unjustified transference-fictions, since a relationship which only has a meaning within the sphere of experience is extended beyond this into the void. As irrational and imaginary numbers like $\sqrt{-a}$ arise through the unjustified transference of mathematical operations, so the fictions of an absolute substance, absolute cause, absolute whole and an absolute essence—in contrast to appearance—arise through the unjustified extension of categorial forms.

The fiction of substance thus arises because one member of the relation, Thing-attribute, is transferred from the given world to a non-existent and imaginary realm. Another example will make this process clearer. In perception the sensation-complex "sweet"—"white" is constantly recurring— in the substance "sugar". The psyche then applies to this combination the category of a thing and its attribute:—"The sugar is sweet." Here, however, the "white" appears also as an object. "Sweet" is the attribute. The psyche is acquainted with the sensation "white" in other cases, where it appears as an attribute; so that in this case too, white is treated as an attribute. But the category thing-attribute is inapplicable if "sweet" and "white" are attributes and no other sensation is given. Here language comes to our help, and, by applying the name "sugar" to the whole perception, enables us to treat the single sensations as attributes. Thus the "thing" leaves the sphere of actually perceived sensations, and is thought of as a special carrier (ἐπινοῖται μονον).

To thought, in its earliest manifestations, this seems a very innocent procedure; but from our present attitude to nature and the world we must regard it as a very doubtful alteration and a falsification of pure experience. Who authorized thought to assume that "white" was a thing, that "sweet" was an attribute? What right had it to go on to assume that both were attributes and then mentally add an object as their carrier? The justification can be found neither in the sensations themselves nor in what we now regard as reality. What then is the true state of affairs? What are these sensations which the psyche projects as attributes of an object? The sensations which the psyche turns into attributes of an objective thing are processes in the psyche itself. In any case the psyche has proceeded in a very arbitrary manner; for its real experiences are sensations and sensations alone.

From the mechanism of sensations the form "thing-attribute" has developed, and this certainly is not to be found in the sensations themselves. Even if this form does correspond to some type of reality, a question with which we are not here concerned, we could only remark that the Thing is an addition made by the psyche, which sets up the sensations as attributes of things. Thus the process of thought is initiated, and the scaffolding is erected.

We must, above all, remember that what is given consists only of sensations, and that everything which is not mere sensation is the work of the psyche itself. But the very process of working the sensations into categories is an alteration of experience, a falsification of reality as given. The creation of categories passes through various processes, the description of which constitutes the special task of psychology. What primarily interests us here is the fact that by analysis and addition an alteration of our immediate data takes place, a result that brings us materially further than the mere combination of sensations in perception. For here we are already in the domain of conceptual and discursive thought. Analysis, comparison, abstraction and combination are the psychical processes by means of which this theoretical elaboration proceeds.

But what is gained thereby? If we examine the matter carefully we shall find that this type of conceptual knowledge has very great value as a means to practical action but no value whatever for real scientific knowledge. The error has always lain in attributing to the means value which really belongs exclusively to what is achieved by the means.

All that is given to consciousness is sensation. By adding a Thing to which sensations are supposed to adhere as attributes, thought commits a very serious error. It hypostasizes sensation, which in the last analysis is only a process, as a subsistent attribute, and ascribes this "attribute" to a "thing" that either exists only in the complex of sensations itself, or has been simply added by thought to what has been sensed. We must clearly realize that when thought subsumes a sensation-complex under the category of object and attribute it is committing a very great mistake. Where is the "sweet" that is ascribed to the sugar? It exists only in the act of sensation. Where is the "sugar" that is supposed to be "white," "sweet," "hard", and "fine", whose "essence" is supposed to consist in these qualities? Thought, in fact, deals with the sensation complex twice, once as Thing and again as Attribute. The succession of sensations alone is given and out of these two entirely different conceptual values are developed.

Thought not only changes immediate sensation thereby, but withdraws further and further from reality and becomes increasingly entangled in its own forms. By means of the "imaginative faculty"—to use this scientific term—it has invented a Thing which is supposed to possess an Attribute. This Thing is a fiction; the Attribute as such is a fiction; and the whole relationship a fiction.

But further: by isolating both members of this relation, the logical function magnifies the error it has made. The relationship itself is of a twofold nature; the object is isolated and its attributes are regarded as separated and as separable from it. We must admit that the logical function thus lays itself open to the charge of making a series of arbitrary acts and errors.

These isolated factors and elements strive to re-combine, and demand to be re-united; disunited they are a contradiction, a tension. Such is the case here. A contradiction exists between the thing and its attributes thought of in isolation. For what can "thing" be without "attribute", or "attribute" without "thing"? The tension is here released in the judgment—"The sugar is sweet"; and we believe that this constitutes understanding, knowledge. But is anything really gained by this judgment except a mere subsumption under an empty category? Certainly; for thought has now corrected its first error. It first duplicated the sensation into a thing and its attributes and then separated the attribute from the thing. Now, in the proposition, it unites them again.

It is generally claimed that a proposition gives us understanding and knowledge. This seems to us to be claiming too much. The tension is indeed released, and the contradiction between thing and attribute (apparently) removed by the equation, but nothing is attained thereby except a subjective feeling of satisfaction. In actual fact nothing whatever is attained for knowledge, but something of great practical utility. All this activity of the logical function has, in general, been looked at far too much from the point of view of knowledge. But, in the first place, no understanding is actually attained thereby, and, secondly the whole process does not serve theoretical but practical purposes. By its means, communication on a large scale is made possible, for how otherwise could the sensation-complex be communicated? Communication became possible only when the means of communication, the word, expressed an entire sensation-complex of this kind and when some new word especially stressed one part of this complex as an attribute, so that the duplication found in the proposition was cancelled. Thus to the separation there corresponds a union. Both concept and proposition serve merely as a means of communication; they also assist in securing an order in the psyche which, it may be mentioned, heightens the power of memory. A third purpose is that of explaining and understanding. We have shown above what is involved in this. The object is indeed attained, but the psyche believes that it has grasped something when it has merely applied its fictional categories to the sensation-complexes.

Concepts as well as judgments are, then, to be regarded only as means to a practical end. Thought creates an object to which it attaches its own sensations attributes and then, by means of this fiction, disengages itself from the mass of sensations that rush in from all sides.

There are various points to note here. First, the fiction has a practical object but is theoretically valueless and even contradictory; for there is no Thing that possesses the attribute of being "sweet". Such a "thing" is self-contradictory; it is an absolutely contradictory construct. It is supposed to be something separated from its attributes, and to be an entity quite distinct from these; and yet we know it only through these attributes. The creation of this fictional thing has, however, an enormous practical value, for it serves as the nail to which the sensations are attached as attributes. Without its aid it would not have been possible for thought to create any order at all out of the confusion of sensation.

This assumption of a Thing would never have been possible without the assistance of language, which provides us with a word for the Thing and gives the attributes specific names. It is to the word that the illusion of the existence of a Thing possessing attributes attaches itself, and it is the word that enables the mistake to become fixed. The logical function selects a complex of sensations from the general stream of sensations and events, and creates a thing to which these sensations, possessed by the psyche alone, are to adhere as attributes. But Thing, Attribute, and the Judgment in which they are combined, are simply transformations of reality fictions; in other words errors—but fruitful errors.

The contradictions and errors in this sensory view of the world become noticeable only later on and act as a stimulus for the elaboration of the intuition. At the same time, these immanent contradictions not only do not prevent the forms and formulæ from acting for many centuries as intermediaries between internal (psychical) and external happenings, but do not disappear even when recognized as errors full of contradictions. Indeed even then they are not merely remnants of a former attitude, but are and remain absolutely necessary for communication and for purposes of logical arrangement. They thus develop from involuntary, fictional constructs to conscious, scientific fictions recognized as necessary.

Our error consists in regarding such logical instruments as ends in themselves and in ascribing to them an independent value for knowledge, whereas they are, as we know, only logical devices for the attainment of purposes which we have already frequently enumerated. We must not, however, always suppose that the purpose of logical thinking is knowledge. Its primary object is a practical one, since the logical function is an instrument for self-preservation. Knowledge is a secondary purpose and, to a certain extent, only a by-product, the primary aim being the practical attainment of communication and action.

The same is true for all the other categories by means of which discursive thought is conducted; the whole and its parts, cause and effect, the general and the particular. These are all only conceptual, logical fictions which give rise to no knowledge whatever in the strict sense of the term. Here "the influence "involves "the addition of characters not contained in actual reality, but mentally added by the experiencing subject."

Although scientific thought does not to-day regard these particular intellectual forms, i.e. the categories, as instruments for understanding, for the world of sense they have at all times been both a determining factor and a means of understanding. Mankind spent thousands of years dividing the sensation complexes into compartments arranged according to purely external characters—and this, even if theoretically useless, had yet a practical value.

Kant proved that the categories were only applicable to experience and this demonstration is another way of expressing what we have been insisting upon. All these transpositions had originally a practical purpose. The categories are simply convenient aids for bringing the mass of sensations into subjection. Apart from this they had originally no object. They arose out of this practical need, and their number and special nature were determined by the different forms of expression assumed by reality, to which the psyche adapted itself by means of these forms, though frequently only in a superficial fashion.

Understanding is the well-known feeling of pleasure due to the empirical transformation of sensations into categories. It is quite meaningless to try to extend this feeling of pleasure beyond its possible limits. If understanding actually consists only in this conversion, and if this conversion turns out to be merely a return to an original starting-point, then it is entirely senseless to go beyond it and to attempt to extract a feeling of pleasure from understanding where such a conversion no longer occurs. The wish to understand the world is not only unrealizable, but also it is a very stupid wish. The psychical state of understanding only occurs when something has been successfully included or invested in the uniform of the categories. To desire to extend this feeling of pleasure further, to hope to understand the categories themselves, is an exceedingly stupid wish. Science in the end always leads us back to unalterable sequences and co-existences; and here there is nothing "understandable", for the word "understand" no longer has any meaning.

> The desire to understand the world is therefore ridiculous, for all understanding consists in an actual or imaginary reduction to the known. But to what is this "known" itself to be reduced, especially if in the end it turns out to be something "unknown".
>
> Our world itself is not capable of being understood but merely of being known. Philosophy can arrive only at a knowledge of the world, not at an understanding of it; it will be a knowledge of the world in its naked simplicity, after the destruction of all subjective forms of interpretation and additions, where fictions are consciously recognized as fictions, i.e. as necessary, useful and helpful conceptual aids. To want to "understand" the world as a whole is exceedingly foolish; and foolish not because human understanding is too undeveloped, but because every individual, even one endowed with superhuman capacities, must simply accept the ultimate realities which we can actually attain as the object of knowledge. To desire to understand them also is self-contradictory and childish. The categories, particularly cause (and purpose) can be usefully applied only within sensory material which is given. When applied to the whole, they lose all theoretical as well as practical value and only engender illusory problems as, for example, the problem concerning the origin and purpose of cosmic events.

This treatment of thought and of logical work is the only one calculated to give us a proper idea of its position. By regarding logical products simply as means for a practical purpose, the superstitious admiration of logical forms diminishes and the logical products no longer appear as revelations of reality but as purely mechanical instruments, whereby thought may move forward and attain its practical objects. By thus regarding both logical functions and logical products as mere means, the way is prepared for their interpretation as fictions, i.e. as constructions of thought, thought-edifices deviating from and even contradicting reality but invented and interpolated by this very thinking, in order to attain its ends more expeditiously.

CHAPTER XXXVIII CATEGORIES AS ANALOGICAL FICTIONS

WE may first note that an indefinitely large number of categories are conceivable. We might even say that the mind once possessed a far wider range of categories than to-day, that the present list is only the result of natural selection and adaptation. The traces of earlier categories are evident in all languages and those of to-day show the nature of their origin very clearly. They are manifestly analogies. A priori, however, a very large number of analogies are possible and have been employed in the course of history. Categories are nothing but analogies according to which objective phenomenal events have been interpreted.

They are, therefore, in no sense innate possessions of the psyche, but analogies which have been selected and applied in the course of time, and according to which events have been interpreted. How the analogies arose it is not difficult to guess; from inner experience. The Thing and its attribute is the abstract expression of the most primitive type of proprietary relationship; the relations of reality are regarded as if they were things which had as their "property" certain "attributes". To substantiate this further is a matter for etymology; in the case of the whole and its parts, for example, or the general and the particular. In all probability it will then be found that entirely different analogies are at the bottom of the same categories in different languages. We must therefore modify and restrict our former provisional assumption that the logical function develops these forms from within itself and say instead that the interconnections of sensations cause the logical function to think of a variety of analogical relationships. The logical function discovers that the sensory mass can be far more easily viewed as a whole and brought into order if thought of in terms of certain analogies.

Some important results follow from this. The view already outlined that the fictions cannot possess a theoretical value for understanding is thus confirmed. All these categories are analogies, applications of an analogous, though in the last analysis unfitting, relationship to objective circumstances. Such analogies, where complexes of experience are regarded *as if* reality behaved in a similar fashion, are all pure fictions. All events are understood in the light of these analogies which are continuously refined, and eventually become the abstract ideas that are always quite rightly recognized as analogical fictions. If then the categories have value only in practice and not in theory—namely for purposes of order, communication, and action—then philosophical systems also can have no other value, historically have never had any other. All understanding claimed for them was but a psychical illusion. Fictions have only a practical purpose and all the systems built up on elementary fictions are only more subtle and more elaborate fictions, to which no theoretical value must ever be attributed and which possess all the characteristics that we have so far always found in fictions. Theoretically they are valueless but practically they are important.

Every form of philosophy that naïvely operates with the categories, or with one of them, is *dogmatism*. *Scepticism* is the discovery that nothing can be achieved thereby, and its uncertainty spreads over the whole field of knowledge, and then further extends to the practical purposes of life also and quite arbitrarily assumes that these are not attained. But the theoretical must be distinguished from the practical purpose of the logical function. As soon as doubt extends to this, scepticism is unjustified. We must therefore not call in question the purpose fulfilled by the general application of the category of causality—namely the introduction of order. Doubt, however, is justified as soon as we realize that nothing can really be known through these categories, that they are only analogies which in the last analysis tell us nothing. By means of *Criticism* we can discover the reasons for this, for the critical attitude recognizes the categories as mere analogies, as fictions invented and set up by thought to bring order into the mass of sensations and to give us the illusion of being able to understand and explain. Criticism also enables us to prove that these analogies themselves cannot be understood, and further that they have been taken from fields of knowledge of far too intricate a nature. Even the most useful of the analogies, the category of causality, the only one that in modern science has survived the general ruin, had its origin in a field of knowledge far too complicated to allow it to serve for explanation; for it arose in the realm of inner experience and of action, which is the product of a highly complicated form of being. As is generally recognized, these expressions are to-day only employed symbolically, to designate an unalterable relation of sequence. What we observe is exclusively unalterable sequences and co-existences, and these we apperceive as a relation of causality and inherence without, however, in fact doing more than repeating things in another language. The whole matter then seems more comprehensible, but only a very naive dogmatist could to-day be deceived by it. Thought employs these devices in order to achieve its practical ends, one of which is just this satisfaction of "understanding." For thousands of years man has been content with this and taken great pleasure in indulging in these innocent subsumptions with the enthusiasm of a child.

But the mature man, unlike the child, is not satisfied there by, or, at least, he should not be. Mankind is beginning to realize to an increasing extent that "understanding" is only an illusion, that life and action are based upon illusions and lead to illusions. We feel we have been duped and are annoyed. It is to this that pessimism is due. The psyche is in every way dissatisfied to-day with what has been accomplished, for neither the purposes of action nor those of thought seem to have been attained. Yet in reality they have been attained, that is, in so far as they are justified at all. Pessimism arises out of exaggerated idealistic pretensions.

All dogmatism thus consists in trading with these categories and believing that something has thereby been attained. This was proved once and for all by Kant.

In one respect only was Kant gravely in error, namely in supposing that there was a predetermined number of categories. If the categories actually arose as we have stated, that is to say, as analogies of especial prominence in terms of which the various sequences could most suitably be conceived, then it is obvious that an indefinite number of such analogies is possible. Through natural selection those have been preserved that are most adapted to this purpose. It is therefore natural that they do not form a limited group but that, on the contrary, their number varies; and that while some are fully active, others have been preserved only in a rudimentary form. The evidence for this is to be found most clearly in language.

To-day there are only two categories with a real and vital application, *Object and attribute, Cause and effect*. But there is a constant tendency to eliminate the first and to reduce all relations of attributes to causal connections. Even this last reduction is regarded by the most prominent thinkers as only a method for arriving at subjective clarity and of enabling phenomena to be arranged in a certain way. Science to-day aims more and more at reducing all processes to purely mathematical relations where the true situation is presented in all its simplicity, but where, of course, all that is generally called "understanding" ceases. To understand is to subsume categories; and where this subsumption comes to an end there is also an end of understanding in the ordinary sense.

CHAPTER XXXIX THE PRACTICAL UTILITY OF THE FICTION OF CATEGORIES

ACCORDING to the purely "psycho-mechanical" principles of combination, fusion, interpenetration, association, etc., a kind of knot is formed in the conceptual stream; as for example, by the category of Thing and attribute—a category which tested originally upon an entirely sensory analogy. This category becomes progressively more refined and more abstract until it develops into a separable form whose origin in purely sensory relations is still demonstrable. We have here an excellent example of the instinctive and unconscious purposive activity of the psyche. We may start from the final outcome and try to show how the psyche has achieved its object though we admit this teleological deduction only for heuristic purposes. This allows us to introduce *order* and develop some sort of classification, even if it be only a superficial one. That this is only artificial and preliminary is obvious, for all progressive science is to-day fully occupied in breaking up this provisional grouping and in replacing it by entirely different systems. In the second place, *communication* is thereby rendered possible. We presuppose here, of course, the development of language and would merely note that the communication of an event or of an impression in an intelligible manner was made possible only through the formation of a limited number of categories. By bringing reality under these categories, communication between individuals became possible in terms of some known analogy, which immediately awakened in the recipient an idea of what the speaker wished to communicate. This is related to our third point, namely that understanding is thereby engendered —from our standpoint an illusion of understanding—reality being thought of under some known analogy. The tremendous pressure of the inrushing sensations is reduced, and the tension of these impressions is removed, in consequence of their being apportioned to different divisions. I would add at once that this was only made possible in *extenso* by language; the category is immediately attached to the word and the word becomes more abstract and loses its sensory colouring. That is why language has both such a releasing and loosening influence upon the psyche, since it was only by this means that the division of existence into categories became possible. Finally, it was only in this way that action could be determined. The psyche was no longer merely a helpless and passive spectator of the stream of existence and events, was no longer exclusively dependent upon mere reflex tendencies, but, as the pictures in this way became ordered and grouped according to categories, it was able to determine their re-entry and to arrange its activity accordingly. Such a possibility, however, rested essentially upon the possibility of memory, and this itself was to a large extent simplified by the arrangement of reality under these arbitrary categories.

These categories are not forms with any corresponding objective reality. They are merely combinations of thought, formed in response to some type of objective relationship but of purely subjective origin and of no value for understanding. This grouping of events under categories represents one of those circuitous devices which, though different as regards truth itself, are yet indispensable in investigation (Lotze).

The world of ideas thus formed makes action more and more easy. We must however note that these constructs—object, attribute, cause, effect—drop out as soon as their purpose has been attained. Their aid renders action easier and makes the operations of thought possible; but as soon as the desired sensations have occurred, the conceptual forms lose their value. Man does not want "things" but the occurrence of certain sensations. Fictions, even though they remain theoretically, drop out as far as practice is concerned, as soon as the desired result is attained. But it cannot be denied that thought obtains its practical success only at the price of its logical purity. The logical function—which consists of just these processes—is not afraid of the mistakes and contradictions which result.

Thus thought moves forward through contradiction as we have already repeatedly observed. The conceptual constructs inhere in the psyche even after their purpose is achieved; and though these logical processes have attained their practical results, their forms persist as residues and husks. These forms constituted the subject-matter of philosophy until the theory of knowledge proved them to be mere forms of fictional origin and value.

Logically considered, these psychical constructs are fictions and not hypotheses relating to the nature of reality, as many philosophers supposed until the contradictions they contained proved that there was nothing objective corresponding to them. For our "critical" standpoint they are only fictions, i.e. conceptual and ideational aids.

NOTES

1   Hobbes' *bellum omnium contra omnes* is probably to be regarded merely as a useful fiction. Dühring also takes it as such. He calls it rather aptly "a schematic apex."

2   For a good analysis of the Bonnet Condillac fiction, see Engel, *Philosoph. für die Welt*, No. 21: it serves as a *simplification* of the investigation.

3   Cf. the hypothetical animal of Lotze and his fiction of the man with the microscopic eye. Already in Locke and Berkeley there is something similar.

4   Cf. also Noiré, *Grundlegung*, p. 22: Fiction of the simple case of a conscious atom.

5   For the determination of the fundamental ethical relations Dühring postulated a schema of two people. Cf. *Cursus*, 202 ff. He also, in part, accepted the fiction of a pact, and on page 254 he reduces political rights to such a schema.

6   *Über die Grenzen des Naturerkennens*, Leipzig, 1872.

7   Illustrative fictions are to be regarded as a special sub-division of these concrete pictures for the generalization of abstract conceptions. For example Locke's conceptual aid, a blank, white sheet (cf. Riehl, *Der Kritizismus*, I, p. 23) and Plato's myths, which are a network of such pictures.

8   A critique of these symbolic fictions is to be found in Strauss, *Alter und neuer Glaube*, I [E.T. 1873].

9   And the similar analogy of the world with an organism or a work of art.

10 This address subsequently appeared in print in his *Reden und Aufsätze*, New Series, 1881, pp. 37–75.

11 *Geschichte des Materialismus*, 2nd Ed. Vol. II, p. 498 [E.T Vol. III, p. 285].

12 For the idea of an external world (*externalité*) as *emploi figuré*, cf. Littré, *Fragments*, 201.

13 In general, we may say that many important controversies in the history of science have been concerned with the question whether a given concept was

an hypothesis or a fiction, with the result that both sides grew weary and the disputed construct was, for the time being, accepted.

14 Littré well characterizes the Absolute as the "imaginary constant", *Fragments*, VII.

15 For induction directly attacks the *causae verae* and shows how to reach them and to arrive at the real context.

16 This task was particularly undertaken by Bain's *Logic,* though in part very superficially. We should not, for example, be able to get very far in the natural sciences or world-history by means of fictions. In the former only hypotheses can be used, while for natural history only an artificial classification is appropriate. On the other hand, the fiction is all the more necessary for the other sciences, where it is not possible to make any progress with deduction and induction alone.

17 I would suggest that in the future we call scientific fictions—*fictions,* and the others, the mythological, æsthetic, etc. *figments.* For instance, Pegasus is a figment, atom, a fiction. This would certainly facilitate distinctions. The opponents of the fiction misrepresent it in so far as they regard it as a mere figment. "Fictio," in legal terminology, has already acquired the secondary meaning of practical utility.

18 That is why in the case of a number of hypotheses, all equally possible, the most probable one is always selected. On the other hand, in the case of a number of equally possible fictions, the most expedient is chosen. The difference between the two constructs is here clearly shown.

19 Cf. Papillon, *Histoire de la Philosophie moderne dans ses rapports avec le developpement des sciences de la nature*, Paris, 1876; Vol. II, p. 412. In spite of the difficulties in the idea of an ideal archetype for all animals, the concept has been fruitful in comparative anatomy. "Mais comment d'après ce type idéal de tous les êtres, comment representer l'éternel exemplaire morphologique? Lá est la grande difiiculté. Le poète mème la sentait bien quand il disait: Cela se peut s'exprimer et non se démontrer. En effet, le type est une de ces notions spéculatives, tellement générales qu'elles échappent à la détermination!" For Goethe's indebtedness to Diderot, the same author may be consulted.

20 According to Roman law an unworthy son and heir is treated as such, even if there is nothing in the will to that effect.

21 We thus see how well Aenesidem interpreted Kant, when he said that Kant had shown that no conclusion about *reality* should be drawn from the fact that something must be thought: i.e. that Kant had proved the fictional nature of ideational forms.

22 Thus Drobisch in his *Logik,* 3rd Edition, pp. 65 and 193, where we also find some very noteworthy remarks about the infinitely small and similar ideas,

which, though indispensable as a means for certain purposes, are yet not free from inner contradictions. Newton, too, regarded *actio in distans* only as a fiction *(mathematicus conceptus),* as "a mere conceptual aid."

23 If it is assumed that the difference between *x* and *x+e,* the quantity in question, is very small, then the equation is approximately right. If it is assumed that the difference is as small as possible, then the equation becomes progressively more correct. And if *e* is taken to be infinitely small, then the difference is infinitely small. Finally if *e=0* then the difference also equals 0. The quantity *e* is therefore imagined to be something although it really is nothing; in other words an unreal thing is interpolated and then taken to be a real thing. We thus have an anticipation of the differential calculus.

24 Mathematicians will here be at once reminded of the well-known general reservations to the effect that, for instance, δx, δy, have no meaning in themselves but only in relation to a given operation, etc.

25 Such a circular process can often be observed. The best example is the idea of God.

26 So Engel, *Phil. für die Welt,* Section *24,* says: "What has now become a mere poetical fiction was formerly a real popular belief," etc.

27 Dühring's remark, *Krit. Gesch.,* p. 101, that "Ideas deteriorate in the very hands of their creators," is much to the point.

28 Lange, *Geschichte des Materialismus,* Vol. II, p. 453 ff. [English Trans., Vol. III, pp. 233 ff.].

29 In the same paper in which he communicates the discovery of antithetic operations, *Silzungsberichle der sachs. Gesellsch. d. Wissenschaft,* 1859.

30 In this connection let me refer to a remarkable and instructive book by A. Mouchot, *La réforme Cartésienne étendue aux diverses branches des mathematiques pures* (Paris, 1871). On the analogy of the theory of the two coordinates, invented by Descartes for dealing with curved lines, Mouchot regards every real point as consisting of two imaginary points. He also treats imaginary numbers from this point of view. He then formulates a "Principle des relations contingentes," that bears some relationship to Herbart's "Method of chance aspects," and proceeds to speak of *cordes idéales,* of *rayons et centres imaginaires,* of imaginary variables, imaginary triangles, imaginary dimensions, angles—all of which are deduced from the theory of imaginary points. The object here is to approach reality by contingent and arbitrary methods and thus to see it in various lights and render it amenable to treatment. The author relates his theory to that of Charles (*Apperçu historique,* etc.) in order to explain the connection of the imaginary and the contingent. The *relations contingentes* are the key to the imaginary. In this sense the

comme si plays an important part in Mouchot's work. What is imaginary is regarded as if it were real and is substituted for the real. Mouchot speaks of various conceptions which serve as *utiles secours en géometrie supérieure.*

31 Descartes created methodological fictions. Dühring in his *Kritische Geschichte der Philosophie,* p. 261, well calls the idea of a deceiving god a valuable fiction, and also other "tropes." Absolute doubt is for Descartes also merely a methodological fiction.

32 Here belongs the conception of "consciousness in general" which Laas so well elaborated, combining with the conception of "space in general" a "time in general." No one would contend that these conceptions are *hypotheses,* but that they are very *useful fictions* is clear from the excellent use to which Laas has put them. Cf. *Ibid.,* pp. 94–96.

33 This has now been rectified by F. Kuntze in his great work on Maimon.

PART 2
AMPLIFIED STUDY OF SPECIAL PROBLEMS

§ 1

Artificial Classification[1]

As a substitute for actual reality, in this case for a group of objects with a common constitutive complex of characters, we find one arbitrarily selected character. This selected character cannot, of course, be anything unreal. But it is not the true principle of classification. Thus, in place of the highly complicated reality, we obtain a simplification which is substituted for it. Phenomena in all their variety are then arranged according to this character as though it were the real and adequate principle.

The botanical system of Linnæus is the most famous example of this method. He took as a basis of classification the number of stamens and pistils. Classes and orders were formed in accordance with these, but as a result, organisms were sometimes grouped together in one species which possessed only this character in common, and not all their essential and unalterable characters. Of course, where the type of plant organization was of such a nature that the constituent elements were modified according to their specific characters, related forms were properly grouped. But where this was not the case, heterogeneous plants (the oak and the violet) were brought together and forced into an uncomfortable proximity, whereas homogeneous plants were separated and placed at points far removed from one another in the system, merely because they differed in respect of some particular organ that had been used as the basis of classification. In these instances, the *differentiae*, which are the modifications of the selected principle of classification x, are not those which actually determine and form the species; so that, instead of collecting individuals similar in their totality, those are grouped together that share only a limited number of characters. In other words, the relationships of the species, as far as their position in the system is concerned, do not correspond to their actual relationships. Yet this system with its 24 classes and 117 orders is of great advantage, for plants can be easily identified by these readily recognizable characters which are not difficult to find.[2]

Classifications based on the colour of the flowers, the serration of the leaves, etc. are just as artificial.

Those attempted by Jussieu and Tournefort are, in part, also based upon single organs (anthers, corona) instead of upon the organism as a whole. It was de Candolle, Endlicher and others who first used the internal anatomical structure, growth, etc. as the basis for a systematic classification.

The same holds for all other fields of natural science. The artificial systems of grouping found in mineralogy[3] were formerly, and are still, based upon more or less arbitrary external characters. So long as there is no natural system based upon chemical constitution, etc., such an artificial system has considerable practical value. Aristotle's classification of animals according to their toes and claws, or that of Linnæus according to their teeth, are other examples.

In many fields we are thus forced to give up, either temporarily or finally, the hope of constructing a natural classification, and as Taine[4] says in connection with his classification of the sensations, to remain content with a sort of *revue*, the manufacture of "un casier commode garni de cases où l'on retrouve aisément ce qu'on veut considérer; on n'a rien fait de plus". These auxiliary groupings, which form very ingenious constructions are, indeed, often only of service as an easy method of registering and arranging things.

As regards the extent to which the authors of these classifications were conscious of their artificiality, at any rate since the time of Linnæus, who was well aware of the arbitrary nature of his system, the difference between a natural and an artificial classification has been generally recognized; and since methodology has concerned itself with this particular point, these classifications are for the most part treated to-day as artificial. In other instances, on the contrary, these non-natural groupings were first accepted as hypotheses, i.e. it was believed that the natural system of classification had been discovered until it was realized that the grouping was unreal. But even when such an hypothesis is recognized as false, it can still render good service as a fiction.

In his inquiry into the races of man, Kant turned his attention to this subject and in his monograph, *Über den Gebrauch teleologischer Prinzipien in der Philosophie* he distinguished between natural and artificial species. The former he called *species naturales*, the latter *species artificiales*. "The academic system is based on classes which are arranged according to similarities, while the natural system is based on families, and classifies animals according to their relationship from the point of view of their origin. The former gives us an academic system for mnemonic purposes, the latter a natural system which appeals to our intelligence; the first aims only at arranging creatures under race names, the second endeavours to bring them under laws." He warns us against regarding this purely external similarity in characteristics as an indication of similarity in powers and so falling into the error "of transferring ideas into observation itself" and "confusing the purely logical differentiation which reason makes between concepts for purposes of comparison only, with the physical differentiation made by nature in their laws from the point of view of their origin." A natural classification should be built up on the "common cause" which lies behind groups of entities of the same type; it is a matter of natural history. Artificial or schematic classification, on the other hand, is based merely on the comparison of external characters and is a matter of description; and so forth.

Ampère should also be mentioned here, for on this point he remarks[5] that in artificial classifications certain arbitrarily selected characters serve the purpose of determining the place of every object; we abstract from all the other characters and thus either group objects together or tear them asunder in the strangest fashion. A natural system of classification, however, is based on all the essential characters, and the importance of each is determined; results are only recognized as valid when the objects that possess the greatest similarity are really brought together in the same class. The "arrangement le plus naturel" says d'Alembert,[6] "serait celui où les objets se succéderaient par les nuances insensibles qui servent tout à la fois à les séparer et à les unir."

Artificial systems are thus "one-sided systems, for since the grouping is made on the basis of special characters, it cannot be a true reflection of the richness of the whole." But such classifications, made on the basis of external, infrequent, secondary and accidental characters, afford a very practical aid to thought by enabling it to gain a temporary general view. In relation to the state of our knowledge, they are often all that is possible or practically useful.

As Taine says, the application of our instinct to classify is not always successful: "plusieurs de vos démarcations demeurent artificielles et ne sont que commodes."[7]

Certain corrections must be made in an artificial classification. These may either be purely ideal—in the conscious admission that our system does not entirely correspond with reality; or in particular cases real—as when the inconsistencies resulting from the artificial or forced grouping, in themselves a notable indication of the fictional nature of the whole process, are cancelled by some further inconsistency. Contrary to strict rules of method, the same type of grouping is not adhered to throughout, and instead of a rigid application of the principle, empirical similarities come into their own.

§ 2
Further Artificial Classifications[8]

It cannot be denied that there are many cases where we have made purely arbitrary divisions in objective nature without sufficient justification. For instance, on the ordinary view, animals and plants, organic and inorganic, life and death are very definitely and strongly contrasted; yet on closer examination they merge into one another so that a separation is impossible. This is proved by the many transitional cases where science cannot decide to which realm they should be assigned. Between plant and animal, inorganic and organic, there are intermediate forms which cut across the old classifications so that they are only retained for convenience. All these controversies about dividing lines should remind us that it is not nature that has drawn these lines and demarcations but our limited interpretation. As soon as these fictitious boundaries are treated as true limits, all kinds of disputes arise as to whether a given form belongs to this division or to that, and we get all the well-known contradictions, which recur in all classification as soon as we can no longer distinguish the real from the fictional. The vast majority of classes into which things have been arranged, and also separated and distinguished from other groups, have been proved by modern science to be unjustified and they are only retained to-day for convenience, for their practical utility, and not for their theoretical value. This is the case, for example, with the group "metal". Whereas it was once firmly believed to designate a quite definite natural group of elements this concept is retained in pure science to-day only because it affords us a convenient comprehensive term. New elements which, according to some of their characters, should be included in this group, in other respects resisted inclusion under this traditional concept and it is clear that nature itself knows nothing of such a classification. No character satisfies all the conditions or is fundamental; neither weight, hardness, malleability, elasticity nor transparency; not even simplicity, for, as Berzelius once said, it would not be a contradiction to find a "metal" that was not a simple element. In these instances we cannot help making an arbitrary classification or forming divisions that nature does not even suggest. There are no partitions in nature. It was Berzelius himself who, with reference to the earths, alkalies, metal-oxides, etc., called our attention to the fact that all our divisions are artificial and that no natural dividing line can be detected.

Passing to other fields, the difference between matter and force, for instance, has, for modern science, become so uncertain that here too any dividing line has become purely arbitrary and conventional. Such divisions are helpful aids to science, but are not science itself. Only the less important workers in science really believe that they gain from them any absolute or objective knowledge; true scientists are quite conscious of the fact that these and similar distinctions are only provisional fictions which play a minor auxiliary role. Yet in spite of their inaccuracy and partial erroneousness they render great service to science.

§ 3
Adam Smith's Method in Political Economy[9]

ADAM SMITH laid down as an axiom the fictional proposition that it appears *as if* all economic and commercial behaviour were dictated solely by egoism. He put it in the forefront of his system and developed therefrom deductively and with systematic necessity all the relations and laws of trade and commerce, as well as the fluctuations in these complicated fields. In view of the importance of this question both for method and for practice the views of important authorities may also be cited here. The question is all the more interesting because a violent controversy has arisen as to whether Adam Smith formulated his assumption as an hypothesis or as a fiction (if not in these terms, this sufficiently covers the facts). And quite apart from this historical point, the question is of great interest from a systematic standpoint.

In Lange's *History of Materialism*, that remarkable monument of a mind both clear and deep, there is an excellent section devoted to this problem. His comments we shall reproduce here. In dealing with the struggle against what he terms the "dogmatism of egoism". Lange is confronted by Adam Smith, the founder of modern political economy, and instead of indulging in vapid remarks on this great genius, as so many writers have done, he attempts to investigate the methodological principles of the problem. It is well known that Adam Smith, the Scottish author of a Moral Philosophy and the friend of Hume, wrote in addition to his *Wealth of Nations*, another work, *The Theory of Moral Sentiments*. It has recently been shown that *The Wealth of Nations* does not strictly form an independent work or a unit in itself, but is merely one portion of a complete moral philosophy.[10] The one work examines mankind from the standpoint of egoism, the other from that of sympathy and altruism. He was unwilling to make an absolute distinction between ethics and economics any more than between economics and politics. "He only made this separation in abstraction and in the interests of method."

"In the doctrine of the 'Wealth of nations'", Lange adds (E.T., Vol. III, p. 234), "the axiom is completely asserted that every one in pursuing his own advantage at the same time furthers the good of all. But the Government has nothing further to do than to maintain all freedom for this struggle of interests. Starting from these principles he reduced the play of interests, the marketing of Supply and Demand, to rules which even yet have not lost their importance. All the time this market of interests was not with him the whole of life, but only an important side of it. His successors, however, forgot the other side, and confounded the rules of the market with the rules of life; nay, even with the elementary laws of human nature. This cause indeed contributed to give to political economy a tincture of strict science, by greatly simplifying all the problems of human intercourse. This simplification consists, however, only in this, that men are conceived as purely egoistic, and as beings who can perceive perfectly their separate interests without being hindered by feelings of any other kind.

"And, in fact, not the slightest objection could be made to this, if these assumptions had been made openly and expressly for the purpose of giving an exact form to theories of social intercourse, by imagining the simplest possible cases; for it is precisely by abstraction from the entirely manifoldly complicated reality that other sciences too have succeeded in gaining the character of exactness. . . . A relative truth, a proposition which is only true on the basis of an arbitrary presupposition, and which deviates from entire reality in a carefully defined sense—just such a proposition is incomparably more capable of permanently advancing our comprehension than a proposition which endeavours at one stroke to come as close as possible to the nature of things, and in doing so carries with it an inevitable and, in their full range, unknown mass of errors.

"As geometry, with its simple lines, surfaces and bodies, helps us forward, although its lines and surfaces do not occur in nature, although the mass of real things is almost always incommensurable; so too abstract political economy may help us forward, although there are in reality no beings who follow exclusively the impulse of a calculating egoism, and follow it with absolute mobility, free from any hindering emotions and influences proceeding from other qualities. Of course, abstraction in the egoistic political economy is much more thorough than in any other science, since the opposing influences of indolence and habit, as well as those of sympathy and of the sense of community, are extremely important. Yet abstraction may be boldly ventured, as long as it remains in our consciousness as such. For when we have found how these mobile atoms of a society encouraging egoism, which is hypothetically assumed, must behave on one supposition, we do not merely gain a fiction which is consistent in itself, but also an exact knowledge of one side of human nature. We might at least know how man comports himself, in so far as the conditions of his activity correspond with the supposition, even though this will never be completely the case." (This last sentence describes the fiction rather inaccurately from the formal standpoint. A more exact formulation is given on page 243, E.T., Vol. III, with reference to the question "how man *would* act if he were only egoistic.")

Lange has here, with that methodological clarity so distinctive of his genius, admirably characterized the nature of the abstractive, neglective method, taking political economy as an example. It speaks well for his heart that he declared the essence of practical materialism to consist in a confusion of this abstraction with reality.

Buckle's attitude was that the two main works of Adam Smith, the *Theory* and the *Inquiry*, were two connected parts of one and the same system. In order, therefore, to understand the philosophy of by far the greatest of all Scottish thinkers, both works must be considered together and regarded as one, for they are in fact two divisions of a single subject. In the first he examines human nature in its altruistic aspect and in the second from the point of view of self-interested behaviour.[11] As we are all both sympathetically and egotistically disposed, this separation was the only possible way of elevating the study of human nature to the position of a science by means of the deductive method. The independent treatment of elements in reality united, does, it is true, rest upon an abstraction, upon a logical artifice, in that we separate in thought certain inseparable facts and proceed to argue about events that actually possess no real and independent existence and are encountered nowhere but in the mind of the investigator. Nevertheless such an artifice is quite legitimate, and may always be employed where a subject is not open to experimental treatment, or where too much confusing detail has grown up around it.

As far as the method of Adam Smith is concerned, these remarks, as Oncken quite correctly points out, hit the nail on the head.

According to Oncken this method is a characteristic feature of Adam Smith's work. The problem involved, he continues, is none other than that of the nature of rational method in general, and it is the peculiarity of this method that it separates things, in imagination, from all external influences in order to regard them as entirely isolated and with reference to a particular purpose. This, he rightly adds, is the method introduced into science by Descartes for the examination of single objects, and it was later extended by Kant and Adam Smith to whole branches of philosophy. He might even have gone further and pointed out that this method had been frequently employed in the eighteenth century, and that in the course of time, particularly in the nineteenth century through the operation of the "law of ideational shifts," the fictions of the masters developed into the dogmas of their followers.[12]

§ 4
Bentham's Method in Political Science[13]

ANOTHER very instructive example of the fictional method of abstraction is offered by Bentham's treatment of the problems of political science. In this instance the historical question as to whether Bentham applied his method consciously, i.e. whether his assumption was a fiction and not an hypothesis, is to be answered in the sense that his own statements certainly appear to have been intended by him as hypotheses, and that it was his successors who first recognized in assumption, false as an hypothesis, an important and useful fiction. Bentham bases his general theory of the state on the comprehensive presupposition that the actions of men are always dictated by self-interest, by purely personal and selfish considerations. In order, however, to represent constitutionalism and parliamentarism as necessary forms of government, Bentham had to make the following deduction from this axiom:—if men's actions are essentially determined by selfish interests, then the only rulers who govern in the interests of their subjects are those whose self-centred interests coincide with those of the people. This, however, only occurs when the interests of the rulers are brought into harmony with those of the people through responsibility, i.e. through the dependence of the rulers upon the will of the ruled. From this it follows that the wish to retain power and the fear of losing it are the only motives that can be regarded as the source of a policy in agreement with the general interests of the people. The feeling of identity of interest can only be called forth and conserved by responsibility. From this Bentham deduces representative government, the responsibility of ministers, and so forth.

§ 5
Abstractive Fictional Methods in Physics and Psychology[14]

IT is well-known that *abstractio logica sive mentalis* is particularly employed in mathematical physics and that there can be no question here of an *abstractio physica sive realis*. The latter is used when, for instance, a piece of wood is split up into parts, the former, when we speak of bodies, for instance, without weight, and imagine that they exist. It also occurs, however, when we neglect the question of the medium, and, "for the convenience of the physicist, agree to treat the relatively empty space as absolutely empty." Here, "the mathematician, in particular, who is accustomed to leave out of his calculation the higher powers of an infinitely small magnitude, can have no reason to demur" (Lange). If the scientific explanation of nature presupposes discrete particles of matter, "which move in what is at least a relatively empty space," it thereby disregards influences due to the medium continuously filling space; and this neglect of elements of reality actually present and in fact always inseparable is of very great service in simplifying calculations. Here too we must include the fact that in physics, molecules are "for the sake of simplicity treated as spherical," an assumption that appears not to be fully in agreement with the demands of chemistry. Possible irregularities in geometrical shape are therefore neglected and, merely for the sake of simplification, a far simpler behaviour is assumed than that which actually occurs. If theoretical mechanics and physics are to proceed deductively at all, any other treatment of reality is impossible. For here the empirical phenomena are so complicated that by excluding subsidiary factors which are, however, always at work—abstract relationships are made the basis of the method, and the behaviour of phenomena is then treated *as* if it were dependent only upon these abstract factors and the others did not come into consideration at all.

This same method is of great use not only in the field of applied psychology—and in this we must include the social sciences since the time of Adam Smith and Bentham—but also in the study of primary psychical phenomena. Here, too, the complicated nature of phenomena makes it necessary for us to substitute only a fraction of reality for the whole range of causes and facts. Psychological relations are of so intricate a nature that fictions which bring one element into prominence and neglect others in order thereby to facilitate theoretical procedure, are valuable here. This method has made great strides since psychology carried through the analogy of psychical phenomena with mechanical processes. Lange, in particular, with his discerning eye for method, recognized the formulæ of Herbartian psychology as mere fictions, false as hypotheses, but not without their auxiliary value. Herbart himself did not believe that he had reached reality by means of them, for he, in part, ascribed to his formulæ a methodological character. In his excellent monograph *Die Grundlegung der mathematischen Psychologie, ein*

Versuch zur Nachweisung des fundamentalen Fehlers bei Herbart und Drobisch (Duisburg, 1865), Lange marshalled the evidence, and only a few of Herbart's formulæ were allowed any utility. Drobisch also used this method and he too made similar fictional assumptions. He declares in the preface to his *Grundlehren* that the fundamental assumptions of mathematical psychology were only provisional assumptions which, although they approximate to reality, do not correspond with it.

Steinthal later employed this method and laid down theoretical formulæ in psychology that were obtained only by neglecting numerous empirical factors.[15] He calls them "abstract pictures" of psychic processes.

§ 6
Condillac's Imaginary Statue[16]

A REMARKABLE example of the fictional method of abstraction is the well-known fiction of Condillac which has made his *Traité des Sensations* so famous and so valuable. The purpose of this fiction is the foundation of what was afterwards called "idéologie," i.e. an analysis of ideas and a reduction of all beliefs and concepts to their origin in experience, in short a theory of the formation of ideas out of sensations. With this object Condillac imagines (*imaginer, supposer*), a statue, which is to be thought of as similar to a living human being whose mind as yet is devoid of ideas. In order to be able both to admit and exelude impressions at will, this imaginary man is enclosed in a marble case which prevents him from using his sense-organs. In this way Condillac was able to isolate the particular world of ideas that would result from each of the senses, if this hypothetical man were limited to but one sense at a time. He limits his statue to the sense of smell and then in succession to those of hearing, taste, of sight, and finally touch. Then he combines the various senses by opening or closing, as desired, the means of access to the statue. By this method he abstracts at will from certain of the factors that usually form a part of the complicated texture of psychical life, and he can then show the contribution of each particular sense. In this way he constructs successively an olfactory man, an auditory man, etc., and shows what kind of a world of ideas would, or might, arise in a man thus partially endowed. By means of this statue, organized like a man and provided with a mind which is as yet without ideas, with senses which are called into existence one after the other, he demonstrates the development of consciousness, attention, memory, judgment, the imaginative faculty, abstraction, reflection, etc. It is obvious how this ingenious fiction simplifies the inquiry. "We know," says the unknown author of a small work called *Die Bildsäule* in Engel's *Philosoph für die Welt* (No. 21), "the reason which led Bonnet and his predecessor Condillac to create such a statue. They thought that they could thereby simplify and facilitate the study of the way in which our psychical powers gradually developed in connection with sense-impressions."[17]

Of course, the fiction gives rise to a number of absurdities: "language before the ear is open, consciousness at the very first stimulation of one of the vaguest of our senses," etc. We must, however, take into consideration, as Condillac himself remarks, "that the uncertainty and even the erroneousness of some of the suppositions will not affect the basis of the work. I observe this statue, not so much to discover what is occurring in it as to discover what takes place in us. I may err in crediting it with activities of which it is not as yet capable, but such errors are of no further consequence if they enable the reader to observe how these operations take place within himself." Objections have been raised to this method, unjustly, I think, by Liebmann for instance.[18]

In the work cited above, Condillac repeatedly makes use of the fictive method. One more instance is relevant here. In his fiction he further supposes that his statue-man lives alone, and he attempts to show how the needs, abilities and ideas of such a man would take shape, according as nature provided for all, for some, or for none of his needs. By varying the possibilities which he imagines for this man left to his own devices, he is able to make a series of very subtle psychological observations. This is all then applied *mutatis mutandis* to real men. The fiction was already known both in the ancient world and in the Middle Ages. Arnobius[19] (circa 300 A.D.) created the fiction of a man who had lived from birth in complete isolation, and used it to disprove Plato's theory of knowledge.

This fiction of Arnobius was revived by Lamettrie in the eighteenth century; it appears as the "belle conjecture d'Arnobe" in an abbreviated form in his *Histoire naturelle de l'âme* (1745),[20] and is used against the Cartesian doctrine of innate ideas. "Let us assume," says Lange in his discussion of this fiction, "that in a faintly-lighted subterranean chamber from which all sounds and sense-impressions have been excluded, a new-born child is being scantily nourished by a naked and silent nurse, and that it is thus brought up until the age of twenty, thirty, or even forty, without any knowledge of the world or of human life. At this age let him leave his solitude. And now let him be asked what thoughts he has had in his solitude, and how he has been nourished and brought up. He will make no answer; he will not even know that the sound addressed to him has any meaning. Where then is that immortal particle of divinity? Where is the soul that enters the body so learned and enlightened? Like Condillac's statue," which Lamettrie seems to have inspired, "this being, which has only the shape and the physical organization of a man, must be supposed to have received sensations through the use of the senses, etc."

This fiction was also employed by Avempace (died 1138) in the interests of religious philosophy, in his *Régime of the Solitary*, and particularly by Abubacer (1100–1185) in his *Haji Ibn Jokdhân*. Abubacer shows in this way the gradual evolution of man's capacities until his intellect merges with the divine, and makes his "solitary" man develop into an independent being, apart from the institutions and opinions of human society. As Überweg says, "he allows the individual to develop from within himself; he frees man's independence of thought and will, to the acquisition of which he has been helped by the whole course of history, from this necessary condition and implants it in his natural man as a non-historical ideal" (as Rousseau also did in the eighteenth century). Stories of the Robinson Crusoe type, so popular in the eighteenth century, also belong here, stories wherein, as Pfleiderer somewhat too wittily expresses it, "the isolated basis of abstract and inwardly reflected thought is schematically clothed in the picture of a desert island in an immense ocean and serves as an excellent experimental field for theory." As with Condillac, the fiction serves here also to simplify investigation and exposition by omitting factors which are invariably co-operative, in this case the community with other living beings. Both educationists and psychologists frequently use this fictional abstraction for their particular purposes.

Here too belong those examples of artificial isolation where not merely a single individual but a whole city or community (an island, etc.) is thought of as shut off from the rest of the world, e.g. Fichte's isolated commercial community.

§ 7

Lotze's 'Hypothetical Animal'[21]

THE extent to which psychology itself advantageously employs this method, is shown by the well-known "hypothetical animal" introduced by Lotze in his *Medisinische Psychologie*.[22] This animal, it will be recalled, is supposed to possess just one single sensitive and movable point in its skin, say at the end of an antenna.

Laas[23] calls this "hypothetical animal" "a sounder, more organic and illuminating abstraction and fiction[24] than Condillac's statue with only the olfactory sense, and a tactile sense given it last of all." He calls Lotze's fiction organic, because the tactile sense is really the first to develop in animal evolution and is even found alone, unaccompanied by other organs, a fact already noted by Aristotle.'[25] Laas's expression leads me to the methodic observation that such fictions must indeed be "sound and organic," i.e.— and this can only be expressed negatively—they should not form ideational constructs that are too far removed from the actual facts but, on the contrary, such as conform most naturally and aptly to the objective data.

The value of this fiction consists in the fact that it simplifies the problem of epistemology and psychology, namely, the nature of the processes through which the idea of the external world arises and the share of the mere succession of perceptions in our picture of the world. The perceptions of this "animal" are only successive, for simultaneous perceptions are excluded by the very nature of the fiction. What follows from these succcssive perceptions of an antenna, moving about and occupying a number of different positions?" If this hypothetical animal is psychically organized like ourselves, it will regard what runs parallel to its arbitrary decision as "subjective," and what is found to be independent of it as "objective," strange and external. And if it has the power of receiving perceptions both with the organ at rest and in motion, and possesses, as we do, memory and associative capacities as well as the faculty of spatial interpretation, then it must, like ourselves, in spite of its defective sensory apparatus, arrive at the point of distinguishing between a stationary and a changing, a resting and a moving object." Laas thinks that this fiction is of great value for the theory of knowledge, because by means of it, by developing the consequences of an impossible assumption, a false Kantian doctrine can in this case be disproved, namely that an intelligence automatically provided with categories was necessary in order to arrive at objective knowledge. "Lotze's animal, endowed with our understanding, would be in a position by means of the actual data to arrive at some idea of objective rest and motion" without those categorial functions which Kant regarded as necessary.

Physiological psychology, in view of the highly complex nature of its subject-matter, makes use of such fictions readily and with success; among them should also be included the assumption made by Helmholtz of a being who is all eye, or that of a man with only one eye and that in the middle of his forehead (the fiction of a Cyclopean eye). The assumption of a fictional man with microscopic eyes also belongs here. Helmholtz, Aubert, and others, make frequent use of this method.

§ 8
Other Examples of Fictitious Isolation[26]

THE ideal isolation and breaking-up of actuality, its logical separation into different divisions, is one of the favourite devices of thought; a complex, in reality inseparable, is split up into ideal elements and parts, and each of these ideal elements is then treated in isolation.

Such cases of isolation, where an object is torn from its natural context and regarded as independent, are frequently found. We may perhaps even treat Galileo's axiom of inertia as such, for "it presupposes an ideal case that is not found in isolation in any material unit nor in any system of such units". It was determined thereby how a moving body would behave if unaffected by any influence whatever—but the if includes an unreal case. This, after all, is only an abstract view that can never be realized, for the law is based on an assumption which contradicts all and every reality, since no body exists alone, but a multiplicity of things is always given. The schematic isolation of a single body in motion presupposes a case which never occurs in reality, can never be observed, and, given the existing organization of the world, is absolutely impossible. But it is only through the neglective method, by means of the fiction of "simple cases," that the simplest laws can be maintained.

As an additional example of the ideal isolation of an element from the circumstances which are in fact always associated with and necessarily accompany it, let me quote a passage from Taine.[27] In order to investigate the conditions and discover the laws under which and according to which sensations are re-awakened in memory, he isolates a single sensation and subjects this single case to an examination. He observes, however, "c'est qu'à vrai dire, il n'y a pas de sensation isolée et separée; une sensation est un état qui commence en continuant les précédents et finit en se perdant dans les suivants; c'est par une coupure arbitraire et pour la commodité du langage que nous la mettons ainsi à part." Psychology is especially fond of making such isolations.

Attention may here also be called to the fiction made by Leibniz in his *Systéme nouveau de la nature*, where he looks upon his monad "comme s'il n'existait rien que Dieu et elle", by thinking of it as isolated (*comme si*) from all other monads which together with it form the whole system of nature. He adds: "pour me servir de la maniére de parler d'une certaine personne d'une grande élévation d'esprit, dont la sainteté est célebrée". The reference is to the celebrated mystic, Saint Theresa, as is proved by a passage in the *Acta Sanctorum*, quoted by Leibniz in a letter to Morellius (1696). Saint Theresa says: "animam corporis concipere res debere non secus ac si in mundo nil esset nisi ipsa et Deus; quam ideam non modice juvat ante oculos in philosophia habere; atque hanc utiliter adhibui in hypothesibus meis"—I would only add here that the purpose of this fiction of Saint Theresa lies in the field of ethics, whereas Leibniz gives the matter a theoretical turn and utilizes it for his Monadology. In the first sense the fiction has a certain ethical value; as used by Leibniz the extent of its significance is dependent on the value of the theory of monads itself.

Methodological interest attaches to the controversy between Curtius and Pott as to whether the roots that are assumed by comparative philologists ever really existed as such without flexions and transformations, whether there ever was a period in which the roots postulated by the grammarians were actually used or whether, on the other hand, these roots were only a generalized abstraction from the so-called derivations. In other words, were they historically hypotheses or grammatical fictions, and was the separation of the stem, so essential and necessary for the grammarian, ever actually an isolated root or not? This question whether the uninflected roots are only starting points, so to speak, for grammatical calculation or whether they correspond to an historical reality, is of considerable methodological interest.

§ 9
The Fiction of Force[28]

ONE of the most important fictions that arise through isolatory abstraction is that notorious and frequently dangerous product of the imagination, the concept of force. In one of its meanings, for instance, that of vital force, we not only find many particular phenomena grouped summarily together but also the idea that a force is something with a special existence.

If two events, one preceding and the other following, are united by a constant bond, we call that peculiarity of the antecedent event, which consists in its being followed by another event, its "force," and we measure this force in terms of the magnitude of its effect. In reality only sequences and coexistences exist, and we ascribe "forces" to things, by regarding the actual phenomena as already possible and then hypostasizing these possibilities and peculiarities, and separating them from the rest as real entities. "Par malheur," say Taine, "de cette particularité qui est un rapport nous faisons par une fiction de l'esprit, une substance; nous lui appelons d'un nom substantif, force ou pouvoir; nous lui attribuons des qualités; nous disons qu'elle est plus ou moins grande; nous l'employons dans le discours comme un sujet; nous oublions que son être est tout verbal, qu'elle le tient de nous, qu'elle l'a recu par emprunt provisoirement, pour la commodité de discours et qu'en soi il n'est rien, puisqu'il n'est qu'un rapport. Trompés par le langage et par l'habitude, nous admettons qu'il y a lá une chose réelle et refléchissant á faux, nous agrandissons á chaque pas notre erreur." This particular essence is a "mere nothing," and by an "illusion" we convert it into a pure incorporeal essence; regard it as an essence of a higher order. And yet in itself it is only a character, a peculiarity, a relationship existing between two events, "détachée par abstraction, posée á part par fiction, maintenue á l'état d'étre distinct par un nom substantif distinct, jusqu'á ce que l'esprit, oubliant son origine, la juge indépendante et devienne la dupe de l'illusion, dont il est l'ouvrier." Taine refers frequently to this fiction. The forces that objects are supposed to possess are nothing but a necessary consequence of succession, "posées á part et considerées isolement, des maniéres d'étre extraites de l'événement, et isolées par une fiction mentale."[29] They are raised to the rank of substances and placed as the permanent background, as a constant fountain-head in contrast with transitory events, and are thus given a separate existence. In summarizing the conditions for a given event, we call it the force necessary for this event, and we represent it as something actual and special: "la condition, dégagée, isolée par une fiction de l'esprit devient ainsi tout-á-fait générale et abstraite."[30]

Taine here is only emphasizing one side of the problem. He points out the theoretical valuelessness and falsity of the concept of force, by exhibiting its psychological origin, but lays far too little stress on the utility and convenience of these conceptual constructs for ordinary scientific practice and in his eagerness to prevent the fiction from being taken as a reality, he omits to recognize the excellent services that this fiction has rendered to thought. This side of the question must not, however, be neglected; critical insight into the theoretical worthlessness and deficiency of the concept of force must be supplemented by the methodological recognition of its practical utility and convenience. That this abstraction, whereby the part that has been separated is also personified, is a useful fiction, I would like to demonstrate by reference to a writer who combines a critical mind with a feeling for the methodological requirements of science.

Lange[31] severely criticizes Moleschott for saying "that wherever, at any time, oxygen may happen to be, it has a relationship to potassium," and thinking of force as something permanently seated in oxygen. He calls such conceptions "the ravages of the concept of possibility," and deprecates the personification of a human abstraction. He agrees with Du Bois-Reymond who concluded that fundamentally there is neither force nor matter, since both are only abstractions. And he agrees with that famous passage where Du Bois-Reymond speaks of force as a rhetorical device of our brain, which seizes upon a metaphor because it lacks the clarity necessary to express an idea directly. Force, so far as it is thought of as the cause of motion, is nothing but a disguised outlet for the irresistible tendency to personification. The idea of force as an excrescence of matter, a sort of instrument like a hand or arm, is certainly a device to whose application neither natural science nor methodology can take exception, so long as we remain aware of the technical nature of the concept, which facilitates rapid calculation in thought. If, however, supersensuous forces are assumed, we introduce what Lange calls a false factor into our calculations. This view of force as something added to and dependent on matter is quite legitimate provided the idea is used only to aid the process of thought, and provided we are sufficiently adept in method to rid ourselves, when the time comes, of the false factor thus introduced into thought.

§ 10

Matter and Materialism as Mental Accessories[32]

ALL this holds of another one-sided abstraction whose influence has been incalculable; indeed the whole method of the natural sciences, which are founded on the assumption of an independent external world, is only a one-sided abstraction. This is what Lange meant when he constantly stressed the methodological validity of materialism, but dwelt with equal emphasis on its metaphysical (or rather its epistemological) invalidity. The materialistic conception of the world is a necessary and useful fiction, but it is false as soon as it is taken for an hypothesis. Lange's contention, so frequently misunderstood because he seemed to be fighting against materialism and also to be in sympathy with it, is thus seen in a new and, as I believe, an instructive light. Not only the sensations of the so-called higher senses but also those of the lower ones must not be assumed to have an absolute existence apart from ourselves as subjects. Not only does the world of colour and sound exist merely through and in our sensations, but touch too reports nothing more than modifications of our psychological organism. The old truth already established by Democritus that the so-called secondary qualities are merely relative has been extended within recent times to the primary qualities also; but just as Goethe in his theory of colour speaks of colours as though they enjoyed objective existence, so materialism speaks of matter, substance and tangibility as though they were real things existing apart from our sensations exactly as they do when we are aware of them. And just as this method of interpreting colours can make convenient abstraction of the presence of the subject, as is unavoidable, for example, in æsthetics and the theory of art, so natural science has to speak of qualities as though they were absolute and objective. For the sake of a more convenient presentation it dispenses entirely with the subject and with the fact that, after all, all these apparently objective properties have only a relative value in relation to the subject; and it proceeds *as if* the external world did assuredly exist outside ourselves and *as if,* even without a subject, things were as they appear. Although in reality all that we experience is merely our sensations which thus always have validity only in relation to the ego, in the natural sciences we entirely disregard this state of affairs as well as the subject, and proceed on the basis of relations far simpler than those actually presented to a careful observation of reality itself.

This separation of our sensations from the matrix of our subjectivity, following on the lines laid down by Berkeley and Hume, was subjected to a thorough examination by Mill and Taine, and was stressed in Germany by Lange in reviving the doctrines of Kant. The fine analytical sense of the English philosophers enabled them to trace the consequences of this separation in their most subtle psychological details. Lange, on the other hand, was more concerned methodologically and systematically to defend the necessity of making the separated material external world the basis of scientific procedure against unreasonable criticism; though at the same time he constantly called attention to the fact that materialism is only an accessory concept, provisionally and methodologically legitimate but not to be confused with metaphysical reality.

§ 11
Abstract Concepts as Fictions[33]

IN abstract ideas, factors of reality that are actually of a dependent nature "are given the form of objective independence, although it is realized that this is only a fictitious and not a real form."[34] The particular existence observable and apprehended in independent objects is provisionally transferred to dependent and partial concepts. These are then *made substantive*, and thus there arise such concepts as sweetness, redness, space, causality, identity, ground, consequence, relation, virtue, beauty, love, omnipotence, hatred; in other words a very large and important portion of our conceptual stock-in-trade owes its origin to this fiction. "Abstraire," says Condillac,[35] "c'est séparer une idée d'une autre á laquelle elle paroit naturellement unie . . . voilá l'artifice des idées que nous nous formons."[36] "Nous pouvons done les observer *comme si* elles existoient séparées de la substance qu'elle modifient . . . c'est ce qu'on nomme une idée abstraite."[37] Condillac here uses the formula for the fiction which we have already met—*observer comme si*—and Bachmann remarks: "To abstract from anything is to dismiss it from our consciousness and retain something else. If A and B are combined in a single object, then we abstract from A if we think of B alone and unalloyed, *as if* A did not exist at all."[38]

Condillac fully recognized the law of antithetic operations, and it is therefore pertinent to consider his ideas on this subject in some detail.

To abstract, he says, is to decompose; it is to separate one thing from another of which it forms an integral part. Abstract concepts are therefore partial concepts, torn from their context. By logically abstracting colour or form from its corporeal substratum, we get special branches of sciences which are concerned only with these qualities, apart from the substances in which alone they manifest themselves.

But this process involves great risks and easily leads to serious mistakes with dangerous consequences. "Many philosophers have fallen into this error; they have converted all their abstractions into realities or regarded them as entities with a real existence apart from that of objects." Relations, modifications and forms are hypostasized. As our mind is too limited to study a large number of modifications at the same time, it takes them one after another and separates them from their substance, thus actually depriving them of their reality. But, continues Condillac, since these abstract qualities that have been torn from their matrix are to become mental objects, this can only be done by regarding them as realities.

"Whenever it has found these qualities with their objects, the mind has been accustomed to see them with a reality from which they could not at the time be distinguished; and it retains this reality for them as much as possible even when it separates them from their substratum (or rather when it arbitrarily sunders them in idea from their permanent context as a complex of qualities). The mind here contradicts itself, for on the one hand it regards these modifications without any relation to the real object, and in this case they are strictly speaking no longer anything; or, on the other hand, since non-existence cannot be apprehended, it treats them as a thing[39] and then proceeds to give them the same reality with which they were at first observed, although they are no longer entitled to it. In a word, although these abstractions are only partial ideas, they have united with the idea of an independent object."

"However erroneous this contradiction may be, it is nevertheless necessary."[40]

Abstractions which we are compelled to regard as something real, are thus children of our imagination;[41] and the cardinal error of all scholastic philosophy consisted in converting these fictions into independent entities. The *qualitates occultae* (Vital force, for instance) are the result of this fatal confusion: "les abstractions sont done souvent des fantômes que les philosophes prennent pour les choses mêmes" (*Ibid.*, p. III).[42]

Another example is the psychical faculties. Locke had already expressed the fear that the manner and fashion in which we speak of these faculties would awaken in many people the confused idea that we were dealing with so many separate agents, which in the form of special entities dominated definite fields. This confusion has led to numerous futile disputes, and to obscure and doubtful investigations of the assumed psychical faculties; whether, for instance, judgment appertains to the intellect or the will, whether both are equally free and independent, whether the will is capable of knowledge or whether it is a blind force, whether the will directs understanding or the reverse, etc. In this manner the psyche became multiple, through the conversion of convenient abstractions into realities. And these faculties are abstractions, for in reality, no single act of the will can take place without some intellectual activity and no intellectual activity without volition or feeling. In all such cases the main protective rule is to avoid all hypostasization and to return to the real elementary processes out of which these abstractions were first formed; in other words, to return to the observation of the particular and the real in all its phenomenal multiplicity and its insoluble combinations.

These fictional abstractions find their clearest expression in language, for we speak of them as though they were single substances. We apply adjectives to them and add verbs; we say that space has three dimensions, that war destroys men; we speak of qualities and deeds of fame, of virtue, wisdom, justice, etc. We thus impart substantiality to these abstractions *as if* they were something special existing independently of the objects with which they are always in fact connected.

This connection of abstraction with language was especially emphasized by Gruppe (following Condillac), who produced a searching critique of the disastrous effect on philosophy of the confusion of abstractions, i.e. of fictions, with reality, a confusion directly encouraged by linguistic usage.

His *Antäus*, a remarkable monument of independent and original thought, in spite of its author's youth, appeared in 1831, or fifty years after Kant's *Kritik d. r. V.* He here undertook to "examine the influence of language, and of linguistic means and methods of expression, upon thought." We make use of a number of abstract expressions and only by means of them is speculation possible. Do they, from their very nature, allow of such an application?

In ordinary linguistic usage, not only are abstractions not misleading or harmful, but they are wholesome and lead to quicker results. It is only speculative philosophy which tears them from their context and converts them into realities. "In ordinary usage they are nothing but *ingenious abbreviations;*

they have developed from linguistic practice and admit of practical application only. Nothing theoretical can be deduced from them and nothing can be extracted from them; they are only a means, not a content; only abbreviations and auxiliary expressions." Abstractions are aids to procedure and spare us a good deal of prolixity. With their assistance we are able to obtain a subtler insight into the nuances of objects, by making characters, apart from the objects where they are found, the subject of our assertions. But we must always return in the end to the living reality—hence the title, *Antäus*—where the properties, from which we have made our abstractions, are to be found. Otherwise all thought would move in the air, instead of on the basis of experience. As soon as abstractions are misused for the purpose of making assertions which appear meaningless when concrete things and relationships are substituted for them, it is a sign that the necessary protective rules have been neglected. We have only to recall the abuse made in the Hegelian system of such abstractions as Number, Magnitude, Speed, Quantity, Quality, Negation, Nothing, Being, Becoming, Unity, Difference, etc. These are all, as Gruppe very properly observes (p. 285), perfectly comprehensible abstractions, "entirely harmless and honest words, but if for one moment we forget what should be meant by them, then they are no longer part of our own mother-tongue but a jargon of thieves, a gibberish to deceive us; they become will-o'-the-wisps leading to a morass." No philosophical torture can extract anything from them.

But however necessary abstractions may be for thought and speech, they do not unlock the world of reality for us; and as soon as we hypostasize them and picture them as special entities invested with life and attributes— as does all speculative philosophy, with Hegel—then we have committed the fundamental error of converting fictions into reality and the elements of a provisional logical scaffolding into real definitive entities. From this error there arise those *questions frivoles*, as Condillac calls them, those tortuous yet apparently profound questions whose falsity and perversity is only recognizable when we have returned to the realm of concrete things. "An evil spirit," Gruppe exclaims, "gave mankind this weapon—and yet it was the spirit of culture itself, which could have made no advance without its aid." Abstractions, in fact, are a necessary aid to thought and meet a practical need, but they furnish no theoretical knowledge, twist and turn, define and differentiate them as we may. We confuse fact and fiction, means and end, if we attempt to deduce anything from such linguistic aids. It would be a complete misunderstanding of the instrument we are using; it would be taking the instrument for the thing which it assists us to make.

Gruppe states the law of fiction in a very general form in these memorable words, "Scientific inquiry is always a *regula falsi*;[43] in order to make a start on its problems it must begin with some presupposition and assumption which it then tries to correct and modify." Abstractions themselves, and the uses to which they are put, must be regarded as an example of this general rule. We start with errors which must subsequently be corrected. We substitute the abstract for the concrete and we must afterwards replace the abstract by the concrete again. What we take away in constructing abstractions, what we subtract, must later, in our definitive logical procedure, be restored and added again.

Although Hegel fully recognized the emptiness of the abstract ideas, although he realized that thought was led to contradictions by means of them, he yet found in them the essence of the real. While Plato regarded the abstract substances as higher entities endowed with a privileged reality, Hegel finds in them active cosmic forces. These abstractions are really mere methodological aids, logical devices. "The question of their reality," as Gruppe rightly observed, "has no meaning whatever here, and the impossible can perform its service as a transient expression like the expression $\sqrt{-1}$ in mathematics. Just as the latter is an imaginary quantity, i.e. a mere fiction, so language must often be regarded as nothing more than a paper-currency."[44] Gruppe was thus fully aware of the true nature of the fiction so far as abstract ideas were concerned, though he did not obtain a hearing at the time.

§ 12
General Ideas as Fictions[45]

A FAVOURITE device of thought, closely connected with abstraction, are the summaries that lead to general ideas.[46]

Words are fruitful aids in the fixation of general images. They help the abstract type which thereby gains a new kind of clarity, a sensuous support by means of the audible word.[47] But no perception, covering, let us say, the word "tree", can be shown to exist. We either perceive a green or a barren tree, a high or a low one, etc. The word "tree," on the other hand, designates something that appears in all the perceptions of a tree but which cannot be further determined; it means a tree that is neither with nor without leaves, that possesses many branches or few, etc.

What however, in relation to actual reality, is the general picture, the concept? Objectively, only the particular, the discrete, exists. We have just seen that the concept "tree" corresponds to nothing real. In other words here, too, thought deviates from reality. Only individual "stars" exist, not "star" in general; individual "dogs ", not "dog" in general; individual "men", not "man" in general. All these ideas represent nothing real; only the individual happening that is brought to the psyche and is received and elaborated by it actually exists. In this general flux certain prominent characters form a nucleus and create centres.

"Star","dog", "man" are thus concepts with no corresponding realities.'[48] These concepts are psychical constructs extracted by thought from the material given. Nevertheless these purely mechanical products of psychical life fulfil a most important purpose. Concepts, general ideas, contain, as such, no knowledge; separated and isolated from their context they are fictional constructs to which no reality corresponds.

Yet the general idea links itself up with the proposition and strains automatically towards expression in the proposition. By means of this proposition united with the general idea, the real purpose of thought is attained; only thus does a general judgment become possible, and it is upon this that all classification, ordering, understanding, demonstration and deduction are based.

What, however, is this general picture under which a particular case is subsumed? It is a pure fiction, for nothing real can be proved to exist or correspond to it in the external world. The advantage gained through this device of thought is, however, considerable. General ideas make general judgments possible; such, for instance, as "stone is hard", "the dog is faithful", "man is mortal". On closer study, however, we realize that this manner of speaking and of thinking, however much it may simplify expression and thought, is, after all, based entirely upon an artifice. We speak in the above examples of things and ascribe properties to them, but they are things, all the same, that do not exist. We apply the category of Thing to what are purely ideational constructs, that is, they are treated as though they were objective entities possessing attributes. This method of expression is certainly convenient and fruitful, for it permits the synthesis of numerous particulars; but we must nevertheless insist that concepts formed by abstraction are only ideational constructs, i.e. are fictions.

It would not be necessary to waste any words on this subject if it were not for the fact that in philosophy it has been held that there is something objective corresponding to these constructs, that they are not fictions but hypotheses; and if the general and the conceptual had not been substituted for what alone really exists, namely the particular. Here we have an example of how a purely formal artifice of thought has led to an error.

By means of this fiction of a general thing, thought is enabled to operate more rapidly and safely than would be the case if it always had to enumerate all the particulars. It is this practical grouping that makes the real construction of science possible: the proof, inference, deduction, and the general propositions first made possible by general ideas—that is what brings about scientific intercourse. Yet we repeat; it must not be forgotten that general judgments, when connected with a general subject, only represent convenient methods of expression. There is no such thing as a general subject in reality.

The dangerous consequences of the opposite view are manifest from the fact that from Plato to Hegel and from Hegel right up to the present time, philosophers have regarded their concepts as endowed with an objective existence, and have supposed that there were Things-in-themselves corresponding to them as such. As opposed to particulars, they have been regarded as the permanent essence, and this permanent essence has been hypostasized into an energic thing interpreted as the general basis of particular phenomena. The thing thus becomes the foundation and essence of everything that is perceived. The more general, the more powerful, and more efficient this foundation is supposed to be, the more it is hypostasized. General ideas thus come to be regarded as the subjective counterpart of actually existing substances endowed with powers which are interpreted as the forces behind and above individual things, as the sources from which the particular takes its origin.

Here we have the extreme of misuse to which logical forms, which are, after all, only artifices of thought, can be subjected. The products of thought are hypostasized and actual reality despised, though, in fact, the individual phenomena, the successive and coexisting phenomena, are the only real things. So here again we find the mere husks of thought substituted for the real kernel. A veritable hierarchy of ideas is evolved, the lower being continuously grouped into higher ones until we finally reach the stage where only the most general and all-embracing idea, that of Something, is left. These artificial and ingenious ideas not only form a complicated network in which the individual meshes are intertwined with one another, but also serve as a ladder whose rungs lie one above the other. Thought, in this way, creates for itself an exceedingly artificial instrument of enormous practical utility for the apprehension and elaboration of the stuff of reality; but a mere instrument, although we often confuse it with reality itself.

Nominalism in its extreme form rejects the employment of forms of thought, upon which, after all, the whole of human science is based, and fails to recognize the practical utility of such logical artifices. Conceptual realism, on the other hand, follows the equally unreasonable and unalterable human tendency to objectify the subjective, and hypostasize the purely logical. This human tendency towards personification so frequently noted by Lange in his *History of Materialism*, also plays a part in the attribution of reality to general ideas: we place the general under our favourite category of substance and interpret it as a Thing possessed of properties and forces. The uncritical use of language has taken over this method of expression, which dates from the childhood of the human race when everything was personified; and just as the astronomer still speaks of the rising and the setting of the sun, so do we still apply these convenient aids, the general ideas, as if the General were real and existent. If the psyche regards the general idea as a thing with attributes, it need not be deprived of this convenient and useful game; but the game should not be taken seriously so that the *as if* becomes a rigid *it is*. Otherwise we should be transforming the husk into the kernel and be taking as subsidiary what is the essence of reality, namely the particular phenomenon and the particular event. From this point of view Mill was quite right in looking upon the general as a logical point of transit for the particular. In short, the general, the formation of general ideas, is a convenient instrument of thought. Having performed its service the work of the general idea is over and it will vanish from the operation if we succeed, by means of it, in discovering the particular, which is what interests us. In other words general ideas and general laws play only a sub-servient rôle.[49]

Much of what we have said about abstract ideas also holds for general ideas. In particular, most of what was said in connection with Condillac applies to them too, for Condillac did not separate the two types. He calls general ideas, "des idées sommaires et des expressions abrégées," to which we are not to ascribe more reality than they actually possess. They are necessary aids to thought, necessary because of the limitations of our intellect;

it is only the logical understanding that requires them, not the intuitive and divine. Condillac compares them to levers[50] employed by the understanding in order to overcome nature. By means of it our spirit advances, rises, attains the unknown and thus brings order into its knowledge. And this means that general ideas are only fictional aids to thought.

The same errors that arise from the misuse and misunderstanding of abstract ideas are also found here. Conceptual realism is not entirely vanquished even to-day, and species are still frequently regarded as independently existing forces or substances.

According to Condillac, the *formae substantiales*, the *species intentionales*, the *Essentiae*, the essence, etc. were all due to this confusion of fiction with reality. The concepts, body, animal, man, metal, gold, silver, etc., contain in the eyes of the philosophers, as Condillac remarked, essences hidden from the rest of mankind. From these there arise "questions frivoles" such as, whether ice and snow are water, whether an abortion is a human being, whether spirits are substances, etc., which presuppose that the questioner believes in the existence of certain *essentiae*, certain realities, designated by the general ideas. The belief that through a classificatory definition of an object, by indicating its generic concept, knowledge can be gained is—as Condillac rightly remarks—another error which results from such a procedure.

Locke[51] had already treated general ideas from this point of view. General ideas are fictions or contrivances of the mind. Locke points out that these general ideas "carry difficulty with them," because a triangle, for instance, "must be neither Oblique, nor Rectangle, neither Equilateral, Equicrural, nor Scalenon; but all and none of these at once." A general idea would therefore be something that could not exist, for all kinds of contradictory ideas would be included in it. But, he adds, "the Mind in this imperfect State has need of such *Ideas*, and makes all the Haste to them it can for the Conveniency of Communication and the Enlargement of Knowledge."

In these words Locke clearly and consciously expresses the nature of the fiction; and, in fact, general ideas do bear the mark of real fictions: they are contradictory constructs, logically impossible inventions, but they are nevertheless indispensable and useful means of thought; logically useful because they are logically impossible. Thought can only use them for its purposes because they are, from a strictly logical standpoint, theoretically contradictory. By an oxymoron we may say that they are only useful logically because they are—logically useless.

§ 13

Summational, Nominal, and Substitutive Fictions[52]

THE same process that lies at the root of the formation of general ideas is also often used in a very similar manner in other connections and thus gives rise to summational fictions. The idea of substance, i.e. the Thing, might be adduced as a prominent example of this class. We speak of things with attributes; we say that the tree, this tree standing before me, has the characters of dimension, hardness, smoothness, a given shape and a given size. Now what is this object that possesses these characters? This substance, as Taine very correctly observes, is absolutely equivalent to the indefinite series of its known and unknown properties. If all these attributes were successively removed, then no substance would remain. Substance represents a summation and its attributes are the individual elements in this summation: the subject is the sum of these attributes. "My idea of substance is therefore only a resumé; it is the equivalent of the sum of the ideas of which it is composed, just as a number is the equivalent of the sum of the units for which it stands, and an abbreviation the equivalent of the objects for which it is used as a shorthand symbol."[53]

The concept Thing, then, is merely a *summational fiction*, and when we say that an object has certain attributes, we are making use of an auxiliary concept, as though this summation were something outside of and apart from the attributes, just as if a genus were thought of as something outside of and apart from the multiplicity of the particular things of which it is formed.

Abbreviations by means of auxiliary words, which might therefore be called verbal fictions, are employed in all the sciences. A whole series of well-known concepts, such as "soul," "force," the various "psychical faculties," etc. belong here. Although these conceptual constructs were formerly, and are still to-day, regarded as expressions for real and existing entities, they are, in truth, nothing but summational expressions for a series of interconnected phenomena and interconnected processes. An instructive example of this type is "attraction." Newton expressly says that he is far from assuming that such a force exists as something apart from the phenomena; he regards the term merely as a summational and abbreviated method of expression for the sum of all the relevant phenomena and events subject to natural laws.

In the same way "Vital force"—in modern science—is only an abbreviation for the sum of all the causes that determine the phenomena of life. It is only in the brain of the dilettante that the vital force still lives as a special reality, so that the conceptual construct has the value either of an hypothesis or of an established dogma. An exact physiology and medicine employ this expression only as a convenient auxiliary expression. Such a concept has no practical value other than that of bringing together the Many and simplifying the method of expression. No more is stated in these *nominal fictions* than what the single phenomena could tell us themselves, and if we believe that we have understood or actually said anything in using these words—a naïve view that still survives—we are simply forgetting that these expressions are *purely tautological*.

Force in general is another such tautological fiction. Force is nothing but a mere reduplication of the facts, viz. of the causal relations of succession. We interpolate this construct in our imagination and then believe that our work is finished. For positive science and a philosophy built upon it this idea has merely the value of a convenient fiction which simplifies our method of ideation and of expression. The assumption of hidden forces that determine the sequence of phenomena in no way aids us in giving a theoretical explanation, and for that reason cannot be recognized as an hypothesis, even though, historically, it has almost always appeared in that form. As the critical attitude develops, these abortive branches on the tree of knowledge wither and fall off, and their only practical use thereafter is to support ideation. A true and exact science is content to collect the facts in order to determine their common basic principles and causal sequences. The delusion of earlier ages that certain kinds of phenomena were under the influence of particular forces has been recognized as a delusion, and this whole way of thinking is now only retained because it represents a convenient vehicle for presentation and expression. The duplication of phenomena by making them also appear as forces is of no value scientifically, although it has a certain practical utility.

In the scientific world to-day everyone is agreed that the concept of "soul" is only a fiction. We still speak of a soul as if there were such a thing as a separated, integral and simple soul-entity, though we are quite conscious that it is only a fiction. The "soul" is simply a summational fiction without any reality. The law of ideational shifts can be readily studied in connection with this concept: the "soul" was first a dogma, then an hypothesis and then a fiction. For Hume and Kant the soul is only a fiction. Kant's successors, incapable of maintaining the fiction in its labile condition and at the same time craving for more stable concepts, frequently transformed the fiction into an hypothesis or even a dogma. On our "critical" view, the "soul" is simply a convenient aid for indicating the totality of psychical phenomena. We speak *as if* a soul existed.

It is to such auxiliary words that Goethe's lines in *Faust* apply, that where ideas are lacking, words appear at the opportune moment. If, for instance, in chemistry, a number of inexplicable processes are ascribed to a "catalytic force"[54], all that has here occurred is that by means of this nominal fiction a convenient expression has been devised, to serve provisionally until the proper explanation has been discovered. Such words represent mere husks holding together and preserving the real kernel. And just as the external shell takes on the form of the kernel and provides us with a duplicate of it, so these auxiliary words are to be taken as pure logical repetitions without any true value. The best-known examples are, of course, the *vis dormitiva* and the *nisus formativus*. To reject such expressions, however, is to misunderstand their practical utility and convenience, and unnecessarily to deprive ourselves of a convenient instrument. This is the more unjustifiable because the danger of misuse is no longer so great to-day and can be completely eliminated by methodological insight.

In the above expressions a substitution occurs, a summational phrase taking the place of real particulars. This substitutional method is of use as a convenient aid to thought in other respects too. Indeed, in a wide sense, all fictions may be regarded as substitutions, in that an unreal element is provisionally put in the place of reality. In the narrow sense of the term we must here include all those substitutions in which an idea functions vicariously as a *symbol* for something else.

This substitutive method is particularly common in mathematics. The formation of such substitutive symbols is one of the most frequent mathematical devices. All algebra is based on the substitutive employment of letters in place of numerals, and if u, for example, is subsequently put for x+y—to simplify the operation—this too is a *substitutive artifice.*

198 PART 2: SPECIAL STUDY

§ 14

Natural Forces and Natural Laws as Fictions[55]

IN the domain of natural phenomena we are frequently in need of comprehensive expressions to serve as convenient handy formulæ for a series of
phenomena, no matter whether they cannot be investigated or are already
known. Such, for instance, is the concept of *affinity*. For scientific chemistry
this expression is merely "a mere comprehensive notion for a class of accurately observed and rigidly defined phenomena."[56] Affinity was originally a
typical scholastic quality, a part of the favourite apparatus of the alchemist.
"At the beginning of the eighteenth century many scientists, particularly the
physicists, protested strongly against the use of this term, fearing that its use
might involve the recognition of a new *vis occulta*. This happened particularly
in France, and St Geoffroy, at that time (1718 and onwards) one of the chief
authorities on chemical relationship, avoided its use. Instead of saying: Two
united substances are decomposed if a third element be added which has
more *relationship* to one of the two bodies than they have to each other, he
said: If it has more *rapport* to one of them."[57]

The concept of force in general, together with its abstractive function to
which reference was made above, is merely an auxiliary expression, a fact
strongly emphasized by Fechner in particular. "All that is given is what can
be seen and felt, movement and the laws of movement. How then can we
speak of force here? For physics, force is nothing but an auxiliary expression
for presenting the laws of equilibrium and of motion; and every clear interpretation of physical force brings us back to this. We speak of laws of force;
but when we look at the matter more closely, we find that they are merely
laws of equilibrium and movement which hold for matter in the presence of
matter. To say that the sun and the earth exercise an attraction upon one another, simply means that the sun and earth behave in relation to one another
in accordance with definite laws. To the physicist, force is but a law, and in no
other way does he know how to describe it. . . All that the physicist deduces
from his forces is merely an inference from laws, through the instrumentality of the auxiliary word 'force'."

But "law" too is, in the end, merely an auxiliary expression for the totality
of relations existing in a group of phenomena.[58] Formally, "law" is absolutely identical with the generic concept that we have already recognized as

a comprehensive fiction. If the objects of knowledge in question are processes, we call this concept a law. The generic concept refers to the domain of being (appearing as relatively stable), to a series of identical or similar individuals; law refers to the domain of happenings and the uniformities of the regularly recurring changes. A "law" is simply the summation of constant relations where the chance variations and the apparent irregularities in detail are disregarded. *A "law" is therefore a summational fiction.* And if this is true, it must also have the characteristics of such a fiction. It must be valuable and indispensable in practice, but in theory a comparatively worthless construct. And further, like all fictions, it must be very liable to confusion with reality.

§ 15
Schematic Fictions[59]

ONE of the main uses of this method is in connection with the schematic drawings so popular in the descriptive natural sciences. Ordinary drawings are, of course, already, as such, abstractions, since the third dimension is omitted. In the case of schematic drawings, the simplification goes even further, by representing only the essential features and main lines. We find this method in use in botany, physiology, zoology, etc. To prove that in this case too the same psychologicological process predominates, let me quote some remarks from the botanist De Bary, although the whole question, by reason of its simplicity, does not really require any further examination. In connection with schematic drawings De Bary expressed himself as follows: "The figure represents the two successive periods in the blossoming of the birthwort described in the text, sketched schematically as if the flower were transparent." "The outline of the calix of the sage is represented in side-view, and the other parts of the flower that interest us are drawn as if the flower were transparent." Here again we find the characteristic "as if" which, as we saw before, indicates that something is being equated with unreal assumptions. The assumption of something unreal—transparency—serves the purpose of making possible a convenient representation of the whole situation.

We must also regard as a characteristic schematic fiction the so-called "schematic eye", and the so-called "reduced or demonstration-eye", two related physiologico-ophthalmological fictions that have played a great part in recent physiological optics. We owe much to both Listing and Helmholtz for introducing and elaborating this peculiar and fruitful fiction.

§ 16
Illustrative Fictions[60]

FREQUENTLY the fictive activity serves the purpose of converting abstract ideas which are, for that very reason, difficult to retain within our mind, into concrete ones which are easier to realize. This is done with the full consciousness that a picture has been substituted for a concept and that, with the picture, a more or less false element has been added to the concept. This is especially the case in natural science. Such methods of attaining the sensuous or concrete can be designated as *illustrative fictions*.

As an example of the favourite manner of clothing the abstract in sensuous pictures, we have the various methods of attempting to make force concrete, from the purely anthropomorphic conception to its mathematical representation in the form of lines. Here, too, we must not confuse the pictures with the conceptual element nor with the realities meant by the concept. Our imagination comes also to our aid in connection with the forces of repulsion and attraction, etc., by introducing the idea of bands of force stretching from one point to another, auxiliary ideas that must, of course, never be transformed from mere imaginary existence into reality.

§ 17
The Atomic Theory as a Fiction[61]

AN excellent example of the illustrative fiction is furnished by the atomic theory. Observation shows us that chemical combinations take place according to definite and very simple numerical relationships. This fact demands theoretical elaboration, and the question arises, upon what these quantitative phenomena depend. Dalton propounded the theory that these simple numbers of the combining weights depended upon the atomic nature of the elements. He believed that he could best picture the striking regularity by means of a corresponding grouping of the atoms. If we think of an atom of one substance united with one or more atoms of another substance, this regularity can be interpreted clearly and simply. F. A. Lange remarks, in connection with this example, that the need for concrete presentation is an indispensable condition for our proper orientation in the phenomena, and that this sensuous intuition almost always attains brilliant results, "often though it may have been shown that all these modes of conception are merely aids, helping us towards complete discovery of causal relationships, and that every attempt to find in them a definitive knowledge of the constitution of matter immediately fails."

To the above we may add the dry remark of Liebig that "The manner in which we imagine the elements to be grouped in chemical combination is based only on convention, which in the case of the dominant view-point has been sanctified by custom," and compare the opinion of Schönbein who says that, "when ideas are wanting, a word comes very conveniently, and assuredly in chemistry since Descartes a gross misuse has been made of molecules and their grouping, under the delusion that by such a play of the imagination we can explain absolutely obscure phenomena and deceive the understanding." In view of the opinions of these two authorities Lange's interpretation cannot be dismissed off-hand. He also made another important methodological comment on this question, whose discussion we cannot evade. Quite correctly, as against Schönbein's destructive criticism, he calls attention to the fact that, in reality, "this play of the imagination" certainly does not serve "to deceive the understanding, but rather to lead it to the maxim which has its foundation deep in the theory of knowledge, that only a rigid adherence to sensuous picturability can protect our knowledge against the much more dangerous playing with words." And he adds the very important remark that an intuition rigorously carried out, even if it is false in fact, frequently serves to a great extent as a picture and provisional substitute for the true intuition. Even Gay-Lussac's view, where the atoms were conceived on the analogy of the differential, indicated that we were only dealing with a fiction, for if there is any conceptual construct that can be regarded as a methodological fiction it is the differential.

If, therefore, following Cauchy, Ampère, Seguin and Moigno, we designate the atoms as centres without extension, we are merely creating substantial basis for the relationships of force, a basis that, upon more accurate scrutiny, turns out to be a very strange construction indeed. For an entity without extension that is at the same time a substantial bearer of forces—this is simply a combination of words with which no definite meaning can be connected. "Simple atoms", that must yet be something material, cannot be *causae verae*, cannot be actual things. Since, however, the physicist does require atoms for his constructions, how is this contradiction to be solved? How are we to rescue science from this dilemma? And to the above we should add the meaningless concept of a vacuum, or of empty interstices between atoms, which, although an extremely concrete idea, suffers logically from the most serious contradictions.

It is a fact hitherto not recognized that Kant was the first[62] to get out of the difficulty by giving the atomic conception the value of a convenient auxiliary idea; though, apart from that, he definitely accepted the dynamic theory of the continuous occupation of space.

In his *Metaphysische Anfangsgründe der naturwissenschaft*, Kant advocates the dynamic theory of matter and assumes an infinite divisibility of the same. Thereby, of course, he rejects the vacuum, for, according to his view, the dynamic occupation of space is continuous. On the other hand, Kant was too much accustomed to thinking about physics not to realize the tremendous methodological advantage of looking upon matter not as continuous but as a totality of separated parts. He therefore declares the mechanical method of explanation, (Ibid. Part II, Note 4), "to be the most amenable to mathematics". But (Ibid. Part II, Section 4, Note 1) he continues, "we quite misunderstand the meaning of the mathematicians and misinterpret their language, if we ascribe to the concept adhering in the object what belongs necessarily to the procedure of forming a concept (he is referring here to the distance of material particles from one another); for, according to them, every single contact can be regarded as an infinitely small distance, which must also necessarily occur whenever a larger or a smaller space is to be imagined as completely filled with just the same amount of matter. For that reason, in the infinitely divisible, no real distance between the parts is to be assumed, and they are to be regarded as forming a continuum in spite of the extension of space as a whole, even though the possibility of this extension can only be concretely represented under the idea of an infinitely small distance."

Thus Kant differentiates between a mathematical (mechanical) idea of matter, which he desires to employ only methodicalJy and not seriously, and a dynamic idea which he regards as the correct one, but which is not so convenient for mathematical calculation.

This solution, first hit upon by Kant, of explaining the mathematico-mechanical conceptions as mere aids to calculation, has been frequently used since his time by other philosophers.

According to Fechner there are physicists and chemists who, "because they do not know how to recognize the higher advantages and excellences of the atomic theory, look upon it with unfavourable eyes, but who admit that it is the most convenient way of representing the matter and that its no-menclature may be used for concretely visualizing the situation; they do not, however, wish to draw any inference therefrom or credit this kind of idea with any reality".[63] Fechner could not refrain from poking fun at these peo-ple. They appeared to him like men who, though they do indeed make use of their real legs because they are the most convenient means of locomotion, are yet careful not to imply thereby that these are their real legs, assuming that the latter are still entirely hidden from view and may eventually emerge into the light of day. I would substitute another image for that of Fechner. They seem to me like the people in a certain part of France where no roads exist, who instead of making use of their natural legs—a manner of locomo-tion very difficult in such a country—employ artificial legs, stilts, and thus make walking both easier and faster.

In his *Anthropologie* (1856) Fichte violently attacked the mechanical atomic theory. Following in the wake of a few scientists, he declared war upon the "common atomic theory", It appeared to him to be a completely contradic-tory hypothesis, utterly without value for explaining reality. He expressly admits however that it is a very convenient and useful fiction, "that it is a very convenient and in itself unobjectionable fiction provided it is regarded as nothing else and nothing more" (204); "it is a permissible fiction for mathematical calculation and measurement" (205); it is indeed "an arbi-trary presupposition" (216), but a "permissible assumption" (215). For that reason Fichte says that "real science makes temporary use of the atomic theory as a permissible fiction until the proper explanation has been discov-ered" (22): in order to make this fiction useful natural science must then devise other auxiliary fictions (308). To clarify and justify this conception Fichte falls back upon "the fiction permitted to the geometrician of allowing a straight line to consist of an infinite number of points in contact with one another, and treating the circle as a polygon of an infinite number of sides, etc. Everywhere we find continuity regarded as infinitely distinguishable and discrete."

Many, therefore, who recognize the difficulties and contradictions inherent in the atomic theory, make use of it, nevertheless, as a surrogate for an explanation: the majority of the physicists and chemists of our time have regarded the atoms as a provisional aid in concrete expression and calculation.[64] So for instance Preyer,[65] "We may look upon the concept of the atom as we will, but it always remains not an hypothesis which we can hope eventually to demonstrate but a fiction undemonstrable for the very reason that in all the forms it has hitherto assumed, it is entangled in inevitable contradictions. The only reason why the concept of atom has maintained itself so long, is that we have no better means of connecting numerous phenomena. The atomic theory has, therefore, only a provisional existence. The tremendous heuristic and mnemo-technic capacity of the atomic theory has often enough led to a confusion between the methods and the objects of investigation, and earned it an admiration which it does not deserve."

The atomic theory often serves, in particular, to give non-sensuous concepts such as force, for instance, a sensuous basis and enables us to picture in imagination processes still obscure to us, such as chemical combinations, cohesion, crystallization, etc.; but this application does not transform subjective methodological means into an objective-metaphysical reality. We must not look at these methods of visualization and calculation—for as such Faraday, Schönbein, Magnus, Du Bois-Reymond, Fick, etc., regarded the atomic theory—as an objective process of nature. Many scientists speak of atoms without really meaning to assume them: some even reject the reality of empty space and yet continue to speak of atoms, although the assumption of empty space is a necessary consequence of the atomic theory. Unquestionably this conceptual method is the most convenient one, but this constitutes, of course, no proof of its objective-metaphysical validity.

According to the more recent views of physicists, Kirchhoff, for instance, all phenomena are reduced to forces and relative effects of forces. For the physical specialist, matter is in no way dependent upon the assumption of extended minimal particles. Matter forms an entirely empty and meaningless subject for the forces and is but an inaccurate after-effect of a view which has grown accustomed to the idea of extended and separated bodies, and which also assumes substances as bearers of the elementary forces. But this conceptual method provides a simplification of the theory, not only because particles of matter are looked upon as the supporters of these forces, but because they are regarded as infinitely small. The former attitude is of greater value in making the abstract concept of force concrete, the latter in simplifying the calculation. That is why the atoms are allowed to remain, though everything that exists has found adequate expression in the forces. We interpolate this conceptual aid because it is so convenient. It is literally an hypostasized Nothing with which we are dealing, in the case of the atom; for if everything has been dissolved and absorbed into the forces, what becomes of matter? And if the atoms are to be represented as infinitely small, how are they to be distinguished from the mathematical point which is also merely an hypostasized nothing?

§ 18
Fictions in Mathematical Physics[66]

In physics, and particularly in mathematical physics, as well as in mechanics, we make use of a number of fictional constructs which are in part merely convenient, in part absolutely indispensable. Faraday's "lines of force" possessing no mass or inertia, for instance, are to be regarded as auxiliary ideas for the purpose of visualization. Maxwell tried to see in these lines of force something more than mere mathematical symbols.

But that Maxwell in this interpretation was contradicting the intention of Faraday, the actual originator of the concept, that, in other words, he committed the frequent error of transforming a fiction into an hypothesis, a mathematical auxiliary idea into a physical theory, is best proved by Faraday's own words. The lines of the magnetic force of gravitation, the lines of eclectro-static force and the bent lines of force, are all, according to him, imaginary.[67] No special meaning was to be ascribed to these terms: he is convinced that he is not giving expression by means of them to any *real* fact of nature, although this method of conceiving things apparently fits the situation and is very neat.[68] He desires to limit the meaning of the words "line of force" in such a way that they designate nothing except the state of the force with respect to its size and direction, and do not involve any idea concerning the nature of the physical cause of the phenomena. How, for instance, magnetic power is carried through various bodies or through space we do not know.[69] According to these statements of Faraday, Zöllner is unquestionably right in rejecting Maxwell's interpretation of these lines of force as physical entities as a gross misunderstanding. It is also quite clear that Maxwell made this confusion through a lack of methodological insight into what constituted the difference between a fiction and an hypothesis. We know this definitely because Faraday expresses himself quite clearly in a letter to Tyndall (14th March 1855), who, he says, is aware that he (Faraday) treats the lines of force only as *representations* of magnetic power, and that he does not profess to say to what physical idea they may thereafter point, or into what they will resolve themselves. Faraday did not allow himself to be led astray by the great mathematical utility of his new conception, which was of extraordinary value in the analytical deduction of physical phenomena, into seeing in it more than a "representative" idea. He protested against the misunderstandings of his contemporaries, men like the Dutch mathematician van Rees, who also seemed to find a physical hypothesis in this idea, in direct opposition to Faraday's clear declarations.

This differentiation between hypothesis and fiction also coincides with the distinction drawn by Wilhelm Weber[70] between real and ideal hypotheses.

An ingenious artifice of thought is that of the "fictitious mean" of Jevons (we follow his *Principles of Science*), which has been used in various connections.[71] It is exceedingly popular in mathematical physics, in those cases where a chain or group of force relationships belonging together, are thought of as united in an ideal mean point so that, should circumstances demand, this totality can be applied in a computation immediately. Since it would necessitate too complicated a calculation if every relationship were taken into consideration, a single unit is substituted for the many, which are regarded as combined within it.

We owe the first application of this method to Archimedes. He hit upon the very ingenious idea of constructing in a given body, a point in which the weight of all the parts was thought of as being concentrated, so that the weight of the whole body could be accurately represented by the weight of this point. The centre of gravity thus takes the place of the weight of innumerable, infinitely small particles, each of which is active in its particular position. In order to obviate the tremendous complexity in calculation necessitated by this circumstance—for the simplest mechanical problem would otherwise break up into innumerable particular ones—a centre of gravity is imagined which is thought of as a point and treated as if all the forces of the individual parts were united there. Archimedes explained the method for determining this centre. Thus in place of a sphere as centre of gravity, we have its indivisible centre which, in this case, still lies within the body. But in the case of a ring, this centre of gravity is entirely imaginary; for here, instead of having the points of application of the forces in the form of a circle, we find the centre falling in the vacant interspace. The same holds for two or more bodies, whether these are separated or united. Here, too, a point can be found that can be treated *as if* the resultant force of both bundles of forces were concentrated in it. We can, for instance, imagine a common centre of gravity of the earth and the sun, that is, a point that can be regarded and introduced into calculations as though it took the place of both these celestial bodies as an indivisible centre exercising exactly the same influence upon a third point as the two bodies do in fact.

We must also mention here as a peculiar and valuable auxiliary idea, the fiction of an absolutely fixed point.

The empirical perception of all change and motion is always connected with empirical points of reference, and it is only when related to these that we can recognize it as motion. In other words all observed motion is relative, relative to us, to an imaginary origin, relative to a fixed background or relative to the apparently stationary earth or sun. These are all mere points of reference which we must assume in succession. Man begins by assuming himself as a point of reference and science constantly postulates other points of reference because those taken first prove to be illusory, since they turn out to be in motion themselves. In order to prove definitely and absolutely the existence of motion, we must have an absolutely fixed point by means of which the speed and the direction of the motion can be measured. Since, however, according to modern views, no such absolutely fixed body can be discovered in the universe, science is faced with a peculiar difficulty.

Neumann[72] deserves the credit for having first demonstrated that Galileo and Newton formulated their laws in such a fashion that an absolute motion was assumed. Galileo's law of inertia cannot, according to Neumann, possibly remain as a starting point for mathematical deductions. We do not indeed know what we are to understand by motion in a direct line; indeed we know that these words can be interpreted in various ways and are capable of innumerable meanings. Motion, for instance, that takes place in a straight line with regard to one celestial body, will appear as curved with regard to every other. We must therefore begin with a special body in the universe and employ it as a basis for our judgment; use it, in other words, as the particular object with respect to which all motion is to be calculated. Only then shall we be in a position to connect a definite meaning with the above words.

To what body shall we assign this place of pre-eminence? Galileo and Newton give us no answer. They simply assume absolute motion without being clear in their own minds or being conscious of the fact that this pre-supposition involves the existence of such an absolute and fixed point of reference. That this condition is necessarily involved was first clearly brought out by Neumann, though there is a definite reference to this matter in Descartes. It is for that reason that Neumann sets up as the first principle of the Galileo-Newton theory the proposition that all conceivable motions existing in the world are to be referred to one and the same absolutely fixed body, whose configuration, position and dimensions are unalterable for all time. He calls this body "the body Alpha." We are to understand then by the motion of a point, not a change of position with regard to the earth or the sun, but one with regard to this body.

What is attained by this conception? This, that a clear content is given for the first time to the determination of rectilineality in Galileo's law: the rectilineal movement is to be understood in regard to this body alpha. This may also be explained as meaning that every motion from now on is thought of as absolute. The nature and the really essential character of this so-called absolute motion, consists in the fact that all change of position is brought into relation with one and the same object, indeed with an object which, as Neumann expresses it, is spatially extended and unalterable but which cannot be further described. If, however, we do not assume absolute motion, then the whole Galileo-Newton theory falls to the ground; for, in that case, since every body in the universe is actually in motion, motion could only be defined as a relative change of position of two points with regard to one another. We should then arrive at a theory which is fundamentally different from the Galileo-Newtonian, and whose agreement with the actually observable phenomena might be very doubtful. We must insist again, therefore, that an absolute motion in absolute space is a necessary presupposition of the Galilean law of inertia. In order to simplify the conception of absolute space we have the body alpha.

We shall never be able to find an empirical point that will satisfy the above conditions. For that reason we assume an ideal point that serves the same purposes. This is how Neumann understands his body alpha.

We can thus perceive what a very peculiar construct this fiction is. It represents an accretion to reality, an intercalation that is to make conceptual mobility and the determination of concepts easier. In the final examination of reality, this interpolated element must therefore drop out and be eliminated. Indeed, as soon as the connections and mediation, for which the fiction has been created and introduced, have been accomplished, the fiction loses its significance and drops out of the final calculation. We consequently find no mention of this body alpha in experimental physics, for it disappears as soon as the mathematical formulæ have been discovered and applied. The same service is rendered by other auxiliary aids of mechanics and physics; for example, the ether of light and the electric fluid which, according to Neumann, serve only for purposes of visualization and of connecting the calculation; and the intermediate element drops out as soon as this connection has been achieved. These scientific interlopers are not included in the council that definitely determines the relations existing in actual reality and, like all temporary makeshifts, are excluded from the principles in the real and narrower sense.

§ 19
The Fiction of Pure Absolute Space[73]

It is the false assumption that mathematics can proceed in a sense different[74] a priori from that of any other science, and that, in mathematics, everything is magically extracted from the mind itself, which is immediately responsible for a distorted idea of the logical meaning of the space concept. The question is: what is space from the logical standpoint? What logical rank does mathematical space occupy?[75] It is the "presupposition" of mathematics. But "presupposition" is an ambiguous word that does not express any definite logical value. "Presupposition" may mean something that is empirically given and upon which mathematics is essentially based, or it can mean that space is an hypothesis without which mathematics could not exist. Mathematical space is unquestionably an essential presupposition, but in neither of these two senses. It is quite easy to prove that space, in the mathematical sense, namely as a pure extension in three dimensions, is not something actually given, a real fact. Empirically we find only individual bodies possessing the fundamental character of extension but never a general or pure space. It is true that the circumstance that all objects are perceived as detached from a uniform background (generally a light one), and the transparency and colourlessness of the air, make it appear as if individual objects lay in a uniformly perceptible vacant space. This peculiar circumstance has unquestionably facilitated the emergence of an independent and absolute idea of space, but we have no right to interpret this as implying that mathematical space is something empirically given. Indeed, for that very reason, nobody has seriously contended that it is. The mathematical idea of space has not, therefore, the logical value of an experience. Perhaps it possesses that of an hypothesis? But then we encounter even greater difficulties. How can an idea so absurd and so contradictory make any claim to be an hypothesis? Mathematical space is a something that is a nothing and a nothing that is a something. The contradictions inherent in the concept of an unoccupied mathematical space are well-known. A vacuum would be something contiguous and separated where we find nothing contiguous and nothing separated. If space is the relation of co-existence of real objects, then, in the absence of these, it must be nothing and would disappear with them. Since, however, the primary characteristic of a useful hypothesis, is its freedom from contradiction, such a contradictory concept as an absolute, unoccupied, mathematical space cannot be an hypothesis. And it is this very contradictoriness that prevents us from contenting ourselves, without further ado, with the favourite expression of the mathematicians that these and similar concepts are "postulates": for this last concept is vague and indefinite. We are consequently forced to ask the very pointed and embarrassing question: what logical position then can the idea of space occupy?

In view of the fundamental importance of this point for our subsequent argument and the remarkable clarity with which Leibniz in the main treated it, let us pause to examine his controversy with Clarke. This controversy, in so far as it bore on the question of space, turned on the problem whether the concept of an absolute, geometrical or vacant space, was justified or not, i.e. whether there was any actual vacuum in reality. Clarke, together with Newton, defended the existence of an absolute space (and consequently of an absolute motion). Within this absolute space, in a general but definite position, the universe, i.e. the material world, is located; and between these bodies that are, as it were, swimming in space, is also to be found absolute and vacant interspace. This theory Leibniz attacks. "Il n'y a point de vuide du tout" (Erdmann's Edition, 748); such is the thesis that Leibniz tries to establish on theological, physical, mathematical and logical grounds. "L'espace réel absolu" (Ibid. 751), is an "idole de quelques Anglois modernes. Je dis 'idole' non pas dans un sens Théologique mais Philosophique, comme le chancelier Bacon disoit autrefois qu'il y a Idola Tribus, Idola Specus." He repeatedly enumerates the *grandes difficultés* and contradictions to which this concept leads. It is particularly by means of his "Principe de la raison suffisante" that he attempts to disprove the "imaginations," the "suppositions chimériques", and the "fictions impossibles" of his opponents. As a matter of fact, of course, the idea of absolute space and absolute time does lead to peculiar absurdities, and Leibniz' refutation is quite justified. He constantly calls these concepts of absolute time and space "chiméres toutes pures" and "imaginations superficielles." They are "fictions impossibles" (771). We might, for instance, at will think of any spatial position in the world displaced any distance in absolute space; since, however, the two points cannot be distinguished, they will remain merely ideal and imaginary and the presupposition that this displacement is possible, i.e. the presupposition of absolute space, is a mere fiction.[76] The fact that there is no sufficient reason why God should have created the world at an earlier moment than he actually did, proves that this whole method of looking at the matter and the presupposition of absolute time upon which it is based, is false. What holds of time holds also for space. This idea that absolute space is a chimerical supposition and an impossible fiction runs in all possible variations through the whole of Leibniz' correspondence, which is so important for his philosophy.

Let us now attempt to show how this dispute can be adjusted by means of a very simple methodological distinction, for here we are concerned with the logical and metaphysical value of the concept of absolute space. As it certainly is not an experience, the only question which can be involved is whether we are dealing with a justifiable hypothesis or a justifiable fiction, a fiction in the sense we originally fixed. We saw how Leibniz proved that this concept was contradictory and impossible and how, for that reason, he rejected it. On the other hand we shall see that Clarke stressed its practical necessity and utility, based upon Newton's mathematical natural philosophy. Leibniz calls the idea a fiction in a derogatory sense. He uses this concept, indeed, very frequently and, as we pointed out above, in the two different meanings of a good and a bad fiction. Had not his enmity against the Newtonians, and the bad feeling that arose on both sides in consequence, disturbed Leibniz' clear vision, and had his correspondence with Clarke not taken place in the later period of his life when he was isolated and embittered by misfortune, he would probably have applied here, too, the fundamental discovery that he had arrived at in connection with other questions; namely that there are necessary and justified fictions. He might thus, perhaps, have found the correct solution, that the idea of absolute space is an indispensable auxiliary idea, i.e. that, although it is in itself contradictory and therefore imaginary and ideal, it must of necessity be formed for the building up of mathematics and mathematical physics.

This simple solution clears up at one stroke the whole passionate strife between Leibniz and the Newtonians. All the reasons advanced by Leibniz go to show that the concept is imaginary, all the counter-reasons advanced by Clarke that it is necessary. As is so often the case we here find a contradictory conception (whose exact definition we owe to Newton) at first attacked because of its logical difficulties; we then see it pass over into the general consciousness, become an everyday idea, until it is again attacked and, though deprived in the end of its reality, yet admitted and allowed to persist because of its indispensability.

In the ambiguity and double-edged nature of the concept "supposition", we again recognize the duality in logical meaning that gives to these concepts of absolute space, of the atom, etc., so varying and uncertain an appearance. Clarke proceeds from the necessity of this supposition, from the fact that Leibniz himself makes it; Leibniz, on the other hand, calls its chimerical, sophistical and imaginary. In the meaning of "fiction" developed by us, both views are united; the conception is nonsensical but fruitful.

Leibniz, indeed, had this solution in his hand but he did not express it clearly. At one place (769) he himself calls attention to the fact that such "choses purement idéales", even if their unreality is recognized, are useful ("dont la considération ne laisse pas d'étre utile"). This gives us the true idea of the methodological fiction. That Leibniz merely hinted at an idea with which he was quite familiar and did not fully demonstrate it, can only be explained by the fact that he allowed himself to be carried away by passion. Otherwise in a calm discussion he would have recognized that the suppositions of Clarke were necessary and useful fictions.

Considering the fundamental nature of this point, it is of interest to cite other places in Liebniz' writings which show his attitude without ambiguity. Thus, for instance, in his "Réplique aux Réflexions de Bayle" (Erdmann, 189; written seventeen years before the discussion with Clarke) he remarks that the mathematical ideas of time, extension, motion and continuity are merely "des choses idéales." He agrees with Hobbes who calls space a *phantasma existentis*. Extension is "the arrangement of possible coexistences." Of particular importance is a passage (190) where he says that although the meditations of the mathematicians are ideal, this does not deprive them of any of their utility. He consequently knew how to value the usefulness of such concepts (191), although quite conscious of the fact that mathematics does not furnish the most fundamental knowledge and that this is to be sought in the more important calculus of Metaphysics, in the "Analysis of ideas", for which we may substitute—without departing too much from Leibniz' meaning—in one direction, at least, the Theory of Knowledge and a methodology connected with it.

Pure mathematical space is a fiction. Its concept has the marks of a fiction: the idea of an extension without anything extended, of separation without things that are to to be separated, is something unthinkable, absurd and impossible. For mathematics, however, the concept is necessary, useful and fruitful, because the mathematicians only investigate the characteristics and laws of extended objects, *qua* extended, and not their materiality or other physical properties. The concept of pure space arises from retaining the relation of objects after the things themselves have already been thought away. While permitting matter and its intensity to be gradually reduced to zero, we still preserve the relation of material objects. Although, strictly speaking, space should disappear at the very instant in which matter has been reduced to zero and thus disappears, we still retain the relation even after the related things have vanished. If we observe an object in continuous extension and if we mentally allow the matter to become thinner and thinner until it reaches zero, then pure space is the limit when matter is conceived as disappearing and the intensity of the occupying matter is conceived as being consumed and expiring. This is the moment we seize hold of. At the very next moment nothingness begins, the zero is substituted for matter, which is seized and retained at the very last moment of its flight and expiration.

We have so far in the course of our investigation come to the conclusion that the concept of space, i.e. the concept of pure and mathematical space, is formed by a peculiar process of our conceptual faculty in which abstraction and imagination work together in a remarkable manner. Abstraction detaches something which we experience only in something else (whether as property or as relation) from this other entity—from something to which it is so firmly and inextricably bound that when what has been detached is accurately analysed we are forced to admit to ourselves that nothing remains in our hands. Abstraction takes from the substratum and the elements their attributes and relations. Now, strictly speaking, these detached pieces, apart from their original context, have no meaning: they evaporate into nothingness and lead to absurdities. Imagination, by reason of its specific and peculiar gifts, comes to the aid and rescues abstraction which, as described above, has dissolved the given world into nothing and stands looking round helplessly at the result of its activity. Imagination reintroduces into the isolated relation the idea of the related elements, but in a form in which they are only shadows of what we find in reality. It thus provides a support for the product of abstraction and prevents it from falling into the abyss of nothingness.

What we must do, therefore, is to make clear to ourselves that the space of the mathematicians is nothing but a scientific and artificial preparation, which differs from the schematic auxiliary constructs, etc., of other sciences, only in the nature of the objects that are to be investigated and not in the method of investigation. This unity of method must be strongly emphasized. Only a methodological approach can purge us of our old prejudices about the objects of mathematics. Only the methodologist, by following the devious routes of human understanding, can demonstrate how, in mathematics also, exactly the same methodological principles are valid as in the other sciences. The objects of mathematics are artificial preparations, artificial structures, fictional abstractions, abstract fictions, as we shall prove in the following pages in connection with particular mathematical constructs. Here we are concerned with the concept of space in general, with pure absolute space, — a perfect example of a normal and scientific fiction. There is therefore no object in trying to argue away the blatant contradictions inherent in this concept. To be a true fiction, the concept of space should be self-contradictory. Anyone who desires to "free" the concept of space from these contradictions, would deprive it of its characteristic qualities, that is to say, of the honour of serving as an ideal example of a true and justified fiction.

§ 20

Surface, Line, Point, etc., as Fictions[77]

WHAT holds for pure absolute space holds also — *mutatis mutandis* — for the single mathematical spaces and parts of space, and for the idea of the so-called mathematical bodies, such as sphere, cylinder, cube, prism, etc. The psychological and logical foundations of these constructs are the corresponding empirical corporeal objects. And here again we find abstraction and imagination participating in the manner described above. The corporeal is reduced to a minimum, finally to zero; and therewith, from a strictly logical standpoint, the boundaries of these corporeal objects must fade away and, so to speak, merge into themselves. But since we are abstracting only from the occupying content, the form is still retained, and before all these boundaries, completely deprived of their content, collapse, they are supported by the imagination which, as the content disappears and becomes infinitely thin, holds them in place as infinitely thin shells, empty husks, as a skin, a covering, indeed even as a mere frame. Such forms, without a content, are, as such, nothing, indeed worse than nothing, for they are contradictory constructs, a nothing that is nevertheless conceived as a something, a something that is already passing over into a nothing. And yet just these contradictory constructs, these fictional entities, are the indispensable bases of mathematical thought. The boundaries of the empirical bodies are taken as such, and are abstracted and hypostasized; and with these imaginary constructs mathematics, and particularly geometry, operates.

The same—*mutatis mutandis*—holds for the surface, the line and the point. That the surface is the boundary of a body is a very oid definition. Historically and psychogenetically, of course, we are first concerned with real "planes," i.e. flat boundaries. The concept of curved surfaces arises later. There are flat surfaces, i.e., really plane constructs, in nature, as well as the great number due to the primitive participation of man; here we abstract from the material that forms the surface, and the formal element is taken alone in itself and made independent by imagination. In this case also it is a contradiction to speak of a surface as such; and yet scientific thought proceeds unconcerned along its path, in the face of these and even more pronounced contradictions. If thought were to allow itself to be held up by such contradictions it would never be able to move at all.

The same is true of the line—as the "boundary of the surface." Of lines, too, there is no lack, either in nature or in primitive art, but they are, so to speak, immersed in the corporeal. It is abstraction that first picks out these lines as something special, with an existence of their own, and then calls in the aid of imagination to hypostasize these structures. But that they are merely fictional concepts is self-evident. What the mathematician, the geometrician, draws on the blackboard or on paper, and calls a line, is not a line in the mathematical sense, for it always possesses a second (and even a third) dimension even if that has been reduced to a minimum. A line, in the mathematical sense, can never be sensuously represented, for it is a matter of abstraction and imagination and, in all cases, remains a contradictory construct.

The same naturally holds for the point which we are accustomed to call the limit of a line. Here, likewise, mathematics, on the basis of certain sense-experiences of which there are many both in nature and among mankind, has constructed the non-sensuous, we might say the super-sensuous idea, of a point without extension in any dimension—an idea in itself both untenable and contradictory, a monstrous concept despite its infinitesimal size, of a something that is already a nothing, of a nothing that is nevertheless supposed to be a something. The mathematical point is, in all respects, a true and complete mathematical fiction.

A point as a zero-dimensional construct, is, in itself, entirely contradictory, though as necessary as it is absurd. A construct without any dimension is, in itself, a nothing. But the one-dimensional construct of the line and the two-dimensional construct of the surface are contradictory ideas. In reality we know only material, corporeal objects, out of whose peculiar characteristic of extension we abstract the three dimensions. The two-dimensional construct of the surface and the one-dimensional construct of the line that we occasionally appear to observe in these bodies, are only abstractions individualized by the imagination, in other words, fictions with which we operate *as* if there were realities corresponding to them; necessary conceptual aids and auxiliary concepts that help us, indeed, in thinking but which cannot give us any knowledge of reality. We are here operating with unrealities and not with realities; but they are useful and indispensable unrealities. We regard these unrealities as real, however, because we are accustomed to regard everything as real to which we give a name, without realizing that we can bestow a name on unreal as well as on real things. Anyone who realizes this, and who further realizes that certain unreal ideas are necessary and useful, has grasped the true, scientific concept of a fiction.

In the examination of the surface, the line and the point, another point of view can also be applied. Hitherto we have taken these constructs as limits, in the sense that they are limits made self-subsistent by our imagination, although they are, of course, merely limits of a something that has been detached from real objects by our abstraction. But here, too, we can introduce the concept of a flux, of the progressive diminution from something real to zero, and thus allow the constructs in question to arise in such a way that we can stop the process of disappearance at the last moment, as we did above in connection with the origin of pure mathematical space.

§ 21
The Fiction of the Infinitely Small[78]

In order to understand the function of the Infinitely Small it is necessary to examine in detail the nature of the objects with which it is concerned. The mathematical constructs are the abstract forms of spatial and temporal contiguity and succession. One of the fundamental characteristics of the latter, which, in the last analysis, is something definitely given, is their division into genera and species. Thus we have for instance the genus of the conic section which is sub-divided into the various species: circle, ellipse, parabola, hyperbola. We have here clear-cut and accurately definable modifications of the general form of a concept, differentiating a genus into a number of different species. We can only proceed from one species to the other by making a conceptual leap.

Now mathematical constructs possess one property, namely, the possibility of a progressive and continuous diminution and enlargement. To which must be added the property that through this progressive diminution (or magnification) of an element of such a concept, it constantly approximates more closely to a neighbouring element. The conceptual formula of the ellipse demands, for example, the presence of two foci which must be a finite distance apart. This distance itself is undetermined and can be made arbitrarily large or small; so long as the necessary condition is adhered to, we have an ellipse. It is, however, an objective and undeniable fact that the closer these foci approach to each other, the nearer does the ellipse approximate to the circle. From this it follows that when this distance disappears entirely, the ellipse has passed into a circle. This transition from the one type to the other is, however, in the last analysis, only possible by a sudden jump which takes us in one instant into a different field. By definition, the ellipse must possess an eccentricity and two foci F and F', distance m apart. An entirely different form arises as soon as this distance disappears. But between the presence of m and the disappearance of m, absolutely no third form exists. The concept of the ellipse has m as a variable element.

It is a fact, then, that the ellipse gradually approaches the circle through the successive diminution of m; when m becomes 0, the circle takes the place of the ellipse. From these facts our conceptual faculty forms something new, which, however, remains entirely within the domain of conception or imagination. The more I divide m the smaller it becomes. I can continue this sub-division *ad infinitum*. What if I now imagine, i.e. form the fiction, that this infinitely progressing division had been completed? I would, of course, be indulging in a crazy logical contradiction, but I should also secure an advantage. If—I am only assuming this in imagination, fictively—this infinite division had been completed, then the last part would not be finite but infinitely small. And if the distance became infinitely small, F and F' would coincide and yet of course not coincide. There would still be a distance, but it would no longer be a real distance, because it would no longer be finite. Let us imagine this quite chimerical case. What is its purpose, what have I gained thereby?

It was our purpose in the previous paragraphs to show the existence of a constant transition between the ellipse and the circle, in other words, to think of the circle as a special case of the ellipse; we did not want to leave the limits of our species in order to arrive at the circle. But what value can this possibly possess? Is it not mere play? Not in the least. For if I can say the circle is to be regarded as an ellipse, I have the right to apply the laws of the one to the other.

The matter can also be expressed thus: in saying that the circle is an ellipse I make a mistake, for in the ellipse there are two foci, in the circle only one centre. But I am making this error progressively smaller by continually decreasing m, and the error will become infinitely small when m is assumed to be "infinitely small". It is true that in doing this, I am making use of a concept full of contradictions and, in fact, make a second mistake; nevertheless, I attain my goal of being able to treat the circle on the analogy of the ellipse.

We are, then, here dealing with a forced and compulsory analogy, with an unjustified transference. I proceed *as* if the circle were an ellipse and I attain this through the idea—*as* if such an infinitely small distance existed—in other words, I am operating with purely imaginary concepts, which are, however, fruitful fictions.

If we now consider the function of the "infinitely small" from a more general point of view, we shall see that this concept serves the purpose of permitting us to regard as identical, constructs which are closely related and of which one is constantly approaching the other through a diminution (or an enlargement) in one of its conceptual elements, without, however, co-inciding as long as the conceptual element remains at all. But wherever one species of construct can be reduced to another and to the laws of the other, the task of thought is simplified. This concept, then, by creating a forced analogy, serves as a bond between different species with the object of simplifying the thought process.[79]

For that reason the concept of the "infinitely small" must of course be contradictory. There is, as we have shown, a conceptual jump between the mathematical species, for there is an eternal chasm between nothing and something; and so the concept in question must itself be a cross between something and nothing. If it is to be the intermediary between two species that differ by reason of the absence or presence of an element, then if we are to succeed in regarding one as a special case of the other it must be possible to imagine, conceive, or picture either the presence of the element as an absence, or its absence as a presence. This contradictory task the concept under discussion takes upon itself by regarding the absence of an element as the presence of an infinitely small part of this element. In the "infinitely-small" we find, indeed, both the nothing and the something at one and the same time. In order to act as a mediating concept, the infinitely-small must combine within itself these contradictory conditions; and it is therefore a true fiction.

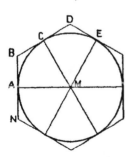

There are cases where this fictive method of approach represents more than mere dialectic play and an unnecessary mediation, namely, where a direct deduction from a formula will not work; this indirect path, this circuitous road, then becomes the only means of attaining our goal. This already holds for the measurement of the area of the circle. We should never be able to arrive at the formula

for the area of the circle from a study of the circle as a circle, simply because the desire to determine the surface of the circle is based upon the
fictional concept that a common measure can be found for rectilinear and
curved figures. Where such a formula cannot be directly deduced, the circuitous path through the infinitely-small renders excellent service; by admittedly regarding the circle, in this case, as a special instance, a limiting
case, of a polygon, we obtain the formula by this fictive treatment. We
act, we speak, we think, we calculate—as if the circle were a regular polygon with an infinite number of infinitely small sides. We create the fiction
of infinitely many, infinitely small sides. Thus the fiction of the infinitely-
small is here not merely useless play but possesses both a meaning and
a justification and is, as we have shown, at least a convenient method of
speech, a convenient concept. From the formula of the arc of a polygon
$F = \frac{1}{2}CM(AB+BC+CD+...+NA)$, (where CM = the radius of the inscribed
circle), we obtain the formula for the area of the circle by considering that,
in this case, if we regard the circle as a regular polygon with an infinite
number of infinitely small sides, the radius of the circumscribed circle (the
side of the triangles into which the polygon is broken up) and that of the
inscribed circle (the altitude of the triangles) differ infinitely little; so that
we are justified in substituting the radius of the circle in question for the
factor CM; by means of which and other modifications we obtain the well-
known formula $F = r^2\pi$

These examples, which can be multiplied at will, prove that the "infinitely-
small" and the "infinitely-large" are both mediating concepts between dissimilar constructs and that there is nothing mysterious to be looked for
behind them.[80] The "passage through the infinite," as this artifice has been
named, is a perfectly transparent methodological process, as our analysis has
shown. The contradiction is absolutely indispensable for these two concepts
since they are to connect fields that are dissimilar, exclusive by definition,
and there is an element absent in the concept of the one that is contained
in that of the other. But we form these contradictory concepts in the full
consciousness of their contradictory nature: fully realizing that we are constructing false and impossible concepts for a practical scientific purpose—in
a word, that they are fictions.

If we now put the question, how we are to explain the riddle that by means of such illogical, indeed senseless concepts, correct results are obtained, the answer lies in what we found above to be the general law of fictions, namely in the correction of the errors that have been committed. (Cf. p. 109 ff.)

Thought obviously makes a mistake, as was sufficiently obvious in the last example. This error consists simply in the fact that the circle is regarded as a polygon at all. Since, as is perfectly clear from the elementary definitions, these two constructs—circle and polygon—are specifically different, it is absolutely impossible logically to subsume the one construct under the other species. The error is therefore manifest. It is self-evident, however, that an error, wherever introduced, is bound to be a disturbing element in the

final result; but since in the case under discussion this does not happen, the result and the inferences drawn from it being specifically true for calculating the area, this can only be explained by the fact that, in some way or other, this error is corrected. And such is actually the case. Let us consider the arc mn which we assume to be equal to the angle mpn (mn = mp+pn). Here the mistake is obvious, and the equation positively false. This error is, however, corrected and made harmless by assuming that both members of the equation are infinitely small, the arc as well as the angle, and that, as remarked above, we infer therefrom that this circle is looked upon as a polygon with an infinite number of infinitely small sides. By the constant diminution of mn and the corresponding multiplication of the number of angles of the inscribed polygon, the error that has been made is just as constantly decreased in size. Because this is thought of as continued *ad infinitum*, the error is made infinitely small, that is, becomes zero. The whole secret consists, consequently, in compensating for an error committed. This correction takes on a specific form in these and similar cases, so that one error is compensated for by another; and for that reason we are justified in calling this whole procedure "the method of double error." This second mistake consists in the illogical assumption of infinitely small or, if it is preferred, an infinitely-large entity (one referring to the size of the sides of the polygon, the other to their number, both being dependent upon one another). The above equation as it stands is false: it loses in falsity as the sides become smaller and their number larger, but its falsity remains finite as long as the quantities connected with it are finite. As we indicated above, the error becomes infinitely small, i.e. equal to zero, as soon as the quantities pass over into infinity, except that the positing of an infinitely-small entity constitutes another error which compensates for the first one committed. After the two mistakes have thus nullified each other, the calculation is freed from both; the result becomes quite correct after the first error has been made good by a second. Now many propositions that hold for polygons can, *mutatis mutandis*, be transferred to the circle; at any rate, those that admit of such a transformation. A definite and useful object has consequently been attained by this fictional analogy. The treatment of the circle *as if* it were a polygon has thus proved itself a fruitful conception: I act, speak, think, and calculate *as if* infinitely small sides of polygons existed, *as if* an infinite number of such sides existed, and could be completely summed into a finite quantity; and with all these false concepts I arrive in the end at a correct result.

As is well-known, our example—the reduction of the circle to a polygon—is not the only one of its kind. The same fictive analogical method is very frequently applied. On the same principles we treat the cylinder as a regular prism with an infinite number of sides and, by means of this fiction, the formula for the volume of the prism $V = h.F$ is, in the form $V = h.r^2\pi$, also applicable to the cylinder. Similarly, we can look upon the cone as a regular pyramid with an infinite number of sides and the formula for the volume of the pyramid $V = \frac{1}{3}h.F$ holds, in the form $V = \frac{1}{3}h.r^2\pi$, for the cone. It is the same in calculating the area of the sphere. For this purpose we first consider the surface described by a polygon rotating round an axis, and transfer the law which we thus discover to the surface described by a semi-circle. To determine the volume we can picture the sphere as broken up into an infinite number of trilateral pyramids with infinitely small bases grouped around a centre.

In all these cases we find the same principle of fictive analogy, according to which the curved line is regarded as made up of an infinite number of infinitely small straight lines. In strict logic, as we have already remarked, we could never subsume the curved under the straight line. All the laws of rectilinear figures hold only for such, and rectilinear figures remain rectilinear even if we increase the number of their angles to infinity. We should never be able to come to any limiting boundary and no point could be given where the rectilinear would suddenly take a leap and become curved. Truly enough both would continually approximate to each other, but approximation does not mean contact, nor is it coincidence. No possible multiplication of the

THE INFINITELY SMALL 223

sides can lead to a coincidence. Thus we see the error that is made by identifying the two. How this is corrected we have already indicated.

There are a number of other instructive examples of this method. It may, for instance, be of value to adopt the reverse process and subsume the straight line under the curve. Since a circular line with a very large diameter closely approximates to the straight line, the latter can be regarded as a segment of a circle having an infinite diameter; a straight line is treated *as if* it were a portion of the periphery of a circle with an infinite diameter.

The same holds for the point, i.e. the mathematical point, where it is of interest to regard it as a surface (or a body). For this purpose the mathematical point is treated *as if* it were a circle or a sphere with an infinitely small diameter. This mediating role here played by the infinite, and particularly the infinitely-small, is taken by the same concept, as we all know, far more extensively in the "infinitesimal-method." In this method, the principle that we have so far employed is further extended, and what characterizes and differentiates it most is the fact that calculation seizes upon this fictive method and makes use of it in a peculiar manner. In the cases so far mentioned, no difficulties were encountered in calculation; as soon as the method of approach had been justified, as soon as a reason had been discovered for the transference, the postulates that held for the polygon could be applied without further consideration to the circle, for the infinitely-small quantities appeared only in the proof and not in the calculation. The matter takes on another aspect, however, in the infinitesimal calculus itself whose most characteristic peculiarity does not lie, as has been frequently assumed, in the conception of the infinitesimal—this was known before Leibniz and Newton—but, far more, in the discovery of an analytical (algebraic) expression for the infinitely-small.

The same fictive subsumption or analogy by means of which the curved can be made subject to the laws of the straight line, we also find employed, though in a different form, in the method of infinitesimals (this form indeed presupposes the well-known Cartesian fictional type of approach discussed above (p. 53). We saw above that the equation of an are with the side of a polygon was false, and that this could only be nullified by thinking of both elements as diminished *ad infinitum*, when the error disappeared. In the present instance we are concerned with another false equation which presupposes the Cartesian system of coordinates. It is well-known that a line (not necessarily a curve) is regarded as determined by the function of two variable quantities. From that we obtain, in a general way, a function-relationship between a definite portion of the main line, on the one hand, and the parts of the coordinates that belong to it, on the other, a fact which (in right-angled parallel coordinates) is directly based on the theorem of Pythagoras.

As the figure shows we have the equation $MN^2 = MR^2 + NR^2$; or if we make the part MN of the main line equal to $S = \Delta s$, the related coordinate portions Δx and Δv (Δx, as the increment PQ of the abscissa $AP = \Delta x$, Δy, as the increment NR of the ordinate MP), then we find $\Delta s^2 = \Delta x^2 + \Delta y^2$. If all these three elements are supposed infinitely small the relationship will not change, and the only difficulty we encounter lies in the concept of the infinitely-small which we have recog-

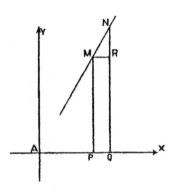

nized to be a fiction. The situation is different in the case of curves or lines which do not arise like those discussed above, from functions of the first degree but from those of higher degrees. If we take as our basis the following example, we again encounter the difficulty mentioned above, that the

curved is incommensurable with the recti-linear. Corresponding to the above example, we should here equate $Mv^2 = Mr^2 + rv^2$ (Mv as a part of the curve s, Mr as the increment of the abscissa x, rv as the increment of the ordinate V); or $\Delta s^2 = \Delta x^2 + \Delta y^2$. But here the incommensurability stands in the way, and the equation is recognized as positively false. In other words, a mistake has been made that must be corrected and this correction can, in this case, only take place by substituting for

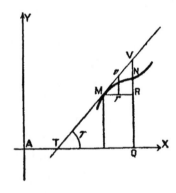

$\Delta s^2 = \Delta x^2 + \Delta y^2$, $ds^2 = dx^2 + dy^2$, i.e. by constantly decreasing the error by a constant decrease of the equated elements, as far as the infinitely-small. If we do this, we obtain as our part of the curve an infinitely small element and have thus attained the possibility of regarding this infinitely small element as straight. Then this equation becomes correct, for the error committed has been made infinitely small by this very diminution.[81]

Another well-known application of the infinite, by a violent subsumption, is the following: Any one of the three corners of the triangle can from the side opposite be gradually extended at will further and further into the limitless. In so doing the two angles of that side naturally become progressively larger, while the corners of the angle in question become infinitely smaller. As the sum of the three angles forms two right angles, the two angles of the side will approximate more and more to two right angles, without, however, attaining this as long as the extension is a finite one. If now we call to our aid the concept of the infinitely-large, by thinking of this corner of the angle as being at an infinite distance, the two sides become transformed into parallel lines and the two angles become exactly equivalent to two right angles. We can therefore regard the two parallel straight lines, together with the piece that has been cut off on the third line, as if it formed a triangle with two infinitely long sides. From this it follows immediately that the so-called eleventh axiom, according to which the sum of the interior opposite angles of two parallel straight lines that are intersected by a third straight line is equal to $180°$, can be looked upon as a special case of the proposition that the sum of three angles of a plane triangle is equal to two right angles. So here, again, we find the same application: the concept of the infinitely-large serves the purpose of subsuming one heterogeneous instance under another of which it can be regarded or imagined as a so-called limiting case. But it is just this assumption of a limiting case that constitutes the error, which is then corrected by introducing the fictional concept of infinity.

§ 22
The History of the Infinitesimal Fiction[82]

THE fictive method of approach enables us, as indicated above, to let lines consist of points, surfaces of lines and bodies of surfaces. This standpoint is at the basis of all mathematics. We particularly wish to call attention here to the fact that lines are looked upon as elements of surfaces and surfaces as elements of bodies.

In particular, mention must here be made of Kepler and his *Nova steriometria doliorum* (1605). In order to express the relation of the circumference to the diameter of the circle he imagines the circumference to be composed of an infinite number of points, of which each forms the base of a triangle, and whose apices meet in the centre (theorem II). He imagines the sphere to consist of an infinite number of cones resting on the infinite number of points forming the surface and with their vertices coinciding in the centre. Here, therefore, we have the idea of the infinitely-small which seems to have been originated by Kepler. The great mind that had busied itself with the infinitely-large, with celestial space, and had studied the movements and laws of the heavenly bodies, had also made a profound study of the infinitely small. Incidentally it is well to point out that Kepler specifically says that he *regards* the circle in such a way, i.e. *as* if it were so, not that it *is* so; i.e. he is conscious of the fictive nature of his procedure.

Just as he regards the infinitely small points as the foundation of the line and, indeed, as the elements of the surface, so we already find in his views the foundations for a treatment of the surfaces as corporeal elements. The cylinder and the parallelopipedon he treats as corporealized surfaces: "sunt hic *veluti* quaedam plana corporata; accidunt igitur illis eadem quae planis; (theorem III). Conus est "hic" "veluti" circulus corporatus; idem igitur a sectione patitur, quod circulus suae baseos (theorem XVI)."

In addition, he wishes to regard surfaces as consisting of line elements. Thus, in theorem XX, he says "secetur area lineis parallelis alicui in aliquot segmenta aeque alta minima *quasi* linearia", i.e. the surface is divided by lines, all of which are parallel to a certain line, into a number of equally high, minimal and, as it were, linear segments, in other words into segments which are looked upon as if they were only lines.

Here, then, we see the marvellous idea of the infinitesimal, as it were in its embryological stage, thrown off and suggested by one of the greatest minds of the world. The valuable part of this view lies in the corollary that "what holds for the body holds also for its constituent lines". For through this method of approach, bodies are reduced to surfaces and the laws of surfaces, the latter to lines and the laws of lines, and these, in turn, to points. The constant repetition of *veluti, quasi*—as-if—is remarkable. Objects are thus subjected to this fictive method, and they are considered from this new and arbitrary point of view.

This fiction whose origin can thus be traced to the great astronomer, became the basis for the mathematical epoch which followed. The next to attack and elaborate the idea was the Jesuit, Cavaleri. He not only described the origin of his views very clearly and concretely (in the Introduction to his *Geometria indivisibilibus continuorum nova quaedam ratione promota*, Bononiae, 1635), but is also quite conscious of the fictive nature of his method.

In order to show that he was methodologically well aware of the significance of his new method, Cavaleri says:

"I use an artifice (tali artificio) similar to that which the algebraists are accustomed to apply in the solution of problems: they add, subtract, multiply and divide irrational roots (radices quamvis ineffabiles, surdas ac ignoratas), provided
only these serve to procure them the desired knowledge of the matter in hand,
and are then convinced that they have done their duty; in the same way, to as-
certain the volumes of continua, I too used the congeries of indivisibilia (partly
lines, partly surfaces), although their number is not assignable (innominabilis,
surda ac ignota), even if their enumeration is confined within concrete limits."

He could hardly have expressed himself more lucidly. In his expressions
"veluti, ceu, quodammodo, effingere, considerare, ponere, contemplari, in-
telligere lineae quales esse existimari possunt", etc., he definitely indicates
that we are dealing here with a methodological fiction. This is even more
evident from his analogy with irrational roots, whose use he quite clearly
designates as a methodological artifice.

Cavaleri's progress beyond Kepler is really very small, but he is clearer and
more consistent. Out of Kepler's idea he makes a consistent body of truth—he
divides the surface not only into, as it were, equal linear segments, but supposes
them to arise through the motion (fluere) of a real line, i.e. of an indivisibile.

Cavaleri, clearly and correctly, defended himself against the logical difficulties that could be advanced against his conception. He mentions both
philosophers and mathematicians as opponents of his method—and their
objections referred to the composition of the continuous, as well as to the
infinite. With regard to the composition of the continuous out of indivisible
elements he well observes that this way of looking at the matter by no means
compels us to regard the continuous as itself composed of indivisibles, for the
only purpose intended here was to show that continua corresponded to the
relation of indivisibles. In other words, he treats these indivisibles as methodological fictions, for he specifically says that he wishes to regard the continua
as if they were made up of indivisibles (lines and surfaces). The fiction must
therefore not be called an hypothesis. For it is indeed impossible to claim that
the continuous is really made up of indivisibles. In imagination, however, this
standpoint is permissible, and even indispensable as a useful fiction.

Cavaleri fully recognized the contradictions in the concept of indivisibilia.
"Many passages . . . prove that Cavaleri himself was quite aware of this contradiction,". . but he knew nevertheless . . . "that by means of his method . . .

truth could be attained, if it were properly employed" (Gerhardt, *Geschichte d. h. Anal.*, Vol. I, 24). "Truth" then, could be attained in spite of "the contradiction"; nay, precisely because of it. In this sense, Cavaleri (*Ibid.*, 22, 24) called his indivisibilia an *instrumentum praecipuum*—i.e., he recognized quite clearly the purely instrumental character of his invention of indivisibilia—they are to him useful fictions.

Cavaleri's method, primarily because of its methodical clarity, was held in high regard by later mathematicians. We find everywhere, beside the attacks of minor doubters, commendations from the great thinkers of his day. Roberval makes explicit acknowledgment to Cavaleri. In his *Traité des Indivisibles* he says: "Pour tirer des conclusions par le moyen des indivisibles, il faut supposer que toute ligne, soit droite ou courbe, se peut diviser en une infinité de parties ou petites lignes, égales entr'elles . . . Par tout ce discours on peut comprendre que la multitude infinie de points *se prend pour* une infinité de petites lignes et compose la ligne entiére . . . . L'infinité de lignes représente l'infinité de petites superficies qui composent la superficie totale. Le grand triligne [a triangle limited by a conchoid] est divisé (selon les indivisibles) en secteurs semblables infinis, qui ressemblent aux triangles, mais par les indivisibles nous les prenons pour secteurs." Elsewhere, too, he praises "le moyen des indivisibles." He is well aware of the purely instrumental character of this method of thought: "in auxilium infinita nostra advocavi." And further: "Lineam *tanquam si* ex infinitis seu indefinitis, numero lineis constet, superficiem ex infinitis seu indefinitis numero superficiebus, solidum ex solidis, angulum ex angulis . . . *componi concepimus* . . . singula enim suas habent *utilitates.*" In other words here too we are dealing with useful fictions.

Pascal approached the matter from the same standpoint (*Ibid.*, 32 ff.). According to him, the new method of Cavaleri was distinguished from the older solely "en la maniére de parler. . . . Et c'est pourquoi je ne ferais aucune difficulté dans la suite d'user de ce langage des Indivisibles: 'la somme des lignes 'ou' la somme des plans', et ainsi quand je considérerai, par exemple, le diamétre d'un demi-circle divisé en un nombre indéfini de parties égales . . . je ne ferai aucune difficulté d'user de cette expression." In other words, Pascal considered the indivisibles, and the infinitesimals, merely as a convenient method of conception and a convenient method of expression respectively.

The same method is employed by Newton to attain the concept of fluxions.[83]

We must here briefly recapitulate the two methods just discussed, namely, those of Cavaleri and Descartes, since they form the necessary presuppositions for the development of Newton's thought.

We saw that Cavaleri derives the line from the expanding motion of a point, the surface from the motion of the line, and the body from that of a surface. It is not difficult to recognize that this attitude is simply the reverse of the view mentioned above for which points, lines and surfaces are originate from lines, surfaces and bodies. The process of movement is similar in character but in the opposite direction. As the process of decrement approaches disappearance, it is checked at the very last moment, the resultant being the *indivisibilia*, i.e. points, lines and surfaces, indivisible because, if they were still further divisible, they could not represent the last moment before complete disappearance. If they could be divided just once more, the motion could still traverse a further section of its course. The last moment is thus imagined as indivisible, and it is at this moment, therefore, that we obtain the nominally indivisible products—point, line, surface. If, now, the movement is reversed, the original condition must clearly be restored, i.e. lines, surfaces and bodies.

Here, finally, comes the Cartesian idea that every line, without exception, can be determined analytically. For every line we can find a function belonging to it that contains in a formula the law for the whole course of the line. This formula $y = F(x)$ is the common magic formula for all lines. Every line is thereupon conceived as determined by the reciprocal relation of x and y, the abscissa and the ordinate.

Newton's method is based upon a combination of the Cartesian conception with that of Kepler-Cavaleri. Taking the idea of Cavaleri, according to which every line is described by a moving point, and further assuming that every line is definitely determined by the relation of the abscissa to the ordinate, the movement of the (Cavaleri) point is thought of as composite, composed of a movement in the direction of the abscissa and the ordinates. Every single forward movement of the point describing the line is accurately determined and prescribed by the law, by the function. The function contains the law of motion of the point. Strictly speaking it is not the formula $y = F(x)$ that holds here, but the expanded formula $y + \Delta y = F(x + \Delta x)$. Every forward movement of the generating point is determined by this fact, i.e. every finite discontinuous and discrete movement. This formula is related to the line, more or less as the finite definite part of a surface is to this line, or this line is to it. Just as I can divide every surface or line (A) into any arbitrary number (x) of finite equal parts (a), so that, $A = x.a$, so I can break up the general path of the line $y = F(x)$ into an arbitrary but finite number of single steps Δx and Δy.

We must lay great stress upon this analogy, for it contains the key to the apparent secret of the calculus of fluxions.

But since, following Cavaleri, we have pictured every line as broken up into a number of infinitely small linear points, it would be useful, in this connection, to substitute for the finite steps or parts an infinite number of infinitely small steps or fluxions.

It is evident that this view can only be properly utilized if we can also succeed in finding an analytical expression for the infinitely-small. To this artifice, the analytical expression of the geometrical conception of the infinitely-small, we owe the tremendous progress made by Newton and Leibniz.

It is, of course, quite clear that no analytical expression can be directly obtained for the infinitely-small. On the other hand an indirect possibility exists through the Cartesian conception.

According to the latter, every progress made by the line or curve is conditioned by two elements, by the relative and mutually dependent progress of the two coordinates.

In order to obtain a proper insight into this method and a correct conception of its nature and use, we must, as Cavaleri had already done with his method, separate carefully the methodological from the metaphysical — which, incidentally, neither Newton nor Leibniz always did. By reason of its philosophical interest, this simple, if somewhat difficult, conception, has been made complicated. In particular we must not see in the absurd something mysterious but firmly adhere to the principle which we have laid down as characteristic, that, as in the case of all fictions, we are here, too, dealing with a logically contradictory assumption which is of practical use. *It is nonsense, but there is method in it.* It is in this, roughly speaking, that the secret of the calculus lies.

In particular, the analytical expression of the fluxion, i.e. of the differential quotients, is nothing mysterious but a mere methodological fiction, a dodge, a subtle device; the fluxion marks a progress that is no progress, or rather an absence of progress that is yet progress.

The method of fluxions has two essential elements, the *geometrical* and the *analytical*. We may deal first with the *geometrical* for it is intimately connected with what has been said above.

It consists simply in assuming that not only is every line to be thought of as consisting in the motion of a point or arising from an infinite number of infinitely small line-points—but that this movement of the describing point is broken up into single thrusts, steps, stages, etc., and is primarily thought of as consisting of any arbitrary number of finite steps. Each of these finite steps can, however, always be imagined smaller and just as the surface becomes, as it were, attenuated to a line, so do these finite step-lines become attenuated to infinitely small step-points. This would indeed be of little assistance if an additional element were not added by the Cartesian method. According to this method, every finite step can be analyzed into the advance of two factors whose relation is exactly fixed. Every individual step can consequently be represented as a right-angled triangle whose hypotenuse is the curve, and whose other two sides are the coordinates. Just as we can let every surface shrink to a line, every line into a point, so likewise we can apply this magic method in the present case.

If we let the triangle decrease gradually, so that it finally only occupies the point M, then we obtain an infinitely small triangle whose hypotenuse, according to the Newtonian conception, is more precisely given by the fact that the ordinate which determines it retains its initial velocity. But since according to the law of the curve, it must change this velocity at every moment, it serves as the best transition to the indivisible moment in which the progress is similarly indivisible.

We see, therefore, that the fluxion triangle is the limit of the triangle of increments, in the same sense the surface is the limit of the body, the line the limit of the surface and the point the limit of the line. Upon this analogy, here first set forth in this way, we must lay great stress, for the internal relationships of all these fictional auxiliary ideas and concepts are thereby illuminated.

What we have said above about the Newtonian fluxion-triangle also holds in exactly the same way for the "characteristic triangle", as Leibniz expressed it. There is no fundamental divergence between Newton's presentation of the matter and that of Leibniz but merely a difference between the formal point of view, which, in the last analysis, is a mere verbal difference. As a rule, it is true, the matter is presented as though Newton's method were stricter and less open to objection than that of Leibniz. Leibniz, it is claimed, following Cavaleri's indivisibility, introduced the contradictory concept of the infinitely-small while Newton, on the other hand, merely applied the old harmless concept of limits. We often find it stated to-day that mathematics must adopt the latter as the safer type and that the conception of Leibniz should be dropped. This view goes back to Newton himself. He maintains a non-committal attitude toward Cavaleri's fiction of *indivisibilia*, the "durior indivisibilium hypothesis, and adds: "Proinde in sequentibus, si quando quantitates

tanquam ex particulis constantes consideravero, vel si pro rectis usupavero li-
neolas curvas, nolim indivisibilia, sed evanescentia divisibilia, non summas et
rationes partium determinatarum, sed summarum et rationum limites semper intelligi, vimque talium demonstrationum ad methodum praecedentium
lemmatum semper revocari." (Gerhardt, *Geschichte der Analysis*, Vol. I, p. 86.)

From all that we have said, however, it is evident that the concept of limits
contains the same contradictions as that of the infinitely-small, only they are
less transparent. The pure concept of the infinitely-small exhibits openly and
directly contradictions that are also contained in the concept of limits, as is
shown by the analysis given above. The latter concept appears more harmless merely because it keeps itself closer to the facts, but all the same it does
conceal within itself all those spikes that the concept of the infinitely-small
presents openly and honestly.

It is, therefore, an entirely vain procedure based upon a complete misunderstanding, if modern mathematicians imagine that they can rid the calculus of contradictions by going back to the concept of limits. Only weak
spirits could be thus satisfied, and a strictly logical thinker must soon discover the same contradictions in the concept of "limits".

If we were to refer here to all that might be said about Leibniz in this connection, our account would soon take on the proportions of a monograph. We shall
limit ourselves to the most essential points, especially to what is of particular
interest here, namely, the purely methodological problem of the new method.
Leibniz did not adequately express himself on this point in the original documents where he specifically developed his discovery of the differential calculus:
this resulted from the custom of his period of keeping new methods secret as
long as possible and making public only their results not their foundation.[84]

Of particular importance is what Leibniz says in 1695 in the *Acta Eru-*
dit. Lips.[85] in answer to the objections of Niewentiit, who pointed out the
logical contradictions in the new method, particularly in the concept of
the infinitely-small. Niewentiit had especially criticized the fact that in the
method the "incomparabiliter minora negleguntur" and that thereby, the
equation, the *aequalitas*, became an inexact one, so that it could no more be
called an *aequalitas*. Leibniz answered as follows: "Si quis talem aequalitatis
definitionum rejicit, de nomine disputat. Sufficit enim intelligibilem esse
et *ad inveniendum utilem*. Itaque non tantum lineas infinite parvas, ut *dx, dy* pro

quantitatibus veris in suo genere assumo, sed et earum quadrata . . . praesertim cum eas ad ratiocinandum *inveninc-dumque utiles* reperiam." We have italicized the most important words in order to draw special attention to them. Leibniz proceeds from the practical utility these concepts possess, and it is only because of this practical utility that he regards these concepts as *verae,* but as he carefully adds, *in suo genere.* He does not think of them as absolutely, but as relatively true,"in their own way". In the same monograph he shows further on that, and why, the infinitely-small can be permitted to become zero; and he remarks that it is "ob talium expressionum raritatem et insolentiam, quae, fateor, tanta est, ut ipse Hugenius eas aegre admiserit", that he had been so cautious in the matter of publication.

Leibniz allows us to see more of what went on behind the scenes in his *Epistola ad Christ. Wolfium,* "Circa scientium infiniti," which has been published as an appendix to the *Act. Erudit. Lips. ad an.* 1713.[86] After briefly explaining his method of the infinitesimal calculus he continues, "Atque hoc consentaneum est legi Continuitatis . . . unde fit, ut in continuis extremum exclusivum *tractari possit ut* inclusivum, et ita ultimus casus, licet tota natura diversus, lateat in generali lege caeterorum, simulque *paradoxa* quadam ratione, et ut sic dicam, *figura philosophico-rhetorica* punctum in linea, quies in motu, specialis casus in generali *contradistinctio* comprehensus intelligi possit, *tanquam* punctum sit linea infinite parva, seu evanescens, aut quies sit motus evanescens, aliaque id genus, quae Joachimus Jungius, Vir profundissimus *toleranter vera* appellasset, et quae *inserviunt* plurimum ad inveniendi artem, etsi meo judicio aliquid *fictionis et imaginarii* complectantur, quod tamen reductione ad expressiones ordinarias ita facile *rectificatur,* ut *error* intervenire non possit". Here again I print the important words in italics. Leibniz, then, realized that in regarding the point as an infinitely-small line, and in general with regard to the whole idea of the infinitely-small, we are dealing with something paradoxical and contrary to sense, permissible, however, as a rhetorical fiction; that we are dealing here with modes of conception which, though fictional, are useful for discovery. He thus clearly grasped not only the actual practical application, but also the theory of fictions, and recognized that the fiction contained an error that had to be made good by being corrected.

Of particular significance in this respect is the reference to Joachim Jungius, in a monograph written at about the same time, *Observatio . . . de vero sensu methodi infinitesimalis,*[87] in the following words: "Tales enuntiationes

(—I esse quantitatem nihilo minorem, modo id sano sensu intelligatur) sunt *toleranter verae*, ut ego cum summo viro Joachimo Jungio loqui solo; Galli appellarent 'passables'. *Rigorem quidem non sustinent, habent tamen usum magnum in calculando* et ad artem inveniendi universalesque conceptus valent, etc."

In this passage Leibniz speaks openly and clearly; he realizes that such methods of conception and forms of judgment are, strictly (rigorose loquendo), not valid (non vera), that they are nevertheless (according to Jungius) *allowed*, because they are useful. He calls all such conceptual constructs, accordingly, mere ways of speaking (modus loquendi, commoditas expressionis); indeed, he explicitly denies the reality of the infinitely-small and of the infinite in general. He fully realizes that we are dealing here only with *analogies*, as in the case of all fictions. He knows that *errors* arise from the application of such methods, but he knows, too, that these errors are subsequently eliminated. In his discussion Leibniz rose to a height of methodological clarity which places him far above all his contemporaries, even above Newton. Especially praiseworthy is the way in which he includes everything relevant to his purpose in one broad view, proceeding from the particular to the general. Thus he begins the monograph just cited with the words: "Cum olim Parisiis Vir summus Antonius Arnaldus sua nova Geometriae Elementa mecum communicaret, atque in iisdem, admirari se testatus fuisset, quommodo posset esse I ad — I, ut — I ad — I, quae res probari videtur ex eo, quod productum est idem sub extremis, quod sub modiis cum utroque prodeat + I: jam tum dixi mihi videri, *veras illas rationes non esse, in quibus quantitas nihilo minor est antecedens, vel consequens, etsi in calculo haec, ut alia imaginaria, tuto et utiliter adhibeatur.*" Thus Leibniz here distinguished clearly between the *verum* and the *imaginarium*, and recognized that the latter, too, has its uses, and to that extent its practical reality.

With extraordinary clarity he also recognized that errors made by the fictional assumption must always be corrected. He frequently mentions this (cf. *Ges. Werke*, V, pp. 218, 350, etc.). This, however, comes out most definitely in his reply to the subtle objections of David Gregorius published in the *Act. Erudit. Lips.* (1699), where at the very end he arrives at the happy formulation "*ut tandem destruentibus sese erroribus perveniretur ad modum apparenter concludendi.*" Here we have a complete formulation of what we have called the Method of Antithetic Error as the methodological principle of the fiction.

§ 23

The Meaning of the 'As-if' Approach[88]

Que melior grammaticus, eo melior philosophus.

THE quotation at the head of this section, in spite of its exaggeration, may well serve as a motto for the pages in which we propose to carry our inquiry further and deeper. In what has just preceded we have again seen the far-reaching significance of "the As-if approach", particularly in the recent history of mathematics. Our logical analysis may therefore now be strengthened by a grammatical analysis.

For purposes of illustration let us first take two passages from Kant's *Kritik der Praktischen Vernunft*.[89]

1. "In testing by practical reason the rule of conduct according to which I am inclined to give certain testimony, I always try to discover how it would be if that principle were to hold as a general law of nature."

2. "We become conscious, through the reason, of a law, to which all our rules of conduct are subjected, *as if*, through our own mere willing, a natural order were bound to arise."

Let us also take the following from Kant's *Grundlegung zur Metaphysik der Sitten*[90].

3. "I hold that every being who can act only under the Idea that he is free is, for that very reason, also in practice free, i.e. all the laws that are inseparably connected with freedom hold for him *as if* his will had been declared free both in itself and by the criteria of theoretical philosophy. I therefore claim that every rational individual, who possesses a will, must necessarily also be endowed with the Idea of freedom according to which alone he acts."

And the explanatory remark which follows:

... "Thus the same laws hold good for a being who can act only under the Idea of his own freedom, that would bind one who was really free".

To take examples from another language, I add the following passages from Diderot, *Entretien d'un Philosophe*, etc.:

4. "On croit, et tous les jours on se conduit *comme si* l'on ne croyait pas. Et sans croire, on se conduit a peu prés comme si l'on croyait."

5. "Aprés tout, le plus court est de se conduire *comme si* le vieillard (Dieu) existait."

Or we may take the following example from Meister Eckart:[91]

6. "We must do our works *as* if no one existed, as if no one lived, and as if no human being had ever appeared upon the earth."

To the above we might add a saying of Saint Theresa (cf. *Acta Sanctorum*, Oct. 15, p. 462 C) recorded by Leibniz in a letter written by him to Andreas Morellius in the year 1696 (a letter that appears to have escaped the eyes of Leibniz scholars):

7. "Jure aestimas Teresiae libros. Equidem reperi illic aliquando pulchram hanc sententiam: animam hominis concipere res debere non secus *ac si* in mundo nil esset nisi ipsa et deus. (Cf. Leibniz, *Opera philos.*, ed. Erdmann, p. 127, b; "*comme s'il* n'existait rien que Dieu et elle").[92]

These examples form a sufficient basis for the following inquiry, whose scope may be defined as an examination into the meaning, the logical value and nature, and the conceptual significance of the compound conjunction "as if".

What logical function, or what type and modification of the general form of a judgment is expressed by the linguistic formula "as if" (as though)? What turn of thought is suggested and given expression to by this phrase?

To take the third of the above examples, we can express its meaning most briefly as follows: man must act, and his acts must be judged, *as if* he were free, *as though* he were free. First we have—this lies in the "as"—quite clearly an equating of two terms, a comparison actually made or demanded. The laws according to which a man is to act are either compared or directly equated with the laws of free beings. The first thought is therefore simply: man must act exactly as free beings do. But to this primary thought another secondary one is added, which is expressed by the conditional phrase. The form of this conditional statement affirms that the condition is an unreal or impossible one. The formula, the acts of man must be judged as though he were a free agent—does not correspond to the simple scheme "if . . . then"; there does not appear to be any apodosis. This apodosis is, however, merely concealed and suppressed. It lurks unheard between the "as" and the "if". In his first example Kant does not make this aposiopesis but, expressing himself at greater length, says, "I regard these principles as they would be, if they had to hold as a general law of nature."

The original form would be—if man were free, then such and such consequences would follow. The necessary connection of the consequence with the condition is definitely expressed, though, at the same time, the possibility of the condition being fulfilled is expressly negated; so that the main clause or apodosis, whose validity is bound up with the condition and which necessarily follows from it, is thus seen to contain something unreal. In this example, therefore, the condition, namely freedom, is denied, and thereby, of course, the consequences following from it. The case is posited but, at the same time, its impossibility is frankly stated. This impossible case is, however, in a conditional sentence of this sort, assumed or posited for the moment as possible or real.

But now the whole hypothetical combination is brought into a new connection. The main clause—the apodosis or 'then' clause—is given a new twist; a second knot is added to the first. This new connection has already been discussed; it is the equating of another case with this consequence. Whereas, however, this consequence in the simple conditional sentence is, as we remarked, an unreal one (because the condition is also an unreal one), this unreal consequence is, nevertheless, taken as the standard for measuring a reality. Thus the equation of a thing with the necessary consequences of an impossible or unreal case, is expressed as a thing demanded. In the above example then, we have: (1) the impossible case; the existence of free beings, or, in shorter form, the statement that men are free.—(2) the necessary consequences (that flow from this impossible case); the laws according to which free beings act; these follow necessarily from the existence of free beings.—(3) the equation of something (with the necessary consequences flowing from the impossible case); the laws, according to which actually existing men ought to act, are equated (in the form of a demand) with the laws which necessarily follow from the (unreal or impossible) existence of free beings.

Thus an impossible case is here imagined, the necessary consequences are drawn from it and, with these consequences, which must also be impossible, demands are equated that do not follow from existing reality.

This can easily be shown in detail by an examination of the examples given. In the first, I posit with Kant the impossible case, that an ethical principle shall hold as a law of nature. From this unreal case Kant draws the consequences, which are here the attributes of a universal law of nature; and these attributes are then transferred to the principle.

The same is true of the second example. The unreal case is stated, that by an act of our will a (general) natural order must arise; from this fictitious case we deduce the law referred to as a necessary consequence; and to this the actual directions taken by the will, the rules of conduct, are subjected.

By the phrase "idea of freedom" and the demand that "every rational being must be endowed with the idea of freedom," Kant means the same thing. By "idea of freedom" is meant the impossible, unreal, ideal, fictitious case existing only in idea; this is to be granted by way of loan, and real individuals are to be regarded as actually free, which they are not, for we should not have to "lend" them the idea, if it really belonged to them as an attribute. From the above we must then draw the consequences that apply in the case under discussion, namely the moral demands that can be made upon a free agent.

The application to the remaining examples may be left to the reader himself. I would, however, mention particularly the instance that we have already so frequently given, the as-if approach to the problem of the circle taken as a polygon. Here the impossible case lies in the assumption that the circle is a polygon; the necessary consequence that flows from this is that the laws of rectilinear figures can be applied to the circle, and with these consequences the method of approaching the real circle is then equated.

§ 24
The Fictive Judgment[93]

THAT the fictive judgment, whose linguistic expression, the *as if*, we have just analyzed, finds no place whatever in the traditional classification of the forms of judgment, affords fresh evidence that this classification, the work particularly of Sigwart and Lotze, requires fundamental corrections. The basic form of this fictive chain of thought is the following: A is to be regarded as if (as though) it were B or: A is to be regarded as if it were B (although it is not B). For example, man is to be regarded (treated) as a free agent; the circle is to be regarded (treated) as a polygon. Is this a positive or a negative, a categorical or an hypothetical, an assertive or a problematical judgment? What kind of a connection is assumed between A and B? In what way is this connection, whatever its nature, to be realized?

The simple, original function of judgment (the so-called assertive, categorical judgment) expresses the equation of A and B in some given direction, asserts that some one of the possible judgemental relations (activity, attribute, identity, etc.), exists between A and B. If we call this judgment the primary, then we find accompanying it a number of secondary modes of judgment, first, the negative and secondly the problematical.

In the *primary* judgment this function is very simply performed: A is B.

In the *secondary* judgment various forms of modification are introduced. The negative judgment either cancels a judgment already completed or repels an attempt in that direction: A is not B. The problematic judgment leaves the choice free between the completion and the cancellation of a judgment, since the subject is not yet clear in his own mind as to its justification or necessity of reversing it: A is perhaps B: A is perhaps not B. Modifications of this are the forms expressed by adverbs, such as probably, possibly, probably not, hardly, etc.

Here the fictive judgment obviously finds its place as a secondary form: the judgment is performed with a simultaneous protest against the idea of its objective validity, but with an express insistence upon its subjective significance. The judgment is made with the consciousness of its non-validity, but at the same time it is tacitly presupposed that this operation is permissible, useful and appropriate for the subject, for the subjective manner of approach. The form, as we observed, is: A is to be regarded as if it were B. Its non-validity is already expressed very clearly by the form of the hypothetical sentence, as we have had occasion to indicate in the foregoing pages. In a hypothetical connection, not only real and possible but also unreal and impossible things can be introduced, because it is merely the connection between the two presuppositions and not their actual reality that is being expressed. "If the circle were a polygon, then it would be subject to the laws of rectilinear figures." This compound statement is just as true and necessary as the two statements which it combines are—strictly speaking—false. "If the diamond were a metal, it would be soluble." "If Caesar had not been murdered, he would have forced his way to the position of Imperator." "If I saw Philip acting justly, I would regard him as worthy of great praise "(Demosthenes). "If we had gone to their help, Philip would not now be annoying us "(*Id.*). These, as we know, are all absolutely necessary connections between the unreal and the impossible. In the creation of fictions such an impossible and therefore invalid case is, nevertheless, assumed as possible for some practical purpose. On closer examination the process is seen to be even more subtle: it is not the impossible case itself, that is assumed to be real, but the manner of regarding the object or case in question is equated with the consequences that flow from it, and are necessarily bound up with it, while the condition itself is designated by its very form as impossible of fulfilment. This is manifest in the expression: "the circle is to be brought under those laws of rectilinear figures to which it would be subject if it were a polygon", or: "the circle is to be treated as if it were a polygon." It is obvious that the invalidity of equating the circle and the polygon, of A and B is, in this form, asserted as unconditioned.

Thus the nature of the fictive judgment is peculiarly complex: it is negative in so far as the equation of A and B is clearly stated to be invalid: it is positive in so far as the possibility of treating this non-valid judgment as nevertheless valid, is affirmed. In this respect it is also categorical, while on the other hand it also contains a hypothetical element, for it states an impossible case and draws from it the necessary conclusions. It is problematic and assertive, eventually even apodeictic, in so far as it simply asserts this method of treatment or lays special stress upon its possibility or necessity. But with regard to the equating of A and B the judgment is not assertive nor even problematical but simply fictive, i.e. we have here to recognize the existente of a new mode of judgment, which has hitherto passed unnoticed.

Joachim Jungius spoke—according to Leibniz[94]—of *enuntiationes toleranter verae*, of judgments strictly speaking false, but nevertheless permissible. Leibniz does not give us any examples from Jungius; he does, however, give the following of his own:

"Punctum est tanquam linea infinite parva".

"Quies est tanquam motus evanescens".

Of such judgments Leibniz says—we will briefly recapitulate, here, the statements which we have already given at length—that they are, strictly speaking, untrue, *rigorem non sustinent*, but permissible for practical purposes: *tolerari posse talia, rigorose loquendo vera non esse possunt, tamen sano aliquo sensu tolerari possunt*. In another connection, Leibniz speaks of such doubtful statements as *expressiones admittendae* (cf. pp. 86, 136). We cannot, strictly, say of a mathematical point that it *is* an infinitely-small line, but we can tolerate this assertion in the sense that the mathematical point is to be treated and regarded *as if it* were an infinitely-small line. This analogy is permissible even if, in a strict sense, it is false. The disjunctively opposed conception of a line is, in such a judgment, predicated of the point as subject. We are concerned here, then, with a predication which, in contradistinction to the categorical and assertive, can only be described as fictive.

Such an amalgamation of contrary concepts, such an identification of different objects, such an equating of unequal things, is probably what Leibniz meant when he spoke of *aequationes inadaequatae*. It is a question of fictive predications in the form of fictive judgments. Leibniz also gives the following as examples:

"Une ligne droite est un angle infiniment obtus."
"Corpus est absolute (= in infinitum) elasticum."

Fermat, as we have seen (cf. pp. 103 ff. above), also spoke of such false equations. He himself simply put $x = x + e$ for definite purposes, and referred to the authority of Diophantus. The latter speaks in similar cases of a παρισότης (compare πάρισος παρισόω, παρισάξω in the Greek writers). Fermat translated this expression by *adaequalitas* and understood by it such fictive equating of unequal things.

The fictive judgment, it is true, is grammatically often made in such an abbreviated form that it is not to be distinguished from the simple categorical-assertive judgment. Strictly speaking, a fictive judgment is of the following form:

"The circle is to be regarded as a polygon of infinitely numerous and infinitely small sides."

From this, by means of a *locutio compendiaria*, we get:

"The circle is a polygon with infinitely numerous, infinitely small sides."

In final form the abbreviation reads:

"The circle is a polygon."

The "ambiguity of the copula" here comes into evidence. The "is" has not two only but many meanings. In this case the "is" is a very short abbreviation for an exceedingly complicated train of thought. In mathematics such grammatical abbreviations are not dangerous because there the means of correcting any eventual erroneous interpretation lie ready to hand.

The situation is different in the other sciences. The judgment that matter is composed of atoms may be intended by the person who expresses it as a conscious fictive judgment, but it may be taken by one who hears or reads it, as a dogmatic assertion, and this without any fault of his. The abbreviation can, therefore, even here become exceedingly dangerous. Such an unexplained abbreviation must lead to the transformation of a fiction into a dogma or, at least, into an hypothesis.

But it is in religion that such abbreviations are most dangerous, most fatal. Many a statement made by the founder of a religion was originally meant by him merely as a conscious fiction. But the poverty of language in primitive times, the pleasure derived from short, pregnant, rhetorically effective sentences, and consideration for the less educated, childlike minds of his hearers, led, or rather misled, the founders of religions into expressing in the linguistic form of a dogma what they themselves took only in the sense of a conscious fiction. And according to the "law of ideational shifts," with which we are now sufficiently familiar (cf. p. 113 above), the conscious fiction of the master became transformed into the unconscious dogma of the disciples. Christ taught: God is our father in heaven. He probably meant: You must regard God (whose existence for Christ was, of course, not a fiction but a dogma), *as if*, just as though, he were your father and as if, just as though, he were present in the heavens as a constant external observer of your actions. His disciples, the people, the children of all times, of all ages, classes, and nations, took this conscious allegory, this fictional assertion, to be a dogma; and not only religious art but the credulity of the childlike mind took and still takes that sentence in a literal, concrete and external sense. At all times, however, more subtle spirits have interpreted spiritually what was meant spiritually, and have accepted such allegories for what they are — that is, fictions. It is, therefore, only right and proper that to-day, according to our "law of ideational shifts," this petrified dogma is very generally becoming a living, conscious fiction once again. Indeed many clergymen (at least in Protestant countries, and not a few elsewhere), when they utter this sentence with their lips, really imply the deeper or higher significance that is so easily lost in the abbreviated form. They realize what they are doing and are, in that sense, making use of a permissible and serviceable religious fiction.

"The ambiguity of the copula" (now in the categorical-assertive, now in the fictive-allegorical sense), played an important part in the historic dispute between Lutherans and Zwinglians over the meaning of ἐστί in the words of the Lord's Supper, the δεῖπνον κυριακόν. The sentences are (Matthew xxvi, 26–29): τοῦτό ἐστι τὸ σῶμά μον. τοῦτό ἐστι τὸ αἷμά μον. Luther and Zwingli disputed the question at the religious conference at Marburg, and this controversy has since then been revived in innumerable treatises. Zwingli, as the more subtle dialectician, took the ἐστί allegorically; for him the sentence was a conscious fiction of Christ: This bread is to be regarded *as if* it were my body; this wine is to be regarded *as if* it were my blood. Luther with his coarse, concrete, popular logic betrayed uneasiness while this explanation was being given, tapping under the table impatiently with his finger, and repeating half-audibly the words *est, est*. He took the "is" quite literally: His hard head, obstinately resentful of the finer implications of dialectic, could not understand that the whole matter turned on the grammatical abbreviation of a conscious fiction. According to Zwingli the "is" did not assert an identity. He translated it as "significat", and according to the "reform" theologians the "is" is to be understood only "allegorically "and "symbolically"; or, in our terminology, as fictive. Cicero, to whom the reformers also appeal, had already said (*De Nat. Deorum*, I, 26) that gods could have only, as it were, body and blood (*quasi corpas quasi sanguis*); and to the Lutherans who, on the contrary, speak of the *verum corpus* and the *verus sanguis*, we might reply, using the language of Leibniz with which we are now familiar, that in the disputed passage we are concerned only with—*toleranter vera*.

The fictive judgment is not an enunciation of theoretical or absolute, but only of practical and relative, truth; of a truth which holds good only in relation to the person who enunciates it and to the end he has in view, and whose content may only with great caution and reserve be described as "true".

§ 25
The Fiction contrasted with the Hypothesis[95]

Now that we have adequately examined the difference between the fictive and problematical judgment both as regards expression and content, we may discuss once more in conclusion the methodological contrast between fiction and hypothesis—which forms the kernel of our whole book.

It is distinctively discreditable to present-day logic, that these two forms of thought have, up to the present, been almost universally confused, though the confusion may find its excuse in the fact that these two forms of thought, in spite of all differences, are in certain respects very close to one another; so that although they are to be sharply distinguished in principle, in practice it is not so easy to keep them apart.

The best example, both for the ease with which they can be confused as well as for their essential difference, is Goethe's concept of animal and plant archetypes which we have already used so frequently as an illustration (cf. pp. 24 and 78 ff.). Goethe postulated the conceptual construct of an archetypal animal, i.e. the archetype of all animal forms in general, of which all the known animal species were to be regarded as modifications, transformations and metamorphoses. Goethe, as we have already remarked, was himself not quite clear as to the methodological character of his construct. Sometimes it appears to him to be a hypothetical assumption, so that he seems to wish to assert the actual existence or at least the former actual existence of such a being; at other times he clearly regards the archetype as a purely mental entity without any implied assertion of its existence or even of the possibility of its existence.

Once when Goethe was discussing these ideas with Schiller, the latter, as is well-known, remarked: "That is not an experience. It is an idea".

The distinction which the Kantian Schiller, using the Kantian terminology, here makes, coincides with the distinction between hypothesis and fiction in the language of the methodologists.

When Schiller says that the animal archetype and the plant archetype do not represent an experience, he does not, of course, mean to say that such archetypal forms have hitherto not been found in experience but may perhaps be experienced at some future date. What he wishes to say—in accordance with the Kantian concept of experience—is that plant and animal archetypes as such are never to be found in any experience; that they cannot possibly be objects of experience, whether already discovered, or eventually to be discovered and therefore assumed in the meantime as valid hypotheses. The archetype represents "an idea", i.e. a mere concept of reason invented by us, one which is necessarily formed by us, it is true, but which is, nevertheless, imaginary and to which no empirical being can ever or anywhere correspond. Schiller, then, correctly recognized that the significance of Goethe's assertion lay in the fictive judgment it expressed that all plant and animal species were to be regarded *as if* they had been formed according to the standard of an animal or plant-archetype. Goethe's animal archetype is a schematic fiction, whereas the Darwinian theory of evolution is an hypothesis.

Let me take another example to illustrate this distinction. The constitution of matter is one of the most important questions of science. Here we meet the view that the elements to which matter has hitherto been reduced' are not the ultimate factors but that they can be reduced to an even smaller number of elements, or even to one original primal substance. This conjecture has been often expressed, and in principle there is no objection to it. Opposed to it we find the view that matter consists of infinitely-small indivisible particles, in themselves actually without extension,—namely atoms. The first theory has regard to the qualitative, the second to the quantitative factors of matter. If the former is open to few objections in principle, the latter is full of contradictions. Whereas the first theory need not despair of a reduction such as it envisages being some day achieved, Atomism, at least in the above form, is absolutely undemonstrable; indeed, by contrast, it is theoretically objectionable, because the atom is a contradictory conceptual construct. Unextended centres of energy that are to be the basis of extension, are absolutely contradictory constructs. Something without extension, that nevertheless in its summation is to give us extension, is a contradiction.

The idea of a reduction of matter to atoms is, then, a fiction. On the other hand the idea of a reduction of the types of matter to a single primal substance is a plausible hypothesis.

This particular example is particularly well adapted to explain the methodological difference of the two forms; the first assumption finds its highest expression in the fictive judgment that matter is so to be regarded, treated and reckoned with *as if* it consisted of atoms. The other assumption, on the contrary, is expressed in the problematical judgment: It is *possible that* the elements of matter so far discovered will all be reduced to an original substance; up to the present, however, it has not been possible to verify this plausible assumption. It is quite otherwise with the fiction: it is absolutely impossible that matter, in the last analysis, should consist of point-atoms without extension; but it is possible, and indeed useful, to make this assumption provisionally, in order more readily to calculate the weight-relationships of matter.

Whereas every hypothesis seeks to be an adequate expression of some reality still unknown and to mirror this objective reality correctly, the fiction is advanced with the consciousness that it is an inadequate, subjective and pictorial manner of conception, whose coincidence with reality is, from the start, excluded and which cannot, therefore, be afterwards verified, as we hope to be able to verify an hypothesis. For that reason a fiction can never be expressed in the form of a problematical judgment but must claim as its proper form of expression the fictive judgment.

The methodological rules which are laid down for the hypothesis do not, consequently, fit the fiction at all. Kant well stated the conditions which must form the fundamental, rigid and logical discipline of hypothetical thinking, in his *Kritik d. r. V.*[96] "The two things required to make an hypothesis acceptable" are first, "that only such objects and reasons be adduced for the explanation of given phenomena as can be brought into connection with reality, and therefore themselves correspond to the general laws of reality"; and secondly, "the adequacy of the assumption for the explanation and empirical deduction of the phenomenal field in question". Only an adherence to these conditions can provide us with a guarantee that the hypothesis has any claim to truth: for reality, and only reality, is the goal of all hypothetical assumptions.

With fictions the situation is quite different. "The two requirements" in the case of hypotheses, have no place here. The condition of correspondence with the general behaviour of reality and the laws of thought is not adhered to, for the fiction assumes something unreal or impossible. In the case of true fictions, that of the infinitesimal for example, conceivability is so little a condition that it might be said that *inconceivability* is rather their characteristic mark; for these fictional concepts are full of contradictions and logical impossibilities. This inner contradiction is shown in the antinomies which arise through the hypostasization of fictions when *Non-Entia imaginaria* are erroneously transformed into *Entia*—a mistake against which Spinoza already warns us in his *Cogit. Metaph*, I, i.

An idea constructed in imagination must first be examined as to whether it is fictional or hypothetical. Man's natural tendency is to take his thought for the direct expression of reality, to see in the forms of thought forms of existence.[97] Natural and naive thought takes all concepts and methods of the subjective conceptual world to be representative of an exactly corresponding reality. If a fairly thorough methodological education is necessary before we can distinguish the hypothetical from the actual, far greater acumen is necessary to distinguish between fictions and hypotheses. The thinking of most people (including not a few scholars of average attainments) is as yet of too coarse, too blunt a type, to be able to grasp this distinction at all, or, if grasped, permanently to hold it fast. Nevertheless mathematicians and jurists, by means of the fictions used in their respective fields (particularly the jurists, through their treatment of the fiction of juristic persons) have prepared the ground for a general acceptance of the distinction between the fiction and the hypothesis. The scientists too, and particularly the evolutionary theorists, have sharpened the consciousness of this distinction through their controversy about schematic drawings that deviate from reality. Nor must we forget the theologians who in all ages—openly or tacitly have distinguished between dogma and picture, between philosophical concept and conscious anthropomorphic expression.

NOTES

1 *Supplementary to Part I, Chapter I.*
2 Drobisch, *Logik,* 18. "The fact that in the Linnæan system, plants of very different kinds have been placed in the same class because of the similarity of their sexual organs, has led to this classification being regarded as unnatural; but it cannot be denied that it is exceedingly useful for obtaining a general view of the manifold forms found among plants"
3 *De l'Intelligence,* II, 27: En minéralogie, il n'y a pas encore de classification veritable.
4 *Ibid.* I. 196.
5 *Essai sur la Philosophie des Sciences,* p. 9.
6 *Discours sur L'Encyelopédie.*
7 *De l'Intelligence,* II, 217.
8 *Supplementary to Part I, Chapters I and II.*
9 *Supplementary to Part I, Chapter II, p.* 17 *ff*
10 Aug. Oncken, *Adam Smith und Immanuel Kant,* Leipzig, 1877, pp. 9–16.
11 *History of Civilization,* Vol. II, pp. 432–3.
12 The method of Adam Smith is related to the fables and Utopias so popular in the eighteenth century, particularly to Mandeville's fable of the Bees, as Karl Marx says (*Das Kapital,* I, 339, note 5).
13 *Supplementary to Part I, Chapter II.* [See pp. xxxi-xxxii of *Bentham's Theory of Fictions* (1932) in this Library, for an account of the relation of Bentham's work to *The Philosophy of 'As if'. Trans.]*
14 *Supplementary to Part I, Chapter II, p.* 18 *ff.*

15 Glogau, in particular, has emphasized this repeatedly in his work *Steinthal's psychologische Formeln.*

16 *Supplementary to Part I, Chapter II, p.* 18.

17 *Traité des Sensations,* I, X, 6.

18 On account of its utility this method was frequently employed in the eighteenth century by Bonnet and Buffon as well as by Condillac, and before Condillac by Diderot in his *Lettres sur les aveugles.* Indeed Condillac became involved in a controversy on this question with Diderot as regards priority.

19 Cf. Arnobius, *Adversus gentes,* II, 20 (Ed. Hildebrand, Hal. Sax. 1844), p. 150 *ff.*

20 Lamettrie, *Œuvres.* The work we refer to is there given as the *Traité de l'âme.* The Appendix, § 7, contains this fiction under the title of a "conjecture." Lange in his *History of Materialism* (E.T., Vol. II., p. 63) describes it incorrectly as an "hypothesis" instead of a fiction.

21 *Supplementary to Part I, Chapter II, p.* 162, *note 3.*

22 § 33. p. 420f.

23 *Kant's Analogien,* 297.

24 The term "hypothetical" animal ("hypothetical" case, etc., *Ib.* 297) had consequently better be replaced by "fictional".

25 *De An.,* II, 4136, 2, 37.

26 *Supplementary to Part I, Chapters II (p.* 18 *ff.) and III.*

27 *De l'Intelligence,* Vol. 1, p. 162.

28 *Supplementary to Part I, Chapters II and VI, pp.* 18 *and* 32 *ff.*

29 *Ibid.,* Vol. II, 49. Cf. pp. 32–33, 52–53, 176, 190.

30 *Ibid.,* Vol. II, p. 280.

31 *Geschichte des Materialismus,* Vol. II, 203 (E.T., Vol. II, p. 377).

32 *Supplementary to Part I, Chapters II and XIV, pp.* 18 *ff. and* 58 *ff.*

33 *Supplementary to Part I, Chapters I (p.* 20 *f.) and VII.*

34 Ueberweg, *Logik* § 47

35 *Trailé des sensations,* § 96.

36 Condillac, *L'art de penser,* pp. 93–4.

37 Condillac, *Grammaire,* lxx, lxxii.

38 Bachmann, *Logik,* 1828, § 44.

39 "L'esprit les regarde comme quelque chose," or as he also says "comme des étres" (*De l'art de penser,* p. 103). On the following page we read, "nous sommes forcés á considérer ces idées comme quelque chose de réel."

40 "Quelque vicieuse que soit cette contradiction elle, est néanmoins nécessaire," *Ibid.,* p. 104.

41 "C'est cette nécessité qui est cause que bien des philosophes n'ont pas soupconné que la réalité des idées abstraites fut l'ouvrage de l'imaginalion" *Ibid.,* 104: and compare 112, where he speaks of *feindre* as an activity of the imagination.

42 Condillac instances Space and Time as particularly characteristic of such abstractions. These are only artificially separated partial qualities of bodies; "nous pouvons diviser nos notions": we think of the body as annihilated and its space preserved. "Il est á craindre que ce ne soit ici qu'un effet de l'imagination, qui, ayant feint qu'un corps est anéanti, est obligée de feindre un espace entre les corps environnans "(Ibid., p. 112). Condillac makes special reference to the different "suppositions" necessary for the construction of such abstractions, and calls them "une maniére artificieuse." He also repeatedly stresses the indispensability of this artificial aid and its necessity for our thought. The very title of Chapter VII of the *Art de penser*, speaks (p. 93) of the *necessity of* these ideas and warns us against the "abus des abstractions réalisés" (p. 113). They are, however, also indispensable, "pour les discours les plus sérieux comme dans les conversations les plus familiéres."

43 Cf. Condillac, *Traité des systémes (Œuvres*, Vol. II), p. 329.

44 Gruppe, *Wendepunkt der Philosophie im 19. Jahrhundert,* Berlin, 1831, pp. 98–9.

45 *Supplementary to Part I, Chapter VII.*

46 Abstract and general ideas must be carefully distinguished in principle. "Goodness, colour, smoothness, equality", are abstract ideas, for the properties in question are separated *by isolation* from concrete things, but in reality do not constitute independent qualities of objects: "stone, plant, pine-tree, ship" are general ideas that are formed *by generalization* from many similar particular phenomena. This differentiation is one of principle but only of principle, for in practice the two operations of isolation and of generalization almost always occur together. For the sake of clarity in exposition, however, it is expedient theoretically to keep these two types rigidly apart.

47 In this sense the *generalia* are only *"nomina"*, as the Nominalists correctly insisted. And in fact the Nominalists had already called the *generalia* mere *ficta*.

48 Nominalism occupied the same rôle with regard to general ideas that the Critical Philosophy does to categories. With the former as *"figmenta"*, Occam closes one period in the history of English philosophy, and with the latter as fictions Hume closes another. This parallel provides material for reflection. In both cases, however, only the negative sense of "fiction" was stressed; the positive and practical justification of these fictions did not then occupy the foreground of the discussion.

49 *De l'art de penser,* Chap. VIII, p. 96.

50 "L'entendement a ses leviers; avec leur secours il suit, il suspend, il hâte, il soumet la nature," says Condillac, *De l'art de penser,* p. 100.

51 *Essay* IV, 7, 9. Condillac also refers to him in his *De l'art de penser,* p. 109.

52 *Supplementary to Part I, Chapters VI and VII.*

53 Taine, *De l'Intelligence,* Vol. II, p. 12.

54 Cf. Hüfner, *Lebenskraft*, p. 24.

55 *Supplementary to Part I, Chapters VI and VII.*

56 Lange, *Op. cit.*, II, 186. [E.T., Vol II, p. 357.]

57 Kopp, *Geschichte der Chemie*, II, 290.

58 Lange, *Op. cit.*, II, 219.

59 *Supplementary to Part I, Chapters III and XVI.*

60 *Supplementary to Part I, Chapters III and IV.*

61 *Supplementary to Part I, Chapter XV.*

62 Kant seems, however, to have had a precursor in the person of Toland, who explained the particles as mere verbal aids. Cf. Berthold, *Toland*, p. 48.

63 A. von Humboldt, too, declares the atomic theory to be "a primeval symbol". Gruppe (in *Op, cit. Antidus*, p. 418) regards the atomic theory merely as a metaphorical auxiliary idea without which the physicist could neither talk nor think; but be holds that from what is simply provisional.no principles should be deduced.

64 Cf. Wundt, *Über die Aufgabe der Philosophie in der Gegenwart*, p. 6.

65 *Über die Aufgabe der Naturwissenschaft*, Jena 1878, p. 7.

66 *Supplementary to Part I, Chapter XVI.*

67 "Experimental Untersuchungen," § 1304, in Zöllner's *Wissenschaft., Abhandlungen*, 82.

68 *Ibid*, 84.

69 *Ibid*, 84.

70 "Elektrodynamische Messbestimmungen insbesondere über Diamagnetismus", *Abhandl. d. Sachs. Ges. d. IV.*, *I*, 560. Cf. Zöllner, *Prinzipien einer elektrodynamischen Theorie der Materie*, 1876, I, 91; and the same author's *Wissenschaftliche Abhandlungen*, 1878, I, 45.

71 The fictitious mean is employed in other sciences too, whenever the need arises of taking the average of a number of gradually varying phenomena and making this the basis of further calculation or consideration; for instance, in statistics, meteorology, etc., where it is important to substitute for a large number of quantities that oscillate around an ideal point, a common quantity valid for them all. An average is therefore constructed, by means of which we make our computation as if every one of the phenomena in question corresponded to it. A famous fiction of this type is that of Quetelet, namely, his "homme moyen", i.e. the fiction of a normal average individual.

72 Neumann, *Über die Prinzipien der Galilei-Newton schen Theorie*, Leipzig, 1870.

73 *Supplementary to Part I, Chapters X and XVI, p. 47 ff. and p. 66.*

74 The a priori and deductive procedure of mathematics does not differ from the deductive procedure possible in other sciences in essence or quality, but quantitatively and in degree.

75 We are not concerned here primarily with the psychological question nor with the epistemological, but more particularly with the logical problem.

76 We see here clearly how, in Leibniz, "imagination" and "fiction" are sometimes used in a derogatory sense, as when he rejects the above idea as unreal in the metaphysical sense, and sometimes in a good sense, as when he yet recognizes that an idea is methodologically justified and expedient.

77 *Supplementary to Part I, Chapter X, p. 46 ff.*

78 *Supplementary to Part I, Chapters XII (p. 50 ff.) and XIII.*

79 As soon as this principle has been grasped it can be very extensively applied. For instance, the line can be regarded as a surface whose second dimension is infinitely small and the surface as a body whose third dimension is infinitely small. Similarly, the straight line can be regarded as a so-called extended angle by thinking of the line *ab* as divided at any selected point *x* and regarding the parts *ax* and *xb* as the sides of an angle whose inclination is infinitely small.

80 With regard to the infinite let me add here what Gauss says about it *(Briefwechsel, Vol. II, 271)*. He says that the infinite "is merely a *façon de parler*, for we are really speaking of limits to which certain relations approximate as closely as we wish them to, while others are allowed to increase without limitation." *Façon de parler*—so too Leibniz had already designated the infinite in every respect as a *modus dicendi*.

81 The method of treating a construct as a border case of a construct of another type than that to which it belongs, by positing certain definite elements as infinitely small (or, in certain circumstances, as infinitely large) certainly celebrated what might be called an historical triumph, in connection with the famous tangent problem. By regarding the tangent as a border case of a secant, where, accordingly, the points of intersection are found at an infinitely small distance from one another, i.e. coincide, we obtain that very important formula, which could not have been obtained directly, for the angle at which the tangent is to be drawn for any curve whatsoever.

82 *Supplementary to Part I, Chapters XII, XIII, XXVI (p. 106 ff.), XXXIII (p. 135 ff).*

83 The concept *fluere* is already found in Cavaleri (cf. above, p. 227); *incrementa, decrementa* and the infinitely-small are mentioned by Kepler (Gerhardt, *Geschichte der Mathematik in Deutschland*, p. 112).

84 These documents are published in Leibniz' *Gesammelte Werke*, edited by G. H. Pertz (Series III, Mathematik, Vols. I–VII, edited by C. J. Gerhardt), Halle, 1849–1865. We cite this collection as Leibniz, *Ges. Werke*. Only the most important points in this collection are utilized in the following discussion: there is still much to be gleaned from them.

85 Leibniz, *Ges. Werke*, V, 320 ff.

86 Leibniz, *Ges. Werke*, V, 382 ff.

87 *Ibid.*, 387 ff.

88 *Supplementary to Part I, Chapter XXII.*

89 I Teil, I Buch, I Hauptstück: "Von den Grundsatzen der reinen praktischen Vernunft." I. "Deduktion der Grundsätze," Kirchmann, p. 52.

90 3. *Abschnitt* (Kirchm., p. 76).

91 In his sermon "Von dem Adel der Seele", Pfeiffer, *Deutsche Mystik,* II, 416 ff.

92 The As-if view with the specific particles "as if", "as though" etc. is frequently found expressed in this manner among the medieval and later mystics, e.g. in Saint Catherine of Genoa.

93 *Supplementary to Part I, Chapter XXII, pp. 84 ff.*

94 Cf. p. 233.

95 *Supplementary to Part I, Chapter XXI.*

96 In the section on the "Disziplin der reinen Vernunft in Ansehung der Hypothesen" (Kehrb., 586).

97 It is one of Kant's main achievements, as we shall see in Part III, to have shown that the fact that something must be thought does not necessarily involve the existence of the thing thought of.

PART 3
HISTORICAL CONFIRMATIONS

1

KANT'S USE OF THE 'AS IF' METHOD

In our systematic exposition we have made frequent use of historical examples. Moreover Part I contained a large section entitled "Contributions to the History and Theory of the Fiction" and our Part II further studies on the History of the Fiction of the Infinitesimal. This third and last portion of the work will be devoted to the most important historical confirmations of our doctrine to be found in the history of philosophy. In Greek philosophy we must mention in this connection the use of the fiction in Parmenides and especially Plato's use of myths (cf. Part I, Chapter XXVIII above).[1] The medieval doctrine of "twofold truth" also bears on our subject, along with much else of which we have already made incidental mention. But for the most important confirmation we are indebted to Kant, whose As-if approach has remained almost unnoticed and misunderstood for more than a hundred years. In presenting this very important doctrine we shall make use, as far as possible, of the actual words of Kant.

THE FUNDAMENTAL ELEMENTS IN THE PRINCIPAL
CRITICAL WORKS OF KANT

In the *Kritik der reinen Vernunft* (1781) Kant's new doctrine suddenly makes its appearance with all the vigour and purity of a mountain spring. It appears in that part of his great work which is entitled "Transcendental Dialectic."

By way of placing ourselves at once at a favourable point of view for the understanding of Kant's Ideology, we may begin with the classical passage in the methodology, in the section: "The Discipline of Pure Reason in Hypothesis."[2] Near the beginning of the section we find the "rational concepts" described as "mere ideas", as "heuristic fictions", and expressly distinguished from hypotheses. "Hypotheses" are "linked with what is actually given and is therefore certain, as an explanatory element." If there is a break in the series of empirically given facts, we have the right to fill in this lacuna with some assumed fact whose empirical possibility is vouched for by its connection with the others and in doing this we are forming a scientifically justified hypothesis. The rational concepts ('the soul as a substance' and 'personal God' in particular) are, however, mere ideas without any objectivity, do not come within the range of empirical facts and only serve as the "regulative principle" of "the systematic use of reason within the field of experience; they are "heuristic fictions". Kant himself gives in this connection as specific examples the "incorporeal unity of the soul and the existence of a Supreme Being". To ascribe reality to such rational ideas, would lead us to "hyper-physical" explanations. But only such hypotheses are permissible as enable us to bring the assumed into connection with the given in accordance with known laws of phenomena and with the conditions of possible experience. Such hypotheses these ideas are not. They are indeed nothing but heuristic fictions (cf. p. 35 above).

Had we always had this famous passage before our eyes, Kant's whole doctrine of ideas would have been better understood from the first. We shall now follow this doctrine from the beginning of the transcendental dialectic onward, and briefly elucídate it from our standpoint.

In the preliminary section of the transcendental dialectic where Kant introduces and justifies the term "Ideas", his language is of a prefatory, adumbrative character. In one passage, however, he expresses himself quite clearly (A 328, B 325); we must say of the transcendental rational concepts that "they are only Ideas", i.e. only ideas without objectivity. But they are not, for that reason, "superfluous and immaterial"; they "can serve reason as a canon of usage, capable, not indeed of enabling it to gain cognition of more objects than it would have by means of its concepts, but of furnishing it with better and further guidance in such cognition". In other words, they are heuristic fictions.

For reasons which will subsequently become apparent, we must place the Second Main Division: "The Antinomy of Pure Reason," before the First. In section 8 Kant introduces a new term for what in the passage quoted above, he subsequently called "heuristic fictions": he calls the Ideas "regulative principles of pure reason": they are not "constitutive" principles of reason, i.e. they do not give us the possibility of objective knowledge either within or outside the domain of experience, but serve "merely as rules" for the understanding, by indicating the path to be pursued within the domain of experience, by providing imaginary points on which it may direct its course but which it can never reach because they lie altogether outside of reality (Kant, in another passage to be mentioned later, calls the idea in this sense a *focus imaginarius*).

What he means thereby becomes clear from a passage which belongs here and which occurs in the "Appendix to the transcendental dialectic."[3] He there says, A 672, B 700 "(In cosmology) we must adhere to the conditions both of internal and external natural phenomena in an investigation of this sort which can never be complete, *as if it were in itself* infinite, etc." Further on, in A 684–686, B 712–714, he says that the absolute totality of the series of conditions in the deduction of constituents is an Idea "that serves by way of a rule, and indicates how we are to proceed in relation to them; namely, that in the explanation of given phenomena (retrogressively or progressively) we should proceed *as if the series it were*, in itself, infinite, i.e. in *indefinitum*." In a passage in the doctrine of Antinomies,[4] he further explains in a note on A 472, B 500, that Epicurus had, in all probability, already enunciated the principle of absolute regression, not indeed as an objective statement but as *A* rule of conduct in the speculative use of reason, when he said "that in the explanation of phenomena we are to proceed *as if the field of inquiry were not limited* by any boundaries or by any beginning of the world." This, says Kant, is a principle which still holds good today, although it is little heeded.

Of great importance is the continuation of the passage from the Appendix to the transcendental dialectic (A 685, B 713), with regard to the cosmological idea of totality. This same idea of totality reversed leads, in another connection, to the fiction of an absolute beginning. "Where reason, itself, is regarded as a determining cause (in a state of freedom), in the case, therefore, of practical principles," we must proceed "*as if* we had before us, not an object of the senses, but one of pure reason, where the conditions can no longer be placed among phenomena but may be placed outside them, and where the series of conditions can be regarded as if it had actually (by an intelligible cause) been begun."

This is again illustrated by certain passages in the doctrine of antinomies itself.[5] There (A 555 fif., B 583 ff.) we find the following: In judging any action of a man we can disregard all the psychological conditions of his act; we can "completely put aside" these empirical conditions "and consider the series of conditions that have occurred as not having taken place and the deed itself as entirely unconditioned, so far as any anterior situation is concerned; *as if* the performer of the deed thereby himself originated a series of effects." Again and again he repeats that it can, may, and must be so regarded but that objectively it is not so. And this does not imply "the reality of freedom." "Freedom is here treated as a transcendental idea"—in other words only as a heuristic fiction.

The fiction of the *freedom* of the soul serves as a convenient transition to the fiction of the *soul* itself. In the First Part of the transcendental dialectic ("Von den Paralogismen der reinen Vernunft") this standpoint is only indirectly hinted at. This is also true of the presentation found in the second edition, where (B 421) the fictive standpoint as applied to the problem of the soul and immortality appears but once: Kant, in speaking of the ethical aim of life, says that our moral endeavour, "even if always directed towards objects of experience, yet derives its principles from a higher source and determines our behaviour, *as if* our destiny extended infinitely far beyond our experience, and therefore far beyond this life." This fiction is naturally only possible on the basis of the assumption of a "non-corporeal soul"; and this assumption, in its turn, is as we shall presently show at greater length, for Kant himself, only a fiction.

On the other hand, the nature of the concept of the soul as a regulative idea along with the idea of God, is very clearly and definitely shown in the Appendix to the transcendental dialectic, where the two ideas are almost always coupled together. What is said of the idea of God is, *mutatis mutandis*, also applied to the idea of the soul. So, for instance, it is said, A 671, B 699, that in accordance with the psychological idea, "we are inclined to attach

all the phenomena, activities and impressions of our spirit, to the thread of
inner experience, as if that spirit were a simple substance possessing personal identity, permanence etc. Cf. also A 682, B 710: "I, myself, regarded
merely as a thinking entity (soul), am the first object of such an Idea." "In
this matter, reason has nothing in view except principles of systematic unity
for the explanation of the phenomena of the soul; *treating* all determinations
as existing in a single subject, all powers, so far as this is possible, *as* deducible from a single basic force and all change *as* referable to the states of one
and the same continuous entity", etc. "This simplicity of the substance, etc.
should merely be the scheme of this regulative principle, and is not presupposed as if it constituted the real ground of the attributes of the soul." We are
dealing here, he says, with a "mere Idea", but "from a psychological Idea of
this kind, only advantage can be derived," etc. Here again Kant quite clearly
indicates the utility of the soul-fiction. The advantages to be obtained from
this fiction are then enumerated, and he continues, "all this is best effected,
indeed can only be effected, by means of such a schema, *regarded as if it were a
real entity*".

Following Kant's divisions, we shall now pass on to the discussion of the
idea of God given in the section, "The Ideal of Pure Reason" (A 567 ff.,
B 595 ff.). There we find it stated at the very beginning that an ideal is something "which only exists in the mind", for instance, the ideal of a sage: Kant
also refers in the same place to schematic average-fictions, when he speaks of
"an outline or sketch suspended in the midst of varied experience", (cf. p. 20
above). In the second section he speaks specifically of "the transcendental
ideal", i.e. of the idea of God as the ideal of *omnitudo realitatis*: A 580, B608:
"This Idea, regarded only as the *concept* [Kant's italics] of all reality, reason
sets at the base of every determination of things whatever, without demanding that all this reality be objectively given and itself constitute a thing. This
last is a piece of pure imagination by means of which we bring togeter and
realize the manifold complexity of our idea in one ideal as one particular
entity, a proceeding for which we have no authority—nay, we have not even
the right to assume the possibility of such an hypothesis." "How does reason come to regard all possibility of things as deducible from a single basic
reality, and that the supreme reality?" We are subject to "a natural illusion"
when we in this way "hypostasize" and "personify" the dependence of the
empirical particular "upon the totality of all empirical reality," "This ideal
of supremely real being . . . is a mere idea", he says in the concluding note.

Again at the beginning of the third section, A 583, B611: Reason, it is said, far too easily perceives "the idealistic and purely imaginary elements in such a presupposition, to be persuaded by them alone to accept at once as a real entity what is merely its own creation". Reason thinks that it possesses dogmatic proofs of the reality of such an entity, of its right "to endow a mere idea with reality"; but these proofs are all broken reeds, as Kant shows in his refutation of the proofs for the existence of God.

From this difficulty some seek to escape by representing the idea of God as "inscrutable". But on this question Kant remarks in the fifth section (A 614, B 642): "An ideal of pure reason cannot be said to be inscrutable on the ground that it can show nothing to substantiate its reality except reason's need to complete all synthetic unity by means of such an ideal. Since then it is not even given us as a conceivable object, neither is it, as such, inscrutable; on the contrary, it must, as a mere idea, have its seat and its resolution in the nature of reason, and must therefore be open to investigation".

This passage contains a disavowal of the traditional view of the Kantian doctrine of ideas, which represents Kant as having, in the *Kritik der reinen Vernunft*, taught the inscrutability of the intelligible world, whereas, in the *Kritik der praktischen Vernunft*, he had, on moral lines, proved the reality of the ideas relating thereto, such as those of God, freedom and immortality. With regard to the latter point we shall have something to say in Section II *infra*. With regard to the former, the passage quoted above shows that here, at least, Kant will have nothing to do with this "inscrutability" of God, of which, it is true, he elsewhere occasionally speaks: the concept of God, as well as that of the whole intelligible world, has been created by our reason and must therefore be capable of being analyzed and resolved by the same reason.

In the Appendix to the fifth section,[6] again speaking of the concept of a necessary, supreme reality, he says that it is by "a natural illusion" that we hypostasize and make real this conception—a thing which can, after all, only be an idea. The principle of seeking a necessary first cause for all that exists is merely "heuristic and regulative"; and he adds, "You should philosophize about nature *as if* there were a necessary first cause for everything that exists, simply in order to bring systematic unity into your knowledge." And, summing up: "The ideal of the Supreme Being is according to this view nothing else than a regulative principle of reason, according to which it regards all connections in nature as if they had sprung from an all-sufficient, necessary cause," etc. "This is not to assert an absolute necessary existence. It is, however, at the same time, inevitable that we should by means of a transcendental subreption represent to ourselves this formal principle as constitutive and think of this unity as hypostatic."

In the sixth section (A 623, B 651), the "advantageousness," in other words, the utility of this idea in the use of our reason within the domain of experience, is especially emphasized—and it was utility which we recognized as the characteristic mark of fictions.

Then follows the "Appendix to the transcendental Dialectic," first the section "on the regulative use of the Ideas of Pure Reason "(A 642 ff., B 670 ff). There, at the very beginning, ideas are spoken of as "having an excellent and indispensable regulative use, that namely of directing the understanding towards a certain end, in pursuit of which the guiding lines of all its rules converge upon one point. And although this point is only an Idea (focus imaginarius), i.e. a point from which the rational concepts do not in reality originate, since it lies entirely outside the limits of possible experience, it yet serves the purpose of obtaining for them (the rational concepts), a maximal unity together with a maximal distribution." The same thought is afterwards repeated in various connections.[7]

In the final section,[8] which follows there are many decisive passages.

Of particular importance are the first three paragraphs. Kant wishes to correct the rather natural mistake of supposing that the ideas, which in the dialectic had been proved to be null and void, were mere illusions, ignes fatui, and therefore valueless and even harmful. No, he says, they have, in spite of that, "their good and useful purpose"; the expediency of these ideas, the distinguishing mark of true fictions, is again stressed. In the proof of this expediency lies what Kant calls their "deduction," i.e. the proof of their right to exist, their "vindication" as he calls it in the third section, their justification, as we named it above (pp. 80, 95) or, as the eleventh paragraph puts it, "their rightness is established". In this way it is shown that they "are not mere creations of thought". This might however be misunderstood. "Creations of thought" they are and remain, their deduction cannot alter this; such a deduction can, however, show that they are not mere empty thoughts, i.e. valueless, as is the case with many other thoughts. They are, in other words, valuable and important thoughts: important heuristic fictions and fictions not in the bad but in the good sense. This proof "completes the critical work of pure reason".

If they are "deduced" in this manner, it is clear that they possess, "at least some objective validity, even though this be indefinite." This passage of the second paragraph is exceedingly important and is explained in the third paragraph, where we read that "the concept of a Supreme Intelligence is a mere idea, i.e. its objective reality does not consist in the fact that it specifically relates to an object (for in this sense we could not vindicate an objective validity). It is merely a scheme[9] of the concept of a thing in general, arranged to suit the requirements of a maximal rational unity, a scheme which only serves the purpose of maintaining a maximum of schematic unity in the empirical use of our reason, etc." It is in this, therefore, that the peculiar "objective reality" of these ideas consists; they have a certain reality but it is only heuristic and practical. Careful attention should be paid to the use in this passage of the expression "objective reality" in application to the ideas; for shortly afterwards, in the fifth paragraph, Kant himself, in accordance with his unfortunate habit, obscured these clear definitions. He there draws a distinction between cosmological ideas and psychological and theological ideas and is of the opinion that nobody can "deny the objective reality of the latter, since we know too little of their possibility to be able either to deny or affirm it." In writing thus, however, he throws over his former argument, which assigned to all ideas an "indeterminate objective validity or reality", consisting precisely in their serviceable character. Unfortunately, still further to increase this confusion, the "objective reality" of a rational concept is presently used in paragraph seven in an absolute-theoretical, instead of in a relative-heuristic-practical, sense. Nevertheless this purely practical "objective reality" of the ideas, with which we were concerned above, was still maintained by Kant. In this sense, "the Idea (though it designates a non-existent object), always retains its rightness" (A 694, B 722). In spite of the fact, therefore, that we cannot bestow absolute objective validity upon the idea of a Supreme Being, we are nevertheless "justified in making use" of this idea "which must be the regulative principle of the investigation of nature by reason"; to make use in this manner of God, the original ground of cosmic unity, "or better, of his Idea"[10] is both possible and desirable; in this practical use "you have the confirmation of the rightness of your idea" (A 696 ff., B 724 ff.).

We find further,[11] that "the concept of a Supreme Intelligence is a mere Idea": "this scheme merely serves the purpose of maintaining the greatest systematic unity possible in the empirical use of our reason". The object of experience is, as it were, derived from the imagined object of the idea as from its principle or cause. For instance, things in the world, he continues, must be so regarded as if they derived their existence from a Supreme Intelligence. In this way the idea is really a heuristic and not an ostensive concept, etc.

In the fourth paragraph immediately following ("I wish to make this clearer"), the expression "as if" is repeated a number of times in the same sense, especially in connection with the theological idea: "We must regard everything that can possibly find a place in the nexus of possible experience, as if this experience constituted an absolute unity . . . at the same time, however, as if the totality of all phenomena (the actual world of sense) had a supreme . . . cause . . . namely an, as it were, independent, original and Creative reason . . . as if the objects themselves had sprung from this archetype of all reason", and so forth: "just as we do not deduce the inner phenomena from a simple thinking substance but from the Idea of such a substance, so we have no right to deduce the world-order from a Supreme Intelligence but only from the Idea of such an Intelligence", i.e. we are allowed to make use of these concepts as heuristic fictions

In the fifth paragraph he says of the idea of the soul and of that of God: "We cannot be permitted[12] to introduce. . . thought-entities as real and definite objects. They should not therefore be accepted as really existent. Their reality is to be taken as a scheme of the regulative principle of the systematic unity of all knowledge of nature; accordingly it is merely as *analoga*[13] of real things, not as real things in themselves" . . . that they can be made the basis of deductions. Of a "thought-entity" ("ideal entity") we can, of course, predicate nothing further, since it is only a product of imagination, yet "we think of it as having a relation to the totality of phenomena that is analogous to the relation existing between the phenomena themselves." Kant goes on at once to speak more specifically of the idea of God: "God only furnishes us with the idea of something upon which all empirical reality bases its highest and necessary unity, and which we cannot picture to ourselves otherwise than on the analogy of a real substance that is the cause of all things according to laws of reason." In the same manner we have in paragraph 9: "I shall therefore, on the analogy of the realities of the world, substances, causality, necessity, picture to myself an entity that possesses all these things in their highest perfection"; "under the protection of such a primal cause I can make possible . . . systematic unity of the manifold of the cosmic whole, by looking upon all interconnections *as* if they were the orderings of a supreme reason." In the twelfth paragraph we have again: "This rational entity is, of course, a *mere Idea*, and is not simply and in itself to be accepted as anything real but is only problematically assumed . . . in order that all the connections in the world of sense may be regarded *as* if they had their basis in this entity, simply and solely however with the object of building thereon a systematic unity . . . which may be indispensable to the reason and is in every way helpful to the empirical understanding" (here Kant again lays stress on usefulness as the distinguishing mark of the fiction; immediately afterwards, in the thirteenth paragraph, he speaks in this sense, of this "so wholesome unity").

These principles are then applied in the next three paragraphs (14, 15, 16), to the three main divisions of metaphysics. The As-if passages bearing on the idea of the soul have already been quoted above, p. 256, and those referring to cosmology on p. 255. With regard to the theological idea, we are once more told in the same connection (A 686, B 714) that the idea of God "like all speculative Ideas, merely means that reason commands us to approach all the connections of the world according to principles of a systematic unity, and therefore *as* if they had all sprung from a single all-embracing unity as a highest and all-sufficient cause," etc. We are concerned here with "nothing but" a subjective, formal rule of our reason.

Stressing the teleological point of view he continues: "the speculative interest of reason makes it necessary to look at all arrangement in the world as if it had originated from the purpose of a Supreme Reason"; such a view can "at all times be of use to reason"; "we can make a number of discoveries in this way" (for instance, in regard to "the shape of the earth, of mountains and of the sea"). The presupposition that this has all been arranged with an object—the presupposition of "teleological inter-relation" —is "nothing but a regulative principle of reason enabling it to attain to the highest systematic unity, by means of the Idea of causality of the supreme cosmic cause adapting means to ends, *as* if this cause, as Supreme Intelligence working with infinitely wise purpose, were the origin of all things." Here the character of the idea of God as a heuristic fiction is very happily expressed. Kant then goes on to show that this idea must not be transformed from a regulative principle into a constitutive one, for otherwise we should be open to the reproach of "indolent reasoning" (*ignava ratio*) and of "perverse reasoning" (*perversa ratio*).

Summing up he again says at the end, it is permitted to us to picture such a Divine Entity "on the analogy of objects of experience", "but merely as an object in Idea"; nay, "we can frankly and without fear of reproach allow a certain anthropomorphism in this Idea that is advantageous to the regulative principle in question, for it is after all only an Idea", etc. This Being then "is thought of on the analogy of an intelligence"; but "it is simply an entity in Idea that we are dealing with. In this sense therefore I may "regard arrangements suggesting an end, as purposes, deducing . . . them from the Divine Will." "I merely posit the Idea of such a Being in order, on the analogy of a causal determination, to look upon phenomena as systematically interconnected."

His final words are: "For that very reason we are also justified in thinking of the cosmic cause in Idea . . . with a subtle anthropomorphism . . . namely, as a Being that possesses understanding and the capacity to be pleased or displeased, as well as commensurate desire and will, etc." "The regulative law of systematic unity demands that we study nature as if everywhere, ad infinitum, a systematic and appropriate unity were to be found in combination with the utmost multiplicity." This view-point, it is said, is "advantageous," another reference to utility, the characteristic of all fictions!

The solid foundations thus laid receive further confirmation of a valuable and definitive kind in the "transcendental methodology", particularly in the section on "The Discipline of Pure Reason in Hypothesis". In this section occurs that classical passage which we have already quoted above; there, ideas are expressly designated as heuristic fictions and are clearly and precisely distinguished from "hypotheses"; the latter are assumptions of objects which stand in an eventually demonstrable connection with empirical phenomena and thus serve to explain and complete our fragmentary experience—in other words, objects whose reality is assumable. Ideas, on the contrary, are rational concepts without objectivity, mere thought-entities that simply serve to guide our reason in certain respects; and are therefore not an assumption of something real, such as hypotheses are, but of something unreal with the consciousness of this unreality—"heuristic fictions".

Among these same rational ideas, which are not legitimate hypotheses but would be quite unjustified as such, is to be reckoned, for example, according to the same passage, the assumption, fully justified as a fiction, of an "understanding possessing the faculty of perceiving its object without the aid of the senses". Thus intuitive understanding or intellectual intuition is here characterized clearly as a mere methodological fiction.[14] In the same sentence Kant cites as further examples of such fictions the idea of a substance which, "without being impenetrable, should nevertheless be present in space", in other words, the idea of the soul, and connected with it, the idea of a supersensuous "community of substances", the idea of "presence otherwise than in space", the idea of "duration otherwise than in time",—i.e. the whole stock-in-trade of the old dogmatic philosophy. These are all, in Kant's penetrating view, not justified hypotheses but useful methodological "heuristic fictions"[15].

The idea of the soul is then selected for further discussion as a particularly useful heuristic fiction: "to think of the soul as something simple is quite permissible in order, by the help of this *Idea*,[16] to make the complete and necessary unity of all spiritual forces, even if they cannot be seen in *concreto*, the principle of our judgment of their inner phenomena. But to *assume*[17] soul as a simple substance (a transcendental concept) is not only to assume something that is undemonstrable (many physical hypotheses are that) but would be a quite arbitrary and reckless procedure "—so again we have a clear-cut distinction between the permissible methodological fiction and the hypothesis. And in the same work "mere Ideas of reason"—fictions are constantly distinguished sharply from "transcendental hypotheses."

With regard to the fiction of the soul, we find in the section "The Discipline of Pure Reason in Proofs", another very important passage, one that is all the more noticeable, in that it has so far never been really noticed. Kant there (A 784, B 812) speaks of the inference from "the unity of apperception to "the simple nature of our thinking substance", and calls this inference a paralogism arising from the fact that we confuse "the simple in abstraction" with "the simple in the object". In elucidation of this he adds: "If I picture to myself the force of a moving body, it is for me, in one respect, an absolute unity and my idea of it is simple; I can therefore also express it by the movement of a point, because the volume of the body is not here involved and, without diminution of the force, can be thought of as as small as we will, and, consequently, as residing in a point." From this I shall not infer, however, that if nothing is given me but the moving force of a body, the body can be thought of as a simple substance, because "the conception of it is abstracted from all dimensional space-content and is therefore simple."

This comparison is exceedingly instructive. For Kant here makes use, as an example, of the well-known fiction according to which the motional force of a body can be thought of as isolated in a point—a well-known methodological fiction of mathematical physics. Quite consciously and with complete methodological clarity, Kant here develops the essence of this abstract fiction and develops from it a practical application in the concept of a simple soul-substance, which, together with all the consequences that follow from it (freedom, immortality, "the communion of saints"), he regards simply as—a mere methodological fiction.

In a later section, "On the ideal of the Highest Good, etc.", the idea of an intelligible moral world, of free and morally-acting spirits, that is, of "a *corpus mysticum* of rational beings" (in other words something corresponding exactly to the religious idea of a Communion of Saints or of an Invisible Church) is expressly referred to by Kant as "a mere Idea, but yet a practical one, which can and should exercise a real influence upon the world of sense, in order to make this world conform as far as possible to this idea." Here then we have nothing but a methodological fiction of ethics.

A variation of this idea is the conception "of an intelligible, i.e. moral world", in the sense that in such a world there reigns the "system by which happiness is bound up with and proportional to morality", the "system of a morality which produces its own reward" (the same thing that later on Fichte—thereby transforming a critical fiction into an uncritical dogma—called "the moral world-order"). That too "is only an Idea" which, in its turn, is only made possible by a special fiction, the fiction, namely, that "all acts of rational beings take place as if they had sprung from a Supreme Will comprehending within and under itself all individual wills".

The idea of such a Supreme Will, balancing merit and happiness, is the "ideal of a Highest Good", the last and highest idea, i.e. the highest of all fictions, which again is identical with the idea of God, or "the concept of a single original Being as the Highest Good", as Kant afterwards puts it.[18]

In the same section he says further: "we must look upon ourselves as belonging to such a world", "we must assume it as our future world (as sensual beings bound to the intuitional form of time)", "we must look upon such a world as one that is to come", "we must see ourselves in the realm of grace";— that "is a practical and necessary Idea of reason"; and in the light of what we now know about Ideas, it is a heuristic fiction, a conceptual aid useful for ethical purposes.

Moreover, that we are dealing here simply with helpful fictional constructions, is obvious from the conclusion of the same section: we may not "presume from the conception of a Supreine Being" to deduce the laws of morality; this would be "fanciful, or even presumptuous"; i.e. we could only deduce the moral laws from the concept of God, if it were a question of a *causa vera*. Since, however, we are dealing only with a fictional concept, we cannot deduce anything from it *realiter*. From an hypothesis something, under certain circumstances a good deal, can be deduced; but from a fiction, nothing. It is therefore a useful and utilizable, nay, a necessary and indispensable idea, though, nevertheless, "merely an Idea".

Finally, the section, "on thinking, knowing and believing", contains an important addition to the foregoing. This section, it is true, is in part self-contradictory, and in part contradicts the preceding one, and probably represents a sketch dating from an earlier period that has been interpolated here. We shall, however, leave aside the contradictory points, and confine ourselves to that which fits into and properly belongs to our theme. Kant refuses (A 827, B 855) to apply the expression "hypotheses" to the rational ideas: "If I were to give to what I accept as theoretical truth the name of hypothesis [i.e, if I chose to apply merely the term "hypothesis" instead of "knowledge" to the ideas], an hypothesis being something that I should be justified in assuming [as real], I should, merely by so doing, be laying claim to a fuller conception of the nature of a cosmic cause and of another world than I could really show. For, even to assume something as an hypothesis, I must have so much knowledge of it, at least in its qualities, as to be able to imagine [i.e. assume hypothetically] not indeed its conception but its existence. The word Belief, however, indicates only the guidance furnished by an Idea in which the concept likewise is fictitious" (cf. in explanation A 770, B 798). Thus "the presupposition that a Supreme Intelligence has arranged everything in accordance with the wisest intent", etc.—all these ideas which are "mere Ideas" Kant desires to designate as "beliefs".[19] In this sense and in this connection therefore belief is equivalent to the assumption that something exists which is not real and cannot be real. It is not only Kant who calls these fictional assumptions "beliefs"—we might go back and prove from the history of religions, particularly from that of Mysticism, that the converse also took place, and that for many believers their world of beliefs was—and still is—a conscious self-deception, i.e. a world of conscious fictions.

With this outlook we close our analysis of the *Kritik der reinen Vernunft*, noting particularly that only those passages have been selected and discussed which spoke in favour of our theory of fictions. But in Kant we also find in the same contexts many passages which permit or even demand a contrary interpretation. Kant, as we know, frequently contradicted himself; that these numerous contradictions constitute no disproof of his greatness is unintelligible only to the Philistine.[20] It is only by a consideration of the nature of Kant's development and of the age in which he happened to live, that we can understand how in him (as in many other great men, e.g. Luther) two tendencies are revealed, a critical and a dogmatic, a revolutionary and a conservative. Kant's two minds are often at variance with one another, and accordingly we find many passages in which he fails to maintain his critical standpoint.

* * *

As an example, we may take the *Prolegomena* (1783), where we encounter a remarkable variation of Kant's doctrine in regard to the Fiction. Only §§ 57 and 58 come into consideration, in the section "On the determination of the bounds of Pure Reason." In the preceding §§ 40–56, Kant has recapitulated the transcendental dialectic of his *Kritik der reinen Vernunft* very briefly, and very much in the form of a "popular version," for all the fine points of his theory of ideas have been lost in the process; it is only a blurred picture which is presented to us. The fact that in the transcendental dialectic we are dealing with concepts that are "mere Ideas" remains quite in the background; it is only rarely that this expression is found. One case in which his doctrine is especially obscured is to be found in the description of the idea of God as a "necessary hypothesis" (§ 55), whereas in the *Kritik der reinen Vernunft* he, with the utmost nicety, distinguished Ideas, as "heuristic fictions", from hypotheses. We see, therefore, that Kant intended his *Prolegomena* only for beginners and as an introduction to the study of his critical philosophy.

This same blurring is also encountered in the two sections 57 and 58. Kant is speaking here almost exclusively of the idea of God, but in consideration of the nature of the public to which he is addressing himself (κατ' ἄνθρωπον), he allows his presentation of this concept as a "mere Idea," to drop quite into the background; the realization, that is, that the very concept of a single original Being is purely fictional, "is only an idea." Here, in the *Prolegomena*, this "heuristic fiction" develops—not indeed for Kant himself but for his reader—into a necessary hypothesis; and henceforth he is only concerned to inquire how this original Being, recognized as real, is to be represented in its relation to the world, i.e. to what extent it is to be endowed with human predicates; it is only in relation to the latter question that the "as if" formula is introduced. In the *Kritik der reinen Vernunft*, at least in the passages quoted above, both the existence and the attributes of God were fictional. Now in the *Prolegomena*, in deference to a wider but not sufficiently advanced circle of readers, the fictional character is attached only to the attributes, while the existence of God is assumed as self-evident, although with a certain amount of hesitation. In § 58 he says: "The appropriate expression for our feeble notions would be this: that we think of the world *as* if it derived its existence and internal determination from a Supreme Reason." In § 59 it is specifically stated that this being is "not merely invented but that, since there must necessarily be something outside the world of sense which is thought only by the pure understanding" and he adds, "this we can . . . of course determine only according to analogy." To this mode of representation Kant (§ 57, end) gives the name of Symbolic (as distinguished from dogmatic) Anthropomorphism, "which in fact is concerned with language only and not with the object itself." "When I say that we are compelled to look upon the world *as* if it were the work of a Supreme Understanding and Will, I am really saying nothing more than that a watch, a ship, a regiment bears the same relation to the watchmaker, the shipbuilder, the commander, as the world of sense . . . does to the Unknown which I know, not in respect of what it is in itself but in respect of what it is for me." Similarly, we "call" the relation of the "Unknown quality in God" to humanity—"love" (on the analogy of the human father). This "symbolic anthropomorphism" then, "is concerned with language only," is only a façon de parler, to use an expression of Leibniz. We simply *talk as* if it were so.

DISCUSSION OF PRINCIPLES IN KANT'S CHIEF WORKS ON ETHICS AND THE PHILOSOPHY OF RELIGION

THE *Grundlegung zur Metaphysik der Sitten* (1785) comes first under this head—one of the boldest and most consistent works of Kant, a worthy counterpart to the *Kritik der reinen Vernunft* and far more important than the weak *Prolegomena*.

We will take first the third and final section, where the "concept of freedom" is treated as "the key to the explanation of the autonomy of the will." In the fourth paragraph (ed. Kirchm., 76)[21] we read:— "Every being who can act only under the notion that he is free is, for that very reason, also in practice free, i.e. all the laws hold for him that are inextricably bound up with freedom *as* if his will should be declared free, both in itself and in a sense valid in theoretical philosophy. I therefore claim that every rational being possessing a will must necessarily also be endowed with the idea of freedom, in virtue of which alone he acts. For to such a being our thought assigns a reason which is practical, i.e. which possesses a causal force in relation to its objects . . . (Such a reason) must regard itself as the originator of its principles . . . and in consequence it must . . . be regarded as free, i.e. its will can only be its own will, in virtue of the Idea of freedom, and must therefore in practical respects be ascribed to all rational beings." In a note (p. 76) Kant again expressly justifies the line he has taken here, "of assuming . . . freedom only as posited merely in Idea by rational beings in regard to their actions," for "the same laws hold good for a being who can act only under the Idea of his own freedom, that would bind one who was really free."

This is only a short passage but it is of far-reaching importance; for here Kant clearly and unambiguously declares freedom to be but a mere idea without reality. The heading of the whole passage runs (p. 76): "Freedom must be *presupposed* as an attribute of the will of all rational beings";— "presuppose" here is manifestly equivalent to "look upon as", "assign to", "ascribe to", in short = "imagine"! Immediately afterwards (p. 77), we find: freedom "we cannot . . . prove to be anything real; all we have seen is that we have to presuppose it";—here then "presuppose" does not denote an hypothesis but a fiction. In the same sense, a little further on, we find (p. 79), "we assume ourselves to be free in the order off efficient causes" and "we have ascribed to ourselves freedom of the will."

Now here another idea makes its appearance, which, as is so often the case with Kant, is presented in an uncertain light: in looking upon ourselves "as free", "we think of ourselves as a priori effective causes" (p. 79) and, thereby, we adopt the "standpoint" (pp. 79, 81–82) of "regarding ourselves" as parts of and partners in "the world of reason" (the *mundus intelligibilis*), and thus "as intelligence" (p. 81). On the one hand Kant maintains energetically that we know nothing at all of the world of things as such. When, on the other hand, he says that the world of things in themselves, consists of "intelligences", we see in this only a piece of "symbolical anthropomorphism", as Kant had previously expressed it. The world of things is regarded *as* if it consisted of intelligences, and we "think" ourselves as members of this fictional world of intelligences. This line of thought is not always clearly and unambiguously expressed; but there are passages in which it stands out, if not as the only meaning of Kant, at least as the most important of his meanings for us.

Further on (p. 82), he says, "Man can never think of the causality of his own will except under the idea of freedom";— "the idea of freedom" is, however, an idea like others, therefore "merely an idea", a "heuristic fiction". "If we think of ourselves as free, we transport ourselves into a world of reason" as parts thereof (p. 82). These are modes of expression which can be interpreted dogmatically as well as critically, dogmatically in the sense of an assumption of reality, critically in the sense of a heuristic fiction. Kant proceeds (p. 82): "Independence of the determining causes of the world of sense (which reason must always ascribe to herself) constitutes freedom. Now, with the Idea of freedom, we find inextricably bound up the concept of autonomy and, with this, the general principle of morality, which in Idea . . . is at the basis of all the acts of rational beings"; and further on, he says again, "when we think of ourselves as free, we are transporting ourselves as members thereof into a world of reason". In other words. freedom is an idea, autonomy is an idea, the general law of morality is an idea—ideas are "mere Ideas": all morality, consequently, is based on fictions. Further on (p. 83), he says: "The idea of freedom makes me a member of an intelligible world"— but if freedom is "merely an Idea", then the intelligible world is also a mere idea. Then (p. 84), it is said that a human being "with a will that is quite free from the impulses of sense, transports itself in thought into an entirely different order of things"; "it believes itself to be this better individual, by transporting itself to the standpoint of a member of the world of reason to which the idea of freedom . . . unconsciously forces it." That freedom, however, is "merely an Idea of reason, whose objective reality in itself is doubtful", is immediately afterwards (p. 85) clearly repeated: "All human beings think of themselves as free as far as the will is concerned"—but they are not free, freedom being only an "as if" assumption, a fiction. The statement that we, "as intelligences, think of ourselves as endowed with a will", is afterwards repeated several times (pp. 86–87), and also "that we place ourselves thereby in a different order of things". "By thinking itself into the world of understanding, practical reason does not overstep its bounds, but would do so if it sought . . . to reach that world by way of intuition" (p. 88). "The concept of a world of understanding is consequently *only a standpoint*[22] which reason finds itself compelled to take up outside phenomena, in order to think of itself as practical" (pp. 88–89)—in other words only a *point de vue*, only an accidental attitude, only a mere fiction. "Freedom is, however, a mere Idea" (p. 89)— and a "mere idea" is, as we know, a heuristic fiction. At the conclusion of the *Grundlegung* (p. 93) he says clearly: "Moreover, the Idea of a pure world of understanding as a totality of all intelligence . . . always remains a serviceable and permissible idea for the purpose of a rational belief . . . in order by means of the glorious ideal[23] of a universal realm of absolute purposes as such . . . to awaken in us a lively interest in the moral law."

The omitted subordinate clause, referring to the concept of a realm of purposes, runs: "to which we can belong as members only if we carefully observe the rules of freedom, *as if they were laws of nature*" (p. 94). We here encounter a thought that is frequently repeated in similar form, in the second section of the *Grundlegung*; for instance, on p. 62, where "the ethical imperative is formulated in the statement that the rules are to be selected precisely *as if they were to function as general laws of nature*"; or, on p. 44: "act *as if the principle of your action were, through your will, to become a general law of nature*"—a new and peculiar fiction. I know very well that the rules of my conduct are no laws of nature, that they are not even laws for the majority of mankind, but I think and I act *as if* they were universal laws of nature! In the same sense, we have, on p. 64: "Accordingly, every rational human being must act as if he were, at all times, by means of his rules of conduct, a law-giving member of the universal realm of purposes. The formal principle of these rules of conduct is: Act as if your rule of conduct was at the same time to serve as the general law (of all rational beings)." Further on (p. 65), he says of this "realm of purposes": "this is only possible on the analogy of a realm of nature": the expression "on the analogy", however, means, according to the usage of Kant discussed before (cf. p. 261 above), a fiction. This "realm of purposes" is "merely possible" because, before it could come into existence, it would be necessary not only that all rational beings should act unanimously according to the rule in question, but also that the realm of nature should "be in tune" with the realm of purposes—an absolute Utopia. The "realm of purposes" is therefore "a mere Idea".

If, however, as he says further on, "the realm of purposes" is thought of as united under a supreme head, then the latter would thereby not remain a mere Idea any more, but acquire a true reality" (p. 65). But the idea of such a supreme head is, as we know, itself merely a fiction of "symbolic anthropomorphism". And even if we wished to assume such a "supreme head", we should nevertheless have to imagine this sole unfettered law-giver as judging the worth of rational beings according to the unselfish conduct prescribed for them by this mere Idea": i.e. the idea of a realm of absolute purposes of rational beings, or, in other words, the idea of the "dignity of man". That this, too, is a "mere Idea", Kant states on p. 65, in the following incisive words: "And herein lies the paradox, that the mere dignity of mankind as a rational nature, apart from any other purpose or advantage to be obtained thereby—the respect therefore for a mere idea[24]—should, nevertheless, serve as the constant prescription of the will; and that precisely this independence of the rule of conduct from all such motives should constitute its superiority and the claim of each individual rational subject to be a law-giving member in the realm of purposes."

In this fine passage Kant reached the high water-mark of his critical philosophy: the "dignity of man", the "realm of purposes"—this Kant acknowledges and teaches—are "mere ideas", concepts, that is, without any reality, only "heuristic fictions", only modes of approach, only a standpoint; we can, should, and must look upon the thing as if it were so. But in spite of this realization of the fictive nature of this mode of representation man, as a "rational being", orders his conduct in accordance with these fictions. Here we reach the highest pinnacle attained by Kantian thought, or, indeed, by any human thought. Only a few, only an élite, can continue to breathe at all at this altitude: the vast majority need a different, a less rarefied atmosphere.

* * *

In the Kritik der praktischen Vernunft (1788) Kant adopts a different tone. The daring radicalism of the Grundlegung has given place to an increasing dogmatism. Whereas in the Grundlegung the critical-radical themes stand out prominently while the conservative-dogmatic tendency is but an undercurrent, here in the Kritik der praktischen Vernunft the position is reversed. The radical elements do not, indeed, disappear entirely even here. With an eye to our theme, we shall lay stress on the radical elements alone, and on these only in so far as they find decisive expression.

In the first section, § 7 (ed. Kirchmann, 1870, pp. 37–38), the idea of holiness is introduced as a practical idea: "In the all-sufficing intelligence (God), free will is correctly represented as being capable of no rules of conduct that could not, at the same time, be objective laws ... this holiness of

the will is a practical Idea which must necessarily serve as an archetype "—
that is, a fictional ideal (cf., on the other hand, Ibid., p. 148).

Yet the"intelligible order of things", or "supersensuous nature", as it is
now often called, appears in quite a dogmatic form in this work. But there
are also passages that seem to have a more critical character; for instance, in
the section, "On the Deduction of the Principles of pure Practical Reason"
(p. 52. ff.): "The law of autonomy is the moral law and, therefore, the basic law of supersensuous nature and of a pure world of intelligence whose
counterpart . . . must be supposed to exist in the world of sense. The former
might be called the archetype, which we apprehend only through reason,
the latter, because it contains the possible influence of the Idea as the determining basis of the will, might be called the copy. For indeed the moral law
carries us in Idea into a nature where pure reason, if it were associated with
the appropriate physical faculties, would produce the highest good . . . that
this Idea does really form a kind of model set up for the determinations of
our will is confirmed by the most ordinary observation of ourselves. In testing by practical reason the rule of conduct according to which I am inclined
to give certain testimony, I always try to see how it would appear if my rule
were to hold good as a universal law of nature. . . . We become conscious,
through the reason, of a law to which all our rules of conduct are subject,
as if through our mere willing a natural order of things were bound to arise.
This must, therefore, be the Idea of a nature not empirically given but possible in virtue of freedom and consequently supersensuous; to which we, at
least for practical purposes, ascribe objective reality[25] because we look upon
it as an object of our will, in our character of pure rational beings." After all,
therefore, an "objective reality"! Not purely fictional therefore? But observe
the context: "objective reality" we ascribe to this supersensuous nature only
because and in so far as we "regard" it as "the object of our will"—that is we
ourselves create this supersensuous nature by our own will and only in so
far as our will is determined by this "Idea";—in other words, we find here
no escape from the fictional. In the same sense, he says very characteristically
further on (pp. 53–54): "The two problems: how pure reason is, on the one
hand, to recognize a priori objects (the problem of the Kritik der reinenVernunft)
and how, on the other hand (the problem of the Kritik der praktischenVernunft)
it can be an immediate determining basis of the will, i.e. the causality of
rational beings in respect to the reality of objects (merely by the thought
of the universal validity of its own rules of conduct as laws); these two

problems are quite distinct." In other words, practical reason simply creates its own object, the realm of the good, "merely by thought," merely then by virtue of the idea; and the object created by it is the realm of the good, which exists only in and through the idea. Here Kant has expressed himself very clearly, at least for anyone who can read him rightly and who can realise these high thoughts in his own experience.

* * *

Die Religion innerhalb der Grenzen der blossen Vernunft (1793) contains very valuable material for our subject. The "introduction" first uses the expressions "assume" (p. 37) and "objective though only practical reality" (ed. Kirchmann, p. 7) rather indefinitely, but at the end of the introduction it becomes quite clear that Kant in what follows "conceives the relation of the good to the bad principle as that of two independently existing efficient causes". How this is meant will soon become clearer.

Near the beginning of the first part (p. 22) we find a similar, though not very definite, expression. More definite is the passage on p. 45: "Every evil act, if we look for the rational origin of it, must be treated *as if* the individual had passed to it straight from a condition of innocence"—in other words, we have here a variation of the fiction of liberty.

The second part contains shortly after the beginning (p. 66) a very characteristic apology for the devil and hell—as fictions. "It should not therefore surprise us if an apostle conceives this invisible enemy (the evil instincts within us), who is only known by his effect upon us, and who destroys our principles —if he conceives this enemy as outside us and in the form of an evil spirit . . . an expression that seems to have been designed not to extend our knowledge beyond the domain of the senses, but only to make more concrete for practical use the concept of what is for us unfathomable." Kant suggests therefore that this fictional mode of representation was consciously and purposely adopted by the apostle in question. Further on he says: "It is characteristic of Christian morality that it represents the morally-good as separated from the morally-bad, not as is heaven from earth but as is heaven from hell: a conception which, though figurative and as such objectionable, is nevertheless philosophically correct in meaning. It serves in fact, etc." Hell and the devil are then expedient fictions, which met with Kant's entire approbation as religious modes of expression. Contrasted with the devil or "the evil spirit" (p. 68) we find "the personified Idea of the good principle"—i.e. "the ideal of moral perfection", "the archetype of the moral attitude of mind" naturally also taken as an expedient fiction. We can say of this fictional archetype "that it has come down to us from heaven";[26] "Son of God" is thus an expedient religious fiction. "We can also regard his union with us as a condition of degradation for the Son of God" and it is also quite right to represent this ideal of the moral attitude as "contending with obstacles and, in face of the most tremendous assaults, still triumphant"—in other words a towering structure of expedient religious fictions.

"In his practical faith in this Son of God (in so far as he is represented as having taken the shape of man), man may accordingly hope to find favour in the sight of God (who naturally remains a fiction only)"; the "practical faith" consists, indeed, only in the recognition of this Idea as a useful religious conception and its "assimilation" to the "archetype of humanity". In this sense Kant says on p. 71: "And the belief in the practical validity of this Idea which lies in our reason . . . possesses a moral worth." Although then "the archetype of such a truly divinely-minded being" "is to be sought nowhere else than in our reason,"(p. 71) nevertheless "this Idea, in practical respects, has its reality entirely in itself" (p. 70); indeed the whole section from which these last quotations have been taken has the characteristic title: "Objective Reality of this Idea."This has great importance for us, for "objective reality" as applied to an "Idea" is equivalent not by any means to "reality of existence" but to "reality of validity".This throws a remarkable light upon those earlier passages in which there was mention of the "objective reality" of the ideas of God and immortality, and of freedom (cf. above pp. 260, 273). Had there been any doubt as to what the "objective reality" of ideas meant, doubt is now quite impossible: the expression means not unconditional existence, but unconditional value.

A note of Kant's on the above section is also of great value for us (pp. 73 ff.); the fact that we have to "hypostasize" (p. 72) these ideas and "make them conceivable in human ways", is a "limitation[27] of human reason" which compels us "to have recourse to an analogy with the natural world in order to bring within our grasp spiritually-moral, supersensuous entities", although in doing so we do not mean to assert that it is so in an absolute sense ($\kappa\alpha\tau$' $\dot{\alpha}\lambda\dot{\eta}\theta\varepsilon\iota\alpha\nu$). What we have here is simply "the schematism of analogy (of illustration) which we cannot do without. But to transform this into a schematism of objectivation (for the extension of our knowledge) is anthropomorphism,[28] which, from a moral standpoint (in religion), has the most noxious consequences." Religious fictions, then, must not be transformed into dogmas, the 'as-if' must not be converted into a 'that' and a 'because'. "Advantageous" though these conceptual methods are as fictions, they are equally noxious as dogmas. It is quite wrong to take this whole conceptual edifice ($\kappa\alpha\tau$' $\dot{\alpha}\lambda\dot{\eta}\theta\varepsilon\iota\alpha\nu$) as true, i.e. objectively and theoretically. It is a castle in the air, a *fata morgana* but, nevertheless, a necessary and serviceable mode of expression and conception and, in this sense, it has the value of a subjective, practical "truth"; cf. above p. 657 note.

Kant develops this idea again in connection with the idea of the eternity of punishment in hell. That is a useful "conception", which "is strong enough to counteract the evil one"; but it must not be presupposed "dogmatically and objectively" as a principle, i.e. not "as a dogma." Against this Kant argues at length. Such a conception "must not proclaim itself as a dogma. It is merely a principle, by means of which practical reason, in the employment of its concepts of the supersensuous (i.e. of the moral commandment which transcends the sensual nature of man), prescribes the rule".

A further application of the method of fictions follows immediately, p. 82ff.: "the deduction of the Idea of a justification of man who, although erring, has nevertheless attained to an attitude of mind pleasing to God" (p. 87). This idea, then, needs a "deduction". It is remarkable that this term, which is so important and characteristic for the doctrine of categories in the *Kritik der reinen Vernunft*, and which, as we saw (p. 259, above) is also used in the doctrine of Ideas, should recur frequently here also. In other words, the (Pauline) idea of justification is here "deduced" by Kant: he shows in detail, particularly on p. 84, how every thing must be "thought" "regarded", "conceived" in such a way that the "divine justice" (itself a fiction) "may be satisfied"—again a heaping up of religious fictions.[29] The "deduction" of these idea-fictions is said expressly, p. 88, to be due to "utility" which, as we know, is the characteristic mark of all fictions.

Further study of the *Religion innerhalb der Grenzen der blossen Vernunft* reveals a very interesting remark in the final section of the second part (p. 93): "To imagine a person free from the inherited disposition towards evil, and to accept his birth of a virgin mother, is an Idea at which reason arrives by adapting itself to a sort of moral instinct hard to explain but yet not to be rejected."[30] Kant then explains the justification and the "fitness" of the "idea of the (virgin) birth, not dependent upon any sex intercourse, of a child possessing no moral defect". He even discusses the scientific difficulties of the idea in this sense but closes the discussion with the following characteristic words: "But why all this theorising for or against, if for practical purposes it is enough that we should regard the Idea as the symbol, set up for our imitation, of a humanity lifting itself above the temptations of evil (triumphantly resisting it)?" In other words the "Idea" of the virgin conception is another expedient religious fiction, a beautiful, suggestive and useful myth!

In the same way he gives a general approval to the "presentation in the form of a history" of the struggle between the evil and the good principle in man, "whereby two principles in man, as antagonistic as heaven and hell, are represented as persons existing outside of him"(p. 91); "the evil principle is called the ruler of this world", "physical suffering, etc. are conceived of as persecutions by this bad principle" (p. 97). "It is easily seen that if we were to free this vivid and popular mode (which, for its time, was perhaps the only possible form of representation) of its mystical husk, it (its spirit and rationality) would be practically valid and binding on all the world at all times "(p. 97)." This being so, nothing is gained by . . . attacking these stories, seeing that true religion [the critical Religion of Right Action] is once for all with us . . . though originally it had to be introduced by such expedients" (p. 99); "nay, we can still honour even the husk which has served to bring a doctrine into being . . ." (*Ibid*) . . . All these religious fictions may therefore be retained for the people; and for the people, not in the usual somewhat contemptuous sense, but as the community in general.

It is true that "the sensible theologian must beware" not to push these religious fictions too far. He must be careful not to fill "the heads of those entrusted to his spiritual care" with miraculous stories "or to let their fantasy run riot" (p. 102). Practical people "use miracles only as phrases"; "so the physician says that a sick person can be saved only by some miracle, i.e. he will most certainly die". "Wise governments have, therefore, at all times, admitted, nay have given a place in the body of legally authorized religious doctrines to the belief that in ancient times miracles occurred, but they have not sanctioned modern miracles", i.e. the state has permitted the conception of miracles as an expedient religious fiction, but forbids us to draw therefrom inferences that would affect social life.

In the third portion we also find many passages relevant to our thesis: there the idea of the Kingdom of God is introduced, which "may also be called a Kingdom of Virtue (of the good principle), the Idea of which has in human reason its well-grounded objective reality (as the duty to form part of such a State)", (p. 111). This passage is of particular importance for us: this idea, like all ideas of this kind, has "its well-grounded objective reality". But where? "In the human reason." And how? "As the duty to form part of such a State." Here the expression "objective reality", which is also applied to the idea of God and of immortality, is explained with all desirable clarity. This "objective reality" has nothing whatever to do with an external existence theoretically demonstrable, or assumable, cf. pp. 260, 273 above; the "objective reality" of the ideas consists in their inward existence in the human reason as practical, ethical norms, values, ideals, fictions. This passage is a classic one for Kant's whole theory of Ideas.

The heading of the first division runs as follows: "Philosophical Conception of the Victory of the Good Principle and Foundation of a Kingdom of God upon Earth." The antithesis to this is the idea "of an ethical 'state of nature'", more or less the Kingdom of the Devil on earth, where human beings are regarded "as if they were the instruments of the evil one" (p. 114). In the Kingdom of God "all laws are regarded as the commands of a common law-giver "(p. 116); they are" thought of", "conceived" in this way (p. 117). "Such a people of God may be matched by the Idea of a rabble of subjects of the evil principle . . . although here, too, the principle antagonistic to virtue lies within ourselves and is only figuratively conceived as an external power" (p. 119). The idea of a people or a Kingdom of God, then becomes that of the "Invisible Church", which is "merely the Idea of the union of all righteous people under a divine . . . world-government" (p. 119). "It might also be compared with that of a family under a . . . moral father" (p. 121). And then follows Kant's celebrated and as yet so little understood definition of religion. "All religion consists in the fact that in respect of all our duties we regard God (a mere idea), as the law-giver to be universally reverenced" (p. 122)—the stress is on "regard"; we regard the matter as if a God existed and as if this God had prescribed our moral code; in this double fiction lies the essence of the religious manner of approach. "The fulfilment of all human duties as divine commands constitutes the essential element in all religions" (p. 130). That has a double meaning: (A) All historical and empirical religions consist in the fact that our human duties have, in all seriousness, been taken and explained by the peoples as the commands of higher beings, i.e. the peoples assumed that this was so; (B) The religion of Pure Reason consists in the fact that man takes his duties as seriously *as* if they had been imposed by some higher being.

The first of these is a still undeveloped condition. "The coverings, under which the embryo first develops into the man, must be laid aside, before he can be born into the light of day," says Kant (*Ibid.*, p. 144). "The leading-strings of the sacred tradition, with all its appendages, statutes and observances, that did good service in their time, become gradually less and less indispensable, indeed, act as a clog, as man reaches adolescence." So long as he (the human race) "was a child, he had the wisdom of a child ... but now that he is become a man, he must put away childish things." Therewith Kant closes this very remarkable passage (p. 144). As soon as the human being reaches the stage of thinking manhood, he transforms the 'that' (dass) of the dogmas into the 'as if' of the fictive standpoint.

The second division of the third part (pp. 148–186) does not afford much support for our thesis. The Resurrection and Ascension are regarded as "rational ideas" (p. 153), i.e. they are given a moral meaning, and in the same way the second coming of the risen Saviour to his kingdom is explained as "symbolic representation" (p. 160). The doctrine of the Millennium, too, is a "beautiful ideal", and together with the associated apocalyptic conceptions may "have its valuable symbolic significance for the reason". If we "put only an intellectual construction" upon these symbols, they are always "useful as vehicles" and "swaddling clothes" (p. 162)— these, too, therefore, are useful fictions: on the other hand, to take them as dogmas would be a "harmful[31] anthropomorphism" (p. 169). Even the concept of the Trinity, when morally "purified" (p. 169) is recognized as another practical idea (p. 170), as a "not inappropriate expression"; 'calling', 'atonement', 'election', these are all recognized in the moral sense "as practical and necessary religious ideas" (p. 174). Simpler than these complicated religious fictions is the primary and basic religious fiction: "we must continually examine our conscience *as if* we had been called to account before a judge" (p. 173).

CONFIRMATIONS AND APPLICATIONS IN THE OTHER WORKS OF THE CRITICAL PERIOD (ESPECIALLY OF 1790)

IN the Kritik der Urteilskraft, Part II, which treats of the teleological faculty of judgment, Kant again comes back (in § 86 "Of Ethico-theology") to the statement that "we must think of a God as the supreme head in a moral kingdom of purposes"; "the mind which is anxious to extend the field of its moral feeling, is here merely voluntarily conceiving an object that is not in the world, in order, where possible, to evince its duty before such an object"; for the man who acts ethically "feels a need within himself both to execute commands imposed upon him and to obey a supreme master."[32] "His severe self-reproach will speak to him *as* if it were the voice of a judge to whom . . . he had to give account". Our moral capacity, as a subjective principle," has just this tendency to ascribe to the world which it contemplates a Supreme Cause governing nature according to ethical principles". "To be in harmony with the final purpose of an intelligent cosmic cause (if such there be)" we regard as our duty. Thus does "reason" conceive for itself "a deity". There is an old half-truth (which Kant occasionally cites) that "fear created the gods" (*timor fecit deos*). Here, however, it appears that reason, in the same way, creates God—so that we may say with Kant, *ratio facit Deum*. And we are only dealing here with "a *concept* of God created by our reason" Kant himself shows clearly. He even goes so far as to speak in the same passage of God as an "object represented in such a shadowy outline" where, however, "object" does not mean something absolute or transcendental, but only the intentional-immanent object of conception.

* * *

A very consistent, daring and frank presentation of the As-if doctrine is found in the work *Uber die Fortschritte der Metaphysik*. Kant, as is well-known, planned this work for the prize offered by the University of Berlin in 1791. He never published it, and it is to this circumstance, perhaps, that we owe the frank and daring language of the essay, which has up to the present received insufficient attention. In the section on the Third Stage of Metaphysics (p. 137) Kant links his argument directly with the *Kritik der Urteilskraft*. Of the concept of fitness for a purpose, he says that it does not relate to what is in the object but to what we put into it; that we consequently "only insert or interpolate this concept by a quasi-rational process"; "the concept of purpose is, at all times, made by us". Connected therewith is the concept (also "made" by us), of an end in general, the concept of the highest good; and connected with this are other "fabricated concepts"—freedom, God and immortality (or "the supersensuous *within us, above* us and *after us*"). Further on in the essay (in the "Solution of the Academic Problem"), he goes on to say that we "must not investigate the supersensuous from the point of view of what it is in itself, but only of how we have to conceive it and imagine its character, if we are to be in harmony with the final purpose, which is the supreme good" (p. 141). We are not to undertake investigations into the nature of things, "which we make for ourselves, and make only for necessary practical purposes, and which perhaps do not exist at all outside of our idea, perhaps cannot possibly exist." In this connection Kant also justifies in detail the expression "faith" for assumptions of this kind with practical object. "The proof of the correctness of this faith is no proof of the truth of the assumptions when considered theoretically; nor is it any objective indication of the reality of their objects—in regard to the supersensuous, this is impossible—but only a subjectively and practically valid, though for this purpose adequate, indication that we are to act *as if we* knew that these objects were real" (p. 143). What really takes place here is that, "in order to strive towards that to which we have already committed ourselves, namely the furtherance of the highest good in the world, we supplement, merely by means of rational ideas, the theory of the possibility of this highest good; we make for ourselves objects, strictly in accordance with the demands of moral law, and arbitrarily endow them with objective reality, viz. God, Freedom of the practical order, and Immortality". Further on, p. 144, he says: "Practically we create these objects ourselves, according as we consider the Idea of them to be helpful to the purpose of our pure reason[33]; and this purpose, because it is morally necessary, is able to produce the illusion that what possesses reality subjectively, namely for the use of men (because it has been exhibited to experience in actions which conform to its laws), is to be taken[34] for knowledge of the existence of the object corresponding to this form." In reality, however, "these ideas have been arbitrarily created by us" (p. 145). In other words, the moral proof for the existence of God is an argument "from the rationality of *assuming*[35] such (a being)." Man is justified in permitting an idea that he has himself constructed according to certain moral principles, to exercise an influence upon his decisions, exactly as if he had derived it from a real object (p. 151). These ideas serve "to represent[36] man's life on earth as if it were a life in heaven"; that is to say, we can and should assume the world on the analogy of physical teleology (i.e. as in the nature of a 'moral teleology'). Considered theoretically this "is not, as the Leibniz-Wolff philosophy holds, a tenable but overstrained concept. It is, from a practical-dogmatic standpoint, a real concept, and one which is sanctioned by practical reason for our sense of duty" (p. 154).[37] But this "practical reality" must not be misunderstood by uncritical readers of the Critical Philosophy and again applied, in a theoretical and dogmatic sense; i.e. the fiction must not be transformed into a dogma. Kant once more repeats expressly and distinctly that "we observe a certain organization of the practical reason in which (1) the subject of universal legislation, as originator of the world, (2) the object of the will of mundane beings, as conforming in their end to the subject, (3) the condition of these beings, in which alone they are capable of attaining that end [God, freedom and immortality]—are in the practical aspect self-made ideas" (p. 156). In other words, these concepts are and remain—self-made ideas.

Here too we see clearly the immeasurable difference between the Kantian justification of religious ideas and that of the pre- and post-Kantians. The Kantian justification of religious ideas is a purely fictive, or better perhaps, a fictionalistic one. They are for him practical, expedient fictions, whereas the pre- and post-Kantian justification of religious concepts and judgments is a rationalistic one; they are rationally grounded hypotheses. A variety only of this rationalism is the *Kantianismus vulgaris*, the popular version of Kant's doctrine, which represents Kant as justifying the principal ideas of religion on the basis of moral facts; for according to the presentation of this popular Kantianism that has become customary since Reinhold, theoretical inferences have been drawn from moral phenomena as to the existence of God, etc., i.e. we are again making hypotheses. The real and genuine Kantian criticism draws no theoretical inferences whatever, but says: You must act *as* you would if a God existed, etc. Therein lies Kant's critical Pragmatism.

A very important passage for the elucidation of Kant's meaning is contained in the treatise *Von einem neuerdings erhobenen vornehmen Ton in der Philosophie* (1796). There we find the expression "belief" fully explained in a note: Taken theoretically "to believe" means, "to regard a thing as likely", and is "something half-way between thinking and knowing." With regard to empirical things and empirical evidence such theoretical belief is a fact, but with regard to the supersensuous no judgment whatever is possible and, therefore, no judgment of probability: "there is therefore no such thing as theoretical belief in the supersensuous."

"But from the practical (moral-practical) point of view, not only is such a belief in the supersensuous possible. It is inevitable." For the categorical commands of the "voice of morality within me" require of us that we should co-operate in realizing the unconditioned purpose of the highest good (which, of course, is only an idea): and this highest good is, in its turn, only realizable "by means of the power of a world-ruler" (which again is only an idea). "To believe in such a ruler practically and morally, does not mean first to assume his reality as true, in order that we may realize the end imposed. For that purpose the law of reason is in itself objectively sufficient. No, it means that, in accordance with the ideal of that purpose, we are to act as we should if such a world-government really existed." "This is an imperative which enjoins not belief, but action." In other words, in the Kantian sense, in the sense of the Critical Philosophy, the expression, "I believe in God", means simply that "I act *as* if a God really existed." As a moral agent the man who thinks in the Kantian, the critical manner, acts *as* if the Good possessed an unconditioned value, such as to render it the decisive factor in the world; and the Good would be the decisive factor in the world if there were a world-government to bring about its final triumph. In spite of the fact that my theoretical reason *forbids* me to assume such a moral world-order—this concept would have no content—I yet act as if such a moral world-order might exist, since my practical reason *bids* me do good unconditionally. In following this command of practical reason I am, in strict theory, acting irrationally,[38] for my theoretical reason tells me that such a moral world-order is merely an empty, even if a beautiful, concept. But I do actually find within me the command of practical reason to do good, and this command impresses me as though it were something sublime. I act according to this command. But in acting thus, I am, at the same time, acting as if I did make this assumption of a moral world-order which I recognize to be theoretically impossible, nay even contradictory. Not in the sense of supposing that it is the assumption which gives the command; far from it; my soul does not think of that at all. The command meets with our approval and impresses us for its own sake; it is indeed part of the content of my practical reason. In other words, to the normal moral man, the moral world-order and the author of the moral order of the world, God, are not in the least a presupposition necessary to his voluntary submission to the moral commandment. On the contrary, in obeying the moral commandment Kant's normal man not only behaves just *as* if this obedience had not only to a certain extent empirical consequences in time and in the phenomenal world, but as if this moral action of his extended into an intelligible supersensuous world and, on the one hand, helped toward the attainment of a general eternal supreme good and, on the other, were incorporated by a divine power, as

an expedient element in a system of purposes. Such is always and everywhere the nature of unconditioned, ethically-good action; for to act morally
means, in contradistinction to the empirical conditions, to act *as if* the good
had an unconditioned value, *as if* it had the power to extend into a super-
empirical world in which a supreme ruler provided for the harmonizing of
good and evil. In this sense good action is identical with a belief in God and
immortality. In this sense the atheist who acts morally also believes *practically*
in God and immortality, since he acts *as if God* and immortality existed. All
ethical conduct, therefore, involves the fiction of God and immortality—this
is the meaning of the practical rational belief in God and immortality. In
this sense, too, and only in this sense, must we understand the conclusion
elsewhere established by Kant regarding "a morally earnest and therefore religious endeavour towards good". The morally-good can say to himself and
to his kind: "Your acts are good and, for that reason, you are, in your way, a
believer, for you act as though a God existed: in short, your actions are good
and therefore you believe." This Kantian *recte agis, ergo credis* is the basic axiom
of practical philosophy and, as such, the counterpart to the basic axiom of
Descartes' theoretical philosophy as rightly understood: *cogito, ergo sum*.

* * *

With the question of practical conduct it is perhaps best to connect the
discussion contained in Kant's *Metaphysik der Sitten*, Part I, in his "Rechtslehre"
(1797). At the very beginning of the work, particularly in the section on
private law, there figures prominently the idea which is described as "the
original community of the soil in general" (§ 6, note, § 10, § 13). In order to enable himself to construct or deduce the possibility of an original
acquisition of landed property, Kant makes the following fiction: "All individuals were originally (i.e. previous to any freely-willed juridical act), in
rightful possession of the soil, i.e. they had the right to live wherever nature
or chance (without their volition) had placed them. Possession (*possessie*) as
distinguished from occupation (*sedes*) (or voluntary and acquired permanent
possession) is possession in common, on account of the connection of all
places on the earth's surface. . . . The possession proper to all men on earth,
which is antecedent to any juridical act (constituted, that is, by nature itself)
is an original possession in common (*communio possessionis originaria*) . . . a practical concept of reason, which contains a priori the principle according to

which alone man can make use of the spot on the earth which he happens to occupy in accordance with the laws of Right" (§ 13). We may not, for instance, say that the soil is "by nature and originally, previously to any jurid-ical act, free" (§6), "for that, too, would be a relation to objects, in this case to the soil, which would refuse possession of itself to anyone . . . because this freedom of the soil would constitute a prohibition to every one against making use of it. In order that use may be made of it, common possession is necessary, which could not be effected without a contract. But a soil that can only become free by means of a contract must actually be in the possession of all those (associated together) who mutually forbid each other its use. . ." (§ 6). Here then another fiction is introduced, that namely of an original contract which declares the original common possession of the soil.

Kant then continues: "This original common ownership of the soil. . . (*communio fundi originaria*) is an idea which possesses objective (practical juridical) reality"—another example of the sort of phrase with which we are now so familiar ("objectively, practically real idea") and for which we substitute the equivalent but clearer expression, *expedient fiction.*

To the idea of a state of nature there thus corresponds the correlative idea of an original contract already propounded simply as a rational idea by Hob-bes, Spinoza, Locke and Rousseau—the famous *pactum originarium* of which Kant speaks in § 52 (and before that in § 41). Whatever contradicts "the spirit of this original contract" and is "not fully compatible with this Idea", is contrary to Right and must be done away with.

With this fiction of a contract is also connected the fiction of a General will (which has a certain similarity to the fiction mentioned above of a "general consciousness"): Kant introduces this "collective will" (also called "the will of the people") in §§ 34, note, 39, 41, 49, A D, 51 and elsewhere. The idea of this common will is expressed in the following principle (§ 49 D): "What the people (the whole mass of the subjects) cannot deter-mine in regard to itself and its co-citizens, that the sovereign cannot deter-mine in regard to the people", and this is to be equated with "the Idea of a general legislative will" (§ 1).

The oath, too, rests on a fictional basis. Kant discusses this subject in § 40, with which must be taken the "verdict" of the "Tugendlehre", § 53—the Athenians banished Protagoras as a disbeliever in God. "In so doing the Athenian judges did, indeed, do him an injustice as men, but as judges and state-officials they behaved quite legally and consistently; for how would the taking of an oath have been possible, had it not been ordained by high authority (*de par le senat*), in a public and legal manner, that gods exist?" The belief in gods and in God is, consequently, an official fiction, serving as a basis for the oath, without which justice could not operate. It is, "in itself", perhaps "fundamentally unjust" to compel citizens to take an oath, but "this spiritual compulsion, this *tortura spiritus*", is an indispensable "expedient" for jurisdiction, from which no citizen can be exempt; for of religion "it has to be presupposed that every individual possesses it" i.e. each individual must regard his duties as no less sacred than if they had been ordained by a God. We take an oath "on the theory that there is a God". It is probably in this sense that all honest and well-considered oaths are sworn. On this subject, as we shall see, Kant speaks more definitely in his *Opus postumum*.

The "Tugendlehre" (1797), the second part of the *Metaphysik der Sitten*, begins (Introduction II) with the positing the fictional "ideal of the wise man": "virtue, as an ideal to which we must continually approximate, is personified under the name of the wise man. A further elaboration of this fiction is given in section fourteen: "Virtue, regarded in all its completeness, is *conceived* not as if man possessed wisdom but *as if* wisdom possessed man". "The personification of virtue and sin is an *æsthetic mechanism* . . . and for that reason the æsthetic of morals does not indeed form a part of but nevertheless constitutes a subjective presentation of the metaphysic of morals."

To this "æsthetic" machinery the idea of God also belongs. Kant had already spoken of it at the very beginning, in the general introduction to the *Metaphysik der Sitten* (IV at the end): "the law, which binds us unconditionally and a priori by our own reason, can also be said to emanate from the will of a supreme law-giver, i.e. from one who has only rights and no duties (consequently, from the divine will), which signifies, however, only the idea of a moral being whose will is law for all, without it being necessary to think of him as the author of the law" — in other words, we are dealing here merely with a method of expression, a *façon de parler*, a "heuristic fiction".

Quite at the end of the "Rechtslehre", he says in continuation, that there can really be no actual duty toward the supreme moral being "because that would be a transcendental duty, i.e. one to which no external duty-imposing subject can be shown to correspond; so that the relation would, from a theoretical standpoint, be merely ideal, i.e. simply a *thought-entity*"; this mental-entity "we *make* (italicized by Kant) ourselves" not "by means of an empty idea, but of one that is fruitful in relation to ourselves and the maxims of our inner morality, and therefore also fruitful in a practical, inner sense" "Accordingly our whole immanent (feasible) duty consists in this merely conceived relation"—in other words the nobler type of man regards morality as a *duty*, i.e. *as* if it were commanded by some higher being.[39]

In this sense it is also a duty of man to have religion, which is equivalent to "the recognition of all our duties regarded as (*instar*)[40] divine commandments." But as § 18 says, this is a duty towards ourselves and not "the consciousness of a duty towards God. For since this idea springs entirely from our reason and . . . is *made* (italicized by Kant) by ourselves, it is not a given entity that we have before our eyes, or one towards whom we could have any duties . . . but it is man's duty towards himself, to apply this Idea, which is inevitably present in reason, to the moral law within us, where it possesses the greatest ethical fruitfulness. In this (*practical*) sense we might, therefore, say that to have religion is a duty of a man towards himself."

In this sense man regards his conscience as another and a higher being existing within himself (§ 13): "The conscience of man will necessarily think of itself as, in respect of all duties, another person,—as himself in the character of judge of his acts . . . and this other person may either be a real or a mere ideal person, created by reason for itself. Such an ideal person (the authorized judge of conscience) must understand the hearts of men: for the tribunal is set up within the heart of man" (and that is why we find in § 9: "the inner judge who is thought of as another person"): "at the same time, however he must be a universal fount of duties, i.e. he must be thought of as being such that all duties whatsoever are to be looked upon as his commandments "This does not, however, mean that man is authorized through the Idea to which his conscience inevitably conducts him—still less that he is bound by his conscience—to assume such a supreme being outside of himself as real. For this Idea is not given him objectively by a theoretical reason, but merely subjectively by a practical reason which imposes on itself the duty of acting in accordance with this idea; and all that man obtains, by means of it (on the analogy merely of a law-giver of all rational world-beings) is a certain prompting to represent to himself Conscience, also called Religion, as responsibility to a Holy Being, different from but intimately present to ourselves, and to submit himself to the will of that Being as the rule of righteousness. Here the concept of religion in general is for man merely a principle of judgment, in virtue of which he regards all his duties as divine commandments." In other words, the idea of God is only a regulative principle, a heuristic fiction.

Finally the fiction of the idea of God reaches its climax in the idea of God as a judge who punishes the world. As Kant puts it in his "final note", the idea of a divine penal justice is here personified: "it is not a special being who administers it, for in that case conflicts would arise between it and legal principles. It is justice regarded as substance . . . which passes judgment. . . ." We are therefore dealing with "justice as such, conceived as a superlative principle ascribed to a supersensuous subject". But reality cannot be assumed of such a being, who, as judge of the world, would also have[41] to be creator of the world—to be "in contradiction with the principles of practical reason, according to which the creation of the world, of a product so antagonistic to the object of a loving Creator, might better not have taken place at all"—a passage overlooked by E. von Hartmann, who has represented Kant, not without justice, as "the father of pessimism".

But is it not, from an ethical standpoint, a reprehensible lie to speak in this manner of a "belief in a future world-judge" whose reality we do not assume? This important question is discussed[42] in § 9 where a sharp distinction is drawn between the necessary rational belief in the idea of a God and the lie of the hypocrite. It is a lie, "if a person persuades himself that it would not do any harm and might possibly do some good, to recognize such a future-world-judge in thought, as a being who knows the hearts of men, in order to insure against risk by hypocritically gaining his favour". It is a lie, if anyone "flatters himself that he has a sincere veneration for the moral law, when the only incentive he really feels is the fear of punishment". In such a person the idea of an ethical law-giver is not effective and consequently not "real", and of such a man it may justly be said that "he is falsely claiming a belief in a future world-judge, since he does not possess such a judge in himself". For the truly ethical man really finds this belief in himself, in the sense that it is efficacious within him to such a degree that the moral law is as sacred to him as if there really were a divine law-giver; and, in this sense, he sincerely believes in God. But he is guilty of "an inner lie", to whom the moral law is an inconvenient chain but who yet pretends to himself and to his God that he loves the moral law. But anyone to whom, in the true sense of Reason and the Critique of Reason, the moral law is as sacred as if it were a divine commandment, possesses the philosophical inner belief in God and does not, like the ethical pilferer, deceive himself with lies. And he who has this true inner belief in God may say with propriety even in an external sense that he believes in God, without being guilty of an "external lie". But the man who has the name of God always on his lips, when God is to him not the sacred author of an ethical code which embraces the whole spirit-world, but an arbitrary and capricious tyrant whose favour he attempts to gain by flattery—this man is guilty of an "external lie". When he speaks of a sacred God, he "does not really believe what he says to others"; and such a liar "insults the dignity of man in his own person".

KANT'S POSTHUMOUS PAPERS

KANT's *Opus postumum* "deserves neither the over-valuation nor the under-valuation which it has received from opposite quarters"—arguments in support of this judgment will be found in the *Arch.f Gesch. d. Philos.*, 1889, Vol. IV, 732–736. In the same article it is also demonstrated that the post-humous manuscript really contains two distinct unfinished works.[43] The two works are promiscuously thrown together and were published in this form (unfortunately incomplete) by R. Reicke in the *Altpreussische Monatsschrift*, 1881–1884, Vols. XIX, XX, XXI. They contain, particularly Vol. XXI, some re-markable passages.[44]

In Vol. XIX we find on pp. 572–578 and 620 some very important state-ments which show that Kant recognized the Ding an sich to be a fiction and indeed regarded the whole separation of Appearance and the Ding an sich as fictive. This is the view taken above on pp. 67–70 and 137–139, though when these passages were written (1876–1877), the *Opus postumum* of Kant had not yet been published (1882–1884), so that it offers a very valuable confirmation of our view.

"The object in appearance . . . flows from the synthetic concept . . .": "the Thing-in-itself is a mental entity (*ens rationis*) forming the link between this manifold whole and the unity which the subject constitutes itself. The object-in-itself = x is the sense-object in itself, not however as another ob-ject but rather as another mode of conception" (p. 573). In this sense Kant calls the entity of perception "a unit of perception, which objectively is a mere appearance, to which the object as Thing-in-itself is thought of as cor-responding purely in idea" (572). "The Thing-in-itself is not another object but another manner of becoming the object. It is not an *objectum noumenon*. The act of reason which makes[45] of the object of sense-perception a mere phenomenon, is the intelligible object." (*Ibid.*) "The transcendental mode of conception is that of intuition as appearance, transcending that of the object as Thing-in-itself, which is only an *ens rationis*, i.e. only a thought-entity and not objectively but only subjectively determinant, a *conceptus infinitus* (*indefinitus*)" (577). "The Thing-in-itself = x is merely a thought-entity, *ens rationis ratiocinantis*" (578). Cf. also p. 332 note 12.

These exceedingly interesting passages contain a further important elaboration of the Kantian doctrine of the Thing-in-itself and confirm, in a remarkable manner, the interpretation adopted not only by the author, but also by a large number of neo-Kantians, particularly by the so-called Marburg school, as also by Windelband and Rickert. That these remarks of Kant are not mere passing notions, is evidenced by the fact that the same standpoint reappears again repeatedly, and if possible, more clearly and emphatically, in the drafts published by Reicke, in Vol. XXI, on pp. 549–568, 582–599.

"With the concept of a thing as appearance is contrasted the concept of a Thing-in-itself [as] its necessary counterpart (pendant) = x, not as that of an object (*realiter*) differentiated from it but as merely conceptually differentiated (*logice oppositum*) ... which only forms a member of the division subjectively as *objectum noumenon*. This *noumenon*, however, is nothing but a rational conception"; ... "that which corresponds to the Things-in-themselves is not a separable counterpart ... but really the same thing regarded from another viewpoint. The *noumenon* as opposed to the *phenomenon* is the object thought by reason in appearance, in so far as it contains the principle of the possibility of synthetic propositions a priori ..." (567 and in more detail 568). "Objects must be regarded as appearances, not as Things-in-themselves, if the determination of this manifold is to take place a priori" (582–583). "Objects are conceptions in appearance and the distinction from the Thing-in-itself is not a distinction of the objects as Things-in-themselves, but only a scientific (ideal) distinction, for the subject and not to the object" (585). "A phenomenon to which its counterpart (*noumenon*) corresponds, not as a separate thing but as an act of reason = x, which, outside of reason, is simply an object in general and exists only in the subject" (599).

That is clear enough. The division into appearances and Things-in-themselves is thus a mere "standpoint", "point of view", "only subjective", "ideal", "scientific"—simply *a heuristic fiction*, "for purposes" of "approach". The Thing-in-itself is clearly and unquestionably seen and recognized by Kant to be a fiction, a method of approach useful and necessary for reason, a product of consciously fictive abstraction, where the ἀφαίρεσις must not develop into a χωρισμός—in other words, simply a fiction and nothing else.

In the same Volume, XXI, 310 ff., we also find innumerable passages in which the fictional nature of the idea of God is stated in new and ever more striking variations. We could fill many pages with them: here we can only reproduce the most important. As before, we shall pay no attention to passages which strike a dogmatic note, of which there are, as a matter of fact, very few.

We may begin with the emphatic passage on p. 325: "The principle of the recognition of all human duties as (tanquam) universally valid commandments, i.e. as the commandments of a supreme, sacred and powerful law-giver, raises . . . the subject to the rank of a unique being endowed with power: i.e. from the Idea which we ourselves form of God, we cannot, it is true, infer the existence of such a being, but we can infer the existence 'as it were' of such a being, and that as emphatically as if such a dictamen rationis were united in substance with our being. . . . The . . . statement: There is a God, must be as much respected and observed in its moral-practical reference as if it had been uttered by the Supreme Being, although . . . it would be madness either to believe in or to wish for the appearance of such a Being, to mistake ideas for perceptions." In the same sense he says on p. 331: "On this principle all human duties can likewise be expressed as divine commandments and even formulated as such, even though no such reason-determining cause be assumed as substance. Indeed practically speaking, it is quite immaterial whether we place the divine nature of the commandment in human reason or in such a person, because the difference is more a question of phraseology than a doctrine enlarging the limits of knowledge." The difference involved in regarding duty as a commandment of God, does not bring about any synthetic extension of our knowledge but gives us merely an analytical elucidation of the sacredness of the law of duty as a commandment of reason. This important formulation we have already encountered. The same thought is expressed in a different and very striking way by Kant on p. 159: By this analogical mode of conception, he says, our outlook is no doubt extended but not our insight. "It is not here practicable to assume the existence of a substance of this kind." (369.) "God is not a substance existing outside of me [Kant's italics] but merely a moral relation within me" (414). This latter statement, that God is not a substance but a relation, and a relation within me, is especially definite; we are consequently dealing in this concept only with a relation between the acting and the commanding part of my reason.

Further important passages are the following: "the categorical imperative does not assume a substance issuing its commands from on high, conceived therefore as outside of me, but is a commandment or a prohibition of my own reason. Nevertheless it is to be regarded as emanating from a being who possesses irresistible power over all" (570); "the categorical imperative represents human duties as divine commandments, not in a historical sense as if [a divine being] had once given certain commands to man, but in the sense that reason . . . has power to command with the authority and in the guise of a divine person" (571); "the ideal person who exercises the highest authority, God," is not a "substance different from man"; and, for that reason, "there can be no controversy as to whether there be a God in substance or not; that is not a subject for controversy (*objectum litis*). We are not dealing with existing entities outside of the discriminating subject, the nature of whose attributes might be matter for controversy, but with a mere idea of pure reason examining its own principles." This Kant (*Ibid.* 571), in contrast to the "technical-practical" view, which assumes an active God in nature, called the "pragmatic-moral" view—another anticipation of "pragmatism", even in phraseology. Further on he says: "the existence of such a being can only be postulated practically, in view, that is, of the necessity I feel to act as if I were under this terrible but salutary guidance, which is at the same time a guarantee, recognizing all my duties as divine commands (*tanquam, non ceu*). Consequently, the existence of such a being is not postulated in this formula. It would, indeed, be self-contradictory" (613.) The assumption of contradictory and yet practically useful concepts constitutes, as we know, the essence of the true fiction. The same idea is also expressed in the words: "in the Idea of God as a moral essence we live and move and have our being, spurred on by the recognition of our duties as divine commands. The concept of God is the Idea of a moral being which, as such, judges and issues universal commands. This is not a hypothetical thing but pure practical reason itself. . ." (613–614). "It is not at all necessary for the categorical imperative that a substance should exist whose duties are also the commands of reason; on the contrary [when we regard our duties as divine commands, we thereby understand] merely the sacredness and inviolability of these commands" (614). It is "merely a judgment according to analogy. We look upon all human duties as they were divine commands" (*Ibid.*). "The Idea of such a being

before whom all bend the knee, etc., arises out of the categorical imperative and not *vice versa*; and, subjectively in human practical reason, a God is
necessarily thought, although not objectively given. It is upon this that the
principle of the recognition of human duties as divine commands is based"
(615). The "*ens summum* . . . is an *ens rationis*. . . . It is not a substance outside
of me . . . the conception of duty underlying a general practical principle
is identical with that contained in the concept of a Divine Being as an ideal
of human reason" (616). This "legislative power gives force to these laws,
although only in Idea" (617–618). For we are dealing here with commands
"which the subject really prescribes for itself, although it treats them as rules
laid down by a personal being other and higher than itself" (619). "But in
the case of man we are able to make conceivable the dictate of reason as it
bears on the concept of duty in general and on the recognition of duties as
(*tanquam non ceu*) divine commandments, because this imperative is conceived
as ruling and issuing absolute commands, i.e. as something proper to a ruler,
i.e. as something to be attributed to a person; the ideal of a substance which
we ourselves create"—these words are found at the end (620) of the manuscript
published by Reicke in 1884, where the same and similar expressions frequently recur.

Finally Kant propounds the daring question: "whether religion without
the assumption of the existence of God is possible?" (619) and answers:
"religion is not the belief in a substance of especial holiness, rank or power,
from which we can by flattery obtain favours and rewards" (410), "it is
conscientiousness (*mihi hoc religioni*), the sacredness of a man's assent, the
sincerity of his self-confession. Confess it to yourself. For this the concept of
God is not required, still less the postulate: There is a God" (370)—but only
the dogma, for Kant holds fast to the idea of God as Idea. In this sense he
says on p. 610; "the principle of performing all duties as divine commands,
is religion", for "that all human duties are to be prescribed as divine commands is inherent in every categorical imperative" (614). Kant sees in this a
justified "anthropomorphism" (356) and it is in this sense that "the moral
imperative can be regarded as the voice of God" (577, cf. 414). Cf. also
p. 283 above. This expression is frequently repeated in the *Opus postumum*: so
also, "to judge as", "conceive as", "treat as", "think as", "for practical purposes", etc.

In conclusion I may mention a very important practical consequence
drawn by Kant from his examination. We all know that there is but one

single case in which a man who thinks in this way about his own thoughts, expressed orally or in writing, is compelled as a citizen to perform an action which directly requires the idea of God; and that is the oath. Can an individual who thinks thus take the oath demanded of him by the state (as witness, expert, official, Member of Parliament, etc.)? To this question Kant, after a little reflection, p. 383—unhesitatingly and consistently replies with an emphatic Yes. "We can swear by God without admitting his existence. To swear by God without admitting (affirming) his existence, simply indicates conscientiousness", "is simply a conscientious affirmation: juro i.e. per Deum testem affirmo. That statement does not directly imply that I know that God exists. I simply take upon my conscience the risk of being called a liar if I utter an untruth", 414, 416, 417. In explanation of which Kant then adds, jurare = ju orare; ju is Jehova, Jupiter, to whom man's heart is an open book, who "knows the hearts of men Of the Being who "knoweth the heart" Kant speaks frequently, e.g. 577, as a necessary idea of reason; indeed the whole As-if philosophy that we have been discussing has Him in view "as the Supreme Idea." "God" is an expedient, a necessary idea, and ideas are "heuristic fictions", As-if modes of approach. Kant and others like him act as if such a God were judging them; that constitutes their belief in God, their "practical belief" in a God.

2

FORBERG, THE ORIGINATOR OF THE FICHTEAN ATHEISM-CONTROVERSY, AND HIS RELIGION OF AS-IF

THE overwhelming number of passages from Kant which we have quoted and discussed above sufficiently prove that the As-if view plays an extraordinarily important part in Kant. This side of Kant has hitherto been almost entirely neglected and in those cases where his As-if doctrine has been slightly touched upon (e.g. by Volkelt, Rée, Görland) it has only been brought into relation with his actual doctrine of ideas, without it being suspected that this attitude also has a decisive significance for Kant's view on the philosophy of religion, on ethics and on law, as well as on natural science and mathematics.

Our presentation, particularly with regard to religious philosophy, introduces us to a quite new Kant, a Kant in one respect more radical, in another more conservative than the Kant we have heretofore known. He reveals himself to us as a theoretical non-Theist, in the sense that he comes to regard the existence of a Supreme Spirit, etc. in the ordinary sense of existence, as not only not probable, but extremely improbable—unbelievable indeed and even impossible. The passages quoted above range from the improbable to the impossible, in varying gradations, avoiding the usual escape by way of agnosticism, which teaches that the domain of Things-in-themselves is unknown, though it might very well consist of a World of Spirits with a Supreme Spirit at their head. Such agnosticism, which is indeed also found in Kant, and which the majority of his disciples have adopted, appears as a weak compromise compared with the radicalism of the passages given above, wherein Kant takes his seat on the extreme left of the philosophical parliament: to him all transcendental conceptions are nothing but "self-formed ideas". This radical current in Kantian thought has been given full value and prominence in the passages quoted above. Kant, then, is much more radical than the pantheists, whose sentimental, mystical and vague conceptions were generally abhorrent to him. Moreover, his pessimism, to which E. von Hartmann quite rightly called attention, as well as his doctrine of radical evil, is quite irreconcilable with pantheism. Kant is far more radical: he recognizes that the conceptions of a transcendental world, the whole conceptual apparatus pertaining to them, consist of ideas constructed by ourselves; and, with singular courage and loyalty to his philosophical calling, he develops the full consequences of this view. These consequences have been called negative, although they contain nothing but the positing of existing reality, pure positivism.

But on the other hand the passages we have quoted reveal a Kant far more conservative than he is generally represented. Kant, the rational philosopher, the thinker of the Enlightenment, champions the "permissibility", nay, even the "propriety" of those religious conceptions which, on account of their absurdity, horrified the traditional thinker of the Enlightenment; such for instance as the Virgin Birth, the idea of Atonement, and the idea of the Last Judgment. For Kant these ideas are a serviceable pedagogical expedient, "æsthetic machinery" for the animation and furtherance of moral impulses, a sensuous poetic dress in which to cloth unattractive duties "for practical purposes". But for him all ideas of a transcendental world also belong to this category, to the category of As-if, and it is only from this angle that Kant's celebrated "moral proof for the existence of God" is to be regarded, namely an As-if standpoint adopted for practical purposes. It is not the reality, in the sense of existential value, of the idea of God which is therein demonstrated by Kant, as we remarked above on page 260; but its reality, in the sense of ethical significance and validity, in fact its moral value. True critical philosophy is concerned with the idea of God and only with the idea. This Kant refuses to abandon: indeed he cannot abandon it, because it is immanently or, as he call it in his academic language, analytically contained in the categorical imperative. Kant not only teaches us to act *as* if our duties were divine commandments; he teaches that anyone, who acts morally behaves *as* if automatically a God had dictated this behaviour to him. From this again follows the rule that, if you wish to act morally, you must act *as* if you were under the orders of a God, of your God.

———————

Throughout the whole period between Kant's appearance and the present day, only a very few people have realized that this was the real Kant.

Some—disciples as well as opponents—were more or less clearly aware of it; others noticed it but had not the courage to speak out. The only writer to recognize and expound Kant's true doctrine in this respect was Forberg.

Forberg's name is well known in the history of philosophy. In all treatises on the subject we are told that Forberg published an essay in the *Philosophische Journal*, edited by Fichte and Niethammer (1798, Part I) under the title "The Development of the Concept of Religion", to which Fichte prefixed an explanatory essay "On the Ground of our Belief in a Divine Government of the World." These two essays gave rise to the "Atheism-controversy", in consequence of which Fichte resigned or lost his professorship at Jena. The whole interest of the historians of philosophy has, naturally enough, been concentrated upon Fichte, a major luminary in the philosophical heavens, beside whom the entirely unknown Forberg, as a very modest little planet, was quite insignificant. This was so, even at the time of the "Atheism-controversy" itself, which falls mainly in the year 1799. In all the numerous writings on either side of this controversy, which agitated the whole of intellectual Germany, only Fichte's name was mentioned. And so it was later on. The historians of philosophy, when the essay of Fichte appeared in his Complete Works in 1845 (Vol. III), had no longer any occasion or facilities for looking at the old original copy printed on blotting-paper, in which alone Forberg's essay was to be found. This remarkable essay thus remained unread and forgotten, so that although Forberg's name survives in the history of philosophy his ideas have been buried.

These ideas are, however, quite remarkable. Forberg clearly grasped and presented, at least in its basic principles, Kant's As-if doctrine, particularly in relation to the philosophy of religion. Not a single one of the countless contemporary— and later—Kant scholars has really understood what it was that Kant was ultimately aiming at in his religious philosophy. But this man, with his clear understanding and his intellectual courage, went to the very root of the matter. We may here reprint the most important passages of this forgotten treatise, after an interval of more than a century.

"Just as the idea of a future possible *consensus* of all men in all their judgments continually floats before the eyes of thinking people, so there floats before the vision of all morally good men the idea of a general *consensus* in Good, the idea of a universal extension of justice and good-will" (p. 30). But in regard to the former it has to be observed that "the reign of truth is an ideal. For in view of the infinite variety of capacities which nature seems to have taken such pleasure in scattering broadcast, it can never be expected that an agreement of all people in all judgments will take place. The kingdom of truth will almost certainly never come, and the final aim set before itself by the republic of scholars will, in all likelihood, never be attained. Nevertheless, the unquenchable interest in truth that burns in the breast of every thinking man will demand, for all eternity, that he should combat error with all his power and spread truth in every direction, i.e. behave exactly *as if* error must some day be completely extirpated and we might look forward to a time when truth will reign in undisputed sovereignty. This indeed is characteristic of a nature like that of man, designed to be for ever approximating to unattainable ideals" (p. 29 f.).

As with the kingdom of truth, so it is with the kingdom of the good. The "good man" "works toward the coming of a kingdom of God on earth, the kingdom of truth and justice: but, at the end of his career, he sees it as far off as ever . . . what can he, a single individual, do against an immoral world? Shall he too cease to struggle against the stream of wrong? Shall he henceforth let the world go its own gait, and cease to exert himself, or, it may be, sacrifice himself for an ideal end that is never attained?" (p. 34 f.). "No—his good heart loudly admonishes him—you shall do good and never weary of it! Believe that virtue in the end will triumph! . . . Believe that no good action done or even merely designed by you, no matter how small and obscure and humble it be, will be lost in the haphazard course of things! Believe that somewhere in this course of things there is a plan, imperceptible to you, it is true, but calculated on the ultimate triumph of the Good! Believe that the kingdom of God, the kingdom of truth and of justice, will come on earth; and do you but work for its coming! . . . It is true that in all this you cannot scientifically demonstrate that it must be so. Enough that your heart bids you act *as if* it were so, and merely by so acting you will prove that you have religion!" (pp. 34–36).

"This is the way, the only way, in which religion is born in the heart of a good man. The good man desires that good should prevail everywhere on earth, and he feels compelled by his conscience to do all that he can to help towards the attainment of this end. . . . He accordingly believes that the end he sets before himself, the supremacy of the Good, is an attainable end. . . . As a matter of *speculation*, he may leave on one side the question whether this end is possible or impossible; but when he *acts* he must behave *as if* he had decided in favour of its possibility, and he must endeavour gradually to draw nearer to that end." Even if he is convinced that "it is after all impossible to make angels out of men" he must not on that account give up the struggle; for he "could not but admit to himself that to act on the opposite principle gives proof of a great and exalted mind" (pp. 36–37).

"Religion, therefore, is not a matter of indifference, about which we can do as we like. It is a duty. It is our duty to believe in an ordering of the affairs of this world such that one can calculate on the final success of all good plans, and that the striving to advance the Good and oppose Evil is not quite in vain; or, what comes to the same thing, to believe in a moral world-government or in a God who rules the world according to moral laws. Yet this belief is by no means a duty in virtue of its being theoretical, i.e. an idle speculation, but simply and solely in so far as it is practical, i.e. in so far as it is a rule of actual conduct. In other words, it is not a duty to believe that there exists a moral world-government or a God as a moral world-ruler; our duty is simply to act *as if* we believed it. In thinking over the matter or discussing it, we can take what position we will, declare in favour of theism or atheism, according as we think we can justify ourselves in the forum of speculative reason; for here it is not a question of religion but of speculation, not of right and wrong but of truth and error. Only in real life, where we must act, is it our duty" to act in the foregoing sense, in the spirit of this As-if view (pp. 36–38).

To act on the opposite principle is bad; for "on that principle we should be acting against our own conscience." "That principle (the principle of irreligion) is consequently opposed to our duty and is sinful. No one can justify to his conscience any other principle than that of doing good and preventing evil wherever it is possible. We must not allow ourselves to be misled by the feeling that success is after all not within our power—we must regard every good and beautiful and noble inspiration as money entrusted to us, which we have to put out at interest; we must work unceasingly towards the extension of the true and the good in our own sphere . . . work for ideals in the hope that chance (or the Divinity, albeit a power unknown to us) will remove all difficulties from our path. . . . These principles are the principles of religion, and religion is therefore nothing but a belief in the success of the good cause, just as irreligion is nothing but despair of the good cause. Religion is by no means a temporary expedient of human weakness (though this it becomes, so soon as we think of religious belief as a theoretical belief); the power of the moral will is nowhere more wonderfully and sublimely manifested than in the principle of the religious man: I will have the world better, whether or no it be Nature's will" (pp. 39–40).

"Can we expect every man to possess religion?

Answer: Unquestionably, just as we can expect every man to act conscientiously..."

"Can a person be upright without believing in God?

Answer: Yes. For here we are unquestionably dealing with a theoretical belief."

"Can an atheist possess religion?

Answer: Certainly. We can say of a virtuous atheist that in his heart he recognizes the very same God whom he denies with his tongue. On the one hand practical belief and theoretical unbelief, on the other, theoretical belief (which then becomes superstition) and practical unbelief can very well exist together" (pp. 42–44).

This Religion of As-if, as we may now call it for short, brought upon the author (who was Rector of the Lyceum at Saalfeld) a disciplinary inquiry which, however, had no evil consequences since his judges happened to be very sensible. Forberg published a public justification under the title *Friedrich Carl Forbergs Apologie seines angeblichen Atheismus* (Gotha, 1799, p. 181). From this pamphlet, now exceedingly rare, I must quote a few more sentences in illustration of Forberg's standpoint. Theoretical atheism is, as such, a mere question of speculation and in that respect harmless and without danger: indeed "an attack of theoretical atheism is really something that every one should wish to have once in his life, in order to find out by an experiment on his own heart whether it desires the good for its own sake, as it ought, or merely for the sake of some advantage to be expected, if not in this, then in another world" (p. 35). Practical atheism is something quite different (for it the moral law is not so sacred as it would be if a God existed): such "practical disbelief is mean egoism. He who does not believe in God practically, is god less. Virtue without religion is a contradiction (p. 26). In this sense the saying of a great sage, 'Blessed are the pure in heart for they shall see God-contains a true, deep and sacred meaning" (p. 73). In this sense it is every man's duty to have religion.

What this sense is, becomes clear on page 141 f., where Kant's esoteric doctrine, so obvious and yet so little known, is announced in the words: the "kingdom of God", the rule of the good in this world, the moral world-order, is logically possible, but "it may well be that in actual fact, circumstances . . .

might arise in large number which, in spite of our logical possibility would, nevertheless, prove this to be a real impossibility. And even if we admitted the worst, that the actual impossibility of the kingdom of God could, at this very moment, be demonstrated, what would be the consequence? Would all efforts to attain the kingdom of God, i.e. all morality, necessarily cease at once and unselfishness disappear entirely from the face of the earth? Why should it? Does effort become impossible the moment success is seen to be impossible?" The adversary, the representative of the lower elements in human nature, will reply to this, according to Forberg: "No. But it at once becomes irrational." To that the true critical spirit in the person of Forberg answers: "Unquestionably that is so, if success be the final aim of effort, the goal the final aim of the runner. But what if the striving were a final aim in itself! What if there were no goal to be attained or, what is the same thing for the runner, only a goal set at an infinite distance? What if the goal were there for the sake of the race, not the race for the sake of the goal? "

If a man who "regards such optimism as completely chimerical", who is convinced that the world is "full of stupidity, falsehood and wickedness", convinced consequently of the presence of an immoral world-order . . ." if such a man nevertheless neglects none of his duties to his fellow-men and consistently behaves according to principles which indicate the greatest consideration for the rights of his fellow-men and for the common good, this is true and genuine religion; and it is so only because it is the attitude of a man who does not believe and yet acts. In other words, it is not the (theoretical) belief that the kingdom of God is coming, which constitutes religion; but the endeavour to make it come, even if we believe that it never will come. This and this alone is religion". In this sense religion is a practical belief in the "kingdom of God", it is to act *as if* by our action it could be brought into being.

Here we have the religion of As-if in its most clearly defined and purest form.

Forberg definitely denies the existence of a moral world-order; for the high dignity and sublimity of this form of the religion of As-if lies precisely in the fact that a good man does good although theoretically he does not believe in a moral world-order; he acts as if he did believe in it. This religion of As-if is built up on a positivistic and at the same time pessimistic basis.

Fichte, on the other hand, is convinced that such a moral world-order, such a divine world-government, actually exists: his conviction is speculative, is based on speculation and leads to speculation. Fichte is not satisfied with the practical belief in the kingdom of God demanded by Forberg. Fichte's belief in this kingdom, even though it had grown up naturally on a practical basis, is itself theoretical. To Forberg this moral world-order is only a fiction, to Fichte it is a philosophical axiom, a dogma. What is to Forberg merely an 'as if', is to Fichte a 'that' and a 'because'. We are, in other words, dealing with two entirely different views of the world, with two entirely different types of man. The Fichtean man says: I cannot act ethically if no moral world-order exists; I can only act ethically because such an order exists. The Forberg man says: I behave ethically even if there is no moral world-order; nay, although there is none, I act as if there were one. For Fichte this standpoint of For-berg, i.e. the real Kantian standpoint, is unattainable and for that reason incomprehensible.

Forberg was the clearer and more consistent thinker. But from the point of view of historical teleology, it is perhaps better that it was Fichte and not Forberg who determined the further development of German philosophy, which was eventually to work out the various potentialities contained in the far greater genius of the former. But the "flights of genius", as Kant says, often lead us astray and, for that reason, it is perhaps no less teleologically justifiable that after the very brilliant errors of German speculation we should to-day return to the clear and definite Kant-Forberg religion of As-if which, in spite of its clear definition, is yet not devoid of warmth and poetry, and represents in its radical form the highest point to which the human mind, or rather the human heart, is capable of raising itself.

3

LANGE'S 'STANDPOINT OF THE IDEAL'

IT was almost seventy years before the Kant-Forberg religion of As-if again made its appearance, though not under this name—in the writings of F. A. Lange. During these seven decades, philosophy had been so fully occupied with metaphysical systems and controversies between them, that the more subdued tones of the critical As-if doctrine were completely drowned by the cries of the philosophical market. And yet it was not entirely drowned. In two men, both theologians, it found an echo—an echo, it is true, in which the original meaning was hardly to be recognized. These were Schleiermacher and de Wette. Schleiermacher, whom we have already claimed as a representative of the As-if point of view, was probably very well acquainted with the essays of Fichte and Forberg, as the "Atheism-dispute" occurred in the years of his development. His own standpoint is a kind of combination of Fichtean pantheism with a diluted form of the Forberg doctrine. Fichte, who had originally been influenced by Spinoza, after passing through the Kantian critique, substituted for the Spinozan substance the ego, not the individual ego, but the universal ego which he regarded as, in the end, co-incident with God; the individual-ego is dependent upon the absolute ego which for Fichte is identical with the Godhead. This feeling of dependency upon the Absolute constitutes for Schleiermacher the feeling of piety. But the Absolute, on which the individual-ego feels itself to be dependent, is unknowable. Nevertheless our sentiment of piety feels the need to think of the Absolute in a symbolical manner, on the analogy of human relation-ships. The idea of a system of working symbolical concepts such as Forberg posited as a leading principle for every theology, was actually realized by Schleiermacher. In his dogmatic writings the formula "to conceive as" is often repeated. Even in Schleiermacher himself and far more markedly in his successors, these religious fictions have, according to our Law of Ide-ational shifts become transformed into hypotheses and dogmas. A further elaboraron of Schleiermacher's method is found in Biedermann and Lipsius. To pursue further the historical connections, to show how the conviction of the necessity of religious picture language was gradually formed, lies beyond the limits of our work and must be left to others. For the same reason we cannot occupy ourselves in any detail with de Wette: he had been influenced by Fries, whose doctrine of presentiment has influenced a number of theologians. De Wette, likewise, takes the attitude that the presentiment of the unknown Absolute must be expressed in conscious symbols. The perception that religion, especially religious practice, must necessarily make conscious use of symbolical language, is exceedingly old, as Forberg rightly remarks: the realization that the detailed ideas of religious objects are indispensable fictions is found in early Christianity as in all religions. A history of the varying phases of this realization has so far not been written; but wherever theology had a philosophical basis, it could not be absent. Schleiermacher and de Wette consequently only represent, in this regard, special phases of a continuous development which, beginning in the far past long before their time, has outlived them and is still active at the present day. Nevertheless this method, under the influence of the Kantian religious philosophy, was clearly and strongly developed in these two theologians.

Not unconnected with these two thinkers, but at the same time quite independent of them, stands the figure of F. A. Lange. He emancipated himself from theological influences and, for that reason, the philosophical principle appears in him in its original purity. This explains the fact that in him we find no longer the diluted and innocuous form of the Kant-Forberg religion of As-if, but the radical, more consistent and undiluted form. It is set forth, even in the first edition (1865), and still better in the second (1873–1875), of his well-known *History of Materialism* (*Die Geschichte des Materialismus und Kritik seiner Bedeutung in der Gegenwart*), after completing which this great thinker died. Since that time the book has appeared in many new editions, two new popular ones having been published recently (those of Reclam and Kröner). In spite of its wide-spread popularity, Lange's "standpoint of the ideal", which met with much intelligent appreciation and found many followers among the general public, has, up to the present, not been understood by professional philosophers. He was regarded as a freak; and as Kant's own cognate point of view had not been rightly apprehended, while that of Forberg had been entirely forgotten, the philosophers were unable to grasp the fact that Lange's "standpoint of the ideal" was but a necessary link in a great chain of development.

What does Lange mean by the "standpoint of the ideal"? He expresses himself very clearly and concisely in the introduction to the second volume (I shall refer to the second German Edition throughout) concerning "the lifting of religion into the sphere of the ideal", by which means the old quarrel between science and theology was to be brought to a "peaceful termination". The "overwhelming balance of probability" is against "the dreams of our imagination (the religious ideas of God, immortality, etc.) possessing any reality". Lange specifically declares himself opposed to the agnostic way of shunting religious ideas into the domain of the unknowable, i.e. against Spencer, Tyndall and even J. S. Mill. "Intellectual morality demands of us that in the sphere of reality we shall not cling to vague possibilities, but shall always prefer the greater probability", i.e. in this case, to the assumption that there is no "life after death" and in general no divine "world-government", i.e. no moral world-order any where. But "we should create for ourselves in imagination a fairer and more perfect world", and thereby "idealize life". "If this principle is once conceded, we shall be compelled to allow its value to myth—as myth" ("even the unbeliever" can, in this sense, "make the ideal image of Christ his own"). But it is more important that we shall rise to the recognition that it is the same necessity, the same . . . root of our human nature, which supplies us through the senses with the idea of the world of reality and which leads us, in the exercise of our highest creative and synthetic powers, to fashion a world of the ideal, in which to take refuge from the limitation of the senses, and in which to find again the true Home of our Spirit."

The imaginative and creative synthesis Lange, following Kant's theory of knowledge in an independent way, shows to be that which produces our ordinary conception of the world. The senses provide the material, but it is our synthetic faculty which constructs from this a "causally "arranged world of "things". "Causality" and "substance" are only categorical functions of the *psyche*. When Kant calls the products of this synthetic function "appearances", and contrasts these with the Thing-in-itself, he is himself falling into the error of converting a categorical function, the Thing—into an independent entity,—of hypostasizing it. Lange emphasizes, often and energetically (without however using the expression), the purely fictional significance of the difference between "appearances" and "things-in-themselves", particularly in Vol. 11, 28, 49, 50, 57, 63, 126, 137: the "Thing-in-itself" is "a mere thing of thought", "the consistent application of our laws of thought leads us to the concept of an entirely problematical something", but this is "a mere limiting concept": "if, however, we are asked where these objects are, the answer will be—in the phenomena. The more the Thing-in-itself becomes attenuated to a mere idea, the more does the world of appearances gain in reality". "We may quietly acquiesce in this view (that appearances and Things-in-themselves are to be differentiated), so far as it is a necessary consequence of our use of the understanding, although this same understanding upon further investigation must confess that it has itself created this antithesis"—in other words, we make use of this conceptual apparatus as a useful fiction. "The natural disposition of our reason necessarily leads us to assume, besides the world that we perceive with our senses, an imaginary world. This imagined world, so far as we form any definite idea of it, is a world of illusion, a figment of the brain", and the "intelligible world" falls under the same condemnation (p. 57).

The interpretation of the intelligible world, found in the official Kant and his traditional expositors, Lange declares to be "open to suspicion", "erroneous" and "fatal" (pp. 59–63). "Kant would not see, what Plato before him would not see, that the 'intelligible world' is a world of poetry, and that it is just this which constitutes its value and dignity. For poetry in the high and comprehensive sense in which it must be taken here, cannot be regarded as the capricious play of talent and fancy diverting themselves with empty imaginations. It is a necessary birth of the spirit, welling forth from the deepest vital reservoirs of the race, the source of all that is sublime and sacred, and a valid counterpoise to the pessimism which arises from a one-sided preoccupation with the actual. Kant was not devoid of a feeling for this attitude toward the intelligible world, but . . . his education and the age in which he lived . . . prevented him from carrying it through."

This judgment on Kant is, as our previous discussion has shown, incorrect. Lange remained imprisoned within the circle of the traditional interpretation of Kant and did not recognize the importance of Kant's 'as-if' teaching. For us, however, that is no loss but rather a gain; for, just because he independently arrived at a "standpoint of the ideal" essentially identical with that of Kant's 'as-if' view (which was unknown to him and which he believed he was the first to develop), Lange is for that very reason an independent witness of the fact that this standpoint must necessarily be adopted by everyone who follows out consistently to their ultimate conclusions the fundamental ideas of Critical Philosophy.

Lange recognizes as his immediate precursor not Kant but Schiller, who, "with the insight of the diviner, grasps the innermost kernel of the Kantian doctrines". Schiller, rightly enough, made the intelligible world visible to sense, by treating it as a poet. In this he follows in the footsteps of Plato, who, in contradiction to his own dialectic, produced his noblest creations when in the myth he made the supersensuous sensible. Schiller, the poet of freedom, might venture openly to transport freedom into the 'Realm of Dreams' and into the 'Realm of Shadows', for, in his hands, dreams and shadows were raised into the region of the ideal. The wavering became a fixed pole, the fleeting a divine form, the play of caprice an everlasting law, as he confronted life with the ideal. The good contained in religion and morality cannot be more purely nor more forcibly expressed than in that immortal Hymn which closes with the ascension of the tortured Son of God. Here is embodied the escape of man from the limitation of the senses into the intelligible world. We follow the god who 'flaming, takes His leave of man', and now dream and truth exchange their rôles—the ponderous dream-picture of life sinks and sinks and sinks". . . "Only what endures when measured by the standard of poetic purity and greatness, can claim . . . to serve as instruction in the ideal" (p. 62 f.).

This is the standpoint of the ideal, which is afterwards further elaborated in two other passages, Vol. II, pp. 484–503 [E.T., Vol. III, pp. 269–291], as well as in the special section bearing this title, Vol. II, pp. 539–562 [E.T., Vol. III, pp. 335–362]. In all these passages Lange combats the idea "that it is all over with religion, now that science has destroyed dogma"; "religion must be maintained, but can only be maintained" by "being lifted into the realm of the ideal"; "religion together with metaphysics must be put on the same footing with art" (p. 494). It is "a contradiction in the nature of our organism, which only gives us things whole, complete, and rounded in the way of poetry; partially, approximately, but with relative accuracy in the way of knowledge." "All poetry, all revelation is, of course, simply false the moment we test their material content by the standards of exact knowledge; but this Absolute is of value only as an image, a symbol . . . and these errors or intentional deviations from reality only do harm when they are treated as material knowledge"—they are, to use our terminology, useful fictions. When "man's sense for reality and verifiable accuracy is fully developed, the credibility of these stories diminishes, because a different standard of what constitutes truth has been adopted; but the feeling for poetry retains its hold on the heart of the natural man through all the stages of his life". In poetry, as is said on p. 540 [E.T., Vol. III, p. 337], "the firm ground of reality is consciously abandoned". The same is the case with the creations of religious mysticism. There too we are dealing with conscious inventions.

Thus "a different standard of truth" is necessary for religious, as distinguished from scientific, ideas, and, consequently, a different concept of truth. "The ancients regarded the poet as an inspired seer, who, being entirely absorbed in his own vision, lived spiritually in a world apart from common mortality. Might not this same absorption in an idea have its place in religion also? And if there are men who live a life of such complete spiritual exaltation that for them everyday realities take a secondary place, how can they describe the vividness, permanency and practical efficacy of their experiences, than with the word 'truth'?" "And since, in actual fact, language belongs to the people, we must, for the present, acquiesce in the double meaning of the word 'truth'." Even "the philosopher may allow the second meaning of the word 'truth,' but he should never forget that it is a figurative meaning. He may even warn us against a fanatical opposition to the 'truths' of religion, if he is convinced that their ideal content still possesses value for our people" (Vol. II, p. 496 [E.T., Vol. III, p. 282]).

Again and again Lange calls attention to the part played "by the poetic principle in religion" (p. 503), of which the ancient world, the Stoics in particular, were already aware (p. 501):[46] for this reason the idea of "a religion purified of all error" (p. 497) is a distorted fancy, for everywhere and at all times, religion consists of a tissue or a structure of imaginations, of an "architecture of our ideas" (p. 496), which "changes its form" according to the needs of the times (p. 494), but which always bears on its face "the character of the absolute" (p. 493). In this sense, "genuine idealism will always set up beside the phenomenal world an ideal world, and will concede to it, even when it is regarded as a product of the brain, all those rights which follow from its relation to the needs of our intellectual life" (p. 530). Theoretical materialism (which rejects everything of which "the truth cannot be demonstrated to common sense," p. 506, which does not understand "the ideal side of religious life" because, for it, "the ideal has no currency" p. 537) cannot, without being inconsistent, raise itself to this standpoint because, in the view of materialism, to start from the whole . . . is an error. The materialist cannot follow Schiller's "Take courage then in erring and in dreaming" (p. 513). Yet this is precisely the "standpoint of the ideal."

This "standpoint of the ideal" has a separate section devoted to it under that title.[47] Lange, in this section, is carrying on a battle on two fronts. On the one hand he attacks dogmatism and orthodoxy: "so long as this tendency reigns, the standpoint of the ideal in religion will never be able to assert itself clearly . . . the symbol involuntarily and gradually becomes a rigid dogma,[48] as the image of the saint[49] becomes an idol and the natural contradiction between poetry and reason easily degenerates in the religious sphere into antipathy to the absolutely True, Useful and Practical." . . . Dogmatic orthodoxy "thinks of the ideal element of life . . . as endowed with ordinary reality, and interprets historically everything that should only be taken as symbolic" (p. 557 f.) And "yet it is always possible to discover in the speeches and writings of orthodox zealots the point where they obviously pass into the symbol" (p. 549), where, in other words, they become inconsistent and are themselves compelled to admit that at least a part of their religious conceptions is only symbolic.[50]

The other tendency against which Lange fights is materialism, not as a scientific method—for in this form he accepts the materialistic mechanistic explanation of existence and events—but in so far as materialism rejects wholesale, as it is bound in consistency to do, the religious world of ideas not only as a system of dogmatic doctrinal teachings but also as useful and tenable symbols, i.e. the materialism which casts religious ideas in general on to the scrap-heap. In opposition to this tendency Lange demands "recognition of the ideal" (p. 559) not only in the sense that the materialist should have noble and ideal strivings—that, fortunately, is generally the case—but in the sense that he should also recognize the great value and the deep meaning of ideal conceptions, in other words, the value of religious conceptions, the value of that conceptual architecture which we have just mentioned, or, as he says on p. 546, of the "architecture of ideals"[51] by which "a temple is erected for the worship of the Eternal and the Divine" (i.e. of his ideals). These metaphysical, religious ideas can be retained "in their ethical efficacy without doing violence to facts". "There is only one way by which mankind can arrive at permanent peace (between religion and natural science). The imperishable nature of all poetry in Art, Religion and Philosophy must be recognized, and on the basis of this recognition the strife between science and imagination must be forever reconciled" (p. 560). A sense of religion as imaginative creation—this Lange demands even of the materialists. "One thing is certain: that

man needs a supplement to reality in the form of an ideal world fashioned by himself, and that the highest and noblest functions of his mind
co-operate in such creations": and the "ideal so fashioned acquires an
overwhelming force when (with Schiller) we openly and unreservedly
transport it into the realm of fantasy" (p. 545). In this sense "we should
accustom ourselves to regard the world of ideas . . . as no less indispensable to any human progress than the knowledge acquired through the intellect, by referring the larger or lesser significance of every idea to ethical
and æsthetic principles" (p. 548). And here it is to be noted that Lange
who, quite correctly, recognized Schiller's poems as being the fruits of the
critical intellect, rightly placed the æsthetic principle beside the ethical,
which had been the only one stressed by Kant. This æsthetic bent is also
discernible when Lange says that the thought of the divine harmony in
which all disharmony disappears, the thought of "the all-surveying divine
vision of the world in which all riddles are solved and all difficulties fade
away, is successfully destroyed by Pessimism; but this destruction affects
the dogma only, not the ideal" (p. 544). We are free, therefore, to retain
this conception as a conscious religious fiction.

The "essence of religion" consists in "overcoming all . . . superstition by
a conscious elevation of our religious conceptions into a region above reality, and in a final abandonment of the falsification of reality by mythology,
which, of course, can never be a means to knowledge" (p. 546). In opposition to crude belief in the crude reality of the religious world of ideas,
"the principle of the spiritualization of religion" thus consists in consciously
reverencing the religious conceptions as myths. So long as the "essence of
religion" was sought in certain "doctrines about God, the Human Soul, the
Creation and its order, it was inevitable that any criticism which attempted
to separate the chaff from the wheat on logical principles must end in complete negation. Everything was sifted till nothing remained". The essence
of religion "should, on the contrary be sought" "in the lifting of the spirit
above reality" into the imagined "home of the spirit", i.e. into the unreal.
The essence of the whole matter in religion lies in the form of the spiritual
process (i.e. precisely in this conscious elevation above reality) and "not in
the logical historical content of particular . . . doctrines" (p. 550). The "ideal
substance and content of religion" (pp. 556–557) is thus preserved for all
time—no longer as a dogma but as an ideal, freely created by ourselves,
which we consciously recognize as a mere ideal, but nevertheless revere to

such a degree that our spirit becomes elevated thereby and that our actions are directed in accordance with it.

It is a very widespread, fundamental error, to which materialists in particular are very liable, to regard such conscious creations as for that reason valueless; whereas it is just in these ideas and ideals that the highest values of mankind lie. The precedence given to these ideas over gross reality, "is not based on greater certainty but on a greater value, against which neither logic, nor the hand that feels, nor the eye that sees, can avail anything, because the idea as form . . . of the constitution of the soul can be a far more powerful object of desire than actual matter" (p. 549). The "true value" of these ideas lies in style, the form, as it were, of the conceptual architecture and in the impression made by it upon the "emotions" (p. 494). With this "world of values", "the world of existence" must be brought into connection, in order by means of the former to invest the latter with "ethical" significance (p. 546). From this it follows, if we think consistently, that "the world of Being" must be supplemented by that of non-Being, the world of the creative imagination; and that a true critical "philosophy of values", of which there has been talk of late, will have to take the form of a Philosophy of 'As if'.

"Reality as man imagines it, an absolutely fixed existence independent of and yet known by us—such a reality neither exists nor can exist" (p. 539)—it is a "creation of the ideal in other words, something nonexistent, although posited as existing. This world is a "creation of free synthesis". The unknown factors in events "we picture to ourselves as Things which exist independently of us and to which, therefore, there is to be ascribed that absolute reality which we have just declared to be impossible. But there is no getting away from this impossibility. For in the very concept of Thing . . . is involved that subjective factor" which Lange characterizes generally as synthesis. "This synthetic, Creative factor of our knowledge extends far back into our first sense-impressions and into the very elements of logic" (p. 539). "But the task of bringing harmony into phenomena and of producing unity from the given manifold, belongs not only to the synthetic factors of experience, but also to those of speculation." In experience the synthetic factor is still bound to the material, and even "the conceptual poetry of speculation is still not wholly free", for "in speculation, form is always preponderant over matter and in poetry it is completely dominant". "From the lowest stages of synthesis . . . up to its creative sovereignty in

poetry, the essence of this activity is at all times directed toward the achievement of unity, of harmony, of perfect form." In these words Lange lays bare
the ultimate and deepest roots of all metaphysical and religious-imagination.

The significance of the synthetic, creative force of human nature in
connection with knowledge Lange, as we saw above, recognized from the
beginning. Above all he realized that even our ordinary view of the world
(and not only the religious-metaphysical, which we have so far been
analyzing with Lange and have raised to the "standpoint of the ideal") is
saturated with imaginative concepts which are none the less necessary to us
as conceptual aids, and continue to be necessary to us, even when we have
recognized them as the work of imagination. To this category belongs, first
of all, the very concept of Thing. In this sense, he says, Vol. II, 214 ff. [E.T.,
Vol. II, p. 390 ff]: "A 'thing' is known to us only through its properties. . . .
But the 'thing' is, in fact, only the resting-place demanded by our thought.
We know nothing but the properties, and their concurrence is an unknown,
whose assumption is a figment of our mind, though as it seems, an assumption made necessary and imperative by our organization." We cannot assume
any attribute without a carrier or any force without substance: "The reason
for this is to be sought only in our psychical organization which causes our
observations to appear under the category of substance."

"The materialists naively take this unknown matter as the sole substance;
Helmholtz, on the other hand, is well aware that it is only a question of
an *assumption* demanded by the nature of our thought and with no validity
for actual reality." Helmholtz calls such an assumption an "abstraction", on
which Lange remarks: "more correctly, a necessary invention, a personification dictated by psychical compulsion"—in other words, a fiction.

A scientific modification of the material Thing, whose fictive nature Lange
here correctly recognizes, is represented by the atom, which he of course
perceives to be also merely a product of the same creative synthesis but, at the
same time, a necessary auxiliary concept. Already in Vol. I, p. 44 (cf. pp. 209,
223 ff., 247. 253, 283) Lange calls the atom "a necessary mode of conceiving an unknown state of things." In this sense Lange compares "the atoms
and their vibrations" with a "scaffolding" that is torn down as soon as the
structure is finished, though it is absolutely necessary for the structure (II,

166, cf. 182–183). When Liebig calls the concept of the atom an arbitrary "convention" and when Schonbein, in this connection, speaks of the "play of fantasy" we must, he tells us, remember that this "play of fantasy", so far from serving to deceive reason, rather guides and aids it. A concrete intuition of this sort, if strictly carried through, even when it is in fact false, is often of considerable value as a picture and as a provisional substitute for the true intuition; "the employment of the imaginative faculty to bring order into our thoughts . . . is therefore really more than mere play" (II, 190). The different ideas of the atom vary according to the "necessities of calculation" (p. 191 ff.). The recognition of this nature of the atom as a mere counter must, of course, not lead us to "a desire to deny to the physicist the primary, i.e. the technical, use of the Atomism" (p. 194 ff.). Lange recognizes quite clearly the purely fictive nature of the atom, although he several times rather inaccurately calls it "hypothetical": pp. 191, 207, 209, 210, 220.

Lange very pertinently attacks those who would use the so-called anti-atomistic dynamism of Kant as a Gorgon's head to terrify the atomists: "The question may be raised whether we might not deduce the necessity of an atomistic view from the principles of Kant's theory of knowledge": there would indeed, be some prospect of success, "for the operation of the category in its fusion with intuition always aims at synthesis in an object, that is to say, an object which is dissociated in our conception from the infinite links that bind it to everything else. If we bring Atomism under this point of view, the isolation of the particles would appear as a necessary physical conception whose validity would extend to the whole complex of the world of phenomena, whereas really it would be only the reflex of our organization. The atom (which according to p. 250 is "a mere conceived unity") would be a creation of the ego but, for that very reason, the necessary basis of all natural science" (p. 211). In this remarkable passage Lange has well characterized the atomic theory as a methodical fiction.

The correlative concept of force (as commonly understood) is also seen to be another methodic fiction of the same sort, "to simplify our treatment," I, 143. This discovery too is connected with the realization that the concept of force, although "it contains obvious contradictions", is nevertheless useful and convenient (I, 264). Lange proves this specifically in reference to the chemical "forces"—affinity in particular (II, 184–187) and shows that such "concrete modes of conception" are "only aids" and not definitive "knowledge": "thus we talk of 'points of affinity' in the atoms, of 'attaching' to them, of 'occupied' and still free points, as if we . . . could see such points in the body of the atom" (200). He cites approvingly the well-known phrase of Du Bois-Reymond that "force" is, as it were, "a rhetorical device of the brain." With the use of this term, as Lange correctly points out (p. 204) "a false factor is introduced into the calculation". He then shows how the errors necessarily resulting therefrom can be avoided, citing a passage from Helmholtz where the latter gives an excellent description of the method of antithetic error. Lange shows how we must proceed if these "aids" (p. 219) are not to become traps—in other words, he elaborates a method of scientific fictions.

On the other hand Lange also recognizes that teleology is only a methodic fiction: in Volume I, p. 373 [E.T., Vol. II, p. 107] he calls attention to the fact that Holbach had already assumed this standpoint: "man may avail himself of these ideas so long as he is not enslaved to them, and if he knows that he has to do, not with objective things, but with inadequate conceptions of them". On which Lange remarks that these ideas, "although in no way answering to the things in themselves, are not merely to be tolerated . . . as convenient . . . habits . . . but belong, in spite—or perhaps because of—their birth in the mind of man,—to the noblest treasures of mankind." In this sense (II, 276) he calls teleology a "heuristic principle" which, following Kant, he formulates as follows: "Through the rational idea of an absolute mutual determination of the parts within the cosmic whole, we are led to regard organisms *as if* they were the product of an intelligence."

F. A. Lange, then, had already recognized that in science and life, imagination plays a part, that erroneous concepts, as measured by empirical reality, must be employed and this with full consciousness of their falsity: he recognized, therefore, as we already saw at the beginning of this work, that to thought and life fictions are indispensable.

4

NIETZSCHE AND HIS DOCTRINE OF CONSCIOUS ILLUSION

(The Will to Illusion)

THAT life and science are not possible without imaginary or false conceptions was also recognized by Friedrich Nietzsche. Nietzsche early observed that such invented and therefore erroneous conceptions are unconsciously employed by men to the advantage of life and science; he was here following Schopenhauer and probably Richard Wagner and his doctrine of "hallucination". But that such false ideas must be employed both in science and in life by intellectually mature people and with the full realization of their falsity is a fact which Nietzsche came to perceive more and more clearly; and it was Lange, in all likelihood, who in this case served as his guide.

Nietzsche, to whom Lange's name was doubtless already known through the philological circles at Bonn, became acquainted with the *Geschichte des Materialismus* which had appeared in October 1865, after his departure from Bonn. He wrote an enthusiastic letter to his friend Gersdorff about the book in September 1866, agreeing with it completely; and on February 16, 1868, he wrote an even more enthusiastic letter to the same friend.[52] He there says that it is "a book which gives infinitely more than the title promises, a real treasure-house, to be looked into and read repeatedly." That in particular Lange's theory of Metaphysics as a justified form of "poetry" made a deep impression upon Nietzsche, is quite clear from Rohde's letter of November 4, 1868.[53] That this notable work long continued to influence Nietzsche is also evident from certain polemical remarks against it, to be found in Vol. XIII, p. 339, and Vol. XIV, p. 14 (cf. p. 156) of his Collected Letters. The following account of Nietzsche's doctrines, as compared with those of Lange, shows that in regard to Illusion Nietzsche must definitely be set down as a disciple and successor of Lange.

Nietzsche, like Lange, emphasizes the great significance of "appearances" in all the various fields of science and life and, like him, points out the fundamental and far-reaching function of "invention" and "falsification" as well as the falsifying influence and poetic "creation", and therewith the value and the justification of the "myth"—not in religion alone. Like Lange he holds that over against the world of "shifting", "evanescent" becoming, there is set up, in the interests of understanding and of the æsthetic satisfaction of the "fantasy", a world of "being" in which everything appears "rounded off" and complete; that in this way there arises an antithesis,"[54] a "conflict" between "knowledge" and "art", "science" and "wisdom", which is only resolved by recognizing that this "invented" world is a justified and "indispensable" "myth"; from which it finally follows that "false" and "true" are "relative" concepts. All this Nietzsche could already have found in Lange. This Kantian or, if you will, neo-Kantian origin of Nietzsche's doctrine has hitherto been completely ignored, because Nietzsche, as was to be expected from his temperament, has repeatedly and ferociously attacked Kant whom he quite misunderstood. As if he had not also attacked Schopenhauer and Darwin, to whom he was just as much indebted! As a matter of fact there is a great deal of Kant in Nietzsche; not, it is true, of Kant in the form in which he is found in the text-books (and in which he will probably remain for all eternity), but of the spirit of Kant, of the real Kant who understood the nature of appearance through and through, but who, in spite of having seen through it, also consciously saw and recognized its usefulness and necessity.

The writings of his youth—which are printed in Vol. I of his works and to which the posthumous pieces of Vols. IX and X also belong—contain a large number of important notes in a rough form. All these early attempts came to a head in the remarkable fragment dating from the year 1873, *Ueber Wahrheit und Lüge im aussermoralischen Sinne* (X, 189–215). "Lying, in the extra-moral sense", is what Nietzsche, with his well-known fondness for forced expressions, calls the conscious deviation from reality to be found in myth, art, metaphor, etc. The intentional adherence to illusion, in spite of the realization of its nature, is a kind of "lie in an extra-moral sense"; and "lying" is simply the conscious, intentional encouragement of illusion.

This is very clearly the case in art, the subject from which Nietzsche started in his first work, *Geburt der Tragödie*, etc., reprinted in Vol. I. Art is the conscious creation of an æsthetic illusion; in this sense art rests upon the "primitive longing for illusion" 35; "drama as a primitive phenomenon" consists "in beholding ourselves transformed before ourselves and then as if we had actually passed into another body and into another character" 60, 168. Drama, in general, operates with "fictional" entities 54. Of the "apollinian illusion" (33, 62) he four times on p. 150 f. (as also 147 and X, 120) uses the As-if formula in this sense. This "æsthetic play" 157, 168, these "countless illusions of beautiful appearance, are what make existence in general worth while" 171, 522. This is "the wisdom of the illusion" 23. For that reason "he who destroys illusion within himself and in others is punished by that most severe of tyrants, nature" 340, for "it is part of the essence of action to be veiled in illusion" 56.[55] The myth is considered from this point of view and commended 147, 160, 411, 511, 560, especially as a mythical fiction, 299. The myth, which the Greeks consciously cultivated, we have lost "in the abstract character of our mythless existence" 170; with us it has become a "fairy-tale", but it must "be brought back to virility" 551; even science cannot exist without myth 102, 106. Cf. Vol. IX, 179, 184, 234, 288, 433; also Vol. X, 88, 128, 139, 203. Appearance, illusion, is a necessary presupposition of art as well as of life. This summarizes Nietzsche's youthful writings. In them we see the idea already developing that this illusion is and must be, for the superior man, a conscious one.

In the posthumous works of his youthful period (Vols. IX and X) this latter point is more clearly made. At first, indeed, Nietzsche speaks merely of "delusional conceptions as necessary and salutary provisions of the instinct" Vol. IX, 69, of a "law of the mechanism of delusions" 100, 124ff. Religion also comes under this heading[56] 130, but particularly "the actual delusional pictures of artistic culture" 148. Of these "delusional constructs" he also speaks on pp. 158, 165, 179, 184. On page 186 he says: "The realm of delusional pictures is also part of nature and worthy of equal study." Thus there arises a whole "network of illusions" 186f. These delusional concepts are created by the will 192, 200, and created by means of "deceptive mechanisms" 106, 210. "Even the recognition of their real nature does not destroy their efficacy" 101. This recognition Nietzsche at first feels as "torture" 101, 126, but the perception of the necessity of these illusions and phantasms for life (76, 108, 185, 189) leads to the conscious, pleasurable affirmation of illusion; in this sense, he says p. 190: "My philosophy is an inverted Platonism: the further it is from actual reality, the purer, more beautiful and better it becomes. Living in illusion as the ideal": this is also the meaning of the utterance on p. 109: "the highest indication of will is the belief in the illusion ("although we see through it"); and theoretical pessimism (i.e. the pain we feel because we are thrown back upon delusional concepts) is biting its own tail".

Entirely in the same sense is Vol. X, 119: "The last of the philosophers . . . proves the necessity of illusion'. The consummation of the history of philosophy is therefore, according to Nietzsche, the philosophy of illusion: the realization of its indispensability and justification: "Our greatness lies in the supreme illusion", for it is there that we are creators (146). Now, however, it is no longer the artistic illusion (the "artistic veil" 110), whose necessity for life is recognized: now the circle of illusions recognized as necessary and consciously grasped is continually widened: "the anthropomorphic element in all knowledge" (121) now makes its appearance, cf. 195 ff. It is not only "life that needs illusions, i.e. untruths regarded as truths" (125 ff.), nor does our culture alone rest upon "isolated illusions" (127); our knowledge also needs them. Thus the "surface-nature of our intellect" 126 ff., leads to the employment of general concepts, already in Vol. I, p. 526 disparaged in the extravagant expression "insanity". In the same line of thought he says on p. 130: "we emphasize the main characters and forget the accessory ones". Concepts we obtain only through "the identification of dissimilars" and "we then act as if the concept of man, for instance, actually were something real, whereas it has been formed only by the dropping away of all individual characters" 172, 195. Our intellect operates with conscious symbols, pictures and rhetorical figures 130, 134, 167, with "coarse and inadequate abstractions" 169, with metaphors 148: "time, space and causality are only cognitive metaphors" 166. "To know is merely to work with one's favourite metaphors" 171, 194. Thus "we live and think wholly under the influence of effects of the illogical, in a world of no knowledge and false knowledge" 173. [57]

All these tentative beginnings lead up to the fragment already mentioned on the Lies in the Extra-Moral Sense, the fundamental idea of which is that not only our language, but also our conceptual thinking, is based upon falsifying operations, i.e. "operations not corresponding to reality" 214. This is once more set forth in detail for the general concept and for "the great structure of concepts", e.g. 195 ff. "The construction of metaphors is the fundamental instinct of man" 203, and by this artistic impulse which is also called on p. 128 simply the "mythical impulse" he is led, even in the domain of the theory of knowledge, to false constructs 213, 505 (cf. 139, 140, 162): these are at first fashioned unconsciously (196) but "for the liberated intellect" (205) they are conscious aids: "scaffoldings."

* * *

The writings of the middle or transitional period, which, be it said, are of a less dithyrambic character, deepen the understanding already gained at certain points.[58] The extravagant expression "lie" now only occurs rarely: II, 5, 162 ("the Greeks intentionally invested life with lies"); III, 105 ("the Muses as liars, the artist as a deceiver") IV, 119; ("the lies and deceits of sensation") V, 309 ("Education, which sanctifies so many lies") XI, 45, 330, 408. He remarks pathetically in XII, 48: "Ah, now we must embrace untruth, now at last error becomes a lie, and lying to ourselves a necessity of life."

The thought that we must consciously make use of "untruth" in our thought still causes him suffering: "One question there is that seems to lie like lead upon our tongues and yet never becomes articulate: the question whether we can consciously remain in falsehood and, if we must, whether death would not be preferable?" (II, 51). Again in V, 142, "the recognition of delusion and error as a condition of knowing and feeling" would without art "be unendurable" and must lead to suicide." But his realization of the fact that ideas, of whose untruth we are conscious, are biological and theoretical necessities becomes more and more clear. At first this realization declares itself in the recognition that "errors and mistakes of fantasy are the only means by which mankind has gradually . . . been able to elevate itself" (47, III, 228; cf. also IV, 97, XI, 36): Man must, however, "understand not only the historical" but also "the psychological legitimacy [which therefore applies also to the living] of such concepts" (38); he must realize that the engine, man, "has to be stoked with . . . illusions, one-sided truths (236). Nietzsche recalls the saying of Voltaire: "Croyez-moi, mon ami, l'erreur aussi a son merite" II, 16: for that reason we must not "destroy" such illusions (368) for they are necessary even to the advanced mind, indeed as necessary as fairy tales and make-believe games are to the child 139 (and for the child too his games are conscious self-deceptions).[59] In the advanced mind there develops more and more "the consciousness of illusion" V, 87, indeed a cult of illusion, "if nothing any longer proves to be divine unless it be error, blindness and lies", since on these "life has been arranged", V, 275 f. This "impenetrable net of errors" is necessary for life XII, 39 ff.

To a mind thus advanced all the customary articles of belief and the convictions even of science, become "regulative fictions" V, 273. He recognizes them as "mere necessary optical errors—necessary if we care to live at all, errors, in so far as all the laws of perspective must by their nature be errors" XII, 42. In this sense he speaks on p. 46 of the "really living untruths", of the "living errors", and adds: "that is why we must allow errors to live and give them a wide domain". Summing up, he says 48: "in order that there might be some degree of consciousness in the world, an unreal world of error had to arise: beings with a belief in permanency, in individuals, etc. Not until an imaginary world, in contradiction to the absolute flux, had arisen, was it possible to erect on this foundation a structure of knowledge; and now finally we can see the fundamental error [the belief in permanence] upon which everything else rests . . . but this error can only be destroyed with life itself . . . our organs are adjusted to error. Thus there arises in the wise man the contradiction of life and of its ultimate determinations: man's instinct for knowledge presupposes belief in error and life . . . to err is the condition of living . . . the fact that we know that we err does not do away with error. And that is not a bitter thought! We must love and cultivate error: it is the mother of knowledge."

Many passages are found in which he summarizes his thought, for instance V, 149: "Such erroneous articles of faith . . . are the beliefs that there are permanent things, that there are equal things, that our will is free . . ." V, 154: "We operate with things that do not exist, with lines, surfaces, bodies, atoms, divisible time and divisible space . . ."; V, 159: "We have arranged for ourselves a world in which we can live—by assuming bodies, lines, surfaces, causes and effects, motion and rest, shape and content; without these articles of faith nobody would now be able to endure life! But that does not mean that anything has yet been proved. Life is no argument; for error might be one of the conditions of life." And XI, 72, he develops the idea that matter, as a mass in extension, "is an hallucination; like things in motion, like Thing in general, like all permanence." So he says XII, 24: "Without the assumption of a kind of being which we could oppose to actual reality, we should have nothing by which we could measure, compare or picture it: error is the presupposition of knowledge. Partial permanency, relative bodies, identical events, similar events—with these we falsify the true state of affairs, but it would be impossible to have knowledge of anything without having falsified it in this way." "At the beginning of all intellectual activity we encounter the grossest assumptions and inventions, for instance, identity, thing, permanence—these are all coeval with the intellect, and the intellect has modelled its conduct of them" 46. And it is in this sense that he says 156: "The intellect is the means of deception, with its forced forms—substance, identity, permanency"; but it is on such opinions as "the belief in identity, number, space, etc. that the duration of mankind is based" 208.

Thinking is dependent upon language, and language is already full of false presuppositions: "we are still continually seduced by words and concepts, into imagining things as simpler than they really are, imagining them separated from one another, indivisible and existing in and for themselves. A philosophical mythology lies hidden in language which breaks through at every moment, no matter how careful we may be" III, 198; these mythical, fictional constituents of language must accordingly be employed with the consciousness of their falsity; cf. XI, 178. It is well said in XI, 180 that "we speak as though there were really existing things, and our science speaks only of such things. But real things exist only for human optics: and from this we cannot escape".

Nietzsche frequently points to artificial simplification as a principal mechanism of our thought; as in Vol. XI, 291 in that very remarkable passage, according to which we "see our infinitely complicated nature in the form of a simplification," etc. Similarly XII, 10: "In what a curious simplification of things and human beings do we live! We have made everything easy and convenient for ourselves . . . and given our thought *carte blanche* to make all sorts of erroneous inferences"; cf. XII, 46.

Next to simplification, isolation plays a leading part, e.g. in mechanics: "we isolate conceptually first the direction, secondly the moving object, thirdly pressure, etc.—in reality there are no such isolated things" XII, 34.

Of logic he says 11,26: it "is based upon presuppositions to which nothing in the real world corresponds, e.g. the presupposition of the equality of things, of the identity of the same thing at different points of time." For this "illusion of identity"[60] see also III, 198, XI, 179 (cf. Lange's similar utterances above (p. 311). He says nothing more about the general concepts, but he has this excellent remark XII, 28, on the "archetype", i.e. the idea corresponding to the universal concept: "the archetype is a fiction, like purpose, line, etc."; cf. 33: "our concepts are inventions."

"Laws of nature" are the remains of "mythological dreaming" III, 18; XII, 30: and in XII, 42 we find the following, so strongly reminiscent of Kant: "It is our laws and our conformity to laws that we read into the world of phenomena—however much the contrary seems to be true." Causality is a "picture", something "that we read in"; what we call "experiencing" is, in this sense, "an imagining" IV, 124.

"The assumptions of mechanics" also rest on ideal inventions, particularly the conception of "force residing in mathematical points and mathematical lines"; "they are in the last analysis practical sciences, and start from the fundamental errors of man, his beliefs in things and identities" XII, 33.

New is his realization of the fictional nature of many mathematical concepts, II, 26: "in nature there is no exactly straight line nor any true circle" 36; "numerals are based on the error that more than one identical thing exists . . . here error already reigns, for here we are already imagining entities and unities that do not exist,"[61] "We introduce a mathematical mean-line into absolute movement and, in general, we introduce lines and surfaces on the basis of the intellect, i.e. of error, the error of assuming equality and constancy", XII, 30. "Our assumption that there are bodies, surfaces, lines, is simply a consequence of our assumption that there are substances and things and permanency. Just as certainly as our concepts are inventions, so certainly are the constructs of mathematics inventions" 33.

The idea of permanent things also belongs here. "It is probably due to our lack of development that we believe in things and assume something permanent in becoming, that we believe in an ego" XI, 185; again in XII, 23: "The only existence for which we have any warrant is mutable not self-identical and possesses relations. . . . Now thought asserts just the opposite as regards reality. It need not, however, for that reason, be true. Indeed this assertion of the contrary represents perhaps only a condition of our conception. "Thought would be impossible if it did not fundamentally misconceive the nature of being: it must predicate substance and equality, because a knowledge of complete flux is impossible; it must ascribe attributes to reality, in order to exist itself. No subject and no object need necessarily exist to make thought possible but thought must believe in both." "The intellect has not been arranged for the understanding of becoming. It endeavours to prove universal rigidity [eternal permanence] owing to its origin in images." The belief in permanence, duration, the unconditioned, is not "the belief that is most true, but the one that is most useful" XII, 24–37, 30. Our conception of space is also based on the belief in the permanent: "our space holds good for an imaginary world", 31. The belief in permanence, which arises of itself within us, and which science maintains in its own way, is the basis of all belief in "reality" (such as bodies, permanence of substance, etc.) 44 f. The permanent individual and his unity is, likewise, something necessarily imagined 128.

Freedom and responsibility are frequently treated as necessary errors; so, e.g., II, 65, 93, 101, 108, 109 ("the illusion of free choice"); III, 31: "We can only dream ourselves free, not make ourselves so" 190, 198; for that reason even "a complete atheist who holds firmly to the fundamentally irresponsible and non-meritorious character of all human action, can experience a feeling of shame when treated *as if* he merited this or that"; he then appears to himself as if "he had forced his way into a higher order of beings," 239; cf. V, 149. Here also, belongs the statement XI, 31: "such a thing as character has no real existence, it is only a helpful abstraction"; and particularly the following trenchant saying 45: "Blame only has meaning as a means of deterrence and subsequent influence as a motive; the object of praise is to spur on, to incite to imitation: in so far as both are given *as if* they had been merited by some act, the falsehood and the illusion present in all praise and blame are unavoidable; they are, indeed, the means sanctified by the higher purpose." But these "moral advantages are still indispensable" XI, 195; and similarly we put it "*as if* we showed the way to nature" in our acts, whereas in truth we are led by her XI, 203, 213. Our freedom, our autonomy, is an "interpretation", i.e. something "read in" 216; XII, 40. Very characteristically he says XII, 224: "I will set down once for all in order everything that I negate: There is no reward or punishment, no wisdom, no goodness, no purpose, no will. [But] in order to act you must believe in error and you will continue to behave in accordance with these errors even when you have recognized them to be errors."

The subject, too, is a self-fashioned concept that we cannot dispense with: "we place ourselves as a unity in the midst of this self-fashioned world of images, as that which abides in the midst of change. But it is an error" XI, 185. He says pertinently in XI, 291 that the ego "is an attempt to see and to understand our infinitely complicated nature in a simplified fashion—an image to represent a thing". That is the "original error" XII, 26. The whole "opposition between subject and object" is an artificial division V, 294.

Nietzsche also recognizes the distinction between Thing-in-itself and Appearance as an artificial one (cf. p. 68 above, on the subject of this separation) and consequently as a conceptual invention: "the true essence of things is an invention of the conceiving being, without which it would not be able to represent things to itself" XII, 22 and V, 294. The entire phenomenal world is a conception "spun out of intellectual errors" II, 33: "the world as idea" is the same as "the world as error", 37, 47; IV, 119, 120,—"the world of phantoms in which we live." "Our external world is a product of the fantasy" XII, 36. "The belief in external things" is one of the necessary errors of mankind, 40. "Matter, stuff, is a subjective form", 71; "the whole perceptual and sensible world is the primordial poem of mankind" 170.

The æsthetic illusion naturally recurs again and again, for instance, II, 157 and twice in the "as if" form, 178[62]; XI, 23 and XII, 175. He speaks of the "artistic deception" in III, 118; V, 311 and XI, 72. Art, "a kind of cult of the untrue," is based on "the will to illusion", V, 149.

We will close with the fine passage V, 88: "What then is 'Appearance' for me! Assuredly not the converse of any real Being—what can I say of any Being except the mere predicates of its appearance! Assuredly not a dead mask that can be put over the face of some unknown and presumably also taken off again! Appearance is for me that which acts and moves . . ."

The works of Nietzsche's third period in Vols. VI–VIII[63] contain (apart from the introductory chapters of *Jenseits von Gut und Böse* in Vol. VII) less that bears on our subject than the posthumous writings belonging to this period in Vols. XII, 235 ff., XIII, XIV, XV; the last two volumes deserve our particular attention.

It is intelligible enough, from what has preceded, that "the problem of the value of truth", ceremoniously introduced in Vol. VII, IX ff. (cf. 471, 482) can now be stated; here Nietzsche places himself not only "beyond good and evil" but also beyond truth and falsehood[64]: "it is nothing but a moral prejudice that regards truth as of more value than illusion . . . there would be no life at all were it not on the basis of perspective valuations and semblances" 55: "the perspective is the basic condition of all life" 4, 11. This expression, seldom found up till now, henceforth occurs more frequently: the perspective is a necessary deception which remains even after we have recognized its falsity. In this sense Nietzsche had already V, 294, given to his philosophy the appropriate title of "perspectivism".[65] This is also the sense in which the often quoted passage VII, 21, is to be understood: "it is now time to substitute for the Kantian question: 'how are synthetic judgments a priori possible?' another question: 'Why is the belief in such judgments necessary'?—to understand namely that, for the survival of beings like ourselves, belief in the truth of such judgments is necessary: for which reason they may, of course, even be false judgments! . . . They are indeed all false judgments. But belief in their truth is necessary as a superficial optical illusion characteristic of the perspective optics of life". "The falsest judgments (among which are to be classed synthetic judgments a priori) are the most indispensable ones for us; without giving validity to logical fictions, without measuring reality by the purely imaginary world of the unconditioned, the "self-identical", without a continual falsification of the world by number, man cannot live—the renunciation of false judgments would be a renunciation of life"[66] 12 f. (cf. XIV, 191, 210). The "will to deception" is to be thus understood 10 f., which indeed is the soul of art (84, 123, 472). "Whatever be the philosophic standpoint we take to-day, from whatever side we look at it, the mistakenness of the world in which we believe we are living is the most definite and most certain thing we see. . . . And why should the world in which we live not be a fiction?" 54–56. Even the most exact and the most positive "science tries to keep us in this simplified, entirely artificial world, invented and falsified to suit us; and willy-nilly science loves error because it is alive and loves life" 41–42. In this sense, for instance, physics makes use of the atomic theory, though it "is one of the most thoroughly disproved things that exist"; but the atomic theory serves the scientist "as a convenient tool, as an abbreviation of his means of expression" 22, 27 f.; the whole of physics is such an artificial, false, temporarily serviceable "arrangement"[67] 24.

Subject and Object are such artificial yet, for the time being, indispensable concepts; the "ego" and the "it" 28–30 are likewise "fictions" 56, as are Cause and Effect. "'Cause' and 'Effect' must not erroneously be made concrete . . . they should be used only as pure concepts, i.e., as conventional fictions for the purpose of defining, understanding and explaining. . . . It is we ourselves who have invented the causes . . . interdependence, relativity, compulslon, number, law, freedom, end: and when we read this sign-world into things as something really existing and mix it up with them, we are merely doing what we have always done, namely mythologizing", 33. Nietzsche attacks in particular the mythical idea of the "active thing": "There is no substratum, there is no 'being' behind the action, behind the 'action on', behind the becoming; the 'agent' has been merely read into the action—the action is all there is"; the atom and the Kantian Thing-in-itself are also such conventional fictions 327. So, too, is that "natural law of which you physicists talk so proudly but which exists—only in virtue of your interpretation . . . it is no fact . . . on the contrary, it is only a naive human manner of arranging things" 34—just a "humanistic" anthropomorphism which for the enlightened man is conscious. He knows more or less clearly "that the thing is not so, and that we merely let it stand at that", 188.

The fragments in Vol. XIV offer a welcome amplification of this, particularly the famous passage p. 16: "The erroneousness of a concept does not for me constitute an objection to it; the question is—to what extent is it advantageous to life. . . . Indeed I am convinced that *the most erroneous assumptions are precisely the most indispensable for us*, that without granting the validity[68] of the logical fiction, without measuring reality by the invented world of the unconditioned, the self-identical, man could not live; and that a negation of this fiction . . . is equivalent to a negation of life itself. To admit untruth as a condition of life—this does indeed imply a terrible negation of the customary valuations."

On page 31 he says more briefly: "My basic concept is that the 'unconditioned' is a regulative fiction, to which reality must not be ascribed", but such fictions are useful and necessary to life, even to the life of "knowledge", for "knowledge is, in its nature, something that invents, something that falsifies", 19; "a fictive, assumptive force must be assumed, just as we must assume the inheritance and perpetuation of fictions", 30. We may recognize the *contradictio* in these fictional concepts,[69] e.g. in the concepts of the Unconditioned, the Existent, Absolute knowledge, Absolute values, the Thing-in-itself, Pure mind[70] (28), but "the intellect is not possible without the positing" of such fictional concepts, particularly that of the unconditioned, 29. These fictions, as we have already seen, Nietzsche calls perspectives: "If we could get out of the world of perspectives we should perish. . . . We must approve of the false . . . and accept it" 13: "the perspective nature of the world is as deep as our 'understanding' can reach to-day" 7: and in this sense he shows that "number"[71] is a perspective form, as are "time" and "space". We no more harbour "one soul" in our breasts than we do "two": "individuals"[72], like material "atoms"[73], are no longer tenable, unless it be as manipulative devices of thought. . . . "Subject[74] and object", "active and passive", "cause and effect[75], "means and end"[76] are all merely perspective forms. Such "perspective falsifications" (323) are necessary for man's existence and indeed for that of all organisms; "Along with the organic world a perspective sphere is given" 324, at first, of course, unconscious; but in the mature man there develops a conscious "will to illusion, the realization of perspectives, i.e. positing of falsehood as truth" 89. The human intellect, with its fixed forms, particularly its grammaticological categories (37) is a "falsificative apparatus" (34)—and yet man makes use of it consciously. For the purpose of life and knowledge—in so far as we can speak of such things—the intellect needs, "as a necessary means, the introduction of full-blown fictions as *schemata*, which . . . enable us to conceive of happenings[77] as simpler than they really are" (47), in other words, to falsify them. Thus it has come about that these errors have made man inventive: and that is why the "cult of error" is necessary 312: indeed a "joy in illusion" develops (366, 389) the "will to illusion"[78] (360), for we recognize "the value of regulative fictions, e.g. the fictions of logic" 322.

That the logical forms rest on fictions is frequently repeated: "Logic is a consistent sign-language worked out on the assumption of the existence of identical cases" (22); and consequently "logicality is only possible as a result of a basic error' 29: "that identical things and identical cases exist is the basic fiction, first in judgment and then in inference" 33, 35, 37: "The invented, rigid, conceptual world" is an important means of thought 46: indeed our practical thinking does not in the least follow the fictional scheme of logic: "Logical thinking represents the model-example of a perfect fiction": "Thus the working of the intellect is to be regarded as if it really corresponded to this regulative scheme of fictional thought" 42 f.—Cf. also the remarks VIII, 78 ff. on logic (and mathematics) as "sign-conventions" and also those on the grammatical forms dominating logical thought, the "metaphysics of language". Cf XIII, 47, 60, 85. Even Plato thought of his "Ideas" essentially in this way (*Ibid.*, 323) —i.e. as mere "regulative fictions".

In one part of the fragments of Vol. XV prominence is given to an aspect of Nietzsche's thought of which we have already had occasional glimpses before: the damage these regulative fictions cause when not used as such but when a character of reality is erroneously ascribed to them, as is indeed generally the case. In this sense these regulative conceptual aids are—fictions in *malo sensu*, "merely" fictions.[79] Thus "the subject, the *ego* is only a fiction" 32; the mind as the agent of thought is fictional, nay, the pure logical thinking of the mind, posited by the theorists of knowledge, is "an absolutely arbitrary fiction" 266 f.: "Mind" and "reason" are "fictional syntheses and unities" 272 and are even deprecated (275) as "useless fictions". "'Subject' is a fiction implying that many similar conditions in us are the effect of a *substratum*. . . . This is to be denied" 282, "the subject is not a thing that has an effect, but merely a fiction", 286; in man "we have imagined a *primum mobile* that does not exist at all" 368. "This artificial freeing and explaining of the *ego* as something in and for itself" has had evil consequences (369), among which is the assumption of an inherent "spiritual causation" which is also only a "fiction"

513 and, with it, the assumption "of free actions", which are then separated, into moral and immoral:—this is all "imaginary, unreal and fictional" 369: particularly the concepts on which morality is based 233, 385. But the *genus*, he contends, is as illusory and false as the ego 341; into the concepts of *genus*, idea, purpose, etc. a fiction has been read, a false reality (284), and that is why these become bad fictions; in this sense generic concepts are "false unities that have been invented" (330) and the same is true also of the "causal fiction", the "schematism of the thing" 271, 281 and, in general, of all "that is thought" (281). In particular the entire world of Things-in-themselves, the true world of the eternally existent in contrast with the world of becoming, is "a mere fiction" 306; cf. also 288, 291, 294, 304, 310, 311, 408; we "imagine" for ourselves a God in this world (288), accomplish our actions "as if they were the commands of God" (26), and thus arrive at the "bad and petty fictions" of the Christian view (91) at the "fictions of the world beyond" (478). But "we must do battle with all the presuppositions upon which a 'true world' has been fictively constructed" 304.

This opposition to the misuse of fictions, dating from the stirring times of the *Götzendämmerung* and the *Antichrist*,[80] must not be misunderstood: the necessary complement to it is furnished by numerous other passages which show that Nietzsche had realized the utility and necessity of fictions. This realization is evident also in many fragments of Vol. XV: thus he speaks on p. 175 of the "necessity of false values" and according to p. 338 "necessity, causality, expediency" are "useful illusions", for such "illusions are a necessity if we are to live"; "illusion has a survival-value,[81] for us" 303. Logic, which, like geometry and arithmetic, holds only for fictive "entities" (278), is nevertheless a "useful" invention, a good "aid", 273, 275, 288. The categories are "falsifications" but "clever" and "useful means for bringing order into the world" 274, 299, 301: the system of categories, the" system of falsification on principle" is, nevertheless, "a serviceable and handy scheme," a system of necessary "manipulations"[82] (300), a "necessary perspectivism". It is with it as with the concept of the atom[83]: there, as here, it is a question of "pure semiotic", but it is not within our power to change at will our means of expression. "The demand for an adequate method of expression is senseless; it is in the nature . . . of a means of expression to express merely a relation" 324. These concepts are therefore inadequate but useful fictions. This is particularly true of the category of causality 318 ff.[84] and still more of the category of substance: the "existent" is a "simplification, for practical purposes" (305) based upon the artificial creation of identical cases (291, 304, 319): it is "a picture" introduced by us for practically useful and perspective reasons (322), for "there lies within us an ordering, falsifying, artificially-separating power" (279) whose products, however,—these numerous "falsifications—are useful and necessary: for "Life is based upon these presuppositions" (287): "The fictional world of subject, substance, reason, etc. is necessary" (279).

This paragraph takes us directly to those thoughts of Nietzsche that might be called the beginnings of a Metaphysic of As-if; with the question, what part illusion plays in the totality of cosmic happenings and how these cosmic happenings, from which illusion is necessarily developed, are to be regarded and evaluated—with this question, the young Nietzsche had already busied himself: we find in the posthumous writing even of the first period the admirable note: "My philosophy is an inverted Platonism: the further it is from actual reality, the purer, more beautiful, and better it becomes. Living in illusion as the ideal" IX, 190: in the same place 198–199 we find Nietzsche struggling with the metaphysical problem of appearance and concluding 205: "The One, in a Greek spirit of gaiety, creates illusion from within itself". In the second period we find the problem deepened: "Our idealistic fantasy-building is also part of reality and must appear in its character. It is not the source, but that is why it is there" XII,3. "We really know only the Being which conceives" with its falsifying activity. What part does this "performing Being play in general Being? Is all Being perhaps necessarily a conceiving and, consequently, a falsifying? At any rate our conceiving, and with it the erroneous but necessary belief in the unconditioned, "must be deducible from the nature of the *Esse* and from conditioned existence in general" XI, 24–25. This question plays a great part in the third period, and in this way Nietzsche finds himself confronted with Descartes' problem of a deceiving God:—the erroneousness of our conceptual world remains a fact: "We find a superabundance of evidence for that which might seduce us into making guesses at a deceiving principle in the 'nature of things'" VII, 54. "What if God is a deceiver, in spite of Descartes?" XIII, 10: "Let us assume that there is something deceptive and fraudulent in the nature of things. . . . We should, in that case, as a reality, have to participate, to some extent, in this deceptive and fraudulent oasis of things and in its basic will . . ." XIII, 52f.: "Descartes is not radical enough. In face of his desire to have certainty and his 'I will not be cheated', it is necessary to ask why not?" (Ibid., 56, 68).

"The starting-point: irony against Descartes: given that there was something deceiving in the basis of things from which we have sprung, what good would it do *de omnibus dubitare!* It might be the best way of cheating ourselves" XIV, 326. From this it follows that: "The will to appearance, to illusion, to deception . . . is deeper, 'more metaphysical' than the will to truth" *Ibid.*, 369 and "the deceptive perspective character belongs to existence" (*Ibid.*, 40); we must "not forget to include this perspective, assumptive force in 'true Being'" XV, 321: "This creating, logicizing, arranging, falsifying, is the best guaranteed reality" *Ibid.*, 281, "so that we might be tempted to assume that there is nothing else but concept-making, i.e. falsifying subjects."—In the same passage Nietzsche sums up his doctrine in the following monumental words: "Parmenides said: 'We do not think that which is not'—we at the other extreme say: 'What can be thought must certainly be a fiction'" Cf. the very similar passages in Lange (above pp. 309, 311) on the value of that which is non-existent and yet thought, i.e. of appearance. From this stand-point, appearance is no more to be censured and attacked by philosophers as heretofore (cf. VII, 55), and illusion, so far as it proves itself to be useful and valuable and at the same time æsthetically unobjectionable, is to be affirmed, desired and justified. "Perspectivism" is "necessary" for us XV, 321.

* * *

This realization of the utility and necessity of fictions would certainly have led Nietzsche, in the course of time, to recognize the utility and necessity of re-ligious fictions also. The question has often been asked where Nietzsche would have been led, in the course of his development, had not the premature ca-tastrophe of 1888 put an end to his development. The answer is: that Nietzsche, after he had so unsparingly revealed the evil side of religious concepts, would necessarily have been led to emphasize their good side also, and to recognize them once more as useful and even as necessary fictions. He was on the direct road thereto. In what has gone before, we have found a number of expressions pointing in this direction, expressions in which he recognizes the historical necessity of the religious conceptual world.[85] Above (p. 338 note 67), we encountered a remarkable passage, quite reminiscent of Kant, in which it is said that man should not indeed believe in the religious presuppositions of tradi-tional morality but should, nevertheless, act according to them and take them "as regulative", i.e. treat them as regulative fictions. That is also the tendency of a few other remarkable utterances in Vol. XV: not only does Nietzsche recognize that we owe to the religious "illusion" an "artificial strengthening" (429) but he finds the "species man" impoverished now that it is no longer in possession of the power to inject such illusion into reality, is no longer in possession of the power "to fashion fictions",[86] has in other words, become "nihilistic" (294). On page 34, he says in his exaggerated language: "Catastrophe: what if falsehood is something divine? Whether the value of all things may not consist in the fact that they are false? Whether we should not believe in God not because he is[87] true, but because he is false? . . . What if it be not just the lying and falsifying, the reading in of meanings, which constitutes a value, a sense, a purpose?" And in a remarkable aphorism he sets to the credit of the nineteenth century, as contrasted with the eighteenth, whose "spectre" was reason, the "strength" of which it gave proof in again becoming "more tolerant" towards religion: "We do not hide from ourselves the obverse of evil things": "Intolerance towards priests and the church" has decreased; even the objection of the rationalists, that it is immoral[88] to believe in God "we regard as the best justification of this belief"—because religious fictions in their capacity as myths[89] should no more be measured by a moral standard than by a logical one.

These utterances are the harbingers of a wider and final period of Nietzsche's development which was cut short by his illness. Nietzsche would inevitably have gained the road taken by the Kant he so completely misunderstood and also followed by F. A. Lange, the Lange by whom he had been so much influenced in his youth. He would not have revoked his *Antichrist*, whose incisive truths had, once and for all, to be spoken, but he would have presented the "obverse of evil things" with the same relentless frankness: he would have "justified" the utility and the necessity of religious fictions.

NOTES

1 And as an essential supplement thereto, the discussion in my monograph "Kant—Ein Metaphysiker?" published in the *Philois. Abhandl, zu Sigwarits* 70 *Geb.-Tag.*, Tübingen, 1900, as well as that in *Kantstudien*, Vol. VI, p. 115 ff.

2 The passages of the *Kritik der reinen Vernunft* are quoted according to the sections found in every edition. Special citations follow the pagination of the two original editions A and B, also indicated in most modern editions.

3 In the section, "Vonder Endabsicht der natürlichen Dialektik der menschlichen Vernunft."

4   In the third section, "Vom Interesse der Vernunft bei diesem ihrem Widerstreit."

5   Especially in the section, "Erläuterung der kosmologischen Idee einer Frei-heil". etc.

6   "Entdeckung und Erklärung des dialektischen Scheins", etc. A 615 ff., B 643 ff.

7   In this section where Kant so clearly and definitely recognizes the ideas as an "illusion at the back of the mirror" (that is, as a useful and beautiful decep-tion on the part of nature), there is also found a most unfortunate confusion of such fictions with hypotheses.

8   "Von der Endabsicht der natürlichen Dialektik der menschlichen Vernunft" (A 668 ff., B 696 ff.)

9   By "Scheme" is here meant the concrete picture of the abstract idea in a conceived concrete substance, and, in relation to the idea of God, is what was described above as the ideal, in contrast to the idea.

10 This remarkable passage, together with the many others cited above, shows that if we desire to retain the popular and quite justifiable view that Kant proved the necessity of the idea of God, we must say not "the necessity of the idea of *God*" but "the necessity of the *idea* of God," for we are dealing here with "a mere Idea". The emphasis is to be placed on the word "idea," not on the word "God"; and this shifting of the verbal emphasis implies a complete shifting of the point of view from which Kant's doctrine is to be regarded.

11 At the opening of the "Endabsicht, etc.", paragraph three.

12 Kant's doctrine of "thought-entities", which has hitherto been almost en-tirely overlooked, has been analyzed by the present author in the *Philosophis-che Abhandlungen Chr. Sigwart zu seinem 70. Geb.-Taggewidmet,"* Tübingen, 1900, pp. 133–158: "Kant—ein Metaphysiker?" (also separately published; cf. my supplementary monograph in the *Kantstudien,* Vol. VII, pp. 116–117, with the concluding words: "Kant—ein Metaphoriker?".) This essay forms an essential complement to the above discussion. The "thought-entity" (occasionally also called "rational entity") is identical with the *ens rationis* which is placed first in the "table of the divisions of the concept of nothing" which is to be found at the end of the transcendental analytic and to which very little attention has been paid. In other words, thought-entity = nothing!

13 Here it appears clearly that, as we said on p. 83, fictions or, at least, many of them, are based on analogy. This view plays, as we shall see, a great part in Kant, and it is in this sense that the phrase mentioned above, "Kant—ein Metaphoriker?", is intended.

14 Another of Kant's methodological fictions is the celebrated "consciousness in general"; see above p. 138. Cf. II. Amrhein, "Kant's Lehre vom 'Bewusst-sein überhaupt' und ihre Weiterbildung bis auf die Gegenwart" *(Kanistudien Ergänzutigsheft No. 10,* Berlin, 1909) with an introduction by the present writer, particularly pp. v-vii and 88–93.

15 Only the former of these two statements is specifically made by Kant. The latter, however, obviously follows from the context.

16 Italicized by Kant.

17 In this passage the word "assume", italicized by Kant himself, expresses an hypothesis. In other passages, pp. 634, 644, 646 ff., "assume" refers to fictions.

18 In this connection (A 813, B 841) Kant lets slip a very characteristic expression; the "moral law" he says, is also "a mere idea"—a very remarkable saying. The whole moral law—merely an idea! What vast perspectives does this not open out before us!

19 Cf. the work of Dr E. Sänger, *Kants Lehre vom Glaubett* (Leipzig, 1903), with an Introduction by the present writer, which contains an important supplement to the above.

20 Compare, in this connection, the additional material in my treatise *Kant—ein Metaphysiker?* (Tübingen, 1900), as well as *Kantstudien*, Vol. VI, p. 115 ff.

21 Cf. above p. 235, where the same passage is treated as a normal case of fictive judgment.

22 In this passage—taken together with that quoted ten lines below—F. A. Lange's well-known "standpoint of the ideal" is anticipated.

23 We must not forget that, in the language of Kant, an "ideal", no matter how "glorious", still remains a fiction: cf. above p. 257. Moreover, Kant expressly adds, in brackets, in the second section of the *Grundlegung* (p. 59), with regard to the "realm of purposes" ("of course only an ideal"). This "of course only" speaks volumes.

24 In the same sense, we have on p. 54: "Man must at all times be regarded as a purpose in himself". That is to say, as a mode of representation, a *point de vue*, an "as if," a fiction.

25 The meaning of "objective reality" shifts in the AV. *d. pr. V.* and the related writings, a fact that is easily overlooked and has generally been overlooked. It is best explained at the end of the section (p. 68), "Von dem Befugnisse der reinen Vernunft", etc. by the interchangeable expression, "practically applicable reality. (We may note what is said in the same passage, at the end of the paragraph, about the purely practical "assumption and presupposition" of supersensuous beings, for instance of God, by an analogy, "but only for a practical purpose".) In another passage (p. 166 in the section: "Wie eine Erweiterung der Vernunft", etc) he says: "the concept of an object of a morally determined will (that of the highest good), and with it the conditions for its possibility, the ideas of God, freedom and immortality, are endowed with reality but always only in relation to the exercise of the moral law (and not for any speculative purpose); i.e. the morally acting person regards himself and feels *as if* he were a member of such a supersensuous world. Cf. above, p. 260.

26 Cf. the expression, p. 67: "this divinely-minded but in reality quite human teacher . . . would be able to speak with truth of himself, as if the ideal of the good . . . were corporeally represented in his person". Notice the phrase, "with truth"; naturally "truth" is not meant here in the theoretical but in the practical sense (cf. above, pp. 259–60, 273), and this latter Kant frequently styles "knowledge." For Kant there is therefore a "double truth", scientific and ethical.

27 The basis for this "limitation of our reason" lies in its connection with the senses. Cf. on this point the excellent remarks of Dr F. Kuberka (*Kant's Lehre von der Sinnlichkeit*, Halle, 1905) which complete what has been said above.

28 Of course this illegitimate, uncritical and dogmatic anthropomorphism is to be carefully distinguished from the anthropomorphism previously admitted and in some cases required by Kant, Cf. above pp. 263, 268.

29 In a note (p. 84) Kant even deduces the idea of the fall of the first man, i.e. that all the evils that man suffers are only "punishments for acts of transgression".

30 In this statement the theory and method of "accommodation" is recognized expressly by Kant as justified and as his own.

31 *Harmful* anthropomorphism: *useful* anthropomorphism is expressly demanded by Kant. Cf. above, pp. 263, 268.

32 Very similar is the famous expression of Goethe, that there is in man a "Will to Service".

33 I.e. the concepts in question are mere conceptual expedients.

34 I.e. the useful fiction is easily transformed into a dogma, owing to the labile nature of these fictional assumptions.

35 Italicized by Kant himself.

36 The traditional text has "anzustellen" in place of "vorzustellen".

37 This type of analogy or symbolism is discussed by Kant in the same work in a special short section near the beginning ("Von der Art den reinen Verstandes—und Vernunftbegriffen objektive Realität zu verschaffen"), p. 120, where he contrasts the schematism of the categories with the symbolism of the ideas. The latter he describes as a "temporary expedient".

38 This is the philosophical basis of the famous theological saying: *credo, quia absurdum*.

39 It would be in the spirit of Kant to add that, for the inferior individual, this 'as-if' must become a 'because'

40 *Instar*, originally *ad instar* = on the model, on the analogy of . . .

41 The idea of a future life, as Kant indicates in a footnote appended at this point, must not of course "be included here even as an hypothesis"; we are dealing in this instance too with a regulative principle, a heuristic fiction.

42 Cf. also the conclusion to the *Ewige Friede in der Philosophie*.

43 1. *Uebergang von den metaphysischen Anfangsgründen der Naturwissen-schaft zur Physik* and 2. *System der reinen Philosophie in ihrem Zusammenhange*.

The title of the second work varies in the different outlines left by Kant. The most remarkable of the titles suggested is *Zoroaster oder die Philosophie im Ganzen ihres Inbegriffs unter einem Prinzip zusammengefasst*; thus Vol. XXI, pp. 418 and 313; cf. also pp. 314, 381, 405 and 311; *Zoroaster das Ideal der physischund zugleich moralisch-praktischen Vernunft in einem Sinnen-Objeht vereinigt*. It is remarkable that Kant should have felt the need of putting his views into the mouth of such an idealized personality; and it is still more re-markable that, like Nietzsche, he should have selected Zoroaster. Strangest of all, however, is the fact that this sketch should have come to light in 1884, at the very time when Nietzsche was writing his book. That it is precisely the 'As-if' theory which forms the meeting-point of Kant and Nietzsche, will be pointed out below.

44 The passages with which we are concerned almost all come from the second work, which is far more important than the first. The selection here given from this second work will show that in the edition of Kant's posthumous manuscripts which has been undertaken by the Berlin Academy, it will have to be represented in some way or other.

45 Italicized by Kant himself.

46 "Of this the wise were clearly conscious, and at least some suspicion of it had found its way into the popular consciousness.

47 The expression "standpoint of the ideal" (though Lange apparently had not noticed it) is already found in Kant as well as in Forberg.

48 A proof of the "law of ideational shifts."

49 It would seem then that Lange did not wish absolutely to discard such images?

50 For that reason it is more or less clearly recognized or divined, "even by the most convinced believers," that the greater part of religion is only a matter of imagi-nation (494). But for that reason also, "the believer is careful not to approach in his inmost soul the border where truth and poetry part company" (554).

51 Kant, in the same way, says that Ideas spring from the "architectonic" instinct of reason.

52 *Gesammelte Briefe*, 3rd Edition, 1902, I, 48, 97.

53 To be found in Nietzsche's *Gesammelte Briefe*, 3rd Edition, 1902, II, 80.

54 For this conflict, which is already apparent in the *Geburt der Tragödie*, cf. especially *Werke*, X, 109 ff. and 216 ff.

55 "There are errors of the most salutary and beneficial kind" (I, 170) and, on the other hand, there are "doctrines which I regard as true but deadly" (367);

hence Nietzsche also approves of Plato's indispensable lie in the *Republic* (376, cf. 487),

56 It is very striking that Nietzsche here already recognizes the freedom of the will "as a necessary delusional concept", e.g. Vol. IX, 186, 188 f.; 207, Vol. X, 213. Man "conceives of freedom as if he could also act otherwise", indeed "the whole process of world-history goes on as if freedom of will existed". "Moral freedom", however, "is a necessary illusion."

57 It is in this sense that we must also understand the following important sentence (Vol. I, p. 128, cf. 110): "The tremendous courage and wisdom of Kant and Schopenhauer accomplished that most difficult of all victories, the victory over the optimism which lies concealed in the essence of logic." Cf. for logical optimism and pessimism, p. 159 ff.

58 These writings are *Menschliches, Allzumenschliches; Morgenröthe; Fröhliche Wissenschaft*—in Vols. II–V, along with the supplementary Vols. XI and XII, 1–233.

59 In this sense he says patiently XI, 21: "Why cannot we learn to look upon metaphysics and religion as the legitimate play of grown-ups?" Similarly of the "illusions of the next world" XI, 66. "There may be necessary errors", he says, XI, 320, in definite contradiction of what Pascal says of Christian dogmas. "We need blindness sometimes and must allow certain articles of faith and errors to remain untouched within us—so long as they maintain us in life" XII, 48. In another passage (XII, 212) he appears to reprobate this "conscious adherence to illusion and the compulsory assimilation of it as the basis of our civilizaton", which he himself finds necessary; but the criticism is directed against a misuse by Richard Wagner.

60 Nietzsche frequently refers, for instance XII, 26 ff., to this "error of identity" which, like the error of permanence, contributes, as he says, to the development of the belief in "things" and "substances."

61 The same passage continues: "Our sensations of space and time are false, for if consistently tested, they lead to logical contradictions. In all scientific calculations we inevitably operate with a number of imaginary quantities, but because these quantities are, at least, constant, as, for instance, our sensations of time and space, the scientific results acquire absolute rigidity and certainty." In other words we always think and compute with constant errors, II, 36 f. Our empirical conception of the world, therefore, is based on "erroneous fundamental assumptions"; "the world as idea means the world as error". In this connection Nietzsche expressly invokes Kant: "when Kant says: 'reason does not derive its laws from nature but prescribes them to nature', this is, in regard to the concept of nature, completely true." This sentence of Kant, as we can infer from other occasional references to it, had made a

great impression upon Nietzsche: it is just this "creative" "active" force of the mind, its "inventive, poetic, and falsifying" activity that Nietzsche, as we shall see, repeatedly emphasizes. There is, then, much more of Kant in Nietzsche than is generally imagined.

62 The As-if also appears in II, 271, as an indication of a conventional fiction, and *(Ibid.,* 333) as an expression of the fiction of the constitutional state; in V, 302, on the contrary, it is the formula of an hypothesis.

63 *Zarathustra, Jenseits von Gut und Böse, Genealogie der Moral, Götzendämmerung, Antichrist.*

64 "Truth does not mean the antithesis of error but the relation of certain errors to other errors such, for instance, as that they are older, more completely assimilated, that we do not know how to live without them, and the like," XIII, 87; (cf. our remarks above, page 98, on "Truth the most expedient form of error"). The antithesis is not "true" and "false" *(Ibid.,* 69). "What is it that forces us to assume an essential antithesis of 'true' and 'false'?" VII, 55.

65 In XII, 43, we find "our poetico-logical power of determining the perspectives in all things," and, in quite a Kantian fashion, Nietzsche speaks of "the abundance of optical errors" which inevitably flow therefrom and which we must consciously maintain. This perspective mode of imaginative creation, found in all organic beings, itself, he says, constitutes a happening, an inner happening accompanying the external one, XIII, 63.

66 Because deception and falsification is necessary for life, at least as necessary as true ideas, not only is man, according to Nietzsche, adjusted to it, but all organic life also: "illusion . . . begins with the organic world" XIII, 228: "thus mankind and all organic beings have made it; they have gone on ordering the world, in action, in thought, in imagination, until they have made of it something that they can use, something that they can reckon with," *Ibid.,* 84; "the capacity to create (to form, invent, imagine) is the fundamental capacity of the organic world" *Ibid.,* 80; "in the organic world error begins: things, substances, attributes, activities . . . these are the specific errors by means of which organisms live," 60, 63. But man is not content with these minor falsifications—" It is the major falsifications and interpretations that in the past have lifted us above mere animal happiness" 29. In this sense Nietzsche in XIII, 37 already calls man "the fantastic animal" and speaks XI, 278 of the "impertinence of our fantasy"; the importance of fantasy is stressed in XII, 36; from it springs our "myth-making instinct," *Ibid.,* 123 and the whole "picture-language" of science, 147, our whole "idealistic phantasmagoria", *Ibid.,* 3, which, however, as conscious "lying", is a necessary element in life XIV, 269.

67 In the posthumous fragments of Vol. XIII these scientific fictions are preferably called "regulative hypotheses", where "hypothesis" (as by Lange)
is employed inaccurately instead of "fiction". Thus XIII, 59: "cause and effect" is not a truth "but an hypothesis by means of which we humanize the
world. By means of the atomic hypothesis we make the world accessible
both to our eye and to our calculation". A "strong" mind is able to reject
the delusion of such absolute concepts and yet keep them as "hypotheses"; so, too, *Ibid.*, 54 f, 59 80, 85. The whole mechanistic view of nature,
especially the "conception of pressure and impact", can be allowed validity
only "in the sense of a regulative hypothesis for the world of illusory appearance"; "the mechanistic conception is to be conceived of as a regulative principle of method" 81–82; in this sense Nietzsche announces to us
the "triumph of the anti-teleological, mechanistic method of thought as a
regulative hypothesis", and as a "conscious one" withal. Thus "the mathematical physicists construct for themselves a force-point-world with which
they can calculate" 84, i.e. "as a provisional truth on the lines of which we
can work" 73 (in other words as a "working hypothesis"), although "the
assumption of atoms" can easily be recognized as purely subjective, 61.
Thus he also says: "in order that we might reckon, we had first to imagine"
XII, 242. In other passages what Nietzsche has here said of calculation is
applied to thinking in general. For the value of regulative fictions cf. also
XIV, 322. Of particular significance is the passage in Vol. XIII, 139: "the
mind has heretofore been too weak and too uncertain of itself to grasp an
hypothesis as an hypothesis and, at the same time, to take it as a guide—it
required faith." To judge from the context this refers to morality. Thus, the
"strong" mind ought to be conscious of its fictive nature and yet "take it
as directive". He need not "believe" it, but he should act on it—quite a
Kantian dictum! Of mechanics with its presuppositions, especially those of
the atom and of empty space, he says, 325: it is "a kind of ideal, regulative
method, nothing more".

68 Cf. above pp. 232, 240 the *tolerabiter vera* of Jungius and Leibniz.

69 The "world of Being" is an invention—there is only a work of Becoming; and
it is because of this invented world of Being that the poet regards himself
also as "being" and contrasts himself with it XIV, 52. Being is, consequently,
a product of thought, substance is an "error" 311, 366. "The royal preroga-
tive, which we assume after the manner of artists, plumes itself on having
created this world", he says quite in the Kantian tradition in XIV, 15.

70 For further remarks about "soul" "spirit," etc. cf. XIV, 27, 338.

71 "Number is an out-and-out invention" XIV, 34. "The arithmetical formulæ
are only regulative fictions" 44. The same holds of the geometrical forms:

"a straight line has never occurred" 42. "The objects of mathematics do not exist" 320.

72 The concepts, "individual", "person", etc. are indeed false, but serve admirably to simplify thought XIV, 37; they are however "deceptions" 325 f.; like all the concepts enumerated above, they are "false yet permanent errors" 326.

73 Cf. for the atomic theory as a mere pictorial construction for purposes of calculation XIV, 325.

74 On the "mythology of the subject-concept" cf. XIV, 329.

75 "Our 'means and ends'are very useful abbreviations for rendering processes tangible and concrete" XIV, 45.

76 On cause and effect, as consequences of an erroneous conception of the relation of subject and predicate, cf. the remarks XIV, 22, 27.

77 Perspectives are principally brought about through simplification: "Life is only possible by means of narrowing, perspective-creating forces" XIV, 45. In this sense Nietzsche also speaks of an "exclusive, selective instinct" 46. The simplifying and therefore falsifying nature of our thought is often emphasized, for instance, in XIV, 34, 320. There are "simplifications of the true facts temporarily permitted" 42. Cf. XIII, 80 f.: simplifying-falsifying-inventing; cf. also 241, 249. "The intellect is an apparatus for simplification" and for analyzing, 245.

78 Of illusion in art, especially epic art, Nietzsche says that the *raconteur* speaks to his admiring audience *as if* he had been present at the events he narrates while his audience knows quite well that it is a deception, etc. XIV, 132; art, in general, consists "of intentional transformation, i.e. falsification" 134.—In this connection let me also quote the following significant aphorism (XIII, 207): "Not to measure the world by our personal feelings but *as if* it were a play and we were part of the play." This pregnant thought, which comes from the later Stoics, is also found *Ibid.*, 282: "To regard our manner of living and acting as a part in a play, including therein our maxims and principles".

79 The expression 'fiction' is also found in the two first periods occasionally, but in a derogatory sense, e.g. in Vol. II, 355 he speaks of the fictions upon which the Medieval Church rested and IV, 99 the fiction of the general concept "man".

80 In these two works (Vol. VIII) we naturally find similar expressions; thus on p. 77 ff. all categories are designated as "prejudices of the reason", as "lies" and as "empty fictions"—that possess in language and "linguistic metaphysics" a "permanent advocate". The Ego, Free-will, Thing, Atom—are "fictions" in the bad sense 94 f., 99. The *Antichrist* attacks all "imaginary" entities, the whole religious "world of fiction" and "the dualistic fiction" 231–233 as mere "lies" in the bad sense (261, 264, 270 f., 281 f., 287, 296 ff.).

Similarly in XII, 21–23, 49, 87, 148. From this standpoint Nietzsche (49) attacks the view that man is, on the one hand, adjusted to "perspective vision" and that he can, on the other, possess a consciousness of this deceptive arrangement—which is elsewhere his own doctrine.

81 Compare in this connection the magnificent Hymn to Illusion, to the "whole Olympus of Illusion" VIII, 209 and XII, 246 f., 290–293, to the "lie" in the good sense=the creation of myths. Compare XIII, 35: it is a "prejudice", he says, "to believe that the philosopher must fight against illusion as though it were his real enemy". Cf. *Ibid.*, 50, 71, 81, 88 (the perspective illusion as a law of conservation). On p. 130 he says, quite in the manner of Kant: "We are adjusted to optical errors" and we may even ask what is the "most useful belief" =error 207, cf. 121, 124, 138. "The inner processes are essentially productive of error because life is only possible under the guidance of narrowing perspective-creating powers" XIV, 45. "Consciousness is something essentially falsifying"—he says in the same place.

82 "Thought is not a means of 'knowledge' but a means of designating, arranging and manipulating events for our use"; "thought is the cause and the condition both of the 'subject' and of the' object', as it is of 'substance' and of 'matter etc." XIII, 51 f. "The inventive power which creates categories is working in the service of our needs, namely of security and rapid intelligibility on the basis of conventions and signs" *Ibid.*, 55. Cf. for such "representative signs" *Ibid.*, 66, 83 ff. Thinking is identical with "creating pictures" 234.

83 Compare in this connection the remarks on pp. 289–297: the concept of the atom is based on the "perspective of consciousness"; "it is consequently, itself, a subjective fiction"; the mechanical view of the world is made possible "by means of two fictions", that of motion and that of the atom. "We need unities in order to calculate, but that does not mean that such unities exist": mechanics is based upon the "picture-language" of "matter, atom, pressure, impulse, gravity" and is, in this sense, a serviceable "semeotic" "for our use in computation". Cf. also XIV, 45 for "the atomic theory".

84 Cf. also XIII, 60 ff. for the necessary "mythology" of the category of causality and the fictional concepts of soul, atom, etc. which flow from it: here also belong "the fictional unities" of the psychical faculties p. 70.

85 The important and beautiful passage VII, 84 to 90, where the religions are raised in detail as "educative and ennobling means" especially belongs here. It is true that Nietzsche, at the same time, points out "the evil obverse side and holds the religions to account for all the damage they have done. Yet he also says: "There is perhaps nothing in Christianity and Buddhism so worthy of respect as their art of exhorting even the lowliest to transport themselves into a higher illusionary arrangement of things through piety" (cf. p. 296

above, for Kant's similar utterances). This art, it is true, springs from a "will to falsehood at any price" but it is just for that reason that the *homines religiosi* "are to be reckoned among the artists, as belonging to their highest order", among whom, also, "the will to deceive is accompanied by a good conscience" 472. Even in *Antichrist* Nietzsche has, from this point of view, a sympathetic word for the "great symbolist", Christ, and for the "primitive symbolism" of Christianity, though he deplores its development in "ever grosser misunderstanding" (VIII, 259–262). Nietzsche has so little against such myths that he makes a demand for a "myth of the future" XII, 400. As a test of such a future-myth we can interpret the idea of the "eternal recurrence". True enough, Nietzsche meant this at first as hypothetical, then as dogmatic, but, in the end, he himself appears to have interpreted it merely as a useful fiction. In this sense he says of this idea XIV, 295: "Perhaps it is not true". And it is thus possible that O. Ewald *(Nietzsches Lehre in ihren Grundbegriffen)* was right in interpreting this thought as a pedagogical-regulative idea, as G. Simmel also does. The idea of the "superman", too, is a heuristic-pedagogical-Utopian fiction of this sort.

86 This creating, logicizing, putting in order, falsifying, simplifying, arranging, artificially-separating, poetizing, imagining (279, 281, 291) "the perspective, assumptive force" 321 he also calls bluntly, but very appropriately, "the error-desiring force within us (291), and (293) "the will to deception".

87 In the printed edition there is a "not" between the "is" and the "true", which is also found in the manuscript, but which is clearly a slip of the pen and is to be corrected.

88 For explanation, cf. VIII, 207.

89 According to XIII, likewise, Nietzsche would like to see the belief in God retained as a "pathetic myth". Cf. also the characteristic utterances XIV, 123, 259 about the "necessity" of "invented" religious concepts. For Nietzsche's theory of knowledge cf. also the two illuminating works—R. Eisler, *Nietzsches Erkenninistheorie und Metaphysik* (1902) and F. Rittelmeyer, *F. Nietzsche und das Erkenninisproblem* (1903).

INDEX

Note: page numbers followed by 'n' refer to end notes.

Vaihinger's education in xxv
Arnobius 178
artificial classifications 15–16, 167–70;
and abstractive fictions 17; as
conceptual aids 106, 109; Kant's use
of 138; as semi-fiction 71, 99–100;
unjustified 170–1
'As If': grammatical form of 86; see also
Philosophy of 'As If'; religion of 'As If'
'As If' approach, meaning of 235–8
assumptions: fictive see fictional
assumptions; and hypotheses 130
atheism, theoretical xxx, 300
Atheism-controversy 297, 303
atoms: as auxiliary idea 250n63; as
fictions 14, 38, 47–8, 64–6, 80, 200–5,
245; Lange on 312–14; Nietzsche on
325, 340n83
attraction, as summational fiction 195–6
auxiliary ideas 57, 66, 200, 202, 205, 207,
212, 250n63
auxiliary words 33, 87, 195, 197–8
Avenarius, Richard xxxiii–xxxiv, xxxvii,
54, 120

Bacon, Francis xviii
Bauch, Bruno xi–xii, xiv
Baur of Tübingen xxi
Being, Parmenides on 126; world of 311,
338n69
Bentham, Jeremy xiv, xix, 175
Berkeley, George 55, 58–9, 106–7, 186
body alpha see Alpha body
Bruno, Giordano 136

calculus: Berkeley on 106, 108; and
curves 53–5; as fiction 73, 80, 96
Carnap, Rudolf x
Cassirer, Ernst xi–xii
categorical imperative 40, 292–3, 296
categorical judgement 239, 241
categories: as analogical fictions 157–60;
as fictions 26–7, 112, 119, 138, 142,
149–57; interpolation of 109; Kant's

doctrine of 276; practical utility of
160–2; sensations worked into 152–4;
shifting and interchangeable nature
150–1
causae verae 163, 202
causality: idea of 262; Nietzsche on 321,
328; purpose of category 158–60; as
real analogy 29, 33; Sextus Empiricus
against 130; as subjective 54, 69, 305
Cavaleri, Bonaventura 226–31, 251n83
centre, indivisible 207
chemistry xxxvii, 33, 136, 176,
197–8, 201
Christianity: dogmas of 25, 106–7; and
ideational shifts 118; Nietzsche on
340–1n85
Cicero, M. Tullius 243
circle: circumference of 138; as ellipse 46,
51, 102, 217–19; as fiction 47; as infinite
number of triangles 125; as polygon
204, 219–22, 238–41
classification: natural system of
15–16, 36, 168–9; see also artificial
classification
collective will 285
communication, and thing-and-attribute
154–5, 160
the communion of saints 265
compossibilitas 50
Comte's law 120
conceivability 246
conception: concrete modes of 313;
modes of 201, 233, 289
concepts: combination of 149–50;
differentiation of 21; as necessary evil
61–2; persistence of 116
conceptual aids 86–7, 156, 205, 216
conceptual realism 193–4
conceptual world: as construction of
thought 60–1; and real world 57–9;
subjectivity of 98; transit-points in 91;
see also world of ideas
condensation 61, 92, 146
Condillac, Étienne Bonnot de 19, 140,
177–80, 186–9, 193–4, 248n18, 249n42
conditional clauses 84–6, 237
conduct, rules of 235, 238, 255, 271–3

85; and logic 29; necessary 319–20, 323–4, 327, 336n58; truth as a kind of 77, 98, 337n64

Essay on the Progress of Metaphysics (Kant) 280–1

ethico-political sciences 9–10, 72

ethics: Kantian 44–5; methodological fiction of 265; practical 137

evil: Kant on idea of 274–7; necessary 61; radical xliv

evil things, obverse of 331

existence, potential 28

expediency 81, 89–90

expedient fictions 35, 43, 274–5, 277, 282, 285

extra-moral sense 316, 318

false factors 184, 314

falsification 151–2, 310, 316, 320, 325–30, 337n66, 339n77, 340n81

fantasy: Nietzsche on 316, 319, 324; play of 313

Faraday, Michael 204–6

Fermat, Pierre de 103–6, 108, 111, 241

Fichte, Johann Gottlieb xxv–xxvii; and analogical fictions 24–6; and atheism controversy 297; on atomic theory 203–4; and ethics 59–60; on morality 301–2; and Neo-Kantianism xlvn11; and utopian fictions 23

fictio (Latin word) 31, 74, 131–4, 163n17

fictio rationis 133

fictional abstractions 179, 188, 214

fictional analogies 29, 119, 222; see also analogical fictions

fictional assumptions 71–4; Greek and Roman terms for 129–30, 132; in mathematics 47; in science 37–8

Fictionalism xiv–xv, xix, xliii

fictions x, 11; in English philosophy xviii–xix; expressions for 87–8; Greek fear of 56; justification of 80–1, 95–6, 211–12, 214; linguistic form of 82–5; and logical mechanism of thought 98–9; main characteristics of 88–90; *in malo sensu* 327, 339n80; method of xxxii,

xxxvi–xxxvii, 138, 276, 313–14; modern use of 133–5; outline of general theory 90–8; psychological genesis of 74; renewed philosophical interest in xv; as valueless in themselves 112

fictive activity 11–12, 61, 72, 200

fictive judgment 74, 86–7, 238–46, 333n21

fictive method 69, 94, 107, 125, 178, 219, 222–3, 225–7

Field, Hartry xiv

figments 87, 163n17, 306, 312

Fine, Arthur xiii–xiv

fixed points 207–8

flux 217

fluxions 55, 106–7, 120, 135, 229–30

focus imaginarius 255, 259

Forberg, F. K. xxxvi, 297, 299–304

force: and atomic theory 204–5; as fiction 32–3, 58, 183–4, 196, 198, 313–14; lines of 205–6

free agents 43, 86, 236–9

freedom, idea of 39–42, 101, 235, 238, 268–71, 274

Gabriel, Markus xv

Galileo Galilei 181, 207–8

general ideas xviii, 3, 30, 34–5, 62; and abstractions 249n46; as fictions 109–13, 132, 190–4; logical 118; necessity of 81; in psycho-mechanics 93, 95

genus 195, 217, 328

geometry xxxii, xxxix, 129, 173, 215, 328

German language 84–5

God: deceptive 329; idea of 85, 164n25, 256–62, 265–8, 278–80, 286–9, 291–4, 332n10; kingdom of 277–8, 298, 300–2; moral proof for existence of 281–4, 296; Nietzsche on 331, 341n89; Son of 275, 307

Goethe, J. W. von 24; and animal archetypes 78–9, 244–5; *Faust* 197; theory of colour 185

grammar 82–3

grammatical fictions 182

gravitation, Newton's laws of 36–7

gravity, centre of 66, 141, 206–7

Greek religion 117–18
Greek scientific procedure 123–8
Gregorius, David 234
Gronemann, Sammy ix–x
Grundlegung see Metaphysics of Models

hallucination 315, 320
Haug, Balthasar xxiii
Hegel, G. W. F. xxiv–xxvi; and Neo-Kantianism xlvn11; on reality and thought 7–8; system of abstractions 189–90
Heidegger, Martin xi, xv
hell, as fiction 274, 276–7
Herbart, Johann Friedrich xxxiii, 4, 19, 58, 118, 141, 164n30, 176–7
heuristic fictions xix–xx, 35–8; animal archetypes as 78; as arbitrary deviation 100; and ideational shift 119; Kant on 254–5, 261–5, 267, 270–2, 286, 290, 334n41; modern use of 140
Hobbes, Thomas xviii–xix, 140, 162n1, 213, 285
holiness 272, 293
Hoppe, J. I. 39–40
Horwicz, Adolf xxviii
human nature xliv, 172–4, 301, 305, 312
Hume, David ix, xviii, xxxi, xxxiv; on fictions 58, 90, 133, 141; on sensation and subjectivity 186; on the soul 197; on unreality of concepts 54, 96–7
husks 112, 162, 192–3, 197, 215, 277
hypostatization 32, 34, 192; of abstractions 183, 188–9; of categories 305; of fictions 246, 257–8, 275
hypotheses: and assumptions 71–2; becoming heuristics 36–8; and fictions 16–19, 76–82, 85–90, 141, 162–3n13, 243–7; Greek word (ὑπόθεσις) 128–32; and ideals 44; Kant's use of 138–9, 254, 266; necessary 267; real and ideal 206; regulative 338n67; transcendental 264; *see also* ideational shifts

hypothetical method 81
hypothetical thinking 246

the Ideal 44; recognition of 309; *see also* Standpoint of the Ideal
idealization xiv
ideas: hierarchy of 192; life-history of 116
ideational constructs: contradictions in 42; equilibration of 115–16; fictive nature of 43–5, 58, 66, 97, 100, 121–2; general 95; and perception 26; reality of 13–16; reduction of reality to 48; utility for thought 34
ideational shifts, law of 113–21, 139, 174, 197, 242, 303, 335n48
identity, illusion of 321, 336n60
illusion: in art 339n78; Nietzsche on 315–19, 324, 327–31; useful 43, 324, 327–30
illustrative fictions 162n7, 200
imaginary numbers 51–2, 66, 68–9, 151, 164–5n30
imaginative faculty: and ideational forms 58; and infinity 57; Lange on 313; and nature 75; and science 48–50; and thought and sensation 153
immortal fictions 120
immortality 44, 113; Kant on 256, 258; as practical fiction 43, 119
impossible terms 109
indivisibilia 227–9, 231–2
induction 10, 29, 72, 163n15
inertia 20, 115, 181, 205, 207–8
the infinite 121; Gauss on 251n80; passage through 220
infinitely small *see* infinitesimals
infinitesimals 55–6, 140, 217–24; as conceptual aid 108–9; in curved lines 74, 83–4; history of 225–34; as *modus dicendi* 86
infinity 56–7; and the Absolute 70; as fiction 20, 136; Greek avoidance of 125
intelligences 269–70
intelligible freedom 42, 120